Third Edition

Family Therapy
An Overview

ch. ~~4~~, 7.

Family Therapy
An Overview

Irene Goldenberg
University of California, Los Angeles

Herbert Goldenberg
California State University, Los Angeles

Brooks/Cole Publishing Company
Pacific Grove, California

Brooks/Cole Publishing Company
A Division of Wadsworth, Inc.

Printed in the United States of America

10 9 8 7 6 5 4

Library of Congress Cataloging in Publication Data
Goldenberg, Irene.
Family therapy : an overview / Irene Goldenberg, Herbert Goldenberg.
—3rd ed.
p. cm.
Includes bibliographical references.
ISBN 0-534-13746-6
1. Family psychotherapy. I. Goldenberg, Herbert. II. Title.
RC488.5.G64 1990
616.89'156—dc20 89-78294
CIP

Sponsoring Editor: Claire Verduin
Editorial Assistant: Gay C. Bond
Production Editor: Linda Loba
Manuscript Editor: Lorraine Anderson
Permissions Editor: Marie DuBois
Interior Design: Linda Loba
Cover Design and Illustration: Lisa Thompson
Printing and Binding: Arcata Graphics, Martinsburg
Credits continue on page 369

For our families of origin
. . . who stimulated our drive and
sensitivities,

And for the family we created
. . . who enriched our understanding
and, above all, taught us
humility,

And for our children's families
. . . whose contributions we look
forward to discovering.

Preface

In the decade since the first edition of this text, the field of family therapy has broadened considerably—more advanced and elaborated theories, greatly expanded research undertakings, a proliferation of clinical intervention techniques. In this third edition, we have attempted, once again, to keep pace with these developments, endeavoring to provide the reader with information that would convey a sense of the increasing complexities that represent the theory and practice of family therapy today.

Consistent with our previous efforts, we remain committed to offering a balanced presentation of the evolving viewpoints, perspectives, values, and intervention techniques, as well as the ethical and other professional issues that we consider to be of greatest relevance and immediacy to today's students and practitioners alike. We have greatly expanded our exposition of the family life cycle framework in this edition, offered a more detailed explication of major theories and a clearer description of numerous specific therapeutic techniques, and have paid closer attention to integrating research findings and clinical practice. At the same time, we have tried hard to retain the goal that others have suggested to be the main strengths of the earlier editions—its concise, readable quality and its unbiased presentation.

To be effective in helping couples and entire families to change, we continue to believe it essential that therapists have some grounding in the general principles of family development and a working knowledge of systems theory. They need some basic understanding of what causes dysfunction within families, and how to distinguish those families that are undergoing a temporarily destabilizing but time-limited crisis, from which they will reorganize and recover independently, from those families who are more seriously dysfunctional and require therapeutic intervention.

Thus, we have organized Part One so as to provide a basic perspective on family development before moving on to considerations of specific family therapy theories and practices, described in Part Two of the text. In Part Three we concern ourselves with research, training and professional issues. Our attention in this section is devoted first to the burgeoning field of research on family theory, classification and the effectiveness of therapeutic intervention. Next we turn to some nuts and bolts issues—where and how to get training and supervision in family therapy, as well as how to regulate, through legal statute and self-monitoring, the rapidly proliferating practices of family therapy today. We conclude with a code of ethical principles adopted by the American Association for Marriage and Family Therapy. A detailed glossary of terms is included at the back of the book to facilitate the reading and minimize interruptions.

We are indebted to a number of reviewers for reading earlier drafts of the text and for making useful suggestions for improving the final product. Specifically we wish to thank: Dr. Vincent D. Foley, Long Island University; Dr. Clarence Hibbs, Pepperdine University, California; Dr. David Lawson, Stephen F. Austin State University, Texas; Professor Uri Ruveni, University of Houston; Dr. Robert Wendt, University of Toledo; and Dr. Carol Werlinich, University of Maryland.

Since the inception of the idea of writing a basic text on family therapy, perhaps fifteen years ago, we ourselves have passed through a number of developmental stages, learning first hand about such things as children leaving home and parents aging, as each of us, separately and together, expanded our personal knowledge base and extended our clinical experiences. We suspect that each successive edition of this text parallels our own growth. If that indeed is the case, perhaps this edition is less blurred, and our elucidation more clear and better differentiated than in the past, as we ourselves grow, deepen, and mature.

Both of us are aware that one of the advantages of being a family therapist is touching so many lives that ultimately enrich your own. Being textbook writers allows us the added joy of touching so many minds and sharpening our own. We are very grateful for the experience.

Irene Goldenberg
Herbert Goldenberg

Contents

Part I

Part I

PERSPECTIVES ON FAMILY DEVELOPMENT

Chapter One

Adopting a Family Frame of Reference

A family is far more than a collection of individuals sharing a specific physical and psychological space. A family is a natural social **system**,[1] with properties all its own, one that has evolved a set of rules, is replete with assigned and ascribed roles for its members, has an organized power structure, has developed intricate overt and covert forms of communication, and has elaborated ways of negotiating and problem solving that permit various tasks to be performed effectively. The relationship between members of this microculture is deep and multilayered, and is based largely on a shared history, shared internalized perceptions and assumptions about the world, and a shared sense of purpose. Within such a system, individuals are tied to one another by powerful, durable, reciprocal emotional attachments and loyalties that may fluctuate in intensity over time but nevertheless persist over the lifetime of the family.

1. Terms in **boldface** are defined in the Glossary at the back of the book.

Entrance into such an organized system occurs only through birth, adoption, or marriage. As Kaye (1985) observes, families create and indoctrinate new members, and although they ultimately give these members autonomy and no longer expect them to live under the same roof, family membership remains intact for life. He contends that the power of the family is such that despite the possible separation of members by vast distances, sometimes even by death, the family's influence remains. Even in the face of a temporary or permanent sense of alienation from one's family, one can never truly relinquish family membership.

As Carter and McGoldrick (1988) point out, no other system is subject to similar restraints. A business organization may fire an employee viewed as dysfunctional, or conversely, members may resign and permanently sever their relationships with the group if the structure or values of the company are not to their liking. The pressures of retaining family membership allow few such exits, even for those who attempt to gain great geographic distance from their **family of origin**.

Further, unlike members of nonfamily systems, who can generally be replaced if they leave, family members are irreplaceable, primarily because the main value in a family is in the network of relationships developed by its members. Should a parent leave or die, for example, and another person be brought in to fill a parenting role, the substitute, regardless of successful effort, can never truly replace the lost parent's personal and emotional ties to the remaining members.

Families are organizationally complex emotional systems comprising at least three, and increasingly today, four, generations. Whether traditional or innovative, adaptive or maladaptive, efficiently or chaotically organized, a family inevitably attempts to arrange itself into a functioning group, structurally as well as behaviorally, to achieve its objectives. Affection, loyalty, and durability of membership characterize all families and further distinguish them from other social systems (Terkelson, 1980). Regardless of format (for example, **nuclear family**, **stepfamily**, **single-parent-led family**) or ultimate success, all families must work at promoting positive relationships among members, attend to the personal needs of their constituents, and prepare to cope with maturational changes (such as children leaving home) as well as unexpected crises (divorce, death, a sudden acute illness). In general, all must organize themselves in order to get on with the day-to-day problems of living. More specifically, all must develop strategies for coping with stresses imposed from outside or from within the family itself.

FAMILY STRATEGIES

Families typically display recurring patterns of interactive sequences—what Kantor and Lehr (1975) refer to as "family strategies"—that largely go unnoticed by outsiders, and that frequently are unstated and not always understood by the participants themselves. Nonverbal exchange patterns between family members, in particular, represent subtle, coded transactions that may transmit family "rules" (for instance, that a son does not speak before his mother, who herself can take her turn only after her husband has spoken). Such family strategies are collaborative, purposeful, highly predictable transactional patterns generated by all family members on cue, as though each participant feels compelled to play a well-rehearsed part, like it or not.

All family members share responsibility for the outcome of family strategies. As Kantor and Lehr (1975) observe, even in the process of a member's being scapegoated or victimized, the **scapegoat** shares a systemic responsibility for his or her role in the process. These authors differentiate three basic family strategies: (1) those intended to maintain the family system by preserving the relationship between members; (2) those that accentuate stress, usually of limited duration, to reach a desired goal; and (3) those strategies aimed at repair, as the family attempts to cope with changing external conditions by modifying its interactive patterns in order to remain a livable, workable system responsive to the changing needs of its members.

Throughout the course of its development, a family fashions fundamental and enduring assumptions about the world in which it lives (Reiss, 1981). Despite any differences or disagreements between members, the core of family membership is based on acceptance of, and belief in, a set of abiding suppositions or shared constructs about the family itself and its relationship to its social environment. Some families generally view the world as trustworthy, orderly, predictable, masterable; they are likely to view themselves as competent, to encourage individual input by their members, and to feel comfortable, perhaps enjoyably challenged, as a group coping with life. Other families perceive their environment as mostly menacing, unstable, and thus unpredictable and potentially dangerous; in their view, the outside world appears confusing and at times chaotic, so they band together, insist on agreement from all members on all issues, and in that way protect themselves against intrusion and threat. (We intend to return to the research of David Reiss and his associates on what he calls **family paradigms** in Chapter 12.)

THE PERSPECTIVE OF FAMILY THERAPY

Scientific models help shape the boundaries of a discipline and set the agenda regarding the subject matter and methodology to be followed in seeking answers. If the individual is the unit of analysis, clinical theories regarding human behavior are likely to emphasize internal events, psychic organization, **intrapsychic** conflict. Methodology in such a situation tends to be retrospective: explanations tend to have a historical basis and to seek out root causes from the past. Typically they attempt to answer the question of why something occurred.

For example, influenced by Freud's theoretical psychoanalytic formulations, most clinicians until recently have focused their attention on uncovering and reconstructing the patient's past, particularly unresolved conflicts from childhood, assuming that such knowledge will produce the necessary insights that lead to behavioral changes. While Freud acknowledged in theory the sometimes powerful impact of family conflict and alliances (the Oedipus Complex in boys is one example) on the development of neurotic behavior in the individual, he nevertheless chose to direct his treatment toward helping that person resolve personal and intrapsychic conflicts rather than attempting to change or modify the properties of the family system directly.[2] By helping bring about changes in the patient's psychic organization, Freud hoped to evoke behavioral changes, including changes in response to others, that would presumably lead others ultimately to change their response patterns to the patient. Thus, most therapists, following the lead of Freud and others, would treat a distressed individual but refuse to see that person's spouse or other family members, believing that as the patient resolved handicapping problems, a corresponding positive change would occur in his or her relationships with family members. Unfortunately, this was frequently not the case.

Without negating the significance of individual internal processes and behavior, today's broader view of human problems focuses on the context in which individual behavior occurs, as well as the interpersonal relationships of which the individual is but one part. While bearing in mind the often complex ways in which individual behavior contributes to that interaction, a more holistic view regards all behavior as part of a sequence of ongoing, interactional, recursive or recurring events with no obvious beginning or end point. Rather than attempt to discover the single answer to why something occurred, this contemporary view stresses reciprocal causality; people and events are assumed to exist in a context of mutual influence and mutual interaction, as participants share in each other's destiny. Their present, repetitive transactions offer the clinician the data for initiating therapeutic interventions.

By adopting such a systematic perspective, family psychology—and its clinical application, family therapy—broadens psychology's traditional emphasis on the individual to attend to the nature and role of individuals in primary relationship networks such as marriage and the family (Liddle, 1987). From this perspective, an individual who manifests **dysfunctional** behavior (for example, substance abuse, depression, schizophrenia) is seen as a representative of a system that is faulty. Moreover, the causes and nature of that person's problems may not be clear from a study of his or her past alone, but can often be better understood when viewed in the context of an ongoing family relationship system that is in disequilibrium.

Recasting the individual as a unit of a larger system, such as the family,[3] enables us to search for recurring patterns of interaction in which that person might engage. Our conceptualization of what that person does, what his or her motives are for doing so, and how that behavior can be changed therapeutically, takes on new

2. Karpel (1986) contends that Freud, by limiting himself to uncovering the experiences, fantasies, and internal perceptions of his individual clients, in effect denied the relevance of the family itself as anything other than a locus and source of trauma for that person. In such an essentially negative and pathology-focused view, the potentially positive and enhancing properties of family relationships are likely to be minimized or overlooked entirely.

3. The family, in turn, is part of a larger system, and its experiences are often profoundly influenced by involvements with the school system, the health care system, the legal system, and so on. Imber-Black (1988) correctly maintains that if individuals cannot be adequately understood without reference to the family system, families themselves are comprehensible only in this still broader social context. We intend to return to these issues in Chapter 3.

dimensions as we shift our attention to the broader context in which that person functions. From this new wide-angle perspective, psychopathology or dysfunctional behavior can be redefined as more the product of a struggle between persons than simply the result of opposing forces within the individual (Haley, 1963). Put another way, from a relationship perspective, the development of symptomatic behavior in a family member can be understood as a manifestation of the transactional processes currently taking place within the family system (Bross & Benjamin, 1982).

A number of therapeutic consequences follow from such a shift of perspective. When the locus of pathology is defined as internal, the therapist focuses on individual processes and behavior patterns. On the other hand, if the dysfunctional behavior is viewed as the product of a flawed relationship between members of a **dyad** or **triad**, then it is the relationship that becomes the center of therapeutic attention and the target of intervention strategies. Helping couples or entire families alter their transactional patterns replaces seeking ways to uncover and decipher just what goes on within "the mysterious black box"—the mind of the individual.

If successful, family therapy changes the system—perhaps repairing the family's limiting and self-defeating repetitive interactive patterns, or opening up the style and manner of communicating with one another across generations, or possibly strengthening the structure of the overall family relationship, or in some cases relieving a family member of symptoms. Within this changed family context, enriched relationship skills, improved communication skills, and enhanced problem-solving skills may lead to more rewarding interpersonal experiences, in most cases extending beyond the family.

A Paradigm Shift

More than simply a new treatment method, family therapy represents a "whole new way of conceptualizing human problems, of understanding behavior, the development of symptoms, and their resolution" (Sluzki, 1978, p. 366). Haley (1971b) and others have argued that the perspective of family therapy demonstrates a **paradigm** shift, a break with past ideas, calling for a new set of premises and methods for collecting and interpreting forthcoming data. Beyond a concern with the individual's personality characteristics or repetitive behavior patterns, beyond even a concern with what transpires between people (where individuals remain the unit of study), this conceptual leap focuses attention on the family as subject matter. It is the family as a functioning system, as an entity in itself that is more than the algebraic sum of the inputs of its participants, that provides the contextual structure for understanding individual functioning.

Sluzki (1978) goes so far as to consider family therapy a major epistemological revolution in the behavioral sciences. Put simply, **epistemology** refers to how one goes about gaining knowledge and drawing conclusions about the world. It refers to the rules used to make sense of experience, the descriptive language used to conceptualize and interpret incoming information. Such rules, not necessarily consciously stated, determine the underlying assumptions we make in our day-today behavior as we attempt to understand what is happening around us and how we can bring about change.

A Cybernetic Epistemology

Family therapy proposes a **cybernetic** epistemology as an alternative to our habitual ways of knowing and thinking (Keeney, 1983). Historically, the science of cybernetics was born during the 1940s in a series of conferences in New York City under the sponsorship of the Josiah Macy Foundation attended by a cross section of the leading scientists, engineers, mathematicians, and social scientists of the time. The conferees addressed, among other things, the study of communication in reference to regulation and control, or **feedback** mechanisms in machines as well as in humans. Norbert Wiener (1948), the mathematician who coined the term *cybernetics* and who was to become a principal player in the development of computers, was especially interested in information processing and how feedback mechanisms operate in controlling both simple and complex systems. Wiener chose the term *cybernetics* from the Greek word for steersman, suggestive of an overall governing or regulating system or organization for guiding or piloting a ship by means of feedback mechanisms.

These Macy Conferences made an important breakthrough by providing a new and exciting epistemology—a way of conceptualizing how systems retain their stability through self-regulation as a result of reinserting the results of past performance into current functioning. Perhaps even more significant, a way was becoming available to change patterns of future performance by altering feedback information.

It was Gregory Bateson, an anthropologist and ethnologist, who took away from these conferences some of these mathematical and engineering concepts and recognized their application to the social and behavioral sciences. Although Wiener himself had begun to reformulate psychological constructs (for example, Freud's idea of an unconscious) in information-processing terms, Bateson (1972) deserves the major credit for seeing how cybernetic principles apply to human communication processes, including those associated with psychopathology (Hoffman, 1981). He introduced the notion that a family might be analogous to a cybernetic system, and while he himself remained outside the realm of family therapy, his cybernetic ideas are credited with providing the field of family therapy with its intellectual foundation (Keeney & Thomas, 1986). Bateson's later contributions to a daring theory of schizophrenia as a relationship phenomenon rather than an intrapsychic disorder (see Chapter 4) were monumental, and were based on the human communication principles he was developing. They were to play a major role in shifting the focus of attention for many clinicians from attempting to gain insight into *why* the individual behaves as she or he does, to examining *what* occurs in the exchange of information and the process of relationships between persons, as in a family.

Gregory Bateson, Ph.D.

Reciprocal Determinism

Adopting a relationship outlook inevitably shifts attention from content to family **process.** That is, rather than dwelling on historical facts as explanations for current problems (Mary: "Our problem began when my husband, Gary, lost his job and our son Greg went to work"), this new perspective focuses on the sequence of linked communication exchanges within a cybernetic family system ("With Gary out of work, our son Greg is contributing more money and seems to be dominating us; I submit to Greg's demands more and more, and I suppose Gary is resentful"). Note how the latter statement shifts attention from the sequential actions of individuals to the transactions occurring between persons. The "facts" of the case (content) are not nearly as illuminating as is the family interactional pattern (process).

Content is the language of **linear causality**—the view that one event causes the next in stimulus-response fashion. While such a view may be appropriate for understanding simple mechanical situations (where the machinery does not have too many parts, and the parts do not interact much), it is woefully inadequate for dealing with situations exhibiting organized complexity, such as what transpires within a family (Constantine, 1986). From a cybernetic or systems standpoint, concerned with wholes, a precise part-by-part analysis is too reductionistic to be of much explanatory value. Instead, parts are understood by the functions they serve in the whole.

In the physical world, the world of Newton, it makes sense to talk of causality in linear terms: A causes B, which acts upon C, causing D. In human relationships, however, this "billiard ball" model, which proposes that a force moves in one direction only and affects objects in its path, rarely, if ever, applies. Consequently, any search for the "real" or ultimate cause of any interpersonal event is pointless. A does not cause B, nor does B cause A; both cause each other. Explanations cannot be found in the action of the parts, but in the system as a whole.

If content is the language of linear causality, then process is the language of **circular causality.** The emphasis here is on forces moving in many directions simultaneously, not simply a single event caused by a previous one. Within a family, a change in one member affects all other members and the family as a whole. Such a reverberating effect in turn impacts the first person, and so forth, in a continuous series of circular loops or recurring chains of influence. Parents who ask quarreling children "Who started the fight?" are almost certain to hear, "He (she) started it; I'm only striking back." Both children are correct, both are incorrect; it all depends on where in the communication loop the parent begins the investigation. Nor is such mutual participation limited to pairs. Within a large family, for example, a multitude of such chains exist, and who started what is usually impossible to decipher.

Goldenberg and Goldenberg (1990) offer the following contrasts between statements based on linear and circular causality:

> *Linear:* A bad mother produces sick children.
> *Implication:* Mother's emotional problems cause similar problems in others.
>
> *Circular:* An unhappy middle-aged woman, struggling with an inattentive husband who feels peripheral to and excluded from the family, attaches herself to her 20-year-old son for male companionship, excluding her adolescent daughter. The daughter, in turn, feeling rejected and unloved, engages in flagrant sexually promiscuous behavior to the considerable distress of her parents. The son, fearful of leaving home and becoming independent, insists he must remain at home because his mother needs his attention. The mother becomes depressed because her children do not seem to be like other "normal" children and blames their dysfunctional behavior on her husband, whom she labels an "absentee father." He in turn becomes angry and defensive, and their sexual relationship suffers. The children respond to the ensuing coldness between the parents in different ways: the son by withdrawing from friends completely and remaining at home with his mother as much as possible, and the daughter by having indiscriminant sexual encounters with one man after another but carefully avoiding intimacy with any of them.
> *Implication:* Behavior has at least as much to do with the interactional context in which it occurs as with the inner mental processes or emotional problems of any of the players.

What should be clear from this example is that family processes affect individual behavior, and individuals within the family system affect family processes, in a recursive manner. As Bednar, Burlingame, and Masters (1988) point out, family functioning is a classic case of reciprocal determinism

> in which every member of a social system, as well as the system's psychological organization (norms, roles), can be influenced by, and influences, every other member of the system in a never-ending cycle. A psychological event in a family cannot be understood without taking into account the simultaneous psychological influences that shaped it. (p. 408)

The Identified Patient and the Family Context

Within a family frame of reference, problems are recast to take into consideration the fact that an individual family member's behavior cannot be understood without attention to the context in which that behavior occurs. Rather than viewing the source of problems or the appearance of symptoms as emanating from a single "sick" person, family therapists view that individual simply as a symptom bearer—the **identified patient** (IP)—expressing the family's disequilibrium or dysfunction.

Satir (1967) contends that a disturbed person's "symptoms" may in reality be a signal that he or she is reacting to family imbalance and is distorting self-growth as a result of trying to absorb and alleviate "family pain." That is, the IP's symptoms can be seen in this view as stabilizing devices[4] used to help relieve family stress and bring the family back into the normal range of its customary behavior. In this sense, the IP's actions may be based on a desire, although not necessarily a planned or premeditated one, to "help" other family members. For example, Haley (1979) describes disturbed young people who do not leave home as willingly sacrificing themselves to protect and maintain family stability. According to Boszormenyi-Nagy and Ulrich (1981), family loyalty may evoke symptomatic behavior when a child "feels obligated to save the parents and their marriage from the threat of destruction" (p. 169). Maintaining symptoms to protect other family members is, of course, not restricted to children and their parents alone, but may occur between marital partners as well (Wachtel & Wachtel, 1986).

Other family therapists, such as Minuchin (Minuchin & Fishman, 1981), consider the symptomatic behavior as a reaction to a family organism under stress, and not particularly as a protective solution to retain family balance. In this view, all family members are equally "symptomatic," despite efforts by the family to locate the problem as residing in one family member.

Minuchin sees the IP's symptoms as rooted in dysfunctional family transactions; it is the family organization that maintains the symptomatic behavior in the

4. We should note here that not all family therapists agree with this "function of the symptom" viewpoint. As we intend to elaborate later, members of the Mental Research Institute (MRI) in Palo Alto in particular maintain that the solutions that families apply to problems may themselves become unsuccessful games without end, repetitive patterns that ultimately become the problem itself. In this viewpoint (Watzlawick, Weakland, & Fisch, 1974), symptoms or problems arise from the repeated use of the same flawed solutions rather than being a sign of family system dysfunction.

identified patient. Change calls for the therapist to understand the family context in which the dysfunctional transactions transpire, and then to attempt with family members as a group to change that existing context in order to permit new interactional possibilities to emerge. As Minuchin and Fishman (1981) argue,

> The therapist, an expander of contexts, creates a context in which exploration of the unfamiliar is possible. She confirms family members and encourages them to experiment with behavior that has previously been constrained by the family system. As new possibilities emerge, the family organism becomes more complex and develops more acceptable alternatives for problem solving. (pp. 15–16)

SUMMARY

A family is a natural social system extending over at least three generations. The way it functions—establishes rules, communicates, and negotiates differences between members—has numerous implications for the development and well-being of its members. Families display a recurring pattern of interactional sequences in which all members participate. Such family strategies primarily help maintain family relationships, but are also called upon to modify transactional patterns in keeping with the changing needs of family members.

Adopting a relationship perspective, family therapists do not negate the significance of individual intrapsychic processes, but take the broader view that individual behavior is better understood as occurring within a family social system. Such a paradigm shift from traditional ways of understanding a person's behavior calls for a cybernetic epistemology in which feedback mechanisms are seen to operate to produce both stability and change. The circular causality involved in what transpires between people within a family forces the family therapist to focus on understanding family processes rather than seeking linear explanations. Within such a framework, the family symptom bearer or identified patient is viewed as merely a representative of a system in disequilibrium.

C h a p t e r T w o

Family Development: Continuity and Change

While family life is an ongoing, interactive process and by no means linear, it does exist in the linear dimension of time. From a multigenerational perspective, such as Carter & McGoldrick (1988) offer, generations have an enduring, reciprocal life-shaping impact on each other as families move through **family life cycle** stages. Within the context of the family's current phase of development, a host of intermingled, intergenerational transactions are occurring concurrently. As one generation moves toward old age, another is attempting to cope with children leaving home, while another may be planning careers or having beginning experiences in intimate adult relationships. Each generation influences and is influenced by the other; development in most families involves multiple simultaneous transitions (Breunlin, 1988).

Family therapists contend that general behavior patterns within a family, or perhaps the family's response to a crisis situation, can become more understandable when viewed within the context of the family's current phase of development.

Similarly, the development of any individual family member can be more fully appreciated only with reference to the developmental path the family has taken. Family development, then, provides the major context and is a major determinant of the growth and development of its members.

THE FAMILY LIFE CYCLE FRAMEWORK

Before we describe the family life cycle concept and evaluate its relevance to family therapy, we need to note that most families, regardless of structure or composition, progress through certain predictable marker events or phases (such as marriage, the birth of a first child, the onset of adolescence, children leaving home, caring for elderly parents). The family, as a developmental system, typically must attempt to deal with the **developmental tasks** that require mastery at each stage. Thus, every family lives in an ever-changing context, and certain key transitional points are universal (Fishman, 1988).

Both continuity and change characterize the family system as it progresses through time. In some cases, the changes are orderly, gradual, continuous; in others they may be sudden, disruptive, and discontinuous. Both call for transformations in the organization of the system. As an example of the latter, a family may suddenly be confronted by unexpected catastrophic events (serious financial reverses, teenage pregnancy, the birth of a handicapped child). Such crises disrupt the family's normal developmental flow and inevitably produce relationship changes within the family system. As Neugarten (1976) points out, the inappropriate or unanticipated timing of a major event may be particularly traumatic precisely because it upsets the sequence and disturbs the rhythm of the expected course of life. To illustrate the point, Neugarten cites the death of a parent during one's childhood, teenage marriage, a first marriage postponed until late in life, or a child born to parents in midlife.

Certain discontinuous changes are so disruptive to family life that they suddenly and profoundly shake up and transform a family system so that it never returns to its former way of functioning. Hoffman (1988) notes particularly those events that affect family membership—events representing gains (children acquired through remarriage) or losses (separation of parents, death). Even a natural transition point that requires major shifts in roles (a child entering kindergarten, a husband retiring from his lifelong work) may produce discontinuous changes and have a similar effect on the family system.

Many family therapists believe that symptoms in a family member are especially likely to appear at these periods of change, signaling the family's difficulty in negotiating a transition. However, not all the difficulties a family experiences coping with change, continuous or discontinuous, need result in symptomatic behavior. The stress on the family system during a transition may actually provide an opportunity for the family to break out of its customary coping patterns and develop more productive, growth-enhancing responses to change.

For example, the continuous change of becoming parents for the first time may be feared (and thus postponed) by the childless couple as restricting mobility, interrupting sleep, constricting their social life, and so on, or may be welcomed as a move to strengthen the family and invest in its future. The discontinuous changes often brought about as a result of remarriage may result in disequilibrium, role confusion, and heightened conflict in the new family, or may provide a second chance to form a more mature, stable relationship. The family therapist has the responsibility to help the family see its choices; belief in the adaptability of the family system and its potential for growth is crucial in helping families engineer change.

The Developmental Stages

Family sociologists such as Reuben Hill and Evelyn Duvall first proposed a developmental framework for studying families in the late 1940s, in an effort to account for regularities in family life over time (Falicov, 1988). Their basic premise was that while families change their form and functions over their existence, they do so in an ordered sequence of developmental stages. These sociologists' focus was on the necessary organizational and adaptational changes a family makes in response to changes in family composition. More specifically, they built their theoretical model on changes in family size due to expansion and later contraction, changes in age composition based on the age of the oldest child, and changes in the work status of the breadwinners.

Duvall, in a text first published in 1957 and now in its sixth edition written with a coauthor (Duvall & Miller, 1985), in particular proposed that the typical development of an intact, middle-class American family proceeds through eight stages, beginning with marriage and ending with the death of both spouses. She portrayed such families in terms of a circle with eight sectors (see Figure 2.1, next page). While no one family is apt to resemble the model in all particulars, the major thrust of Duvall's work was to plot the stages through which families typically pass, and to predict the approximate time (revised with successive editions of her text) when each stage is reached. Within each stage, each individual must perform a series of developmental tasks (for instance, during adolescence, establishing independence) to be better equipped to deal with those tasks requiring mastery at a subsequent stage. At the same time, the family too must succeed in its developmental tasks (for parents of adolescents, balancing freedom with responsibilities) so that it might continue to grow as a unit. In general, making the appropriate role changes over time becomes the family's developmental task.

Although initially arising out of the National Conference on Family Life held in Washington, D.C., in 1948, where it was proposed as a framework for sociological research on marriage and the family (Duvall & Hill, 1948), the life cycle approach was later incorporated by a number of family therapists (Carter & McGoldrick, 1980; Haley, 1971a) as a framework for conceptualizing what transpires within normal and dysfunctional families. As Carter & McGoldrick (1988) have recently formulated this position, the life-cycle perspective "frames problems within the course the family has moved along in its past, the tasks it is trying to master, and the future toward which it is moving" (p. 4).

Individual life cycles take place within the family life cycle, and the interplay between the two affects what takes place in each. The relationship system within a family expands, contracts, and realigns over the family's life span, and the family must be flexible enough to sustain the entry and exit of members as well as bolster the efforts of members to move on in their own personal development. Families that become derailed in their life cycle (and correspondingly derail individual efforts at independence) need help in getting back on developmental track. Carter & McGoldrick (1988) suggest that a major goal of family therapy in such situations is reestablishing the family's developmental momentum.

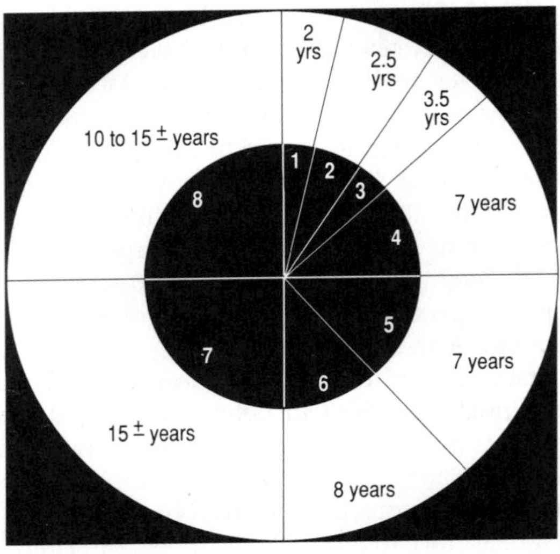

1. Married couples (without children)
2. Childbearing families (oldest child, birth–30 months)
3. Families with preschool children (oldest child 30 months–6 years)
4. Families with school children (oldest child 6–13 years)
5. Families with teenagers (oldest child 13–20 years)
6. Families as launching centers (first child gone to last child leaving home)
7. Middle-aged parents (empty nest to retirement)
8. Aging family members (retirement to death of both spouses)

Figure 2.1 Duvall's (1977) depiction of the eight stages of family life. The duration of each stage has implications for budgeting, housing needs, health care, recreation, education, home management, and various other family resources and services. (Source: Duvall, 1977)

While the family life cycle perspective offers a valuable context for understanding individual and family dysfunction, its shortcomings too require acknowledgment. It is essentially descriptive rather than explanatory. It purports to offer normative data on intact family life at a time in history when a diversity of lifestyles (delayed marriages, cohabitation) and a variety of living arrangements (single-parent-led families, stepfamilies) are prevalent and functional. The approach fails to take individual differences in the timing of nodal events (for example, due to postponed marriages and/or delayed pregnancies) into account, despite the kaleidoscopic array of lifestyles today. To the extent that it suggests that what transpires within the stages is all-important, it does a disservice to the equally important, perhaps more important, transitions between stages, key periods of change.

While we must bear such reservations in mind, the life-cycle approach offers an organizing schema for viewing the family as a system moving through time. Family dysfunction may signal that the family is at a developmental impasse. The appearance of symptomatic behavior may thus be seen as a manifestation of the stress the family is experiencing around a transitional event. Or perhaps the family is rigidly organized and cannot change its organizational structure to accommodate new developmental requirements. Finally, the symptom may serve the function of offering the family a "solution" that helps maintain stability in the face of impending change (Falicov, 1988).

As an example of a family experiencing difficulties in moving on to the next phase of the life cycle, Haley (1973) describes a woman who suffers from postpartum depression following the birth of a child. While she is commonly thought to be experiencing an intense intrapsychic conflict that is producing her symptoms, Haley argues that the entire family may be having difficulty making the transition as it enters this new phase in its development marked by the infant's birth; the mother is simply the identified patient. Haley defines the task of the therapist as helping the family resolve the immediate crisis together in order to achieve a new balance and adaptation to the changed family structure. If successful, the family will resume its developmental course.

Developmental Tasks in Intact Families

There is an invariable order to the stages of family development. Each stage requires that the family face new tasks and learn new adaptational techniques; correspondingly, the family faces new risks of dysfunction. The events occurring at any one stage of the life cycle have a powerful impact on relationships at another stage. Transition points may be especially hazardous. Successful adaptation at any one stage rests heavily on the family's ability to master the tasks required at the previous stage. We might ask, "How well did the family do on its last assignment?" For example, as we note later, a young husband and wife who have not achieved sufficient separation from their parents to be able to establish their own independent marital unit may experience considerable distress, conflict, and confusion when they prepare to enter the next phase of their family life—the birth and rearing of their own children.

Table 2.1 offers an overview of the life-cycle stages for intact middle-class American families, including the second-order changes necessary for the stage to be traversed successfully. (**First-order changes** are changes within a system that do not change the structure of the system itself. **Second-order changes** require a fundamental alteration of the system's structure and function.) Carter and McGoldrick (1988) depart from the traditional sociological view of the family life cycle commencing at the time of marriage, arguing that single young adults must first complete their primary developmental task: separating from the family of origin without cutting off from them and fleeing to a substitute emotional refuge. Separation from parents is made more difficult today because of longer periods of education leading to prolonged financial dependency, increased housing costs, and so on. Delayed marriages due to career demands, fear of sexual experimentation because of AIDS, a general acceptance of later marriages, and apprehension about the longevity of marriage all make commitment to the new relationship more tenuous. Aylmer (1988) contends that the satisfactory resolution of this task, enabling the young person to leave home and begin to establish an identity in the world of work and intimate relationships, is primarily determined by the quality, tone, and degree of completeness reached in original family relationships, with parents, siblings, and **extended family** members.

Table 2.1 Life-Cycle Stages for Intact Middle-Class American Families

Family Life Cycle Stage	*Emotional Process of Transition: Key Principles*	*Second-Order Changes in Family Status Required to Proceed Developmentally*
1. Leaving home: Single young adults	Accepting emotional and financial responsibility for self	a. Differentiation of self in relation to family of origin b. Development of intimate peer relationships c. Establishment of self re work and financial independence
2. The joining of families through marriage: The new couple	Commitment to new system	a. Formation of marital system b. Realignment of relationships with extended families and friends to include spouse
3. Families with young children	Accepting new members into the system	a. Adjusting marital system to make space for child(ren) b. Joining in child-rearing, financial, and household tasks c. Realignment of relationships with extended family to include parenting and grandparenting roles
4. Families with adolescents	Increasing flexibility of family boundaries to include children's independence and grandparents' frailties	a. Shifting of parent-child relationships to permit adolescent to move in and out of system b. Refocus on midlife marital and career issues c. Beginning shift toward joint caring for older generation

(continued)

Table 2.1 *(continued)*

Family Life Cycle Stage	*Emotional Process of Transition: Key Principles*	*Second-Order Changes in Family Status Required to Proceed Developmentally*
5. Launching children and moving on	Accepting a multitude of exits from and entries into the family system	a. Renegotiation of marital system as a dyad b. Development of adult-to-adult relationships between grown children and their parents c. Realignment of relationships to include in-laws and grandchildren d. Dealing with disabilities and death of parents (grandparents)
6. Families in later life	Accepting the shifting of generational roles	a. Maintaining own and/or couple functioning and interests in face of physiological decline; exploration of new familial and social role options b.Support for a more central role of middle generation c. Making room in the system for the wisdom and experience of the elderly, supporting the older generation without overfunctioning for them d. Dealing with loss of spouse, siblings, and other peers, and preparation for own death; life review and integration

(Source: Carter & McGoldrick, 1988, p. 15)

Rather than simply joining two individuals, marriage represents a change in two established family systems and the formation of a subsystem in each. Less formally bound by family traditions than couples in the past, and thus with fewer models to emulate, today's newly married pair must go about differentiating themselves as a couple with primary allegiance to one another and only secondary allegiance to their families of origin. Commitment to the marital partnership is the key to managing the transition of detaching sufficiently from each of their families and forming a new cohesive marital unit (Barnhill & Longo, 1978).

Each mate has acquired from his or her family a set of expectations or rules for marital interaction and family life. Minuchin, Rosman, and Baker (1978) believe that in marriage both paradigms must be retained so that each person maintains a sense of self; the two paradigms must also be reconciled in order for the couple to have a life in common. In the process of reconciliation, spouses arrive at new transactional patterns—compromises or tacit agreements to disagree—that then become familiar and ultimately their preferred or habitual way of interacting with each other.

In developing a marital coalition, the partners must not only provide for their basic physical needs but also continually negotiate such personal issues as when and how to sleep, eat, have sex, fight, and make up. They must decide how to celebrate holidays, plan vacations, spend money, and do household chores. They are obliged to decide which family traditions and rituals to retain from each of their pasts and which they wish to generate as their own. Together they need to determine the degree of closeness to or distance from each of their extended families they wish to maintain. Each has to gain admission to the other's family, perhaps as the first person to do so in many years. In the same way, they must meet each other's friends and over time select those who will become the couple's friends. Together they gain new friends and lose touch with some old ones.

When a couple is first married, the marital system tends to be loosely organized and the roles played by the spouses flexible and often interchangeable. The structure of a family without children allows for a wide variety of solutions to immediate problems. For example, either or both of the partners may prepare dinner at home; they may choose to eat out at a restaurant; they may drop in at a friend's or relative's house for a meal; they may eat separately or together. When there are children to be fed, however, a more formal and specific arrangement will have to be formulated in advance of dinnertime. Beyond making room for children in their lives, psychologically as well as physically, the couple must define more clearly the distribution of duties and division of labor: who will shop, cook, pick up the children at a nursery or child-care center, wash the dishes, put their offspring to bed? The commitment of husband and wife, then, to become mother and father represents a significant transition point in a family's life, changing forever the relatively simple playing out of roles between mates who are childless.

The arrival of children thus represents perhaps the most significant milestone in the life cycle of the family. The partners' lives may not have changed nearly as much when the two married; this is even more likely if they lived together before marriage and/or established a satisfactory premarital sexual relationship. When husband and wife become parents, however, both "move up" a generation and now must provide care for a younger generation. Other members of the family **suprasystem** also move up a notch—parental siblings become uncles and aunts; nieces and nephews now become cousins; the parents of the new mother and father become grandparents. Overall, a vertical realignment occurs for new family and extended family together.

Making this transition, taking and sharing responsibilities, developing patience, setting limits, tolerating restrictions on free time and mobility, all these tasks must be mastered in the expanding family system. Young parents, particularly if both are employed full-time, as is increasingly the case, each must now juggle schedules and attempt to find a comfortable balance between work and domestic responsibilities. At the same time, husband and wife need to redefine and redistribute household and child-care chores. Their previously egalitarian role structure may break down and they may resort to more traditional male/female divisions of labor, which may create unexpected conflicts and additional stress. Older parents must learn to accommodate young children in an already established or perhaps fixed pattern of relationships, often without being able to call upon elderly grandparents for support.

Beyond such practical problems, Bradt (1988) observes that a child's arrival may bring a nuclear family **triangle**[1] into play, challenging the stability of the spousal relationship because of one parent's closeness to the child and distancing from a mate. Bradt contends that the failure of either spouse to change to a parent and at the same time to continue to grow as a spouse may well threaten the couple's intimacy. He argues that "a marriage that has developed intimacy is a marriage better able to respond to the challenge of parenthood, to integrate the lifelong change that parenthood brings, not only to the new parents but to the entire family" (p. 243).

Barnhill and Longo (1978) believe that two crucial transition points for the family involve, first, both parents learning to accept the new personality as the child grows up, and second, introducing the child to institutions outside the family, such as schools, church, and sports groups. According to Haley (1973), a common crisis period occurs within families when the first child starts school; this represents the family's first step toward the realization that the children will eventually leave home. The symptoms of school refusal or school phobia in young children may reflect familial turmoil and restructuring.

When children reach adolescence, the family faces new organizational challenges, particularly around autonomy and independence. Parents may no longer be able to maintain complete authority, but they cannot abdicate authority completely, either. Rule changing, limit setting, role renegotiation are all necessary, often disruptively shifting relationships across two or more generations. As Preto (1988) points out, the struggle to meet adolescent demands may reactivate unresolved parent-grandparent conflicts over child rearing, or perhaps bring similar husband-wife conflicts to the surface. Triangles between the teenager and both parents, or perhaps the teenager, parent, and grandparent, are common and often disruptive to the suprasystem.

Adolescents must strike a balance on their own, forging an identity and beginning to establish autonomy from the family. Teenagers who remain too childlike and dependent or who become too isolated and withdrawn may become problems, putting a strain on the family system. Too rapid an exit from family life by adolescents may also impair a family's ability to adapt. Parents, too, need to come to terms with their teenager's rapidly changing social and sexual behavior.

All of this is likely to occur while simultaneous strains on the system may be taking place: (1) "midlife crises" in which one or both middle-age parents question not only career choices but also perhaps their earlier marital choices as well (for some women, this may represent the first opportunity to pursue a career without child-care responsibilities, leading to family dislocations and role changes); (2) the aging of grandparents, necessitating role reversals between parents and now-dependent grandparents, perhaps calling for changing caretaking arrangements regarding the older generation.

1. Murray Bowen introduced and elaborated the importance of triangles in family relationships, considering them the basic building blocks of a family's emotional system. We intend to elaborate these ideas further in a later chapter devoted to Bowen's transgenerational theories.

Carter and McGoldrick (1988) refer to the next phase of the intact family's life cycle as "launching children and moving on." Unlike in earlier times, today the low birthrate coupled with longer life expectancy means that this stage now covers a lengthy period; parents frequently launch their families almost twenty years before retirement. Parents must come to accept their children's independent role and eventual creation of their own families. The development of adult-to-adult relationships with their children is an important developmental task at this stage, as is the expansion of the family to include the spouses, children, and in-laws of their married children.

Parents also need to reassess their relationship with one another now that their children no longer reside at home. Sometimes couples view this change as an opportunity for freedom from child-rearing responsibilities and perhaps a chance to travel or do other things postponed for financial reasons while they cared for their children. Now, in the absence of children, these families see a chance to strengthen their marital bond. In other families, marital strains covered over while they raised children together may resurface with the children gone. Children leaving may in such cases lead to increased marital strife or feelings of depression and loneliness over life having become empty and meaningless. It is not uncommon for such parents to hold onto their offspring, especially the last child.

Further, parents need to cope with moving up a notch to grandparent positions. At the same time, increased caretaking responsibilities for their own needy and dependent parents, especially by women, is likely. In some cases, the renewal of the parent-grandparent relationship provides an opportunity to resolve earlier interpersonal conflicts; in other cases, it may simply exacerbate unresolved conflict from earlier days. A major transition point for the middle-aged adult is apt to revolve around the death of elderly parents.

The retirement years mean that a husband and wife must cope with a dramatic increase in their daily time together, and, frequently, a reduction in income. Enduring the loss of friends and relatives (and most difficult of all, loss of a spouse), coping with increased dependence on one's children, handling changing relationships with grandchildren, relinquishing power and status, coming to terms with one's own illness, limitations, and ultimate death—these are some of the problems of old age. With the death of one partner, the family must often assume care of the surviving mate at home or in a nursing home, with all family members experiencing a new set of transitional stresses.

Walsh (1988) suggests that changes brought about by retirement, widowhood, grandparenthood, and illness/dependency all represent major adaptational challenges for the entire family system, as it attempts to cope with loss and dysfunction and tries to reorganize itself. The death of a grandparent may be the young child's first encounter with separation and loss and, at the same time, may be a reminder to the parents of their own mortality. How the family deals with the dying process has implications for several generations as all move inevitably toward the aging phase of the life cycle (Brody, 1974).

Developmental Tasks in Alternative Families

Divorce, affecting perhaps half of all couples married today, touches family members at every generation and throughout the nuclear as well as extended families. The divorce process and its sequelae inevitably have a powerful, disruptive impact on three aspects of the life cycle—individual, marital, and family—all of which must be taken into account in gaining a full measure of the subsequent dislocations to all participants (Sager et al., 1983). In family system terms, divorce adds complexity to whatever developmental tasks the family is currently experiencing. Peck and Manocherian (1988) even suggest that with the shape of the family inevitably altered, each ensuing life phase becomes affected by the divorce and therefore must be viewed within the dual context of that stage itself along with the residual effects of the earlier divorce.

Postdivorce families need to go through at least one, and possibly two, additional life-cycle phases before they can restabilize and resume their development (Tables 2.2 and 2.3). In the former case, single-parent-led families where there is no remarriage must cope with a number of thorny issues. The custodial parent, likely to be the mother, must deal with lowered economic status, grief and self-blame, loneliness, lack of an adequate support system, child-care arrangements, custody and visitation problems, and more. The noncustodial parent must cope with diminished relationships with his children, disruption of his customary living experiences, loneliness and self-blame for the failed marriage, custody and visitation conflicts. The children must grapple with shame and embarrassment, less contact with the noncustodial parent, conflicting loyalties, adaptation to visitation activities, and perhaps continued fantasies over parental reconciliation (Goldenberg & Goldenberg, 1990). All three experience problems that affect, and are affected by, problems in the others.

In the majority of cases, one-parent households are a stepping-stone to remarriage, frequently involving stepfamilies. Whiteside (1982) observes that such families must undergo two sets of developmental processes simultaneously: those appropriate to the family's ordinary life-cycle stage, and those related to the stage of the remarriage process. Beyond their adaptation to a single-parent household, here the entire family must struggle with fears regarding investing in new relationships and forming a new family. Visher & Visher (1988) suggest that the majority of stepfamilies have a number of distinctive problems: they are born out of relationship losses and the abandonment of hopes and dreams in the previous family; they are composed of members with separate family histories and traditions that may be in conflict and that need to be reconciled; children are often members of two households, with differing rules and lifestyles; children often experience loyalty conflicts between parents. Goldenberg and Goldenberg (1990) add that there may be difficulties in assuming parental roles with stepchildren, rivalries and jealousies may develop between stepchildren, and competition between the biological mother and the stepmother may occur.

Table 2.2 Dislocations in the Family Life Cycle Requiring Additional Steps to Restabilize and Proceed Developmentally

Phase	*Emotional Process of Transition Prerequisite Attitude*	*Developmental Issues*
Divorce		
1. The decision to divorce	Acceptance of inability to resolve marital tensions sufficiently to continue relationship	Acceptance of one's own part in the failure of the marriage
2. Planning the breakup of the system	Supporting viable arrangements for all parts of the system	a. Working cooperatively on problems of custody, visitation, and finances b. Dealing with extended family about the divorce
3. Separation	a. Willingness to continue cooperative coparental relationship and joint financial support of children b. Work on resolution of attachment to spouse	a. Mourning loss of intact family b. Restructuring marital and parent-child relationships and finances; adaptation to living apart c. Realignment of relationships with extended family; staying connected with spouse's extended family
4. The divorce	More work on emotional divorce: Overcoming hurt, anger, guilt, etc.	a. Mourning loss of intact family; giving up fantasies of reunion b. Retrieval of hopes, dreams, expectations from the marriage c. Staying connected with extended families
Postdivorce family		
Custodial single parent	Willingness to maintain financial responsibilities, continue parental contact with ex-spouse, and support contact of children with ex-spouse and his or her family	a. Making flexible visitation arrangements with ex-spouse and his family b. Rebuilding own financial resources c. Rebuilding own social network
Noncustodial single parent	Willingness to maintain parental contact with ex-spouse and support custodial parent's relationship with children	a. Finding ways to continue effective parenting relationship with children b. Maintaining financial responsibilities to ex-spouse and children c. Rebuilding own social network

(Source: Carter & McGoldrick, 1988, p. 22)

Table 2.3 Remarried Family Formation: A Developmental Outline

Step	*Prerequisite Attitude*	*Developmental Issues*
1. Entering the new relationship	Recovery from loss of first marriage (adequate "emotional divorce")	Recommitment to marriage and to forming a family with readiness to deal with complexity and ambiguity
2. Conceptualizing and planning new marriage and family	Accepting one's own fears and those of new spouse and children about remarriage and forming a stepfamily Accepting need for time and patience for adjustment to complexity and ambiguity of: 1. Multiple new roles 2. Boundaries: space, time, membership, and authority 3. Affective issues: guilt, loyalty conflicts, desire for mutuality, unresolvable past hurts	a. Working on openness in the new relationships to avoid pseudomutuality b. Planning for maintenance of cooperative financial and coparental relationships with ex-spouses c. Planning to help children deal with fears, loyalty conflicts, and membership in two systems d. Realignment of relationships with extended family to include new spouse and children e. Planning maintenance of connections for children with extended family of ex-spouses(s).
3. Remarriage and reconstitution of family	Final resolution of attachment to previous spouse and ideal of "intact" family; acceptance of a different model of family with permeable boundaries	a. Restructuring family boundaries to allow for inclusion of new spouse–stepparent b. Realignment of relationships and financial arrangements throughout subsystems to permit interweaving of several systems c. Making room for relationships of all children with biological (noncustodial) parents, grandparents, and other extended family d. Sharing memories and histories to enhance stepfamily integration

(Source: Carter & McGoldrick, 1988, p. 24)

Visher and Visher (1988) suggest that stepfamily development occurs in stages and that each stage in the process calls for renegotiating and reorganizing a complex and dynamic network of relationships. They conclude from their research that the process is likely to take several years before full stepfamily integration is achieved.

GENDER ISSUES AND FAMILY DEVELOPMENT

A full understanding of the family developmental process must take into account the fact that men and women experience family life differently, both in their families of origin and in the families they form through marriage. Typically they are reared with different role expectations, beliefs, values, attitudes, goals, and opportunities. They enter marriage and, later, parenthood with different ideas of what will be expected of them, and, not surprisingly, have different experiences. As Bernard (1974) suggests, in every marriage there are two marriages—his and hers.

In recent years, a number of studies (Gilligan, 1982; Goldner, 1985; McGoldrick, Anderson, & Walsh, 1989) have faulted family therapy theory for failing to pay sufficient attention to how these differences influence internal family interaction, the social context for family development. In particular, feminists have started to address the social, cultural, and historic conditions that have shaped not only the development and experiences of women, but also their relationships with men. One approach has been to examine traditional and emerging women's roles throughout the life cycle. The Women's Project in Family Therapy, begun in 1977 in an effort to introduce a feminist perspective to the field, has now resulted in a text by the four researchers (Walters, Carter, Papp, & Silverstein, 1989). In it, they stress the intrinsic influence of gender on relationship patterns throughout a woman's life.

Feminists argue that the field of family therapy has by and large ignored gender issues in conceptualizing family life, except to focus on a woman's role as nurturer, caretaker, and helper to her family (husband, children, parents). A woman, according to Gilligan (1982), tends to define herself within the context of relationships on which she in turn relies. Gilligan argues that men, in their theories of psychological development, have tended to downplay or devalue that care, viewing it as weakness rather than an expression of strength. She believes that such theories, because of their inherent male bias, equate maturity with independence, rationality, action. Such qualities as caring for the needs of others, warmth, and emotional expressiveness, which our society defines as necessary for feminine behavior, are at the same time given short shrift as expressions of the inferiority of the "weaker sex."

Hare-Mustin (1987) goes so far as to describe gender as the "basic category on which the world is organized" (p. 15). She suggests that commonly observed behavioral differences simply reflect established gender arrangements in society, rather than any essential set of differences in the nature of men as opposed to women, as Gilligan proposes. A woman's typically greater concern with relationships, according to Hare-Mustin, can best be understood as a need to please others when one lacks power. In this view, a woman's behavior reflects her less-powerful role position vis-à-vis a man's, rather than resulting from an inherent weakness of character. Where the powerful advocate rules and rationality, the weak espouse relatedness.

Hare-Mustin (1987) offers the following example:

> Thus, in husband-wife conflicts, husbands use logic, wives call on caring. But, in parent-child conflicts, parents, including mothers, emphasize rules; it is the children who appeal for understanding. Society rewards rationality, not emotions, but which is used is associated with who has the power, and not primarily with being male or female. (p. 22)

In family life cycle terms, independent young adulthood for women in the United States is a relatively new phenomenon. Traditionally, a single woman lived with her family of origin until married; she had no time in between to experience being independent. In recent years, however, as women have entered the work force, many have chosen to live alone or perhaps cohabit with men or other women. Men have typically found it easier to separate from their families of origin with societal approval.

The entry of women, whether single, married, or heads of single-parent households, into the world of paid work has had a profound effect on family life. In recent years, women have been marrying later (or choosing not to marry at all) and are having fewer children. Young couples who do decide to become parents, as noted earlier, must rearrange the family system and renegotiate the roles each plays, particularly if the wife continues to work outside the home, as more and more do. Breaking out of stereotypic male/female roles regarding domestic and work responsibilities is essential. However, though to a lesser extent than before, working wives continue to bear the major responsibility for child care and household chores. In addition, they are likely to take on the obligation of maintaining contact with both their families of origin, as well as sustaining friendships.

Traditionally, while women's domain has been the management of the home and the raising of the children, men have taken on the responsibility for financial support and, if necessary, the family's physical protection. According to Weiss's (1985) survey, this traditional family organization is likely to persist even when the woman works. While the man might acknowledge the help provided by his wife's income, and might do the dishes or shop or look after the children on occasion, the division of day-to-day responsibilities remains sex-linked. As Gurman and Klein (1980) note, despite sharing more of the household and child-care activities than men have generally done in the past, today's husband is still likely to retain a privately held attitude that he is helping his wife carry out what are essentially her responsibilities.

With the children out of the house and forming families of their own, men and women may find themselves with differing priorities, according to McGoldrick (1988b). She believes that men may wish to seek greater closeness to their wives, while the latter may begin to feel energized about developing their own lives, perhaps through resumed careers or other activities outside the home. If serious marital tension leads to divorce, as it sometimes does at this stage, McGoldrick contends that women are especially vulnerable. Not only are they less likely than men to remarry, but their embeddedness in relationships, their orientation toward interdependence, their lifelong subordination of achievement to caring for others, and their conflicts over competitive success may make them especially susceptible to despair.

Finally, since women are apt to outlive men, many may find themselves alone and financially impoverished. Very likely they will turn to their daughters (or perhaps daughters-in-law) for support and care.

ETHNIC AND SOCIOECONOMIC CONSIDERATIONS

Just as one's family is integral to the life of the individual, so family life itself is dependent in large measure on forces within the social environment of which it is a part. Aponte (1987) emphasizes the interdependence of the individual, the family and the community, arguing that personal problems inevitably are embedded in a "social ecological matrix," the place where the dynamics of the individual, the family, and society interface. In this section, we focus on two underemphasized aspects of the social environment—ethnicity and socioeconomic factors—that impact significantly on family life.

Ethnicity and Family Development

Ethnicity, the unique characteristics of a cultural group, is surely a fundamental determinant of how families establish and reinforce acceptable values, attitudes, behavior patterns, and modes of emotional expression. Transmitted over generations by the family, ethnicity patterns may surpass race, religion, or national origin in significance for the family, particularly because they represent the individual's and the family's psychological needs for identity and a sense of historical continuity.

Our ethnic background influences how we think, how we feel, how we work, how we relax, how we celebrate holidays and rituals, how we express our anxieties, how we feel about illness or life and death. Ethnicity patterns, reinforced by family tradition and perhaps community membership, may operate in subtle ways, frequently outside of our awareness, but their impact may nevertheless be potent. Just as family therapy theory cannot fail to recognize the power of gender or family of origin on individual behavior, so it must also acknowledge the contribution of ethnic background and cultural tradition.

Even the definition of "family" differs in different groups. The dominant white Anglo Saxon Protestant (WASP) focus is on the intact nuclear family, extending back over generations. Blacks expand their definition to include a wide informal network of kin and community. Italians think in terms of tightly knit three-or-four generational families, often including godfathers and old friends; all may be involved in family decision making, may live in close proximity to one another, and may share life-cycle transitions together. The Chinese tend to go even further, including all their ancestors and all their descendants in their definition of family membership (McGoldrick, 1988a).

American Indian family systems are extended networks, including several households. A nonkin can become a family member through being a namesake of a child, and consequently assumes family obligations and responsibilities for child rearing and role modeling. Hispanic Americans, the fastest growing ethnic group in the country, take deep pride in family membership, with a man generally using both his father's and mother's name together with his given name. (The name Jose Garcia Rivera thus reflects that Garcia is his father's family name and Rivera his mother's. If this person were addressed by a single name, the father's family name, Garcia, would be used, reflecting the Hispanic patriarchal pattern) (Ho, 1987).

Family life cycle timing is influenced by ethnic considerations. Mexican Americans tend to have longer courtship periods and extended childhoods beyond the dominant American pattern, but shorter adolescent periods and hastened adulthood. Similarly, different groups give different importance to life-cycle transition points. The Irish wake is a ritual that represents a view of death as the most important transition, freeing humans so that they can go on to a happier afterlife. Polish families emphasize weddings, their lengthy celebration reflecting the importance of the family's continuity into the next generation. For Jewish families, the Bar Mitzvah signifies the transition into adulthood, reflecting the high value placed on continued intellectual development (McGoldrick, 1988a).

Child-rearing practices may also vary greatly. While the dominant American pattern is for the mother to have primary responsibility, blacks often rely on grandparents and extended family members to care for children, especially if the mother is working outside the home. Greeks and Puerto Ricans tend to indulge young infants, but later become strict with children, particularly girls. Adolescent girls from Italian-American families may find themselves in intergenerational conflicts with parents and grandparents as they rebel against traditional female roles of waiting on fathers, brothers, and later, husbands and sons.

The danger in these generalizations, of course, is that they run the risk of stereotyping. Ho (1987) reminds us that there is not only considerable interethnic group diversity, but also marked intraethnic group heterogeneity. It is important to remember that some families are more assimilated than others; some have long histories of intermarriage; and social-class differences play a more decisive role in some ethnic groups than in others. The importance of delineating common family patterns is in emphasizing the often-overlooked role of ethnocultural factors in behavior (McGoldrick, Pearce, & Giordano, 1982).

Since therapists inevitably impose some of their own cultural biases on their work, they need to be aware of their own values as well as the values of client families influenced by their cultural and ethnic backgrounds. Rather than oversimplified pictures to be taken at face value, the diverse ethnic profiles are intended to call attention to the rich variety of human experiences and behavior—to emphasize the fact that family therapists must consider the possible impact of cultural idiosyncracies in assessing and treating families they might otherwise label deviant or dysfunctional.

Poverty, Class, and the Family Life Cycle

Although recognizing the family as integral to the life of the individual, many family therapists fail to pay sufficient attention to the dependence of families on their social environment. By not fully exploring the implications of the interdependence of the individual, the family, and the community, they often overlook the relationship of societal forces to mental health (Aponte, 1987). For example, Belle (1982) points out that one in three female-headed households lives in poverty; those women who live in such financially strained circumstances and who have responsibilities for young children are particularly prone to feelings of hopelessness and depression. The significance of social context in organizing and constraining people's lives cannot be overestimated.

Mednick (1987) estimates that women heading their own families have a poverty rate two and one-half times that of the two-parent family. Beyond such female-led families who are impoverished, there are other unemployed or homeless people whose life cycles consist of a virtually endless series of crises that strain their adaptive capacities to the limit.

As Hines (1988) points out in discussing the family life cycle of poor blacks, those families embedded in a context of chronic unemployment and discrimination are particularly limited in their abilities to function in ways that permit family members to thrive. The decline in marriage rates among blacks, coupled with the increased rate of illegitimate births, particularly among adolescents, has added to the family crisis among black Americans. Edelman (1987), founder of the Children's Defense Fund, argues that the interrelated factors of poverty, male joblessness, and poor, female-headed households operate together to perpetuate generations of membership in America's underclass. In a seemingly endless circle, the loosening of the black family structure has led to increased out-of-wedlock births and, correspondingly, increased child poverty; joblessness and its resulting poverty have led to a decline in the number of marriageable males and the further weakening of the family structure. Thus, children are poor, according to Edelman's analysis, not only because many live in fatherless homes, but also because the single parents with whom they live are likely to be unemployed or, if employed, earn low wages.

Aponte (1987), too, emphasizes the erosion of family structure and the creation of what he terms "underorganized" families. Living in such situations through generations, white and black families alike "learn to view as normal their own impotence" (p. 2). They are forced to accept their dependence upon the community's network of social institutions (welfare, public housing, publicly funded health care) without the necessary political or economic power to influence outcomes. Where fatherless homes predominate, roles lose their distinctiveness, and children may grow up too quickly while being at the same time intellectually and emotionally stifled in development.

Life-cycle progression among the poor is often accelerated by teenage pregnancy. The stages we have described for middle-class intact families (see Table 2.1) are often fast-forwarded; the "launching" stage for a young mother's children, for example, may occur when she is still at *her* mother's home (Fulmer, 1988). In the same manner, a "single adult" label hardly applies to an adolescent mother with children, nor is the parent-child relationship likely to be the central one around which the family is organized. More probably, grandmother-mother-daughter relationships predominate, and several generations of family are likely to be alive at the same time. The basic family unit in such situations is apt to include extended three- or four-generational networks of kin. Such kinship groups at times function as "multiple-parent families" with reciprocal obligations to one another, sharing meager resources as efficiently as possible (Fulmer, 1988).

The family therapist, likely to be middle class (in viewpoint if not necessarily in origin), must be careful not to regard being poor as synonymous with leading a chaotic, disorganized life. It is essential to distinguish between those families who have been poor for many generations (victims of what Aponte, 1987, calls structural poverty), poor intermittently or temporarily (while divorced but before remarriage), or recently poor because of loss (such as the death of the wage earner). It also helps to be aware that some poor people share middle-class values while others embrace the values of the working class as a result of their life experiences. Some lead lives that are a series of crises, and others have forged family and social networks that are resourceful and workable. Above all, as Aponte (1976) reminds us, any efforts to equate poverty with psychological deviance first must take into account the harsh and confining social conditions usually associated with being poor.

SUMMARY

One way of understanding both individuals and their families is to study their development over the family life cycle. Continuity and change characterize family life, as the family system progresses over time. While the progression is generally orderly and sequenced, certain discontinuous changes may be particularly disruptive. The appearance of symptomatic behavior in a family member at transition points in the family life cycle may signal that the family is having difficulty in negotiating change.

Despite certain shortcomings, the family life cycle perspective offers an organizing theme for viewing the family as a system moving through time with specific developmental tasks to accomplish at each stage en route. Passing expected milestones as well as dealing with unexpected crises may temporarily threaten the family's usual developmental progress, causing realignments in the family's organization. Alternative families, such as those led by single parents or those where remarriage has created a stepfamily, may experience disruptions in the family life cycle before resuming their orderly development.

Men and women are reared with different role expectations, experiences, goals, and opportunities, and these gender differences influence later husband-wife interactions. The entry of women in large numbers into the work force in recent years has also influenced traditional male-female roles regarding household and outside work responsibilities.

Ethnicity and socioeconomic considerations also influence family lifestyles. The former may help determine how families establish values, behavior patterns, and modes of emotional expression, and how they progress through the family life cycle. Living in poverty, whether temporarily or as part of poverty patterns extending over generations, may erode family structure and create underorganized families. In poor families, life-cycle progression is often accelerated by early pregnancy, frequently of unwed mothers. The basic unit in fatherless homes is likely to be the grandmother-mother-daughter relationship.

Chapter Three

The Family as a Psychosocial System

We have proposed to this point adopting a relationship frame of reference in studying a family's functioning, paying simultaneous attention to its structure (the way it arranges, organizes, and maintains itself at any given cross section of time) and its processes (the way it evolves, adapts, and changes over time). Families are living, ongoing entities, organized wholes with members in a continuous, interactive, patterned relationship with one another extending over time and space. A change in any one component inevitably is associated with changes in other components with which it is in relation. It is in this most primary sense that a family is a system (Bloch, 1985).

In this chapter we introduce some of the underlying concepts of **general systems theory** as providing the theoretical underpinnings for much of family therapy theory and current practice. Both general systems theory and the cybernetics concepts described in Chapter 1 emerged during the 1940s, and indeed the terms are sometimes used interchangeably to refer to systems theory. However, we believe the terms are not synonymous. While both are built upon the same assumptions (such as recursive sequences and circular causality), the former term is broader, in our opinion, referring to all self-regulating systems and less specifically to feedback mechanisms.

In this family therapy scene, cotherapists work together with a husband and wife who sought help because of their frequent quarrels over disciplining their 6-year-old hyperactive daughter.

Most family therapists appear to acknowledge a theoretical debt to general systems theory, freely (if somewhat loosely) borrowing such systems terms as *homeostasis* and *open system* to describe families or goals of their therapeutic interventions. In actuality, according to Constantine (1986), systems terms are not used by therapists with the precision and rigor with which they were originally formulated, but rather simply allude to the idea of a family as a complexly organized, durable, and ongoing causal network of related components.

SOME CHARACTERISTICS OF A FAMILY SYSTEM

According to Buckley (1967), a system involves a "complex of elements or components directly or indirectly related in a causal network such that each component is related to at least some other parts in a more or less stable way within a particular period of time" (p. 41). That is, a system is an entity with component parts or units that covary, with each unit constrained by or dependent on the state of the other units. There are solar systems, ecosystems, systems of law, electronic systems, and so forth. In each case, the components interact so that each influences and in turn is influenced by other component parts, together producing a whole—a system—that is greater than the sum of the interdependent parts.

The concepts of **organization** and **wholeness** are keys to understanding how systems operate. If a system represents a set of units that stand in some consistent relationship to one another, then we can infer that the system is organized around those relationships. Further, we can say that the parts or elements of the system interact with each other in a predictable, "organized" fashion. Similarly, we can assume that the elements, once combined, produce an entity—a whole—that is greater than the sum of its parts. It follows that no system can be adequately understood or fully explained once it has been broken down into its component parts; and that no element within the system can ever be understood in isolation since it never functions independently.

A family represents one such system, in which the member components are organized into a group, forming a whole that transcends the sum of its separate parts. When we speak of the Johnson family, for example, we are discussing a complex and recognizable entity—not simply the aggregate of Mr. Johnson plus Mrs. Johnson plus the Johnson children. Understanding the dynamic relationships among the components (family members) is far more illuminating than simply summing up those components (Ackerman, 1984). The relationships between the family members are complex, and factions, alliances, coalitions, and tensions exist. Causality within the family system is circular and multidirectional.

As Leslie (1988) observes, because of the system's wholeness, the movement of each component influences the whole and is explained, in part, by movement in related parts of the system. Focusing on the functioning of one element (member) becomes secondary to understanding the connections or relationships among family members and the overall organization of the system. As illustration, Leslie notes that a family with two children does not simply add a new member when a baby is born; the family becomes a new entity with accompanying changes in family interactive patterns.

Should a 2-year-old start to engage in hostile outbursts, linear explanations might attribute the new behavior to jealousy or infer the toddler is reacting to the loss of his mother's attention, since she now must devote a great deal of attention to the baby. A systems perspective, on the other hand, might look at how the family has reorganized after the new birth. Perhaps in reorganizing around the infant, the mother has assumed primary care of the infant, and the father the major responsibility for the older children, while the older son has been designated a helper to his mother with the newborn. The toddler may have lost his customary role in the family. From this vantage point, his hostile behavior may be signaling the family that their reorganization is inadequate or perhaps incomplete in meeting the needs of all of its members. To examine the motives of the toddler alone, without addressing the system's interactive patterns, would be to miss the point that the system requires alteration (Leslie, 1988).

Family Rules

A family is a rule-governed system. The interaction of family members typically follows organized, established patterns, enabling each person to learn what is permitted or expected of him or her as well as others in family transactions. Usually unstated, such rules characterize, regulate, and help stabilize how—and how well—families function as a unit. They form a basis for the development of family traditions, and largely determine expectations of the members vis-à-vis one another.

The observation that family interactions follow certain persistent patterns—rules—was first made by Don Jackson (1965a), a pioneer in family therapy. He observed that partners in a marriage face multiple challenges as potential collaborators in wage earning, housekeeping, socializing, love making, and parenting. Early in their relationship, they begin to exchange views about one another, as well as express expectations about the nature of their relationship. More or less specifically, according to Jackson (1965a), they define the rights and duties of each spouse: "You can depend on me to be logical, practical, realistic"; "In return, you can depend on me to be a feeling, sensitive, social person." Such determinations often reflect culturally linked sex roles—in this case, traditional male and female roles, respectively—but variations are frequent. If it is appropriate for the persons involved, and not too rigidly set so that modifications cannot be made on the basis of their subsequent experiences together, the couple is beginning to develop a division of labor that is intended to help them pursue the sort of life they wish to lead in the future.

Family rules determine the way people pattern their behavior; thus, for Jackson, rules become the governing principles of family life, providing guidelines for future interactive patterns. Addressing the marital dyad, Jackson adopted the concept of **marital quid pro quo** to describe a relationship with well-formulated rules in which each partner gives and receives something in return. Although trained in psychoanalysis and committed to the study of intrapsychic conflict, Jackson began to develop a language of interaction, a schema for depicting human exchanges. By means of descriptive language, he attempted to account for the stabilizing mechanisms in any ongoing relationship (Greenberg, 1977).

Extending his observations to the family at large, Jackson (1965b) hypothesized that a **redundancy principle** operates in family life, according to which a family interacts in repetitive behavioral sequences. That is, instead of using the full range of possible behavior open to them, members settle on certain rules or redundant patterns when dealing with one another. If you understand their rules, you begin to understand how a family defines its internal relationships. Jackson maintained that it is these rules rather than individual needs, drives, or personality traits that determine the interactive sequences between family members.

Rules may be descriptive (metaphors describing patterns of interchange) or prescriptive (directing what can or cannot occur between members). They are formulas for constructing and maintaining family relationships. Within a family group they may be based on individual prerogatives and obligations determined by age, sex, or generation. All members learn the family's **metarules** (literally, the rules about the rules), which typically take the form of unstated family directives offering principles for interpreting rules, as well as family rules for changing rules.

Some family rules are stated overtly—rules such as: "Children allow parents to speak without interruption"; "Children hang up their clothes"; "Parents decide on bedtime"; "Mother makes decisions regarding the purchase of new clothes"; "Father chooses the television programs on Monday night"; "Heavy lifting is done by the males"; "Sister helps set the table but Brother helps Dad clear the dinner dishes"; "Younger children go to bed earlier than older ones"; "Older children have larger allowances."[1]

Most family rules, however, are covert and unstated. That is, they are inferences that all family members draw from the redundancies or repetitive patterns in the relationships they observe at home—for example, "It's best to ask Mother for money after dinner, when she's in a good mood"; "Show the report card to Dad first because Mom might be tougher"; "Don't be a crybaby"; "If you lose your glasses, avoid mentioning it as long as possible because they'll both be mad"; "Stay away from their room on Sunday morning, they like to be alone." Children learn and perpetuate these rules.

Parents act according to covert rules of their own: "Daughters help in the kitchen, but it isn't right to ask a son"; "Boys have later curfews than girls"; "You kids can fight all you want but don't involve us"; "We can trust our daughter with money, but it seems to burn a hole in our son's pocket." Sometimes a family rule, unstated but understood by all, is that decisions are made by the parents and handed down to the children; in other cases, all family members learn that they may state their own opinions freely. In a well-functioning family, rules help maintain order and stability while at the same time allowing for changes with changing circumstances.

Some family therapists, such as Virginia Satir (1972), try to help a family recognize its unwritten rules, especially those that involve the exchange of feelings or that cause family pain. For example, some families forbid discussion of certain topics ("Mother is an alcoholic"; "Father does not come home certain nights"; "Brother does not know how to read"; "Sister should be talked to about sex and contraception") and, as a consequence, fail to take realistic steps to alleviate problems. Other families forbid overt expressions of anger or irritation with each other ("Stop! The children will hear us"; "If you can't say something nice to one another, don't say anything at all"). Still others foster dependence ("Never trust anyone but your mother or father") and thus handicap children as they attempt to deal with the outside world.

Satir argues that dysfunctional families follow dysfunctional rules. She attempts to help such families become aware of these unwritten rules that retard growth and

1. A small child visiting a friend for the first time is apt to be bewildered by observing a family operating under an alien set of rules. Mother and father may greet each other with a kiss, may not get into a quarrel over the dinner table, may include children in the conversation. A visiting child is sometimes startled to learn that, according to the rules in another family, it is not necessary to finish all the food on your plate before you are allowed to have dessert!

maturity. Once these rules have been identified, it may be possible for the family to revise or discard those that are outmoded, inappropriate, or irrelevant to improve overall family functioning.

Family Homeostasis

Physiological studies first carried out by Walter Cannon (1932) led to the concept of dynamic equilibrium to explain the body's ability to operate as a self-regulating system, maintaining a steady state despite possibly drastic changes in the outside environment. For example, whatever the change in outside temperature, body temperature varies little from its customary 98.6 degrees; various body-regulating mechanisms (perspiration, change in water retention, "goose pimples," shivering) are ordinarily called into play to maintain the constancy of body temperature should a sudden change in outside temperature occur. (The same is true for other body mechanisms, such as blood pressure.) The automatic tendency of the body to maintain balance or equilibrium is called **homeostasis**. Restated in cybernetic terms, the body can be seen as a dynamic biosocial system that exchanges information with the outside world and uses feedback processes to maintain internal stability.

Although the end result is a steady state, the process is hardly a static one. On the contrary, a constantly fluctuating interaction of equilibrating and disequilibrating forces is operating, and it is that interaction that generates the bodily pattern we call stability. Just as a tightrope walker is constantly in motion, continuously making body position and weight distribution corrections to maintain balance, so the body strives for dynamic equilibrium (Bloch, 1985).

In family terms, homeostasis refers to those internal, ongoing, sustaining, dynamically interactional processes that take place within a family and help assure internal balance. That is, family members will attempt to restore a stable environment whenever it becomes disrupted. The family, as an error-activated (or excess-activated) system, usually restricts behavior to a narrow range—for example, a quarrel between two children is not permitted to escalate to the point of physical assault. In such a developing situation, a parent is likely to do one or more of the following: scold one or both; lecture one or both; remind them of their family ties and responsibilities; punish one or both; hug them both and urge them to settle the argument; act as a referee; or send each out of the way of the other, until tempers cool. Whatever the attempted solution, the effort is directed, at least in part, to returning the system to its previous balance or equilibrium.

In a similar manner, couples typically monitor the state of their relationship and—usually without being aware of doing so—provide input to return it to a steady state should certain errors or excesses threaten their previous homeostatic balance. Stimulated by Bateson's application of the biological system's homeostatic principles to family systems, his colleague Jackson (1957; 1965b) noted that during the courting period, most couples' behavior is characterized by wondrously varied amorous advances and flirtatious moves. In the course of a long-term relationship, however, most of these behavioral ploys are dropped from their interactional repertoire. What remains is an narrower range of behavior that may require the couple to restore the balance from time to time. Usually a private code develops, each partner learning to cue the other, homeostatically, perhaps with a glance or gesture that means, for example, "I'm hurt by what you just said (or did) and want you to reassure me that you don't mean it and still love me." Such cues are a signal that disequilibrium has been created and some corrective steps are required in order to return the relationship to its previous balanced state.

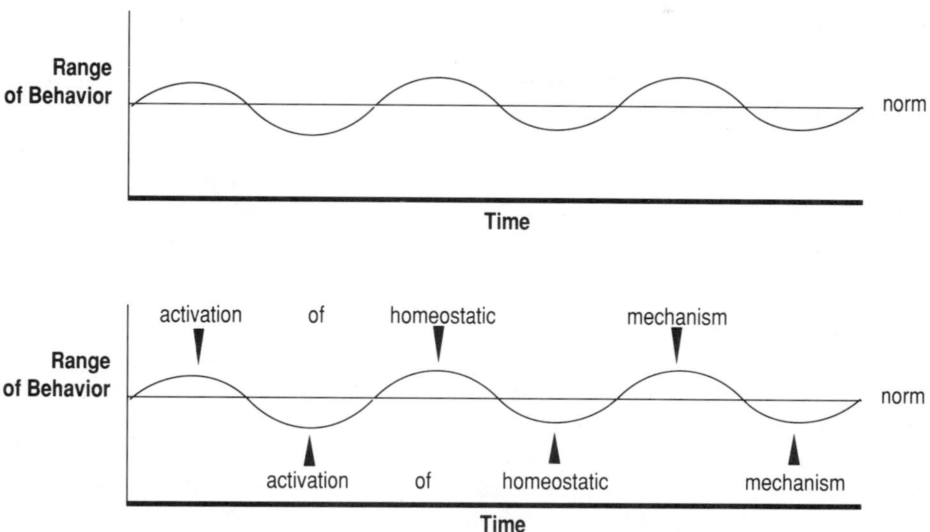

Figure 3.1 The operation of homeostatic mechanisms in the family. In a home heating system, when the temperature deviates from a preset norm, the deviation is registered and counteracted by the homeostatic mechanisms of the thermostat system. Families respond to similar cues to achieve balance and equilibrium. (Source: Jackson, 1965b)

The analogy is often made to a home heating system with a thermostat set to cause the furnace to respond if the temperature in the house drops below the desired level of warmth. Figure 3.1 demonstrates such a situation. Let us say that a temperature of 70 degrees Fahrenheit is desired by the home's occupants. When the temperature in the house dips below that point, that information is fed back into the system, activating the furnace. When the desired temperature is reached again, that new information, once again fed back, alters the ongoing state by deactivating the system until such time as reactivation might be needed to once again warm up the house. Balance is achieved by the system's inclination to maintain a dynamic equilibrium around a set point (called a "bias") and to undertake operations through what cyberneticists call servomechanisms to restore equilibrium whenever it is threatened.

Homeostatic mechanisms help to maintain the stability of an ongoing arrangement between family members by activating the rules that define their relationships. What happens, however, when a family must change or modify its rules? How adaptive or flexible are the metarules for changing established or habitual patterns in a particular family? As children grow up, they often put pressure on the family to redefine its relationships. Many middle-class adolescents expect to be given allowances to spend as they wish, to make their own decisions about a suitable bedtime, to listen to music that may be repellent to their parents' ears. They may wish to borrow the car, sleep over at a friend's, pursue interests other than those traditionally cared about in the family. They may challenge the family's values, customs, and norms; they insist on being treated as equals. All of this causes disequilibrium in the family system, a sense of loss, and perhaps a feeling of strangeness until reorganization restores family balance.

In most cases, a system tends to maintain itself within preferred and familiar ranges. As Minuchin, Rosman, and Baker (1978) point out, a demand for deviation or change that is too great, too sudden, or too far beyond the system's threshold of tolerance is likely to encounter counterdeviation responses. In **pathogenic** families, demands for even the most necessary or modest changes may be met with increased rigidity as the family stubbornly attempts to retain familiar rules. Symptoms in a family member may develop when the family system is not sufficiently flexible to permit change in order to accommodate the changing developmental needs of its members.

While this view of the family operating as a cybernetic system has become axiomatic for most family therapists, a number of influential critics (Dell, 1982; Hoffman, 1981) now believe the simple analogy to a home heating system has outlived its usefulness. Rather than viewing the family as a homeostatic machine with a governor (for example, a family member develops a symptom when a family breakup is threatened), they argue that this descriptive language incorrectly assumes a dualism between one part of the system and another, when in fact all parts together engage in change. Urging the adoption of an new epistemology, they contend that more than seeking to maintain the status quo, homeostasis represents a tendency to seek a steady state when a system is perturbed. That new state is always slightly different from the preceding steady state, since all systems continue to change and evolve.

Here the family therapist may be called upon to do more than help restabilize a system whose stability has been threatened. Dell (1982) sees the therapist's task in such cases not as aiding the family members to return to their former homeostatic balance, but rather as forcing the family to search for new solutions, in effect pushing the family system out of its old state of equilibrium and into achieving a new level of stability through reorganization and change.

A second set of criticisms comes from feminists such as Luepnitz (1988), who insist that what is left out of the simple home heating system analogy is attention to who has access to the "bias." That is, different people have differing degrees of power in altering the setting. A landlord in a large building, for example, may control the thermostat for all the apartments; the system may work neatly for him but not from the viewpoint of the freezing tenants. Luepnitz believes that cyberneticists and general systems theorists fail to take power differentials (say, between men and women) into account in their homeostatic formulations.

Feedback, Information, and Control

Systems are constantly in flux, simultaneously pursuing goals and responding to outside forces. Homeostasis, as we have illustrated, refers to that state in which stability or equilibrium is achieved between the need for change and the need to control change in order to maintain the integrity of the system. The regulatory mechanism by which a system manages to maintain homeostasis, while at the same time monitoring its attempts to achieve certain of its goals, is referred to as feedback (Leslie, 1988).

As we noted in our earlier discussion of cybernetics in Chapter 1, *feedback* refers to reinserting into a system the results of its past performance as a method of controlling the system. That is, information about how a system is functioning is looped back from output to input in a circular manner, modifying or self-correcting subsequent input signals. **Feedback loops** are thus circular mechanisms whose purpose is to introduce information about a system's output back to its input, in order to alter, correct, and ultimately govern the system's functioning. In any self-regulating system, such servomechanisms (pressure gauges, thermostats) help activate the internal interactional processes that maintain stability within a system and ensure a dynamic but steady state of being.

Feedback loops help mitigate against excessive fluctuations, thus serving to maintain and thereby extend the life of the system. Both negative and positive information about the state of the system can be fed back through the system, triggering those necessary changes that serve to keep the system "on track." The process of **negative feedback**[2] is illustrated in Figure 3.2. Here we see how attenuating feedback loops operate in a corrective manner, adjusting the input so that the system returns to its preset steady state.

Positive feedback (amplifying feedback loops) has the opposite effect: it leads to further change by augmenting or accelerating the initial deviation. Like negative feedback, it too is an error-activated process, reintroducing information about a deviation from a previously set state (for example, 70 degrees Fahrenheit) back into the system. In the case of positive feedback, however, the information is accepted (the room is not yet at the desired temperature) and the system continues to respond as it has been programmed to do until it achieves its predetermined goal. In certain extreme cases, however, the escalation may reach runaway proportions, forcing the system beyond its limits to the point of exhaustion or self-destruction. The furnace driven beyond its limits explodes; the car oversteered through an oil slick on the road goes out of control.

2. While *negative feedback* and *positive feedback* are commonly used terms in the systems literature, some critics argue that in light of the everyday use of these terms, they may erroneously suggest value judgments to some readers. Constantine (1986) suggests that for *negative feedback* we substitute *attenuating feedback loops* (loops that promote equilibrium) and that for *positive feedback* we use *amplifying loops* (loops that promote change).

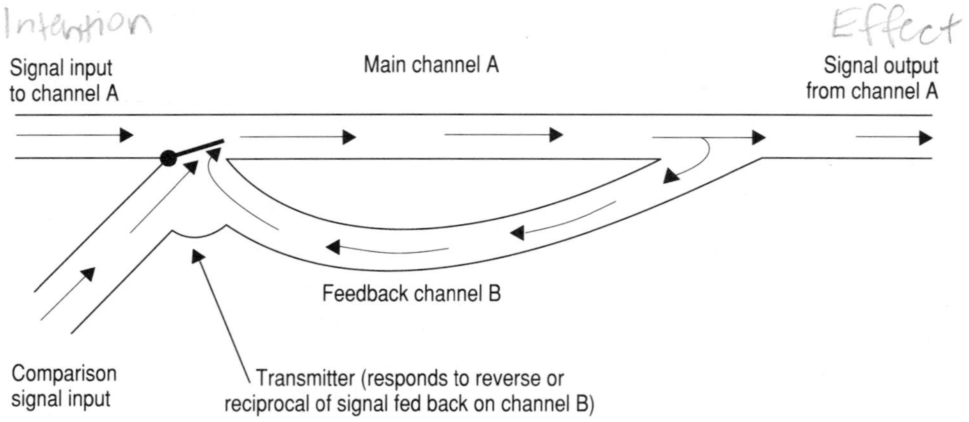

Figure 3.2 In this illustration of negative feedback, part of a system's output is reintroduced into the system as information about the output, thus governing and correcting the process. A negative signal from channel A, fed back to the sender through channel B, alters the signal in A. Feedback loops characterize all interpersonal relationships. (Source: Miller, 1978)

Similarly, within a marriage, exchange of information through feedback loops helps maintain equilibrium, as disturbing or annoying patterns are adjusted and new, stabilizing patterns evolve. A misunderstanding can be corrected (attenuating deviation) or escalated (amplifying deviation). In the latter case, an argument may get out of control, becoming increasingly vicious, ugly, or even violent, reaching the point where neither spouse can (or wants to) control the consequences.

Goldenberg and Goldenberg (1990) illustrate the operation of negative and positive feedback loops in the case of a remarried couple. In the former situation, there is attenuation:

Husband: I'm upset at the way you talked to that man at the party tonight, especially the way you seemed to be hanging on every word he said.

Wife: Don't be silly! You're the one I care about. He said he had just come back from a trip you and I had talked about going on and I was interested in what he had to tell me about the place.

Husband: OK. But please don't do it again without telling me. You know I'm touchy on the subject because of what Gina [ex-wife] used to do at parties with other men that drove me crazy.

Wife: Sorry. I hadn't thought about that. I'll try to remember next time. In the meantime, you try to remember that you're married to me now and I don't want you to be jealous.

In a less blissful situation, instead of the previous attenuation, there is amplification:

Husband:	I'm upset at the way you talked to that man at the party tonight, especially the way you seemed to be hanging on every word he said.
Wife:	One thing I don't appreciate is your spying on me.
Husband:	Spying? That's a funny word to use. You must be getting paranoid in your old age. Or maybe you have something to hide.
Wife:	As a matter of fact, I was talking to him about a trip he took that we had talked about, but I don't suppose you'd believe that. Talk about paranoid!
Husband:	I give up on women! You're no different from Gina, and I suppose all other women.
Wife:	With an attitude like that, I'm starting to see why Gina walked out on you.

The ultimate stability of a system can be maintained by negative or positive feedback processes. Despite the potentially escalating impact of the runaway system in the second example, not all positive feedback should be thought of as damaging or destructive to the system's operations. Homeostatic does not mean static; as a marriage or a family grows, stability calls for acknowledging change, and change often comes about in a family through breakthroughs that push the family beyond its previous homeostatic level. As we have noted previously, at times it may be advantageous to propel a family with stultifying or otherwise untenable behavior patterns to new levels of functioning. In these cases, the therapist may seize the opportunity of disequilibrium to promote discontinuity and the restoration of family homeostasis at a new, more satisfactory level for all.

How deviant must an outcome be before corrective action is initiated? Broderick and Smith (1979), pointing out the necessity for cybernetic control for stable system operation, offer this example: parents may respond to their daughter's return home from a date positively or negatively, depending on whether she has conformed to family rules in the time she arrives home, the condition she is in, and other factors. These authors note that the response will depend on the degree of **calibration** the family has determined—how much deviation it will allow. If the event is calibrated too narrowly, the daughter may not easily achieve a sense of independence and reliance on her own judgment. If it is calibrated too broadly, she may fail to learn limits and a sense of responsibility. Family therapists need to be aware of a family's efforts at calibrating their responses to such events, helping them fine-tune these responses for more effective functioning as a family unit.

Information processing is fundamental to the operation of any system. If faulty, the system is likely to malfunction. The more-or-less free exchange of information within a family and between the family and the outside world helps reduce uncertainty, thus avoiding disorder. The exchange of information is essential to all living, ongoing systems, as new input information is fed back and alterations in output are made in response to the new input. According to Bateson's (1972) elegant definition, information is "a difference that makes a difference." In interpersonal family terms, a word, a gesture, a smile, a scowl—these are differences or changes in the environment comparable to a temperature drop as environmental input. These differences in turn make a difference when the receiver of the new information alters his or her perceptions of the environment and modifies subsequent behavior.

Subsystems and Boundaries

A system, as we have seen, is organized into a more-or-less stable set of relationships; it functions in certain characteristic ways; it is continuously in the process of evolution as it seeks new homeostatic balance. **Subsystems** are those parts of the overall system assigned to carry out particular functions or processes within the system as a whole. Each system exists as part of a larger suprasystem and contains smaller subsystems of which it is the suprasystem.

A family commonly contains a number of coexisting subsystems. The husband-and-wife dyad constitutes a subsystem; so do the mother-child, father-child, and child-child dyads. In a family, subsystems can be formed by generation, by sex, by interest, or by function (Minuchin, 1974). Within each, different levels of power are exercised, different skills learned, and different responsibilities assigned. For example, the oldest child may have power within the sibling subsystem but must cede that power when interacting with his or her parents.

Because each family member may belong to several subsystems simultaneously, he or she enters into different complementary relationships with other members. For example, a woman can be a wife, mother, daughter, younger sister, older sister, niece, granddaughter, and so on, simultaneously. Within each subsystem in which she holds membership, she plays a different role and can be expected to engage in different transactional patterns. Consider this example: While giving her younger sister advice about finding a job, a woman is told by her husband to get off the telephone and hurry up with dinner. She decides how to deal with his demand. Some moments later, she remembers not to be hurt when the children refuse to eat what she has prepared. She even responds diplomatically when her mother, a dinner guest, gives her advice on how to improve the table setting.

The most enduring subsystems are the spousal, the parental, and the sibling subsystems (Minuchin, Rosman, & Baker, 1978). The husband-wife dyad is basic; any dysfunction in this subsystem is bound to reverberate throughout the family as children are scapegoated or co-opted into alliances with one parent against the other whenever the parents engage in conflict. The spousal subsystem teaches the children about male-female intimacy and commitment by providing a model of marital interaction.

The parental subsystem (which may include grandparents or older children temporarily assigned parental roles) has the major responsibility for proper child rearing, nurturance, guidance, limit setting, and discipline. Through interaction with parents, children learn to deal with authority, with people of greater power, while strengthening their own capacity for decision making and self-direction.

Problems within this subsystem, such as serious intergenerational conflicts involving rebelliousness, symptomatic children, or runaways, often reflect underlying family instability and disorganization.

The sibling set represents a child's first peer group. Through participation in this subsystem, a child develops patterns of negotiation, cooperation, competition, mutual support, and later, attachment to friends. Interpersonal skills honed here influence later school or workplace relationships.

Other subsystems, most less durable than those just outlined, exist in all families. Father-daughter, mother-son, father–oldest son, and mother–youngest child transitional alliances are common. Their protracted duration, however, may signal difficulties within the spousal subsystem, alerting the family therapist to the potential instability of the family system.

A **boundary** is an invisible line of demarcation that separates a system, subsystem, or individual from outside surroundings. Within a system such as a family, boundaries circumscribe and protect the integrity of the system, determining who is considered an insider and who remains outside. The family boundary may serve a gatekeeper function, controlling information flow into and out of the system ("We don't care if your friend's parents allow her to ___ ; we don't"; "Whatever you hear at home, you are expected to keep private and not discuss with your friends").

Within a family itself, boundaries also differentiate subsystems, helping define the separate subunits of the overall system. Minuchin (1974) contends that such divisions must be sufficiently well defined to allow subsystem members to carry out their tasks without undue interference, while at the same time open enough to permit contact between members of the subsystem and others. Boundaries thus help safeguard each subsystem's autonomy while maintaining the interdependence of all of the family's subsystems.

For example, a mother defines the boundaries of the parental subsystem when she tells her 15-year-old son, the oldest of three children: "Don't you decide whether your sisters are old enough to stay up to watch that TV program. Your father and I will decide that." However, she temporarily redefines that boundary to include the oldest child within the parental subsystem when she announces: "I want all of you children to listen to your older brother while your father and I are away from home tomorrow evening." Or she may invite grandparents to join the parental subsystem for one evening only, asking them to check on how the children are getting along or advise the oldest son on necessary action in case of an emergency.

These examples underscore the idea that the clarity of the subsystem boundaries is far more significant in the effectiveness of family functioning than the composition of the family subsystems. While the parent-child subsystem may be flexible enough to include the oldest child, or grandmother may be pressed into service when both parents are unavailable, the lines of authority and responsibility must remain clear. A grandmother who interferes with her daughter's management of the children in ways that undermine the parent-child subsystem (and perhaps also the spousal subsystem in the process) is overstepping her authority by being intrusive and crossing family boundary lines.

An important issue here involves the permeability of the boundaries, since boundaries vary in how easily they permit information to flow to and from the environment. Not only must boundaries within families be clearly drawn, but also the "rules" must be apparent to all. If boundaries are too blurred or too rigid, they invite confusion, increasing the family's risk of instability and ultimate dysfunction. A system with a high level of information flow to and from the outside is considered in systems theory to be an **open system**, while one whose boundaries are not easily crossed is considered a **closed system**. In family terms, no system is fully open or closed; if totally open, no boundaries would exist between it and the outside world and it would cease to exist; if totally closed, there would be no exchanges with the outside environment, and it would die. Rather, systems exist along a continuum with regard to the flexibility or rigidity of their boundaries.

While all families operate as open systems, some may appear more closed in the sense of being rigid or insular (Kantor & Lehr, 1975). The more open the family system, the more adaptable and open to change it is. Such a system tends not only to survive but to thrive, to be open to new experiences and to alter or discard no longer usable interactive patterns; thus it is said to have **negentropy**. On the other hand, relatively closed systems run the risk of **entropy**; they tend to make maladaptive adaptations, to seal themselves off from all but necessary exchanges with the outside world, and are destined for eventual dysfunction because of insufficient input. For example, recent immigrants or ethnic groups that live in relative isolation, communicating only among themselves, suspicious of outsiders, and fostering dependence on the family, often tend to hold onto tradition and avoid change, thus operating in the manner of a relatively closed system. Parent-child relationships in such families may encounter problems due in part to culture conflict, and these problems, if serious enough, may lead to the development of an entropic family.

In dyadic terms, even a social interaction as brief and tentative as a first date is concerned with boundaries (Broderick and Smith, 1979). A number of rules apply: it is bad form to pay too much attention to someone other than your date, and rude and insulting to abandon your date and return home with someone else. Moreover, others are expected to respect the couple's boundaries and refrain from cutting in on another's partner. It is also understood that the arrangement—the establishment of the unit—is time-limited, and when the date is over, so is the claim, and the rules just described no longer apply. If the two move to a more intimate relationship and see each other more regularly, they—as well as others such as their friends—behave as though the boundary is more clearly drawn and now operates between dates as well.

FAMILIES AND LARGER SYSTEMS

Families do not exist in a vacuum. All interact with, and are influenced by, one or more of society's larger systems—health care, church, welfare, probation, schools, the legal system. As Imber-Black (1988) observes, for most families such engagements proceed, perhaps with occasional exceptions, in ways that are largely nonproblematic. However, a significant portion of families frequently become entangled with these larger systems in unfortunate ways, impeding the growth and development of family members while at the same time contributing to cynicism and burnout among helpers.

Due to physical handicaps, or perhaps to chronic illness, some families spend a significant portion of their lives engaged with larger systems. In the case of longstanding poverty, the relationship may extend over generations. Problems may develop not only between such families and the public agencies in which they often become embedded, but between these public agencies as well. In a case of wife battering, for example, confusion may result from conflicting perceptions of various professionals attempting to help.

In the example offered by Imber-Black (1988) illustrated in Figure 3.3, a family initially seeking the aid of a family therapist for their son Billy's aggressive behavior, revealed over the course of therapy that Jim, the father, had been physically abusive to his wife, Cathy. Cathy also disclosed to the therapist that she had been sexually abused, as a child and young adolescent, by her father. The referring family physician knew only of the problems with Billy. By the time they consulted a family therapist, the family had become involved with five larger systems: Jim in a local hospital group for men who batter their wives; Cathy in a sexual assault program for women; Jim and Cathy together in a church counseling program for family violence; Cathy in a women's shelter counseling group; the entire family in family therapy.

When the family therapist invited the various participants to meet together and coordinate their efforts, differences in approach and fundamental beliefs among the various helpers turned out to be significant. For example, while Jim's group sought the causes of violence within him and from his past experiences, urging a long-term group program, the family therapist took a systemic approach, recommended a short-term approach, and attempted to locate the violence in the context of the couple's ongoing interactions. By contrast, Cathy felt the women's shelter counselors blamed Jim exclusively, and thought it was he who needed treatment.

Because competing definitions of the problem and approaches to a solution were so apparent in this macrosystem, a consultant was needed to help untangle the various family member–helper coalitions that had developed. Imber-Black argues that conflict between specialized "helping" systems may, in many cases such as this one, contribute to or enlarge the very problems the helping systems were created to fix or alleviate. In this case, the consultant highlighted their differences to the helpers, pointing out the impact of these differences on how the couple interacted. Stressing the macrosystem level, she designed an intervention that made the boundaries between helpers clearer and less rigid. At the same time, couple-helper boundaries were clarified and thus became less diffuse and confusing. The restructuring allowed the couple themselves to determine the amount and source of help they needed on a weekly basis.

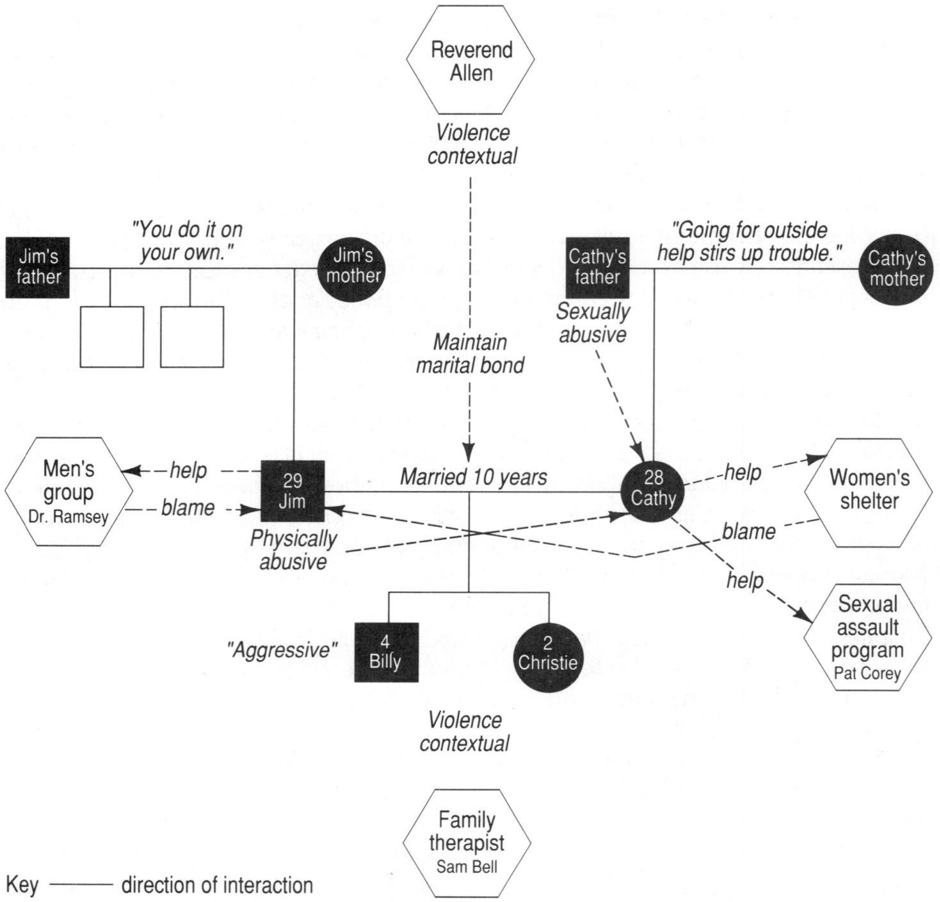

Figure 3.3 Conflicting perceptions and interactions in the Lee family case. (Source: Imber-Black, 1988, p. 117)

SUMMARY

General systems theory provides the theoretical underpinnings for much of current family therapy theory and practice. The concepts of organization and wholeness in particular emphasize that a system operates as a organized whole that is greater than the sum of its parts, and that such a system cannot be adequately understood if broken down into component parts.

A family represents a complex relationship system in which causality is circular and multidimensional. Family rules, for the most part unstated but understood by family members, help stabilize and regulate family functioning. Homeostasis is achieved in a family by means of dynamically interacting processes that help restore stability whenever threatened, often by activating the rules that define the relationships. When changes are called for, negative as well as positive feedback loops may help restore equilibrium, in the latter case by promoting discontinuity and necessitating the achievement of homeostasis at a new level.

Subsystems carry out specific family functions. Particularly significant are the spousal, parental, and sibling subsystems. Boundaries help separate systems, as well as subsystems within the overall system, from one another. Their clarity and permeability are more germane to family functioning than is their membership composition. Families vary in the extent to which they are open systems; relatively closed systems run the risk of entropy.

Family systems interact with larger outside systems, such as the church, schools, or the health care system. In a sizable number of cases, confusion may result from competing definitions of the family problem and conflicting solutions offered by different helpers in this macrosystem. In this broader context, boundaries between helpers, as well as boundaries between client families and helpers, may need to be clarified for the macrosystem to operate effectively.

Part II

HISTORICAL FOUNDATIONS AND CONTEMPORARY PRACTICES

Chapter Four

Origins and Growth of Family Therapy

Having established a family framework integrating both developmental and systems perspectives in Part I, we are ready to turn to the application of these viewpoints to working therapeutically with families.

In Part II we explore the historical as well as theoretical foundations of the family therapy movement. In this chapter, we first examine some scientific and clinical developments that coalesced in the late 1940s and early 1950s to give birth to that movement, before discussing in detail its evolution over the last four decades. In subsequent chapters in this section we will offer a variety of contemporary theoretical models for conceptualizing how and why families establish—or fail to establish—successful adaptational skills and competencies. In each model, the unit of analysis as well as the focus of therapeutic intervention is the family. Accompanying each model will be examples of therapeutic techniques for intervening with troubled or problematic families.

HISTORICAL ROOTS OF FAMILY THERAPY

It is never easy or entirely accurate to pinpoint the beginning of a scientific endeavor. But most authorities point to the decade following World War II as the period when researchers, followed by practitioners, turned their attention to the family's role in creating and maintaining psychological disturbance in one or more family members. The sudden reuniting of families in the aftermath of the war created a number of problems (social, interpersonal, cultural, situational) for which the public sought solutions by turning to mental health specialists. Accustomed to working with individuals, these professionals were now expected to deal effectively with an array of problems within the family. Family members experienced the stress associated with delayed marriages and hasty wartime marriages; the baby boom brought pressures of its own. Changing sexual mores and increasing acceptance of divorce brought new freedoms—and conflicts. Transitions to new jobs, new educational opportunities, and new homes with mortgages meant new tensions within the family. Most significant of all, the family had entered the nuclear age: the atom bomb had challenged its basic security.

In general, psychological intervention became acceptable to people from a broader range of social and educational backgrounds than had been the case in prewar days. Practitioners from many disciplines—clinical psychologists, psychiatric social workers, marriage counselors, pastoral counselors—began to offer such aid, in addition to psychiatrists, the primary prewar providers of psychotherapy. The definition of problems considered amenable to psychotherapy also expanded to include marital discord, separation and divorce, delinquency, problems with in-laws, and various forms of emotional disturbance not requiring hospitalization. Although many clinicians continued to offer individual treatment only, others began to look at family relationships, the transactions between members that needed modification if individual well-being was to be achieved. Eventually, more and more clinicians began to recognize that it was often necessary to alter the family's structure and interaction patterns in order for adaptive behavior to replace problematic, dysfunctional, or maladaptive behavior. In the last three decades, representatives from a wide variety of behavioral sciences and professional disciplines have become involved in examining and better understanding family functioning (see Table 4.1).

Goldenberg and Goldenberg (1983) draw attention to five seemingly independent scientific and clinical developments that together set the stage for the emergence of family therapy. These include (1) the extension of psychoanalytic treatment to a full range of emotional problems, eventually including work with whole families; (2) the introduction of general systems theory, with its emphasis on exploring relationships between parts that make up an interrelated whole; (3) the investigation of the family's role in the development of schizophrenia in one of its members; (4) the evolution of the fields of child guidance and marital counseling; and (5) the increased interest in new clinical techniques such as **group therapy**. We will explore each of these developments in turn to arrive at an understanding of the interdisciplinary roots of family therapy.

Table 4.1 Behavioral Sciences and Disciplines Involved in the Study of the Family

Disciplines	*Illustrative studies*	*Representative researchers**
Anthropology Cultural anthropology Social anthropology Ethnology	Cultural and subcultural family forms and functions Cross-cultural comparative family patterns Ethnic, racial, and social status family differences Families in primitive, developing, and industrial societies	Ruth Benedict Allison Davis Clyde Kluckhohn Oscar Lewis Ralph Linton Helen and Robert Lynd Margaret Mead George Murdock W. Lloyd Warner
Counseling Counseling theory Clinical practice Evaluation	Dynamics of interpersonal relationships in marriage and family Methods and results of individual, marriage, and family counseling	Rollo May Emily Hartshorne Mudd James A. Peterson Carl Rogers
Demography	Census and vital statistics on many facets of family life Cross-sectional, longitudinal, and record-linkage surveys Differential birthrates Family planning and population control	Donald Bogue Hugh Carter Harold Christensen Ronald Freedman Paul Glick Philip Hauser P.K. Whelpton
Economics	Consumer behavior, marketing, and motivation research Insurance, pensions, and welfare needs of families Standards of living, wage scales, socioeconomic status	Robert C. Angell Howard Bigelow Milton Friedman John Kenneth Galbraith John Morgan Margaret Reid
Education Early childhood Early elementary Secondary College Parent Professional	Child-rearing methods Developmental patterns Educational methods and evaluation Family-life education Motivation and learning Preparation for marriage Sex education	Orville Brim Catherine Chilman Cyril Houle Harold Lief Nevitt Sanford Ralph Tyler James Walters
History	Historical roots of family Origins of family patterns Predictions of the future of families Social influences on the family Social trends and adaptations	Arthur Calhoun Franklin Frazier Bernard Stern Edward Westermarck Carle Zimmerman

(continued)

Table 4.1 *(continued)*

Disciplines	*Illustrative studies*	*Representative researchers**
Home economics Family relationships Home economics education Home management Nutrition	Evaluation of practices and measurement of educational results Family food habits and nutrition Home management practices Relationships between family members	Muriel Brown Irma Gross Paulena Nickell Evelyn Spindler Alice Thorpe
Human development Child development Adolescent development Middle age and aging	Character development Child growth and development Developmental norms and differences Nature of cognitive learning Cross-cultural variations Personality development Social roles of aging	Nancy Bayley Urie Bronfenbrenner Erik Erikson Dale Harris Robert Havighurst Lois Barclay Murphy Bernice Neugarten Jean Piaget
Law	Adoption and child protection Child care and welfare Divorce and marital dissolution Marriage and family law Parental rights and responsibilities Sexual controls and behavior	Paul Alexander John Bradway Harriet Daggett Marie Kargman Harriet Pilpel Max Rheinstein
Psychoanalysis	Abnormal and normal behavior Clinical diagnosis and therapy Foundations of personality Stages of development Treatment of mental illness	Nathan Ackerman Erik Erikson John Flugel Irene Josselyn Harry Stack Sullivan
Psychology Clinical Developmental Social	Aspirations and self-concepts Drives, needs, and hungers Dynamics of interpersonal interaction Learning theory Mental health Therapeutic intervention	Rosalind Dymond Gerald Gurin Robert Hess Eleanore Luckey Frederick Stodtbeck John Whiting
Public health	Epidemiology and immunization Family health and preventive medicine Maternal and infant health Noxious materials research Pediatric health education Venereal disease	Cecelia Deschin Nicholson Eastman Earl L. Koos Niles Newton Clark Vincent

(continued)

Table 4.1 *(continued)*

Disciplines	*Illustrative studies*	*Representative researchers**
Religion	Church policies on marriage and family Families of various religions Interfaith marriage Love, sex, marriage, divorce, and family in religious contexts	Stanley Brav Roy Fairchild Seward Hiltner John L. Thomas John C. Wynn
Social work Family casework Group work Social welfare	Appraising family need Devising constructive programs for family assistance Measuring family functioning	Dorothy F. Beck L.L. Geismar James Hardy Charlotte Towle
Sociology	Courtship and mate selection Family formation and functioning Effects of social change on families Family crises and dissolution Prediction of family success Social class influence on families	Ernest W. Burgess Ruth S. Cavan Harold Christensen Reuben Hill Judson Landis Marvin Sussman

*Illustrative of those research workers whose published findings may be available to students of the family in various disciplines; not an all-inclusive listing. (Source: Duvall, 1977)

Psychoanalysis

Psychoanalysis, the theory and set of therapeutic techniques advanced by Sigmund Freud, became the dominant ideology in American psychiatry after World War II. Shortly before the war, a large migration of European psychologists and psychiatrists, psychoanalytic in their orientation, had come to this country to escape the Nazi regime. The American public had been receptive to Freud's ideas since early in this century. With the arrival of these clinicians, psychoanalysis began to gain greater acceptance among medical specialists, academicians, and clinicians in the psychology community, as well as among sociologists and psychiatric social workers.

Freud had been aware of the impact of family relationships on the individual's character formation, particularly in the development of symptomatic behavior. For example, in his famous case of Little Hans, a 5-year-old boy who refused to go out into the street for fear that a horse might bite him, Freud hypothesized that Hans was displacing anxiety associated with his Oedipus complex. That is, Freud believed Hans unconsciously desired his mother sexually but felt competitive with, and hostile toward, his father, as well as fearful of his father's reaction to his hostility.

Hans had witnessed a horse falling down in the street, and Freud speculated that he unconsciously associated the scene with his father, since he wanted his father hurt too. According to Freud, Hans unconsciously changed his intense fear of castration by his father into a **phobia** about being bitten by the horse, whom Hans had previously seen as innocuous. Having substituted the horse for his father, Hans was able to turn an internal danger into an external one. The fear was displaced onto a substitute object, which is prototypically what takes place in the development of a phobia. In this celebrated 1909 case (Freud, 1955), the boy was actually treated by the father, under Freud's guidance.

Historically, the case of Little Hans has conceptual as well as technical significance. Conceptually, it enabled Freud to elaborate on his earlier formulations regarding psychosexual development in children and the use of **defense mechanisms** (such as displacement) as unconscious **ego** devices a person calls on as protection against being overwhelmed by anxiety. Moreover, the case supported Freud's developing belief that inadequate resolution of a particular phase of psychosexual development can lead to neurotic behavior such as phobias. Technically, as Bloch and LaPerriere (1973) point out, Little Hans represents the first case in the history both of child analysis and of family therapy. Note, however, that Freud chose not to work with either the child or the family but encouraged Hans's father, a physician, to treat his own son under Freud's supervision.[1] The clinical intervention remained individually focused; ultimately, Hans was relieved of his phobic symptom.

From the case of Little Hans and similar examples from among Freud's published papers, we can appreciate how family relationships came to provide a rich diagnostic aid to Freud's psychoanalytic thinking.

Four years earlier, in 1905, he had written that psychoanalysts were "obliged to pay as much attention . . . to purely human and social circumstances of our patients as to the somatic data and the symptoms of the disorder. Above all, our interest will be directed toward their family circumstances" (Freud, 1959, pp. 25–26). In practice, however, Freud preferred working therapeutically with individuals; both his theories and techniques stress the resolution of intrapsychic conflicts rather than restructuring interpersonal or transactional phenomena within a family. So strongly was he opposed to working with more than one family member at a time that his negative assessment became virtually a doctrine among psychoanalysts, who for many years accepted the prohibition against analyzing members of the same family (Broderick & Schrader, 1981).

In fact, as Bowen (1975) notes, one psychoanalytic principle that may have retarded earlier growth of the family therapy movement was the isolation of the therapist/patient relationship and the related concern that contact with the patient's relatives would "contaminate" the therapist. Bowen reports that some hospitals went so far as to have one therapist deal with the patient's intrapsychic processes while another handled practical matters and administrative procedures,

1. Unwittingly, Freud was anticipating a technique used by many of today's family therapists, particularly those with a behavioral approach, of using family members, especially parents, as agents of change.

and a third team member, a social worker, talked to relatives. According to Bowen's early experiences, failure to respect these boundaries was considered "inept psychotherapy." It was only in the 1950s that this principle began to be violated—more often for research than for clinical purposes—and that family members began to be seen therapeutically as a group.[2]

Nathan Ackerman, a psychoanalyst and child psychiatrist, is generally credited with adapting psychoanalytic formulations to the study of the family. In what may have been the first paper to deal specifically with family therapy, published as the lead article in the *Bulletin of the Kansas Mental Hygiene Society*, Ackerman (1937) emphasized the role of the family as a dynamic psychosocial unit in and of itself. The constant interaction between the biologically driven person (a psychoanalytic concept) and the social environment (a systems concept) was to preoccupy him for more than three decades, as he attempted to apply an intrapsychic vocabulary to systems phenomena he observed in the family and in society at large. As he summed it up in a paper published shortly after his death (Ackerman, 1972):

> Over a period of some thirty-five years, I have extended my orientation to the problems of behavior, step-by-step, from the inner life of the person, to the person within family, to the family within community, and most recently, to the social community itself. (p. 449)

Ackerman is considered by many to be the grandfather of the family therapy movement. His contribution to both theory and practice will be discussed in Chapter 5.

Another psychoanalytic influence on family therapy is the work of Alfred Adler, an early associate of Freud's; among other accomplishments, Adler helped to found the child guidance movement in Vienna in the early 1900s. Adler insisted that an individual's conscious personal and social goals as well as subsequent goal-directed behavior could be fully understood only by comprehending the environment or social context in which that behavior was displayed. Adlerian concepts such as sibling rivalry, family constellation, and style of life attest to Adler's awareness of the key role of family experiences in influencing adult behavior. Like Freud, Adler did not himself work therapeutically with entire families, but he did influence one of his associates, Rudolf Dreikurs, to expand child guidance centers in the United States into family counseling centers (Lowe, 1982). Classes for teachers, parent education study groups, single-parent groups, even groups for grandparents have been organized in these centers in an effort to facilitate adult-child understanding and cooperation (Dinkmeyer & McKay, 1976).

Finally, the American psychiatrist Harry Stack Sullivan was psychoanalytically trained but was also influenced by sociology and social psychology. Throughout a career that began in the late 1920s, he stressed the role of interpersonal relationships in personality development. Sullivan (1953) argued that people are

2. Just how much change in attitude has taken place in the last 35 years can be gleaned from the fact that family therapists are willing to demonstrate their work with families quite openly, even before a large professional audience, without benefit of one-way mirrors or other devices to shield participants from viewers. Most families report that any initial self-consciousness is quickly overcome.

essentially products of their social interactions; to understand how people function, he urged the study of their "relatively enduring patterns of recurrent interpersonal situations" (p. 110). Working mostly with schizophrenics, Sullivan noted that the disorder frequently manifested itself during the transitional period of adolescence, leading him to speculate about the possibly critical effects of the patient's ongoing family life in producing the confusion that might lead ultimately to schizophrenia (Perry, 1982).

Don Jackson and Murray Bowen, both of whom were later to become outstanding figures in the emerging field of family therapy, trained under Sullivan and his colleague Frieda Fromm-Reichmann. Jackson's work (see Chapter 3) was clearly influenced by Sullivan's early notion of redundant family interactive patterns. Bowen's theories (see Chapter 7), especially those that pertain to individual pathology emerging from a faulty multigenerational family system, can be traced to Sullivan's influence.

General Systems Theory

First proposed by the biologist Ludwig von Bertalanffy in the 1940s, general systems theory represents an effort to provide a comprehensive theoretical model embracing all living systems, a model relevant to all the behavioral sciences. Bertalanffy's major contribution is in providing a framework for looking at seemingly unrelated phenomena and understanding how together they represent interrelated components of a larger system (Bertalanffy, 1968).

A system is a complex of component parts that are in mutual interaction. Rather than viewing each part as isolated and simply adding the parts to make up an entity, this theory stresses the relationships between the parts; the various components are best understood as functions of the total system. (The application of the theory to a family, made up of members, each of whom influences and, in turn, is influenced by all other members, has been discussed in Chapter 3.) According to Bertalanffy, to understand how something works, we must study the transactional process taking place between the components of a system, not merely add up what each part contributes.

General systems theory seeks to classify systems by the manner in which they are organized and by the interdependence of their parts. It thus represents a new approach to scientific knowledge, a new, holistic way of thinking. The traditional reductionistic view of a system (derived from the physical sciences) explains complex phenomena by breaking them down into series of less complex cause-and-effect reactions, by analyzing in a linear fashion how A causes B, B causes C, C causes D, and so on. By contrast, general systems theory presents a new epistemology in which it is not the structure that defines an object but its organization as defined by the interactive pattern of its parts. That is, the component parts of a system are less important than their interrelations (Segal & Bavelas, 1983). A may cause B, but B also affects A, which affects B, and so on in circular causality. Moreover, patterns form and persist over time, since we are dealing with a process as well as a structure.

The behavioral scientist J. G. Miller (1978) views all living systems as special subsets of open systems. According to his set of principles, all phenomena described by the biological and social sciences can be arranged according to a comprehensive schema with seven hierarchical levels (see Figure 4.1). In increasing order of complexity, the levels are cells; organs (composed of cells); organisms (independent life forms); groups (families, committees); organizations (universities, multinational corporations, cities); societies or nations; and supranational systems. Each higher-level system encompasses all lower-level ones and provides the environment for the systems on the level directly below it. Miller's thesis holds that ever since cells evolved about 3 billion years ago, the general direction of evolution has been toward ever-greater complexity.

Nothing and nobody exists in isolation; the world is made up of systems within systems. The emotionally disturbed person is just one part of a subsystem in the family system, but the entire family system is influenced by and influences the disturbed person. Dysfunctional families who seek treatment at a social agency are components in that agency's organizational system. They, in turn, affect disbursement of government funds, training grants for research on family life or educating family counselors, and so on. A human being is a system of many organ subsystems and, as we have shown, is an organism that is part of a larger scheme. Consider an example offered by Bloch and LaPerriere (1973) of a woman who becomes depressed. At what level would her symptomatic behavior be best understood and intervention be most effective? At the organ system level her depression might be related to hormonal changes during her menstrual cycle; at the organism level, to her way of handling aggressive impulses; at the group level, to her way of dealing with her family; at the society level, to the socialization process that teaches females to suppress assertive impulses. Family therapists take the position that intervention at the family level addresses many of this woman's problem areas and offers an effective method for expediting change.

Although systems thinking permeates all aspects of family therapy—its theories, its assessment techniques, its therapeutic approaches—here we want to emphasize the historical significance of systems theory to the emerging family therapy movement. In contrast to psychoanalysis, with its psychopathological orientation, general systems theory views an individual as a complex being operating within a system where concepts such as "sick" or "well" are irrelevant; a symptom developing in one person merely means that the system (that is, the family, community, or society at large) has become dysfunctional. In contrast to the psychoanalyst who remains distant from the patient, a family therapist is apt to intervene more directly and become a participant in the family system. In family therapy, the emphasis is on multiple causality at various levels rather than on defining an individual's unresolved intrapsychic conflicts; on dealing with the present rather than the past. Watzlawick, Beavin, and Jackson (1967) point out that when we focus on an emotionally disturbed individual we are inevitably led to speculate on the nature of that person's mind (what must be going on inside the mysterious "black box"). However, when we look at the effects of the individual's disturbed behavior, the way others react to it, and the context in which this

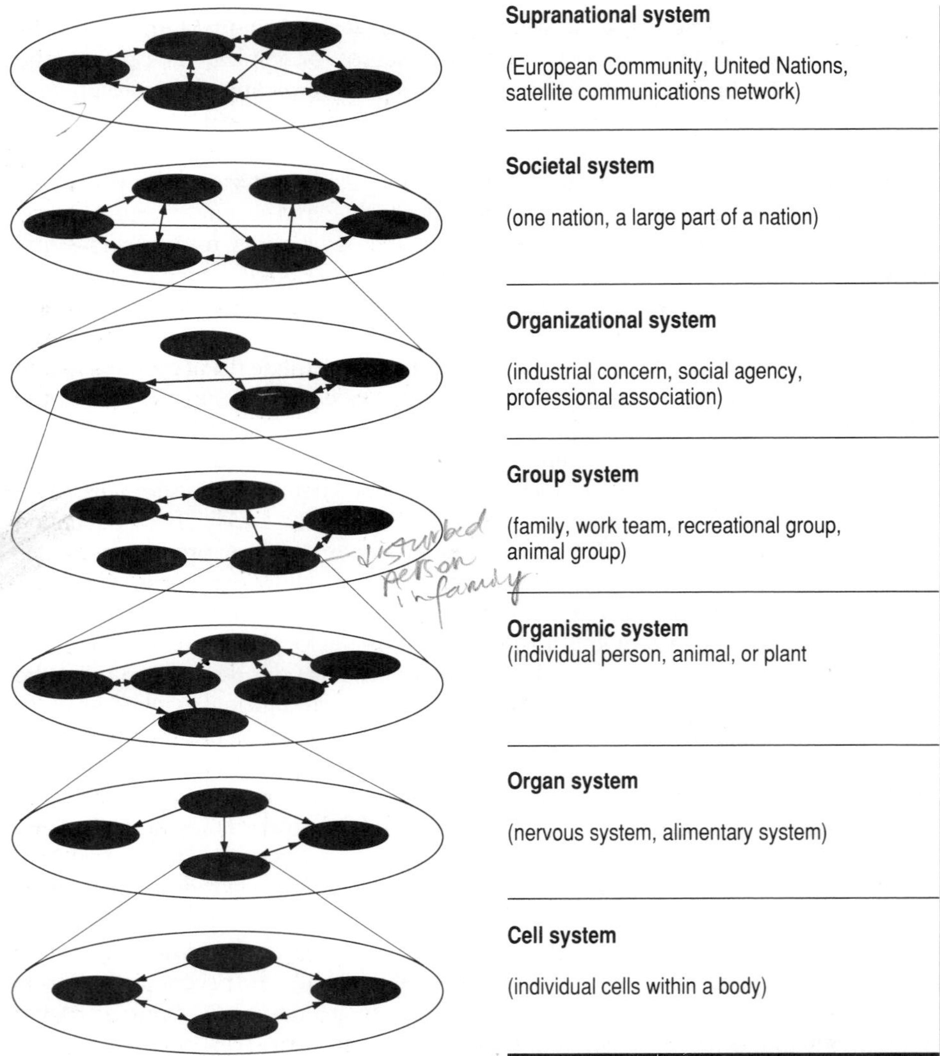

Figure 4.1 Living systems exist in a hierarchy of levels. Each level is made up of subsystems that have a relationship with other parts of their own system and to systems at other levels. Behavior at an individual (organismic) level is different from that individual's behavior at a group or family level, because of characteristics of that higher level (family rules, roles, power structure, ways of communicating). Family members relate to each other with greater intensity than they do to others outside the family boundary, but they also relate to others in society, a higher system. (Source: Sundberg, Tyler, & Taplin, 1973)

interaction transpires, the focus shifts to a consideration of relationships between system parts. Perhaps even more significant for family therapists, the shift represents a change of course from inferential studies of the mind to the study of the observable manifestations and behavioral consequences of interpersonal relationships. As we shall see in the next six chapters, these are the phenomena to which family therapists such as Bowen, Minuchin, Satir, Whitaker, Haley, and Selvini-Palazzoli have paid particular attention.

Studies of Schizophrenia and the Family

What role does a disturbed family environment play in the development of **schizophrenia** in a family member? Lidz and Lidz (1949), among the first to investigate the characteristics of mothers of schizophrenic patients, found serious inadequacies and psychological disturbances in the mother-child relationship. Fromm-Reichmann (1948) introduced the term **schizophrenogenic mother** to denote a domineering, cold, rejecting, possessive, guilt-producing person who, in combination with a passive, detached, and ineffectual father, causes her male offspring to feel confused and inadequate and ultimately to become schizophrenic. These family pathology studies, extending into the 1950s, sought to establish a linear cause-and-effect relationship between a pathogenic mother, an inadequate father, and schizophrenia in the male child. This psychological analysis of the family was soon complemented by a broader and more systematic psychosocial approach to the family as a group of individuals influencing each other and by a sociological perspective in which the family is perceived as a dysfunctional system supporting the disturbed person (Waxler, 1975). The study of family environment and the development of schizophrenia was launched.

During the mid-1950s, the major impetus for family research in the area of schizophrenia came from Gregory Bateson in Palo Alto, California; Theodore Lidz at Yale; and Murray Bowen (and later, Lyman Wynne) at the National Institute of Mental Health. Working independently at first, the investigators did not become fully aware of each other's research until later in the decade. Guerin (1976) maintains that research on the family and schizophrenia was the primary focus of the majority of the family therapy pioneers.

In 1952, Bateson—then affiliated with the Palo Alto Veterans Administration Hospital—received a grant to study patterns and paradoxes of communication in animals as well as in human beings. Soon he was joined by Jay Haley, then a graduate student studying communication; John Weakland, a former chemical engineer with training in cultural anthropology; and later, Don Jackson, a psychiatrist experienced in working with schizophrenics. Among other communications phenomena, they began to study the relationship between pathological communication patterns within a family and the emergence and maintenance of schizophrenic behavior in a family member. More specifically, they hypothesized that the family might have shaped the strange and irrational behavior of a schizophrenic by means of its contradictory, and thus impossible, communication requirements.

Four years later, Bateson, Jackson, Haley, and Weakland published a landmark paper (1956) introducing the **double-bind concept** to account for the development of schizophrenia in a family member. According to their thesis, a double-bind situation occurs when an individual (often a child) habitually receives contradictory messages from the same person, who forbids comment on the contradiction; the individual, perceiving the threat to his or her survival, feels compelled to make some response, but feels doomed to failure whatever response he or she chooses. Their paper reports the following poignant example:

> *A young man who had fairly well recovered from an acute schizophrenic episode was visited in the hospital by his mother. He was glad to see her and impulsively put his arm around her shoulders, whereupon she stiffened. He withdrew his arm and she asked, "Don't you love me anymore?" He then blushed, and she said, "Dear, you must not be so easily embarrassed and afraid of your feelings." (p. 259)*

Note the sequence of the mother's underlying messages: "Don't touch me" ("Go away"); "Don't trust your feelings in regard to how I respond" ("Come closer"); "Don't challenge the contradictions in my behavior"; "You can't survive without my love"; "You're wrong and at fault no matter how you interpret my messages." The authors report that the distressed patient promptly became violent and assaultive when he returned to the ward.

Confronted by expressions of love and hate, with an invitation to approach and an injunction to stay away issued by the same important figure, a person is forced into an impossible situation of trying to discriminate correctly between the messages. Unable to form a satisfactory response (and in the case of a child, unable to escape) and unable to comment on the dilemma without being punished further, such a person becomes confused. Response leads to rejection and failure to respond leads to the loss of potential love, the classic "damned if you do and damned if you don't" situation. If the important figure (a parent, for example) then denies sending simultaneous contradictory messages, this only adds to the confusion. Once the pattern is established, only a hint of or initial step in the original sequence is enough to set off a panic or rage reaction. Bateson and his colleagues suggested that the typical result of repeated and prolonged exposure to this kind of impossible situation is that the child learns to escape hurt and punishment by responding with equally incongruent messages. As a means of self-protection, he or she learns to deal with all relationships in this distorted manner and finally loses the ability to understand the true meaning of his or her own or others' communications. At this point the child begins to manifest schizophrenic behavior. The group led by Bateson thus focused on schizophrenia as a prototype of the consequences of failure in a family's communication system.

At about the same time that Bateson and his colleagues were doing research on the family and schizophrenia on the West Coast, Theodore Lidz on the East Coast (in Baltimore and later in New Haven, Connecticut) began publishing his research on the family's role in schizophrenic development of one or more of its children. These studies (Lidz, Cornelison, Fleck, & Terry, 1957) represented an extension of psychoanalytic concepts to the family, although these concepts were broadened somewhat in the transition. For example, Lidz and his coworkers at the Yale Psychiatric Institute recognized oral fixation—which orthodox psychoanalytic formulations consider a primary factor in the development of schizophrenia—as only one aspect of the disorder. To these researchers, schizophrenia was a "deficiency disease" resulting from the family's failure to provide the essentials for integrated personality development. More specifically, they suggested that a parent's (usually the mother's) own arrested personality development leads to an inability to meet the child's nurturance needs; the child is likely to grow up with profound insecurity and be unable to achieve autonomy. They also postulated that an unstable marriage in which there is considerable conflict between husband and wife provides poor role models for children. As a consequence, a child may fail to acquire the coping skills necessary for interaction with others outside the family and, ultimately, for independent adult living. You can see from this brief description that to Lidz, it was the **psychodynamics** of the parents, rather than the family as a social system, that was primarily responsible for the development of schizophrenic behavior in the child.

Lidz and his associates (1957) described two patterns of chronic marital discord that are particularly characteristic of families of schizophrenics (although each may exist in "normal" families to a lesser extent). **Marital schism** refers to a disharmonious situation in which each parent, preoccupied with his or her own problems, fails to create a satisfactory role in the family that is compatible with and reciprocal to the other spouse's role. Each parent tends to undermine the worth of the other, especially to the children, and they seem to compete for loyalty, affection, sympathy, and support of the children. Neither valuing nor respecting each other, each parent may fear that a particular child (or children) will grow up behaving like the other parent. Threats of separation or divorce are common; it is usual in such families for the father to become ostracized, a virtual nonentity if he remains in the home.

In the pattern of **marital skew**, which these researchers have also observed in families with a schizophrenic offspring, the continuity of the marriage is not threatened, but mutually destructive patterns nevertheless exist. The serious psychological disturbance of one parent (such as psychosis) usually dominates this type of home. The other parent, who is often dependent and weak, accepts the situation and goes so far as to imply to the children that the home situation is normal. Such a denial of what they are actually living through may lead to further denials and distortions of reality by the children. Lidz and his associates (1957) concluded that male schizophrenics usually come from skewed families in which there is a dominant, emotionally disturbed mother, impervious to the needs of other family members but nevertheless intrusive in her child's life. At the same time, a skewed family usually has a father who can neither counter the mother's child-rearing practices nor provide an adequate male role model.

If marital skew is often an antecedent of schizophrenia in a son, marital schism often precedes schizophrenia in a daughter. Here open marital discord is present and each parent particularly wants the daughter's support. However, the father's disparagement of the mother (or perhaps all women), together with his seductive efforts to gain the daughter's love and support, lead to the daughter's confusion about her identity as a woman, as well as doubt about her eventual ability to carry out an adult role as wife and mother. Pleasing one parent means rejection by the other. In some cases, as Shean (1978) notes, such a child may become a family scapegoat, causing problems that mask and divert attention from parental incompatibility. Unfortunately, the diversion is at the expense of the child's own developmental needs.

First at the Menninger Foundation in Topeka, Kansas, in the early 1950s, and later at the National Institute of Mental Health (NIMH) near Washington, D.C., Murray Bowen arranged for family members to move in with hospitalized schizophrenic patients in order to study the family as a unit; Bowen was especially interested in identifying symbiotic mother-child interactions. As he later reported (Bowen, 1960) in a book edited by Don Jackson that brought together for the first time various family theories related to the etiology of schizophrenia, families of schizophrenics often demonstrate interaction patterns resembling Lidz's findings about marital schism. Bowen termed the striking emotional distance between parents in such a situation **emotional divorce**. He described relationships of this kind as vacillating between periods of overcloseness and overdistance. Eventually the relationship becomes fixed at a point of sufficient emotional distance between the parents to avoid anxiety; they settle for "peace at any price." One area of joint activity—and, commonly, conflicting view—is the rearing of their children, particularly of children who show signs of psychological disturbance. It is as if the parents maintain contact with each other (and therefore a semblance of emotional equilibrium) by keeping the disturbed child helpless and needy. Thus adolescence, the period in which the child usually strives for a measure of autonomy, becomes especially stormy and stressful. This is typically the time when schizophrenic behavior first appears. Bowen proposed the intriguing notion that schizophrenia is a process that spans at least three generations before it manifests in the behavior of a family member. He suggested that one or both parents of a schizophrenic are troubled, immature individuals who, having experienced serious emotional conflict with their own parents, are now subjecting their offspring to similar conflict situations (for further discussion of Bowen's theories, see Chapter 7).

Succeeding Bowen as head of the Family Studies Section at NIMH, Lyman Wynne focused his research on the blurred, ambiguous, and confused communication patterns in families with schizophrenic members. In a series of papers (Wynne, Ryckoff, Day, & Hirsch, 1958; Wynne & Singer, 1963), he and his colleagues addressed themselves to the social organization of such families. For example, observing the families' recurrent fragmented and irrational style of communication, these researchers hypothesized that such a family pattern contributes to the schizophrenic member's tendency to interpret events occurring around him or her in blurred or distorted ways. In turn, such confusion or occasional bafflement increases the schizophrenic's social and interpersonal vulnerability, both within and outside the family. Wynne offered the term **pseudomutuality**—giving the appearance of a mutual, open, and understanding relationship without really having one—to describe how such families conceal an underlying distance between members. Pseudomutuality is a shared maneuver designed to defend all of the family members against pervasive feelings of meaninglessness and emptiness.

rule in family?

A person who grows up in a pseudomutual family setting fails to develop a strong sense of personal identity. This lack of identity handicaps the person from engaging in successful interactions outside the family and makes involvement within his or her own family system all-important. According to Wynne et al. (1958), the preschizophrenic doubts his or her capacity to accurately derive meaning from a personal experience outside the family, preferring instead to return to the familiar, self-sufficient family system with its enclosed (but safe) boundaries.

All of these studies were cross-sectional, involving families in which schizophrenia had been diagnosed in a member, usually a young adult, often long before the research was carried out. A common underlying assumption was that disturbances in family relationships are the major cause of mental disorders in general, and that perhaps distinctive patterns of family dynamics can be discovered for each form of psychopathology. Unfortunately, as Goldstein (1988) observes, the major barrier to testing such assumptions was that families were studied long after the major mental disorder such as schizophrenia had affected the family system.

Despite these deficits in research design, however, considerable enthusiasm was aroused by this new field of clinical inquiry into the baffling etiology of schizophrenia. A number of schizophrenia/family researchers met together for the first time at the 1957 national convention of the interdisciplinary American Orthopsychiatric Association. Although no separate organization was formed by this still-small group of researchers, they did learn of each other's work. The subsequent cross-fertilization of ideas culminated in *Intensive Family Therapy* (Boszormenyi-Nagy & Framo, 1965), a report by 15 authorities on their research with schizophrenics and their families. The clinical investigations begun a decade earlier had laid the groundwork for the emerging field of family therapy.

Marital Counseling and Child Guidance

The fields of marital counseling and child guidance, precursors of family therapy, are based on the concept that psychological disturbances arise from conflicts between persons as well as from conflict within a person. Effective intervention requires the therapist to work simultaneously with the troubled marital partners or parent-child pair.

If we assume that people have always been ready to advise or seek advice from others, informal marriage counseling has certainly existed for as long as the institution of marriage. On the other hand, formal counseling by a professional marriage counselor probably began somewhat over 60 years ago in the United States when the physicians Abraham and Hannah Stone opened the Marriage Consultation Center in New York in 1929. A year later, Paul Popenoe (a biologist specializing in human heredity) founded the American Institute of Family Relations in Los Angeles, offering premarital guidance as well as aid in promoting marital adjustment. Family educator Emily Mudd started the Marriage Council of Philadelphia in 1932 and later wrote what is thought to be the first textbook in the field (Mudd, 1951). In 1941, largely through Mudd's prodding, the American Association of Marriage Counselors (AAMC) was formed, bringing together various professionals (primarily physicians, educators, lawyers, and social workers, but also psychologists, sociologists, and clergymen) concerned with the new interdisciplinary field of marriage counseling. This organization has led the way in developing standards for training and practice, certifying marriage counseling centers, and establishing a professional code of ethics (Broderick & Schrader, 1981).

When Gurin, Veroff, and Feld (1960) conducted a nationwide survey on the nature of personal problems for which people seek professional help (as part of the ground-breaking work of the Joint Commission on Mental Illness and Health), they found that in their sample of 2460 individuals only one person in seven had ever sought such help. However, as indicated in Table 4.2, marriage and family problems together were by far the most common reasons given for seeking such help. Nevertheless, by the mid-1960s, it was still possible to characterize marriage counseling as a set of practices in search of a theory (Manus, 1966). No breakthrough research was being carried out, no dominant theories had emerged, no major figure had gained recognition. The AAMC published no journal of its own. If practitioners published at all, they apparently preferred to submit articles to journals of their own professions. By the 1970s, however, the situation had begun to change. Olson (1970) urged an integration of marriage counseling and the emerging field of family therapy, since both focused on the marital relationship and not simply on individuals in the relationship. In 1970, the AAMC, bowing to increased interest by its members in family therapy, changed its name to the American Association of Marriage and Family Counselors (in 1978, it became the present American Association for Marriage and Family Therapy). In 1975, the organization launched the *Journal of Marriage and Family Counseling* (renamed the *Journal of Marital and Family Therapy* in 1979).

What exactly is marriage counseling or, as it is called more and more frequently, marital therapy? Not considered to be as deeply probing, intensive, or as prolonged as psychotherapy, marriage counseling, as initially practiced, tended to be short-term, attempted to repair a damaged relationship, and by and large dealt with here-and-now issues rather than reconstructing the past. Unlike psychotherapy, which probed inner meanings, marriage counseling addressed reality issues and offered guidance to troubled couples in order to facilitate their conscious decision-making processes. As the outlook grew during the 1950s, in conjunction with family research, that problems arise out of a relationship context, a marital therapy approach offering a systems viewpoint began to replace the earlier counseling orientation. Marital therapy offered a broader perspective, focusing on interlocking problems and neurotic interactions between spouses. In particular, how one partner carried the pathology or symptomatology for the other began to be emphasized (Nichols, 1988). Marital therapists today address the affective, cognitive, and behavioral aspects of the husband-wife relationship within the context of marital and family systems.

Most people who seek help for their marriage are attempting to cope with a crisis (such as infidelity, threat of divorce, disagreements regarding child rearing, money problems, sexual incompatibilities, ineffective communication patterns, conflicts over power and control) that has caused an imbalance in the family equilibrium. Each partner enters marital therapy with different experiences, expectations, and goals and with different degrees of commitment to the marriage. Both partners are probably somewhat invested in staying married or they would not seek professional help, but the strength of the determination to stay together may vary greatly between them. Most marital therapy is brief, problem-focused, and pragmatic. In treating the relationship the therapist considers each individual's personality, role perceptions, and expectations as husband or wife (and how each perceives the partner's counter-role), patterns of communication (including sexual patterns, and disruptive and inconsistent patterns of verbal communication), and the couple's ability to function together as a working unit in dealing with problems and reaching decisions (Cromwell, Olson, & Fournier, 1976).

Table 4.2 Nature of Personal Problems for Which People Sought Professional Help (N=345)

Problem area	*Percent**
Spouse; marriage	42
Child; relationship with child	12
Other family relationships—parents, in-laws	5
Other relationship problems; type of relationship problem unspecified	4
Job or school problems; vocational choice	6
Nonjob adjustment problems in the self (general adjustment, specific symptoms)	18
Situational problems involving other people (that is, death or illness of a loved one) causing extreme psychological reaction	6
Nonpsychological situational problems	8
Nothing specific; a lot of little things; can't remember	2
Not ascertained	1

*Total is more than 100 percent because some respondents gave more than one response. (Source: Gurin, Veroff, & Feld, 1960)

As traditionally practiced, marriage counseling was likely to involve a collaborative approach; each spouse was seen by a separate therapist. By collaborating with one another, each counselor could then compare how his or her client saw a conflict situation with how the spouse reported the same situation to the other counselor. Martin and Bird (1963) called it "stereoscopic therapy" to emphasize that each counselor got a double view of each client. While such an approach overcomes some of the pitfalls inherent in seeing a single individual about his or her marital problem, firsthand observation of the ongoing relationship is forfeited. No matter how well briefed by the collaborating colleague, each counselor has a necessarily limited view of the marriage and no view whatsoever of the marital interaction (Bodin, 1983).

In concurrent counseling, a less-common approach, a counselor worked with both spouses, but saw each one separately. The counselor then had to piece together how the couple functioned by hearing two sides of the same event or transaction. Mittelman (1948), a psychoanalyst, was an early advocate of this procedure but he cautioned therapists to remain impartial and to remember what information had been learned from which partner. The counselor also faced the problem of keeping confidential the secrets one spouse wished not to reveal to the other. Although Sager (1966) reports that the concurrent-but-separate rule was occasionally broken (for example, with a couple seeking a divorce), for the most part the spouses were treated separately.

As the focus of marital counseling turned more and more to changing the marital relationship as such, it became clear that couples should be seen together in joint therapy sessions. Jackson (1959) introduced the term **conjoint** therapy to describe the situation where a couple (or perhaps the entire family) worked with the same therapist in the same room at the same time. By the end of the 1960s, Olson (1970) was able to state that marital therapists as a group could be distinguished by their primary emphasis on understanding and modifying the marital relationship and their preference for conjoint treatment. According to Nichols & Everett (1986), collaborative and concurrent counseling are seldom used today, conjoint marital therapy having become the most widely employed technique for treating marital discord.

Turning to historical developments in the child guidance movement, note that the systematic study of early childhood simply did not begin anywhere until early in this century (Kanner, 1962). In a careful survey of the child psychiatry literature before 1900, Rubenstein (1948) found no references to the psychological or developmental aspects of normal childhood. With the exception of some studies of the "mentally defective" child of subnormal intelligence, little if anything that is known today in the fields of child psychology and child psychiatry was published before 1900.

Early in this century, major social reforms and changes in the legal status of children occurred, leading to universal compulsory education, restrictions on child labor, and a greater respect for children's rights. Inevitably, interest grew in establishing groups of experts who might work as a team to help emotionally disturbed children; thus, the child guidance movement was launched (Rosenblatt, 1971). (Earlier in this chapter, we acknowledged Adler's contribution to the development of this movement in Europe and later, through his followers, in the United States.) By 1909 the psychiatrist William Healy had founded the Juvenile Psychopathic Institute in Chicago, a forerunner among child guidance clinics (now known as the Institute for Juvenile Research). Healy was specifically concerned with treating (and if possible, discovering ways of preventing) juvenile delinquency. By 1917 Healy had moved to Boston and established the Judge Baker Guidance Center devoted to diagnostic evaluation and treatment of delinquent children (Goldenberg, 1983). In 1924 the American Orthopsychiatric Association, largely devoted to the prevention of emotional disorders in children, was organized. Although child guidance clinics remained few in number until after World War II, they now exist in almost every city in the United States.

An important innovation introduced by Healy was the formation of a team of professionals from different disciplines to assess both the child and his or her family. The practice of using a team made up of a psychiatrist, a clinical psychologist, and a psychiatric social worker to examine the child through interviews, psychological tests, and history taking, respectively, became standard in child guidance clinics. The same may be said for involving one or both parents in the treatment. The psychiatrist was generally responsible for making most clinical decisions and conducting psychotherapy, the psychologist for developing educational and remedial programs, and the social worker for casework with the parents and liaison with other agencies to help improve the family's social environment. If therapy was undertaken with the child, it was common for the parents (particularly the more available mother) to visit the clinic regularly for therapy also, usually seeing a different therapist from the one working with the child. This collaborative approach, with the two therapists presumably consulting each other frequently, became traditional in child guidance clinics. According to Cooper (1974), direct work with the parents of emotionally disturbed children has three basic aims: (1) to establish an alliance with the parents that would support the child's growth in therapy; (2) to secure pertinent information about the child's experiences and the family situation; and (3) to help change the environment, thus aiding the child's growth and development. This type of intervention implies that the child's disturbance may very likely arise from interaction with one or both parents and that therapeutic change is best brought about by changing the nature of that interaction. Moreover, child guidance clinics function on the principle of early intervention in a child's—family's—emotional problems to avert the later development of more serious disabilities.

Group Therapy

Group therapy has been practiced in one form or another since the beginning of the 20th century but the impetus for its major expansion came from the need for clinical services during and immediately after World War II. The earliest use of the group process in psychotherapy can be credited to the Austrian psychiatrist Jacob Moreno who, around 1910, combined dramatic and therapeutic techniques to create **psychodrama**. Moreno, whose psychodramatic techniques are still used today, believed that it is necessary to recreate in the therapeutic process the various interpersonal situations that may have led to the patient's psychological difficulties. Since this was hard to accomplish in the one-to-one therapist-patient situation, Moreno, in the role of therapist/director, used a stage on which the patient could act out his or her significant life events in front of an audience. In these psychodramas, various people (frequently, but not necessarily, other patients) represented key persons ("auxiliary egos") in the patient's life. At certain junctures, the director might instruct the patient to reverse roles with one of the players so that he or she could gain a greater awareness of how another person saw him or her. In 1925 Moreno introduced psychodrama into the United States; in 1931 he coined the term "group therapy" (Gazda, 1975).

Stimulated largely by the theories developed by British psychoanalyst Melanie Klein, considerable interest in group processes developed during the 1930s at the Tavistock Institute in London. Several therapists began experimenting with group intervention techniques (Bion, 1961). In particular, they emphasized dealing with current problems ("here and now") rather than searching for past causes and explanations or reconstructing possibly traumatic early experiences. Samuel Slavson, an engineer by training, began to do group work at the Jewish Board of Guardians in New York City at about the same time; from this work emerged his activity-group therapy technique, in which a group setting encourages disturbed children or adolescents to interact, thereby acting out their conflicts, impulses, and typical behavior patterns (Slavson, 1964). Slavson's approach was based on concepts derived from psychoanalysis, group work, and progressive education. In 1943 the American Group Psychotherapy Association was formed, largely through Slavson's efforts.

The sudden influx of psychiatric casualties during World War II, along with a shortage of trained therapists to work with these individuals, led to increased interest in briefer and more efficient therapeutic techniques such as group therapy. Shortly after the war, human relations training groups (T-groups)—sometimes referred to as "therapy for normals"—originated at the National Training Laboratory (NTL) at Bethel, Maine. Here the focus was on group discussion and role-playing techniques; these groups were part of an educational effort to provide interpersonal feedback information to the participants so that they could gain a better understanding of the group process, examine their attitudes and values, and become more sensitive to others. (T-groups were sometimes referred to as sensitivity-training groups on the West Coast.) In the 1960s, stimulated by the emergence of various growth centers around the United States, particularly the Esalen Institute in Big Sur, California, the **encounter group** (part of the **human potential movement**) made a dramatic impact on the therapy scene and seemed to gain the immediate approval of large numbers of people, mostly from the upper-middle class. Today that enthusiasm has waned considerably, although traditional group therapies, NTL groups, and, to a lesser extent, encounter groups, continue to exist side by side (Goldenberg, 1983).

Fundamental to the practice of group therapy is the principle that a small group can act as a carrier of change and strongly influence those who choose to be considered its members. A therapy group is a meaningful and real unit in and of itself, more than a collection of individuals, more than the sum of its parts. Another way of putting it is that the group is a collection of positions and roles and not of individuals (Back, 1974). The Tavistock version of group therapy is a good illustration: the group is treated as if it were a disturbed patient who is hurting because certain functions are not being carried out successfully. In a Tavistock group, the leader helps the group to function in a more balanced, coordinated, and mutually reinforcing way so that the group can accomplish productive work more efficiently. The implications for family therapy with a dysfunctional family are obvious.

As group therapy is practiced today (Yalom, 1985), most groups consist of between five and ten members plus a leader, meet at least once a week in 1-1/2 to 2-hour sessions, and sit in a circular arrangement so that each member can see and readily talk to every other member, including the therapist. The groups are usually heterogeneous, although under certain circumstances homogeneous groups are formed (for example, women's consciousness-raising groups, groups composed of rape victims, groups of child-abusing parents). NTL groups, in which participants generally meet over a two-week period away from home, tend to focus on training community, business, and government leaders in organizational development; these laboratories have expanded from their beginnings in Bethel in 1946 to various parts of the world today. Encounter groups are still available in many large cities, although they no longer attract the large numbers of people they did a decade or more ago. Table 4.3 summarizes some unique advantages of group therapy.

Table 4.3 Some Special Advantages of Group Therapy over Individual Therapy

Principle	*Elaboration*
Resembles everyday reality more closely	Therapist sees patient interacting with others, rather than hearing about it from the patient and possibly getting a biased or distorted picture; adds another informational dimension regarding his or her customary way of dealing with people.
Reduces social isolation	Patient learns that he or she is not unique by listening to others; thus he or she may be encouraged to give up feelings of isolation and self-consciousness.
Greater feelings of support and caring from others	Group cohesiveness ("we-ness") leads to increased trust; self-acceptance is likely to increase when patient is bolstered by acceptance by strangers.
Imitation of successful coping styles	New group members have the opportunity to observe older members and their successful adaptational skills.
Greater exchange of feelings through feedback	Group situation demands expression of feelings, both positive and negative, directed at other members who evoke love, frustration, tears, or rage; patient thus gains relief while also learning from responses of others that intense affect does not destroy anyone, as he or she may have feared or fantasized.
Increases self-esteem through helping others	Patient has the opportunity to reciprocate help, to offer others empathy, warmth, acceptance, support, and genuineness, thereby increasing his or her own feelings of self-worth.
Greater insight	Patients become more attuned to understanding human motives and behavior, in themselves and in others.

(Source: Goldenberg, 1983)

DEVELOPMENTS IN FAMILY THERAPY

As the various movements we have been describing began to converge, beginning in the 1950s, each succeeding decade brought further consolidation and maturity to the field of family therapy.

The 1950s: From Family Research to Family Treatment

Most historical surveys of the family therapy movement (Broderick & Schrader, 1981; Goldenberg & Goldenberg, 1983; Guerin, 1976) agree that the 1950s was its founding decade. It was then that the theories and approaches we have been describing seemed to coalesce. Those ideas, to be sure, pertained more to clinical research than to clinical practice. Observation of a family—particularly one with a symptomatic member—could be justified only if it was presented as a research strategy. Observation of a family as a basis for treatment would have been a direct challenge to the prevailing sanction against a therapist's contact with anyone in the family other than her or his own patient.

Family therapy therefore owes its initial legitimacy to the facts that (1) it was being carried out for scientifically defensible research purposes; and (2) the "research" was being done on clinical problems such as schizophrenia that did not respond well to the established psychotherapies of that time (Segal & Bavelas, 1983). As Wynne (1983) notes, Bateson's Schizophrenia Communication Research Project in Palo Alto, the work of Lidz and his coresearchers in New Haven, and Bowen's ambitious effort to hospitalize parents of schizophrenics for residential treatment with their disturbed offspring were all initially research-motivated and research-oriented. Wynne's own work at NIMH with schizophrenics was based on the use of therapy as a source of experimental data. It was the apparent success of the family research that helped give the stamp of approval to the development of therapeutic techniques.

At the 1952 American Psychiatric Association convention, Christian Midelfort, a psychoanalyst, presented a paper that was probably the first to report on the treatment of psychiatric patients and their families. Later expanded into a book (Midelfort, 1957), the paper described Midelfort's experiences and results with family therapy working with relatives and patients in and out of mental hospitals. Unfortunately, Midelfort's pioneering efforts are all but forgotten by most family therapists today since his geographic location (Lutheran Hospital in La Crosse, Wisconsin) and lack of academic or training center affiliation isolated him from the mainstream of activity and the exchange of ideas and techniques then taking place.

John Bell, an academic psychologist at Clark University in Worcester, Massachusetts, was another major architect of family therapy who receives little recognition for his contributions; as an inductive, action-oriented researcher and innovator, Bell was more interested in new ideas and practices than in establishing a reputation. Bell (1975) recalls that a casual remark overheard while he was visiting the Tavistock Clinic in London in 1951—to the effect that Dr. John Bowlby was experimenting with group therapy with families—stimulated his interest in applying the technique to treat behavior problems in children. Bell assumed that Bowlby, a

John Bell, Ed.D.

distinguished British psychiatrist, was treating the entire family, although this later proved to be an erroneous assumption; actually, Bowlby only occasionally held a family conference as an adjunct to working with the problem child. On the basis of this misinformation, Bell began to think through the technical implications of meeting with an entire family on a regular basis. Once back in the United States, a case came to his attention that gave him the opportunity to try out this method as a therapeutic device. Bell's description of his work was not widely disseminated until a decade later (Bell, 1961). That ground-breaking monograph is often thought, along with Ackerman's 1958 text, to represent the founding of family therapy as practiced today. Unlike most of their colleagues in the 1950s, both Bell and Ackerman worked with nonschizophrenic families.

Meanwhile, the Palo Alto group led by Bateson was influenced greatly by the clinical wisdom of Milton Erickson, a Phoenix psychiatrist whose extraordinary powers of observation and therapeutic "wizardry" were becoming renowned among psychotherapists and hypnotherapists alike. (They would become even more celebrated after Haley's 1973 exposition of Erickson's work.) Erickson's gifts were his spontaneity, his quick and intuitive reading of a client's uniqueness, his tactical skills in reaching a resistant person, and his artful use of persuasive communication at several levels simultaneously. His use of paradoxical instruction was to have an impact in general on the communication approach to family therapy and specifically on Haley's later **strategic** techniques (see Chapter 9).

Carl Whitaker, a psychiatrist, worked at Oak Ridge, Tennessee, during World War II. There he developed many of his innovative techniques: the use of a cotherapist; the inclusion of intergenerational family members in a patient's therapy; a highly active style with patients (including physical interaction, such as arm wrestling); and what he later described (Whitaker, 1975) as the "psychotherapy of the absurd." Lovingly carried out by Whitaker, this was a tongue-in-cheek procedure of escalating the incongruity of a symptom or bit of patient behavior to the point that the absurdity was easily apparent to the patient, sometimes by means of the therapist exposing his own absurd behavior or "creative craziness." Whitaker's use of self (stemming largely from his **experiential** view of psychotherapy) is not incidental to the treatment process but consciously intended to help the family achieve a looser, more caring, more intimate set of relationships among its members. Working at Emory University in Atlanta and later the University of Wisconsin at Madison, Whitaker—in spite of his deliberately irreverent style—was considered a key figure in family therapy by the late 1950s. He achieved further recognition for including extended family members in the family therapy process.

By 1957 the family movement had surfaced nationally (Guerin, 1976) as family researchers and clinicians in various parts of the country began to learn of each other's work. At professional meetings, interest focused on families with a hospitalized schizophrenic member; and as noted earlier in this chapter, a number of family-related studies of the etiology of schizophrenia were published together in a volume edited by Jackson (1960). By this time, schizophrenia as well as a number of other severely incapacitating disorders were seen as resulting from a destructive family environment, the so-called pathogenic family (Zuk & Rubenstein, 1965).

By the decade's end in 1959, Don Jackson had founded the Mental Research Institute (MRI) in Palo Alto; Virginia Satir, Jay Haley, John Weakland, Paul Watzlawick, Arthur Bodin, and Richard Fisch would soon join the staff. A year later, Ackerman organized the Family Institute in New York (renamed the Ackerman Institute for Family Therapy after the death of its founder in 1971). Representing the East and West coasts, both institutes have played seminal roles in the family therapy field.

The 1960s: The Rush to Practice

The early 1960s was a time of greatly heightened curiosity regarding family therapy. An increasing number of clinical practitioners began to think of family therapy as a new way of conceptualizing the origins of mental disorders and their amelioration, not simply one more method of treatment. A number of therapists began working with whole families. Those with an individual orientation recognized that the "identified patient" was the victim of family strife but preferred to work with each family member separately. Largely oblivious to any of the results of the theoretical research of the 1950s, these therapists simply extended their familiar and primarily psychodynamic techniques and concepts to family settings and situations.

The more family-oriented therapists did more than treat individuals in a family context; they began to realize that it was the dysfunctional family patterns that needed to be transformed. For this latter group, as Haley (1971b) points out, the focus of treatment was a family's structure and its members' interaction, not on an individual's perceptions, affect, or behavior as such. For these therapists, the goal of therapy shifted from changing the person to changing the sequences of behavior between intimates. At the same time, family therapy programs were established in new outpatient settings (such as community mental health centers) and were directed at new kinds of families (for example, poor families and minority families); family therapy was no longer restricted to the treatment of hospitalized schizophrenics and their families (Zuk, 1981).

Several significant developments in the early 1960s indicated the momentum that the field of family therapy was gathering. In 1962, Ackerman and Jackson founded the first—and still the most influential—journal in the field, *Family Process*, with Jay Haley as its editor. From its beginnings, the journal enabled researchers and practitioners alike to exchange ideas and identify with the field. In addition, several important national conferences were organized. A meeting in 1964 dealt with the application of systems theory to understanding dysfunctional families (Zuk & Boszormenyi-Nagy, 1967); in 1967 a conference organized by psychologist James Framo was held to stimulate and maintain an ongoing dialogue between family researchers, theorists, and family therapists (Framo, 1972).

Family therapy, gaining professional respectability, was becoming a familiar topic at most psychiatric and psychological meetings. As Bowen (1976) later recalled, dozens of therapists were eager to present their newly minted intervention techniques with whole families. In nearly all cases, this "rush to practice" precluded the development of procedures that were adequately grounded in research or based on sound conceptual formulations. In their clinical zeal—Bowen refers to it as "therapeutic evangelism"—many therapists attempted solutions to family dilemmas using familiar concepts borrowed from individual psychotherapy.

One notable exception to the emphasis on practice over theory and research during this period was Minuchin's Wiltwyck School Project, a pioneering study of urban slum families (Minuchin, Montalvo, Guerney, Rosman, & Schumer, 1967), and his development of appropriate clinical techniques for successful intervention with male juvenile delinquents, many of whom were Puerto Ricans or blacks from New York City. From this landmark study of poor, disadvantaged, unstable families, largely without fathers or stable father-figures, Minuchin developed a **structural**  family therapy approach that was practical and oriented toward problem resolution, always mindful of the social environment or context in which the family problems emerged and were maintained. By 1965, Minuchin had become director of the Philadelphia Child Guidance Clinic, originally in the heart of the black ghetto, where he focused on intervention techniques with low-income families. His staff included Braulio Montalvo and Bernice Rosman from Wiltwyck, and in 1967 he invited Jay Haley from Palo Alto to join them. (The Bateson research group had officially disbanded in 1962 when Bateson, an anthropologist more interested in theoretical ideas regarding communication than in their clinical application to troubled families, moved to the Oceanic Institute in Hawaii to observe patterns of communication among dolphins.) The Philadelphia center was soon transformed from a traditional child guidance clinic into a large family-oriented treatment center. By the late 1960s, the Philadelphia group had begun working with psychosomatic families (with particular attention to families of anorexia nervosa patients), applying some of Minuchin's earlier concepts of boundaries and the interplay of a family's subsystems to problems of somatic dysfunction.

During this highly productive period, the MRI on the West Coast extended its earlier studies to include families with expressions of dysfunctional behavior other than schizophrenia: delinquency, school underachievement, psychosomatic disorders, marital conflict (Bodin, 1981). The 1964 publication of *Conjoint Family Therapy* by Virginia Satir, then at MRI, did much to popularize the family approach, as did Satir's demonstrations at professional meetings and workshops in many parts of the world. Toward the end of the decade, the character of the work at the MRI changed as the result of Satir's departure to become the director of training of Esalen Institute, a growth center at Big Sur, California; Haley's move to Philadelphia; and especially Jackson's untimely death in 1968. Although the MRI has continued to focus on family interactional patterns (particularly communication), the Brief Therapy Project, begun in 1967, became its major thrust. In this pragmatic, short-term, team approach to working with families (see Chapter 11), a primary therapist consults with other therapists observing the session from behind a one-way mirror. Geared toward problem resolution, brief therapy helps family members change the kinds of responses they make to problems, since the solutions they have persistently chosen in the past have only served to reinforce their problematic behavior (Watzlawick, Weakland, & Fisch, 1974).

During the 1960s there were corresponding developments in family therapy outside of the United States. At the psychoanalytically oriented Institute of Family Therapy in London, Robin Skynner contributed a brief version of psychodynamic family therapy (Skynner, 1981). The British psychiatrist John Howells (1975) devised a system for family diagnosis as a necessary step in planning therapeutic intervention. In West Germany, Helm Stierlin (1972) called attention to patterns of separation in adolescence and related these patterns to family characteristics.

In Italy, Mara Selvini-Palazzoli (1978), trained in child psychoanalysis but discouraged by her results with anorectic children, was attracted to the new epistemology proposed by Bateson and the Palo Alto group. Shifting to a systems approach that stressed circularity, she was more successful with resistant cases. In 1967 Selvini-Palazzoli formed the Institute for Family Studies in Milan; the Institute would eventually have a worldwide impact on the field of family therapy, particularly with its use of "long" brief therapy in which ten sessions are held at monthly intervals. We will return to the work of the Milan family therapists (Luigi Boscolo, Giuliana Prata, Gianfranco Cecchin, and Selvini-Palazzoli) in Chapter 9.

The 1970s: Innovative Techniques and Self-Examination

For the most part, technique continued to outdistance theory and research in family therapy well into the 1970s. The early part of the decade saw a proliferation of family therapy approaches: treating several families simultaneously in **multiple**

family therapy (Laqueur, 1976); bringing families together for an intensive, crisis-focused two-day period of continuing interaction with a team of mental health professionals, in **multiple impact therapy** (MacGregor, Ritchie, Serrano, & Schuster, 1964); working in the home with an extended family group including friends, neighbors, and employers, in **network therapy** (Speck & Attneave, 1973); treating a family on an outpatient basis in **family crisis therapy** instead of hospitalizing a disturbed, scapegoated family member (Langsley, Pittman, Machotka, & Flomenhaft, 1968). Behavioral psychologists began to turn their attention to issues related to family matters, such as teaching parents "behavior management skills" to facilitate effective child rearing (Patterson, 1971), and to propose therapeutic strategies for working with marital discord (Jacobson & Martin, 1976) and family dysfunction (Liberman, 1970). The newly available technology of videotape allowed family therapists to tape ongoing sessions either for immediate playback to the family, for later study by the therapist, or for training purposes (Alger, 1976a).

In the 1970s the relatively new field of family therapy engaged in its first efforts at self-examination. The so-called GAP report (Group for the Advancement of Psychiatry, 1970) acknowledged clinicians' increasing awareness of the family's role in symptom and conflict formation as well as of the limitations of the traditional psychoanalytic emphasis on intrapsychic processes. The GAP survey of a sample of family therapists found that they belonged largely to three disciplines—psychiatry, psychology, and social work—although practitioners also included marriage counselors, clergy, nonpsychiatric physicians, child psychiatrists, nurses, sociologists, and others. Most family therapists were young, reported dissatisfaction with the results of individual treatment, and were looking for a more efficient method of therapeutic intervention. When asked to select their primary and secondary goals from among eight categorties, over 90 percent of the 290 respondents listed improved communication within the family as their primary goal; not a single respondent said it was rarely or never a goal. All eight of the goals described in the questionnaire were chosen as primary goals (with all or with certain families) by over half of the respondents (see Table 4.4). However, improvement in individual task performance or individual symptomatic improvement was more likely to be a secondary goal (see Table 4.5). This indicates that these objectives had by no means been abandoned but that change in only part of a family was given less emphasis than a familywide change such as improved communication.

The 1970 GAP report also presented the results of a survey of practicing family therapists asked to rank the major figures in the field according to their influence at that time. The practitioners placed them in this order: Satir, Ackerman, Jackson, Haley, Bowen, Wynne, Bateson, Bell, Boszormenyi-Nagy.

In another kind of effort to bring order and self-awareness to the developing field, Beels and Ferber (1969) observed a number of leading therapists conducting family sessions and studied videotapes and films of their work with families. Beels and Ferber then distinguished two types of family therapists based on the therapist's relationship to the family group: **conductors** and **reactors**. Conductor therapists are active, aggressive, and colorful leaders who place themselves in the center of the family group. They are likely to initiate rather than respond, to propound ideas vigorously, to make their value systems explicit. Ackerman, Satir, Bowen, and Minuchin are models for this type. Reactor therapists are less theatrical personalities, more subtle and indirect. They observe and clarify the family group process, responding to what the family presents to them, negotiating differences among family members. Beels and Ferber further divided reactors into analysts (who tend to conceptualize what is taking place in psychoanalytic terms such as **transference**, **countertransference**, or **acting out**) and systems purists (who view families as rule-governed systems). The authors cite Whitaker, Wynne, Boszormenyi-Nagy, and Framo as analyst reactors; Haley, Jackson, Watzlawick, and Zuk as systems purist reactors.

Table 4.4 Primary Goals Stated by Therapists with Families Actually in Treatment (*N*=290)

Primary goals	*Percent of all families*	*Percent of certain families*	*Total percent*
1. Improved communication	85	5	90
2. Improved autonomy and individuation	56	31	87
3. Improved empathy	56	15	71
4. More flexible leadership	34	32	66
5. Improved role agreement	32	32	64
6. Reduced conflict	23	37	60
7. Individual symptomatic improvement	23	33	56
8. Improved individual task performance	12	38	50

Table 4.5 Secondary Goals Stated by Therapists with Families Actually in Treatment (*N*=290)

Primary goals	*Percent of all families*	*Percent of certain families*	*Total percent*
1. Improved individual task performance	16	29	45
2. Individual symptomatic improvement	23	15	38
3. Reduced conflict	17	18	35
4. Improved role agreement	17	15	32
5. More flexible leadership	11	19	30
6. Improved empathy	17	8	25
7. Improved autonomy and individuation	7	5	12
8. Improved communication	8	1	9

Beels and Ferber (1969) contend that each type of therapist is effective in directing and controlling the family sessions and in providing family members with possible new ways of relating to each other; the conductors are more direct in their methods but not necessarily more successful in helping to create a new family experience as the basis for changing its members' interactive behavior patterns.

Another kind of analysis of therapist intervention was initiated in the early 1970s at the University of California at Santa Cruz when mathematician Richard Bandler and linguist John Grinder set out to determine just how master clinicians consistently achieve their desired therapeutic outcomes. They based their inquiry on **neuro-linguistic programming** (NLP), hypothesizing that all behavior results from neurological processes ("neuro"), that these neural processes are represented, ordered, and sequenced into models and strategies through language ("linguistic"), and that the process of organizing the system's components determines specific outcomes ("programming") (Dilts, Grinder, Bandler, Cameron-Bandler, & DeLozier, 1980). Bandler and Grinder studied the linguistic patterns of Virginia Satir, Fritz Perls, and later, Milton Erickson to detect how language produces changes in people and to provide a more systematic explanation for how these therapists worked and how their intervention strategies helped clients reprogram their behavior. The work of Bandler and Grinder (1975) was especially useful in helping to clarify and systematize previously unanalyzed patterns of therapist communication and in discovering how clients reveal what they are thinking and feeling through sensory-based statements ("I see what you mean"; "I'm touched by your offer"; "I like it when you tell me you appreciate what I've done") and behavioral cues (for example, eye movements). NLP practitioners learn to scan word patterns and body language for cues regarding a person's emotional state, preliminary to helping to change his or her behavior. In recent years NLP has developed into an all-purpose self-improvement program for salesmen and executives as well as a technique used by hypnotherapists and family therapists.

Finally, self-examination took the form of outcome research on the effectiveness of family therapy. By the late 1970s the need for such studies was being generally acknowledged. Nevertheless, Wells and Dezen (1978) pointed out after surveying the outcome literature that most family therapy approaches, some of them identified with major figures in the field, "have never submitted their methods to empirical testing and, indeed, seem oblivious to such a need" (p. 266). By the end of the decade there had been some improvement (Gurman & Kniskern, 1981a), but the effectiveness of family therapy still required continuing and systematic evaluation. (For further discussion of this topic, see Chapter 12).

The 1980s: Growth and Professionalization

In the 1980s, a number of signs documented the phenomenal growth of the family therapy field, now in its "over-thirty" adult years. Whereas barely a decade earlier the field had one professional journal of its own, *Family Process*, there were now approximately two dozen family therapy journals, half of them published in English. Once, family therapy centers could be counted on the fingers of one hand; now more than 300 free-standing family therapy institutes existed in the United States alone. Three professional organizations now represented the interests of family therapy. The American Association for Marriage and Family Therapy (AAMFT), which grew from fewer than 1000 members in 1970 to over 7500 by 1979, to 16,000 by 1989, has authority to accredit marriage and family therapy training programs, to develop standards for issuing certificates to qualified persons as Approved Supervisors, to publish a code of ethics for its members, and to actively pursue state licensing and certification for marital and family therapists. In addition, the AAMFT joins other coalitions of mental health and family organizations in advocacy of public policy (regarding such family-related issues as child care, paternal and maternal leave, and mandated minimum health insurance) at both the state and federal levels.

The American Family Therapy Association, founded in 1977, a smaller group of approximately 1000 members by the end of the 1980s, has restricted itself to being an interest group concerned exclusively with family therapy issues as distinct from marriage counseling or marital therapy. The youngest group, the Division of Family Psychology of the American Psychological Association, was established in 1986. As noted in Chapter 1, family psychology offers a broader perspective than the clinical emphasis of family therapy, paying special attention to relationship networks within marriage and the family. By the close of the decade, membership in the Division of Family Psychology was approximately 2000.

Family therapy became an international phenomenon in the 1980s, with active training programs and congresses in Canada, England, Israel, Holland, Italy, Australia, West Germany, and elsewhere. The Heidelberg Conference marking the tenth anniversary of the Department of Basic Psychoanalytic Research and Family Therapy of Heidelberg University in West Germany took place in 1985, with some 2000 participants from 25 countries attending (Stierlin, Simon, & Schmidt, 1987). Bridging east-west differences in 1987, a family therapy conference attended by over 2500 people from all over the world took place in Prague, Czechoslovakia, followed in 1989 by a similar event in Budapest, Hungary.

The 1990s: Integration and Consolidation

Training in family therapy is by now an integral part of most university clinical graduate programs, with students also seeking out family therapy institutes for more advanced study. Workshops are held each month in various parts of the United States and are usually heavily attended. The profession has established superstars (such as Minuchin, Whitaker, or Haley) as well as lesser luminaries who offer demonstrations of their work in different parts of the country throughout the year.

No longer the radical movement it was considered barely four decades ago, family therapy has established itself as a distinctive and important mental health field. Family therapy has become the treatment of choice for a wide range of problems; public awareness of and demand for relationship-oriented services has increased dramatically. Truly, as Olson, Russell, and Sprenkle (1980) observe, marital and family therapy reflects the *Zeitgeist*.

Olson, Russell, and Sprenkle (1980) also note the important consequences for the entire mental health profession that have followed from the growth and acceptance of this new field: (1) the traditional distinction between marriage counseling and family therapy has faded so that it is now more accurate to describe marital and family therapy as one not-quite-unified field; (2) the field has achieved sufficient integrity and stature that workers in the field today are apt to think of themselves as family therapists as much as or more than they identify themselves with their professional disciplines; (3) there is a trend toward treating relationships, whether the intervention be with married couples, cohabiting couples, stepfamilies, gay couples, parent-adolescent dyads, or elsewhere; (4) intervention is now considered appropriate at all stages of a relationship, from premarital counseling to divorce counseling to custody-resolution counseling.

This emphasis on treating problems within a relationship context characterizes the field of family therapy today. The practice has been buttressed theoretically by the acceptance of systems theory, as well as by the renewed coherence of family therapy and family research. For example, the revival of interest in family theory (including the current debate within the field regarding the "new epistemology") is largely stimulated by clinical research observations of the type favored during family therapy's earliest days in the 1950s (Wynne, 1983).

Many of the first general family therapists remain active and continue to have authority in the field. In reviewing the last three decades, Thaxton and L'Abate (1982) named the following figures (not necessarily in order of importance) as having had the greatest impact: Ackerman, Boszormenyi-Nagy, Bowen, Framo, Haley, Jackson, Minuchin, Satir, Whitaker, and Zuk.

In a 1988 survey of 900 family therapists (Rait, 1988), nearly a third described their theoretical orientation as eclectic; of those with a clearly defined orientation, the most popular was structural family therapy, first developed by Minuchin and associated with training at the Philadelphia Child Guidance Clinic. Marital difficulties and parent-adolescent problems were the most frequent complaints clients presented, with drug/alcohol abuse and school problems the next most common. The survey's overall results indicated that "family therapy today is far from monolithic; few beliefs and clinical methods have reached anything approaching broad acceptance" (Rait, 1988, p. 56).

The challenge of the 1990s is integrating the various approaches we are about to consider, using some of each as called for in working with disparate populations.

SUMMARY

We have discussed the diverse roots of contemporary family therapy. Psychoanalysis, as conceived by Freud, acknowledged the role of family relationships in personality development but its techniques of treatment were individual-oriented. Ackerman is generally credited with adapting psychoanalytic formulations to the study of the family and is thus considered a founder of family therapy; Adler and Sullivan also influenced the developing field. General systems theory, as proposed by the biologist Bertalanffy, described seemingly unrelated phenomena as components of a self-regulating total system with feedback mechanisms to govern the process; applied to the family, the focus is on how the parts form a whole, how they are organized, and how they interact. In schizophrenia research, Bateson's and his associates' work on double-bind interactions, Lidz's on marital schism and marital skew, Bowen's on symbiotic mother-child relationships, and Wynne's on pseudomutuality helped establish the role of the dysfunctional family in the etiology of schizophrenia and set the stage for studying interaction patterns in other kinds of families. The fields of marital counseling and child guidance brought pairs of family members (such as husband-wife, parent-child) into treatment, thus modifying the traditional emphasis on treating individual patients. Group therapy used small-group processes for therapeutic gain and provided a model for therapy with whole families.

Stimulated by the research-oriented study of families with schizophrenic members, the family therapy movement gained momentum and national visibility in the 1950s. The pioneering family therapists of that decade were joined in the 1960s by more individual-oriented therapists who were attracted to this new way of conceptualizing and treating dysfunctional behavior. Largely oblivious to the findings of earlier research on the family, many clinicians during this era simply rushed into practice; in the process, they created many new strategies for intervention with whole families. Corresponding developments were taking place in various parts of the world, particularly in Europe. Selvini-Palazzoli's systems-based work with anorectic children in Milan, Italy, is particularly noteworthy.

Technique continued to outpace theory and research well into the 1970s. Additional innovative therapeutic techniques were introduced, including behavioral approaches to family-related problems. The field was growing at a rapid rate and a number of efforts aimed at self-awareness and self-evaluation were undertaken. In the 1980s marital therapy and family therapy became an all-but-unified field. Practitioners from a variety of disciplines made "family therapist" their primary professional identification. The emphasis today is on treating problems within a relationship context rather than working separately with individuals. There is a revival of interest in family theory and the linking of clinical family research and family therapy practice. The challenge of the 1990s is to integrate the various approaches and apply combinations of techniques as needed for different populations.

Chapter Five

Psychodynamic Approaches to Theory and Practice

Family therapists share a common view of the family as the context of and for relationships. However, significant differences exist in the theoretical assumptions they make about the nature and origin of psychological dysfunction, in the way they understand family interactions, and in their strategies for therapeutic intervention. Although their positions do not represent rigid adherence to particular "schools," distinct differences in viewpoint and emphasis are apparent. In this and the following five chapters, we look at approaches to family theory and clinical practice from six perspectives, grouping those that are primarily psychodynamic in orientation; those that pay special attention to the family as a system—the Bowen, structural, and communication/strategic models; and those that are behavioral in their approach.

Before explaining our reasons for such a classification scheme, let us emphasize our belief that the theoretical foundation of the field of family therapy demands to be strengthened lest it become merely a set of clever, even flashy, empirically derived intervention techniques. Important and effective as some of these techniques may be, they require the kind of rationale or justification that only a coherent, unified theory can provide. All theories, of course, are inevitably speculations or hypotheses offered in the hope of shedding light or providing fresh perspectives on the causes of family dysfunction. They are never, in and of themselves, true or false; rather, some are more useful than others, particularly in generating research hypotheses that can be verified through testing. All of these theories are tentative; all are expendable in the sense that useful theories lead to new ways of looking at behavior and to the discovery of new relationships that in turn lead to new sets of theoretical proposals.

At this stage in the development of family therapy—still a considerable distance from a comprehensive theory—we need to examine the usefulness of the various contributions that have already been made to our understanding of family development and functioning. Some models have come from the research laboratory, others from the consultation room of a clinician working with seriously disturbed or merely temporarily troubled families. In evaluating each of the models presented in this chapter, as well as in Chapters 6 through 10, keep in mind the following criteria of a sound theory:

1. Is it *comprehensive*? Does it deal with understanding family functioning and avoid being trivial or oversimplified? Is it generalizable to all families as they behave in all situations (not, for example, only to white middle-class families or only to the ways families behave in special psychotherapeutic situations)?
2. Is it *parsimonious*? Does it make as few assumptions as necessary to account for the phenomena under study? If two competing theoretical systems both predict the same behavior, is it the one with fewer assumptions and constructs?
3. Is it *verifiable*? Does it generate predictions about behavior that can be confirmed when the relevant empirical data have been collected?
4. Is it *precise*? Does it define concepts explicitly and relate them to each other and to data (avoiding figurative, metaphorical, or analogical language)?
5. Is it *empirically valid*? Do systematic empirical tests of the predictions made by the theory confirm the theory?
6. Is it *stimulating*? Does it provoke response and further investigation to enhance the theory or even to demonstrate its inadequacies?

CLASSIFYING THEORIES IN FAMILY THERAPY

Over a decade ago, Gerald Zuk (1976), himself a leading figure in the field, questioned whether family therapy was a "clinical hodgepodge" (of numerous techniques and incomplete theories) rather than a true clinical science. Unfortunately, the question remains almost as relevant today, although a number of scientifically designed efforts are being made to expand theory and to conduct more research relevant to family assessment as well as to therapy.

One scientific endeavor involves classification of therapist styles and/or theoretical stances into groupings based on significant similarities. The first and necessary step in such a procedure is to select the dimensions according to which the different therapists will be aligned. In surveying practitioners in the late 1960s, the Group for the Advancement of Psychiatry (1970) classified therapists from A to Z based on their theoretical orientation. According to this scheme, "Position A will locate those one-to-one therapists who occasionally see families but retain a primary focus upon the individual system and Position Z those who use exclusively a family system orientation" (p. 48).

According to the GAP findings, Position A therapists were likely to be psychodynamically oriented individual therapists for whom family therapy was but one method of treatment among many. If on occasion these therapists worked with entire families, they kept the focus on their individual patients; the other family members might be included to clarify some interpersonal conflict or facilitate the individual's treatment. History taking, differential diagnosis, and the noting of positive or negative affect constituted a major portion of these therapists' initial clinical activity. Position Z therapists were likely to think "systems." These therapists viewed the "identified patient" as part of a dysfunctional family and thus the family's "symptom bearer"; they held conjoint family sessions focusing on the here-and-now family interaction rather than on the past; they directed treatment at resolving relationship problems, rather than trying to uncover affect or make a careful psychiatric diagnosis of the "identified patient." Although readers of the survey may have concluded that the field of psychotherapy was becoming polarized (in many ways, of course, it was), the GAP report did acknowledge that some therapists occupied Position N; these therapists gave the individual and the systems approach equal validity and felt free to use either or both ways of conceptualizing dysfunction and planning treatment.

Rather than classifying therapists by theoretical orientation, Beels and Ferber (1969) focused on personal style; they made the distinction between "conductors" (who are active, direct, dominating, and even charismatic) and "reactors" (who are less active and directive and who prefer to observe and clarify family interaction) (see fuller discussion in Chapter 4). In Beels and Ferber's system of classification, the distinctions between psychodynamicists and systems theorists were blurred. A Position A therapist (or a Position Z) might be a conductor or reactor, depending more on the therapist's individual personality than on his or her theoretical suppositions. For example, Ackerman (psychoanalytic in viewpoint) and Satir (then primarily a communication advocate) were both characterized as conductors; so were Minuchin (structural theory) and Bowen (family systems). Conversely, Framo (psychodynamic) and Whitaker (experiential) were identified as reactors, as were Haley and Jackson (communication approach). Bear in mind that both groups—conductors and reactors—exercise control over what goes on in therapy, the former in more direct and obvious but not necessarily more influential ways.

Philip Guerin (1976) made a later attempt at classification, in part as a reaction to the antitheoretical trend he saw developing in the field. Returning to the central issue of theoretical stance, he again divided family therapists into two basic groups, psychodynamic and systems. The psychodynamic category included (1) individual approaches (similar to Position A in the GAP report), taken by therapists, mostly psychoanalytic in orientation, who might occasionally see families for consultation or informational purposes regarding their individual patient; (2) group approaches, taken by therapists (for example, Bell, Wynne) who define the family as a natural group with the therapist adopting an observer position and directing, clarifying, or interpreting what is taking place during the session; (3) the Ackerman-style approach, taken by a therapist who is aggressive, directive, and crafty and who operates from a psychoanalytic orientation; and (4) experiential approaches (such as those developed during the late 1960s), taken by therapists who attempt to engage the family in a "therapeutic happening" or growth experience by having the members interact in an open, "gut-level," emotionally charged way. Guerin divided the systems group into the following four subgroups: communication-strategic (Haley, Satir, Erickson); structural (Minuchin); Bowen's system theory and technique (probably the most comprehensive of all theoretical formulations); and general systems (a theory-based model without direct clinical application at the time).

More recent classification proposals have come from Gurman (1979), Kaslow (1980), L'Abate and Frey (1981), and Zimmerman and Sims (1983). Gurman's three-part division—psychoanalytically oriented family therapy, systems therapy of the communication and Bowenian types, and behavioral family therapy—was supplemented by Kaslow's suggestion that Boszormenyi-Nagy's intergenerational-contextual approach be added and other, finer distinctions be made. L'Abate and Frey offered what they called an E-R-A model (Emotionality, Rationality, Activity), arguing that the differences in therapist approaches are ones of emphasis along these dimensions. That is, family therapists of the E-school, such as Satir or Whitaker, pay a great deal of attention to how feelings are felt, expressed, and translated within family transactions; R-school advocates such as Bowen or Framo value cognitive activity, rational and relatively unemotional discussion, problem solving; A-school adherents such as Haley, Minuchin, Selvini-Palazzoli, and the behaviorists invite active change outside the therapy sessions by issuing directives and prescribing schedules to be followed. L'Abate and Frey's intriguing typology of family therapy theories is presented in Table 5.1.

Zimmerman and Sims (1983) devised a continuum with psychoanalytically oriented family therapy on one end and behaviorally oriented family therapy on the other, making the major distinction that between a psychodynamic or systems perspective. In our opinion, a system of classification that discriminates according to a single variable cannot do justice to the intricacies of the many theoretical positions formulated and used by family therapists. All of these efforts at classification have limitations; most important, they fail to deal adequately, if at all, with two issues. First, they neglect the sizable number of family therapists, largely influenced by the **existential**, **phenomenological**, and human potential movement outlooks, who were particularly prominent during the 1960s and early 1970s. Intuitive and insistently antitheoretical, they deserve a separate grouping of their own. We have labeled them experiential/humanistic to provide a broad enough rubric to embrace several approaches; Satir, Whitaker, and Kempler are key figures among this group. Second, any serious attempt at classification must acknowledge that no theory or therapist can be compared adequately with any other theory or therapist along one dimension alone.

Table 5.1 The E-R-A Model for Classifying Family Therapy Theories

	Dimension Emphasized		
Variable	*Emotionality*	*Rationality*	*Activity*
Historical background schools of thought	Humanism Existential Gestalt Experiential	Psychoanalytic-Cognitive	Behavioral-Systems
Temporal perspective	Present	Past	Future
Representative theorists	Satir, Bandler & Grinder Napier & Whitaker	Boszormenyi-Nagy & Spark Stierlin Bowen & associates Framo	Adlerians, Palo Alto group, Milano group, Behaviorists, Minuchin, Haley
Preferred therapeutic interventions	Sculpture, non-verbal role-playing	History, genograms	Task assignment Prescriptions
Locus of change	Family feelings and immediacy	Family of origin, inside individuals	Family relationships and problem solving
Predicted length of therapy	Variable Intermediate	Long	Short, fixed
Activity level	Mostly inside office	Least active	Mostly outside office

(Source: L'Abate & Frey, 1981)

As presented in Table 5.2, we propose seven dimensions along which existing—and future—theoretical viewpoints in family therapy can be compared. These dimensions are the time frame (emphasis on the past or present); the role that unconscious processes are seen to play; the extent to which insight into past causes or action in the form of changed behavior is emphasized; the role of the therapist; the unit of analysis (individual, dyad, triad, or whole group); the major theoretical underpinnings; and the goals of treatment.

Thus we offer our own system for organizing the different approaches to family therapy, not to minimize the complexities of the field, but to provide a compre-

Table 5.2 A Comparison of Six Theoretical Viewpoints in Family Therapy

Dimension	*Psychodynamic*	*Experiential/ Humanistic*	*Bowenian*	*Structural*	*Communication/ Strategic*	*Behavioral*
1. Major time frame	Past; history of early experiences needs to be uncovered.	Present; here-and-now data from immediate experience observed.	Primarily the present, although attention also paid to one's family of origin.	Present and past; family's current structure carried over from earlier transactional patterns.	Present; current problems or symptoms maintained by ongoing, repetitive sequences between persons.	Present; focus on interpersonal environments that maintain and perpetuate current behavior patterns.
2. Role of unconscious processes	Unresolved conflicts from the past, largely out of the person's awareness, continue to attach themselves to current objects and situations.	Free choice and conscious self-determination more important than unconscious motivation.	Earlier concepts suggested unconscious conflicts, although now recast in interactive terms.	Unconscious motivation less important than repetition of learned habits and role assignments by which the family carries out its tasks.	Family rules, homeostatic balance, and feedback loops determine behavior, not unconscious processes.	Problematic behavior is learned and maintained by its consequences; unconscious processes rejected as too inferential and unquantifiable.

(continued)

Table 5.2 *(continued)*

Dimension	*Psychodynamic*	*Experiential/ Humanistic*	*Bowenian*	*Structural*	*Communication/ Strategic*	*Behavioral*
3. Insight vs. action	Insight leads to understanding, conflict reduction, and ultimately intrapsychic and interpersonal change.	Self-awareness of one's immediate existence leads to choice, responsibility, and change.	Rational processes used to gain self-awareness into current relationships as well as intergenerational experiences.	Action precedes understanding; change in transactional patterns more important than insight in producing new behaviors.	Action-oriented; behavior change and symptom reduction brought about through directives rather than interpretations.	Actions prescribed to modify specific behavior patterns.
4. Role of therapist	Neutral; makes interpretations of individual and family behavior patterns.	Active facilitator of potential for growth; provides family with new experiences.	Direct but nonconfrontational; de-triangulated from family fusion.	Stage director; manipulates family structure to change dysfunctional sets.	Active; manipulative; problem-focused; prescriptive, paradoxical.	Directive; teacher, trainer, or model of desired behavior; contract negotiator.
5. Unit of study	Focus on individual; emphasis on how family members feel about one another and deal with each other.	Dyad; problems arise from interaction between two members (for example, husband and wife).	Entire family over several generations; may work with one dyad (or one partner) for a period of time.	Triads; coalitions, subsystems, boundaries, power.	Dyads and triads; problems and symptoms viewed as interpersonal communications between two or more family members.	Dyads; effect of one person's behavior on another; linear view of causality.

(continued)

Table 5.2 *(continued)*

Dimension	*Psychodynamic*	*Experiential/ Humanistic*	*Bowenian*	*Structural*	*Communication/ Strategic*	*Behavioral*
6. Major theoretical underpinnings	Psychoanalysis.	Existentialism; humanistic psychlogy; phenomenology.	Family systems theory.	Structural family theory; systems.	Communication theory; systems, behaviorism.	Behaviorism; social learning theory
7. Goals of treatment	Insight, psychosexual maturity, strengthening of ego functioning; reduction in interlocking pathologies; more satisfying object relations.	Growth, more fulfilling interaction patterns; clearer communication; expanded awareness; authenticity.	Maximization of self-differentiation for each family member.	Change in relationship context in order to restructure family organization and change dysfunctional transactional patterns.	Change dysfunctional, redundant behavioral sequences ("games") between family members in order to eliminate presenting problem or symptom.	Change in behavioral consequences between persons in order to eliminate maladaptive or problematic behavior.
8. Major theorists and/or practitioners	Ackerman, Framo, Boszormenyi-Nagy, Stierlin, Skynner, Bell	Whitaker, Kempler, Satir	Bowen	Minuchin	Jackson, Erickson, Haley, Madanes, Selvini-Palazzoli, Watzlawick	Patterson, Stuart, Liberman, Jacobson, Margolin

hensive frame of reference for understanding the similarities and differences within it. Our model comprises six theoretical viewpoints: psychodynamic, experiential/humanistic, Bowenian, structural, communication/strategic, and behavioral.

THE PSYCHODYNAMIC OUTLOOK

The psychodynamic view of individual behavior, based largely on a psychoanalytic model, focuses on the interplay of opposing forces within a person as the basis for understanding that person's motivation and sources of discomfort and anxiety. The neurotic individual may be seen as, for example, someone torn by inner conflict between his or her sexual wishes or urges and a punitive, guilt-producing conscience. Extrapolated to the family level, this view seeks to discover how the inner lives and conflicts of family members interlock and how the binding together affects disturbances in family members.

According to advocates of the psychodynamic view, the two individuals joined by marriage each bring to the relationship a separate and unique psychological heritage. Inevitably, the dyadic relationship bears resemblances to the parent-child relationships the partners experienced in their families of origin. As Meissner (1978) observes, "The capacity to successfully function as a spouse is largely a consequence of the spouse's childhood relationships to his (or her) own parents" (p. 26). The relative success that marital partners experience, as well as the manner in which they approach and accomplish developmental tasks throughout the life cycle, is largely determined by the extent to which they are free from excessive negative attachments to the past. Troubled marriages, then, are seen as contaminated by the pathogenic **introjects** (imprints or memories of the parents or other figures) from past relationships with members of the previous generation residing within each partner. Moreover, the partners' unresolved intrapsychic problems not only prevent them from enjoying a productive and fulfilling marital experience but are also passed along to their children, who eventually bring psychic disturbances into their own marriages. Only by gaining insight into, and thus freedom from, such burdensome attachments to the past can individuals—or couples—learn to develop adult-to-adult relationships in the present with members of their families of origin.

As we present various approaches that belong to the psychodynamic perspective, keep in mind that each one addresses two levels of understanding and intervention simultaneously: the motives, fantasies, unconscious conflicts, and repressed memories of each family member and the more complex world of family interaction and family dynamics.

Psychoanalysis and Family Dynamics (Ackerman)

As early as the 1930s, Nathan Ackerman, a child analyst in the child guidance movement, began to attend to the family itself as a social and emotional unit whose impact on the child needed exploration. By the 1940s, he was making clinical assessments of entire families (Green & Framo, 1981) and devising clinical

Nathan Ackerman, M.D.

techniques for applying psychoanalytic principles to treating preschool children and their families (Ackerman, 1956). In contrast to the collaborative approach practiced by most child guidance clinics, in which parent (usually mother) and child were seen by separate but collaborating therapists, Ackerman started to experiment with seeing whole families together (Guerin, 1976). Although he continued to work with both individuals as well as families for a decade, by the 1950s he had moved explicitly into family therapy and in 1960 opened the Family Institute in New York City. One of the earliest pioneers in assessing and treating families, Ackerman remained throughout his long career a bold, innovative therapist. He also represents early efforts to integrate a psychoanalytic stance (with its intrapsychic orientation) with the then-emerging systems approach (emphasizing interpersonal relationships).

Ackerman (1970b) saw the family as a system of interacting personalities; each individual is an important subsystem within the family, just as the family is a subsystem within the community. Understanding family functioning calls for acknowledging input from several sources: the unique personality of each member; the dynamics of family role adaptations; the family's commitment to a set of human values; the behavior of the family as a social unit. At the individual level, the process of symptom formation may be understood in terms of intrapsychic conflict, a defense against anxiety aroused by the conflict, and the resulting development of a neurotic symptom (a classical psychoanalytic explanation); at the family level, the symptom is viewed as part of a recurring, predictable interactional pattern intended to assure equilibrium for the individual, but actually impairing family homeostasis by producing distortions in family role relationships. In family terms, an individual's symptom becomes a unit of interpersonal behavior reflected within a context of shared family conflict, anxiety, and defenses. Conceptualizing behavior in this way, Ackerman was beginning to build a bridge between psychoanalysis and systems theory.

To Ackerman, homeostasis signifies the capacity of the family system to adapt to change; it means much more than restoring the system to a previous balance or accustomed level of functioning. A disturbed individual's symptomatic behavior unbalances the family homeostasis and at the same time reflects emotional distortions within the entire family. A "failure of **complementarity**," to use Ackerman's terms, characterizes the roles played by various family members in respect to each other. Change and growth within the system become constricted. Roles become rigid, narrowly defined, or stereotyped—or shift rapidly, causing confusion. According to Ackerman (1966), the family in which this occurs must be helped to "accommodate to new experiences, to cultivate new levels of complementarity in family role relationships, to find avenues for the solution of conflict, to build a favorable self-image, to buttress critical forms of defense against anxiety, and to provide support for further creative development" (pp. 90–91).

Family difficulties arise, Ackerman (1966) noted, not only when family roles are not complementary but also when there is stalemated or otherwise unresolved conflict and when a family engages in "prejudicial scapegoating." For a family's behavior to be stable, flexibility and adaptability of roles is essential; roles within the family, which change over time, must allow for maturing children to gain an appropriate degree of autonomy. Conflict may occur at several levels—within an individual family member, between members of the nuclear family, between generations including the extended family, between the family and the surrounding community. Inevitably, according to Ackerman's observations, conflict at any level reverberates throughout the family system. What begins as a breakdown of role complementarity may lead to interpersonal conflict within the family and ultimately to intrapsychic conflict in one or more individual members; the individual's conflict deepens if the internalized family conflicts are persistent and pathogenic in form. One of Ackerman's therapeutic goals was to interrupt this sequence by extrapolating intrapsychic conflict to the broader area of family interaction.

Should the conflict between members become chronic, the family is at risk of reorganization into competing factions. The process often gets under way when one individual—often noticeably different from the others—becomes the family scapegoat or "whipping post." As that individual is singled out and punished for causing family disunity, various realignments of roles follow within the family. One member becomes "persecutor," while another may take the role of "healer" or "rescuer" of the "victim" of such "prejudicial scapegoating." Families are thus split into factions and different members may even play different roles at different times, depending upon what Ackerman considers the shared unconscious processes going on within the family at any particular period of time. Typically, observed Ackerman, such family alliances and interpersonal conflicts begin with a failure of complementarity within the marital dyad; the family is precluded from functioning as a cooperative, supportive, integrated whole. In cases such as these, Ackerman's therapeutic mission was to shift a family's concern from the scapegoated person's behavior to the basic disorder of the marital relationship.

In an early paper, Ackerman (1956) presented a conceptual model of **interlocking pathology** in family relationships, arguing for family sessions in which such entanglements could be pointed out to the family members as they occurred so the family members could begin to work toward eliminating them. Concerned with the impact of the family environment on the development of childhood disorders, Ackerman was one of the first to note the constant interchange of unconscious processes taking place between family members as they are bound together in a particular interpersonal pattern. Accordingly, any single member's behavior can be a symptomatic reflection of confusion and distortion occurring in the entire family. With notions such as "interlocking pathology," Ackerman—by training a Freudian, but personally inclined to attend to social interaction—was able to wed many of the psychoanalytic concepts of intrapsychic dynamics to the psychosocial dynamics of family life. [1]

Ackerman's broadly based therapeutic approach used principles from biology, psychoanalysis, social psychology, and child psychiatry. Unaffected and deceptively casual in manner, Ackerman tried through a series of office interviews and home visits to obtain a firsthand diagnostic impression of the dynamic relationships among family members. Hearty, confident, unafraid to be himself or to disclose his own feelings, he was apt to bring out these same qualities in the family. Soon the family was dealing with sex, aggression, and dependency, the issues it had previously avoided as too threatening and dangerous.

To watch Ackerman on film or videotape is to see an honest, warm, straightforward, provocative, charismatic person at work in the very midst of the family, challenging a prejudice, coming to the aid of a scapegoated child, helping expose a family myth or hypocrisy, vigorously supplying the emotional ingredients necessary to galvanize a previously subdued family. No topic is taboo or off limits, no family rules so sacred they cannot be broken, nothing so shameful as to be unmentionable. Labeled as a "conductor" type of family therapist by Beels and Ferber (1969), Ackerman was said to lend the family "his pleasure in life, jokes, good sex, and limited aggression."

The following brief excerpt is from a therapy session with a family whose crisis was brought on when the 11-year-old daughter threatened to stab her 16-year-old brother and both parents with a kitchen knife. This explosive attack was precipitated by the girl's discovery of a conspiracy among the family members to say that

1. The pattern of interlocking pathology had long been known to therapists, many of whom had made the disquieting observation that sometimes when a patient improved, his or her marriage failed (Walrond-Skinner, 1976). This seemed to suggest that prior to treatment the patient had felt locked into a neurotic relationship; after treatment, he or she was no longer willing to take part in the dysfunctional interaction and felt free—and able—to leave the marriage. If in the course of psychoanalytic treatment a spouse became upset in response to the changes occurring in the patient, individual therapy with another therapist was the usual recommendation. It is not surprising that under this approach, a patient's "improvement" was viewed as a threat to other family members who might proceed to subtly undermine the therapeutic progress. It was not until family therapy began to be practiced that all of the persons involved in a family were treated together.

her dog had died when in reality the mother had taken him to the dog pound. Members of the family indulge in many small lies, then cover up and deny their feelings. Note how Ackerman will have none of this charade. He reveals his own feelings in order to cut through the denial and open up the family encounter. The left-hand column is the verbatim account; the right-hand column is Ackerman's analysis of what is taking place.

Transcript	*Comments*
Dr. A: Bill, you heaved a sigh as you sat down tonight.	Therapist instantly fastens on a piece of nonverbal behavior, the father's sigh.
Father: Just physical, not mental.	
Dr. A.: Who are you kidding?	Therapist challenges father's evasive response.
Father: I'm kidding no one.	
Dr. A.: Hmmm . . .	Therapist registers disbelief, a further pressure for a more honest response.
Father: Really not. . . . Really physical. I'm tired because I put in a full day today.	
Dr. A.: Well, I'm very tired every day, and when I sigh it's never purely physical.	An example of therapist's use of his own emotions to counter an insincere denial.
Father: Really?	
Dr. A.: What's the matter?	
Father: Nothing. Really!	
Dr. A.: Well, your own son doesn't believe that.	Therapist now exploits son's gesture, a knowing grin, to penetrate father's denial and evoke a deeper sharing of feelings.
Father: Well, I mean, nothing . . . nothing could cause me to sigh especially today or tonight.	
Dr. A.: Well, maybe it isn't so special, but . . . How about it, John?	Therapist stirs son to unmask father.

(continued)

Transcript	*Comments*
Son: I wouldn't know.	Now son wipes grin off his face and turns evasive, like father.
Dr. A.: You wouldn't know? How come all of a sudden you put on a poker face? A moment ago you were grinning very knowingly.	Therapist counters by challenging son, who took pot shot from sidelines and then backed away.
Son: I really wouldn't know.	
Dr. A.: You . . . Do you know anything about your pop?	
Son: Yeah.	
Dr. A.: What do you know about him?	
Son: Well, I don't know, except that I know some stuff.	
Dr. A.: Well, let's hear.	

(Source: Ackerman, 1966, pp. 3-4)

Trained as a psychoanalyst, Ackerman clearly retained his interest in each family member's personality dynamics. However, influenced by social psychology, he was impressed by how personality is shaped by the particular social roles people are expected to play. In his approach to families, Ackerman was always interested in how people define their own roles ("What does it mean to you to be a father?") and what they expect from other family members ("How would you like your daughter to react to this situation?"). When all members delineate their roles clearly, family interactions proceed more smoothly, he maintained. Members can rework alignments, engage in new family transactions, and cultivate new levels of complementarity in their role relationships.

Ackerman (1966) described a troubled, perplexed, frightened family coming for family therapy; everyone knows something is wrong but they don't know how or why or what to do about it. By tradition they push one individual forward as "sick," although several if not all of the members are disturbed in various ways and to varying degrees. They are in the office because their previous equilibrium or homeostasis has been upset. The therapist tries to nourish hope, to keep them from feeling defeated. Generally speaking, Ackerman saw the therapist's purpose as offering *reeducation*, *reorganization* through a change in the pattern of communication, and *resolution* of pathogenic conflict as an avenue for inducing change and growth as a family.

Diagnosis and treatment are interwoven in Ackerman's approach. Rather than follow a formal intake procedure, the therapist watches as the family becomes engaged in the therapeutic struggle and listens as relevant historial facts emerge (for example, mental hospitalization of a member, a daughter's abortion never disclosed outside the family circle before, a suicide). The therapist is aware of the family's outer protective mask, the secret pacts to avoid discussing certain subjects, the personalities of each member and their adaptation to family roles, the family emotional climate. Families are usually seen once a week for about an hour each session. According to Ackerman (1966), therapeutic change is often achieved within a period of six months to two years.

Ackerman believed the family therapist's principal job is that of a catalyst who, moving into the "living space" of the family, stirs up interaction, helps the family have a meaningful emotional exchange, and at the same time nurtures and encourages the members to understand themselves better through their contact with the therapist. As a catalyst, the therapist must play a wide range of roles from activator, challenger, and confronter to supporter, interpreter, and integrator. Unlike the orthodox psychoanalyst who chooses to remain a neutral, distant, mysterious **blank screen**, Ackerman as family therapist was a vigorous person who engaged a family in the here and now and made his presence felt. He moved directly into the path of family conflict, influenced the interactional process, supported positive forces and counteracted negative ones, and withdrew as the family began to deal more constructively with its problems.

Diagnostically, Ackerman attempted to fathom a family's deeper emotional currents—fears and suspicions, feelings of despair, the urge for vengeance. Using his personal emotional responses as well as his psychodynamic insights, he gauged what the family was experiencing, discerned its patterns of role complementarity, and probed the deeper, more pervasive family conflicts. By "tickling the defenses," he caught members off guard and exposed their self-justifying rationalizations. In due course, he was able to trace significant connections between the family dysfunction and the intrapsychic anxieties of various family members. Finally, when the members were more in touch with what they were feeling, thinking, and doing individually, Ackerman helped them expand their awareness of alternate patterns of family relationships through which they might discover new levels of intimacy, sharing, and identification.

Throughout his long career, Ackerman remained staunchly psychodynamic in outlook; his death in 1971 removed one of the major proponents of this viewpoint in family therapy (Nichols & Everett, 1986). A collection of his published papers with commentary by the editors (Bloch & Simon, 1982), called *The Strength of Family Therapy*, attests to his trailblazing efforts as well as his broad range of interests (child psychoanalysis, group therapy, social and cultural issues, marriage, and more). According to these editors, Ackerman practiced what he held dear in theory—namely, not to be bound by professional conventions unless they had some definite theoretical or clinical value for the problem at hand.

Nevertheless, despite his importance in family therapy's early years, there are few therapists today who would call themselves "Ackerman-style" in their approach (Luepnitz, 1988). The Ackerman Institute, renamed in his memory, while acknowledging his pioneering efforts, does not operate from a psychodynamic perspective today. Systems theory has by and large replaced psychoanalytic thinking for most family therapists. While many therapists continue to be interested in the "psychodynamics of family life," and may from time to time use psychoanalytic concepts, the psychodynamic view is currently best expressed by **object relations theory**, to which we now turn.

Object Relations and Families of Origin (Framo)

Another first-generation family therapist whose training and early orientation, like Ackerman's, was psychoanalytic, James Framo (1981) stresses the relationship between the intrapsychic and the interpersonal, offering an amalgam of psychodynamic and systems concepts. Framo, one of the few psychologists in the early family therapy movement, was affiliated initially with the Eastern Pennsylvania Psychiatric Institute (EPPI) in Philadelphia, where he began to view family dysfunction as rooted in the extended family system. Ultimately he developed a set of intervention techniques that help couples in marital therapy deal with unresolved issues each partner brings to the marriage from his or her family of origin.

Not wishing to disregard the significant contributions made by psychoanalysis to our understanding of an individual's intrapsychic world, Framo nevertheless believes psychoanalytic theory has not paid sufficient attention to the social context of a person's life, particularly the crucial role played by family relationships in shaping individual behavior. Rather than polarize the intrapsychic and the interactional, Framo maintains that both are essential to understanding the dynamic aspects of family life. As he points out in the introduction to a collection of his papers (Framo, 1982), his orientation to marital and family theory and therapy emphasizes "the psychology of intimate relationships, the interlocking of multi-person motivational systems, the relationship between the intrapsychic and the transactional, and the hidden transgenerational and historical forces that exercise their powerful influences on current intimate relationships" (p. IX).

Framo believes that insoluble intrapsychic conflicts derived from one's family of origin continue to be acted out or replicated with current intimates, such as a spouse or children. Indeed, Framo (1981) contends that efforts at the interpersonal resolution of inner conflict (for example, harshly criticizing a spouse for failing to live up to one's wildly inappropriate expectations) are at the very heart of the kinds of distress found in troubled couples and families. By exploring such phenomena, Framo makes use of both dynamic and systems concepts, providing a conceptual bridge between the personal and the social.

Basic to Framo's outlook is the work of Fairbairn (1954) and Dicks (1967) on object relations theory. Fairbairn, an English psychiatrist, postulated that human beings are object-seeking in the sense that they require relationships. He argued that it is a person's need for a satisfying object relationship—not, as Freud had maintained, the gratification of instinctual drives—that constitutes the fundamental motive of life. Extrapolating from Fairbairn's proposals, Framo (1976) theorized that a young child who interprets parental behavior as rejection, desertion, or persecution is in a dilemma; the child cannot give up the sought-after object (the parents) nor can he or she change that object. Typically, the ensuing frustration is

James L. Framo, Ph.D.

dealt with by internalizing aspects of the "loved-hated" parents in order to control the objects in the child's inner world. These internalized objects, having both good and bad characteristics, are retained as introjects, the psychological representations of external objects. According to Framo, the most powerful obstacle to change is people's attachments to their parental introjects.

To Fairbairn (1954), these internalized objects undergo splits and become part of one's personality structure: good-object introjects remain as pleasing memories, bad-object introjects cause intrapsychic distress. That is, current life situations are unconsciously interpreted in light of one's inner object world of good-bad images. As a result, the person grows up with distorted expectations of others, unconsciously forcing intimates into fitting the internal role models. As Fairbairn illustrates, the earlier the split (resulting, for example, from an early loss of a parent), the more likely it is that the person will yearn for merger with loved ones so that they become a part of him or her. At the same time, he or she may also yearn for independence and separation, a normal part of growing up, although too much distance may lead to feelings of loneliness and depression. As Framo (1976) confirmed, the more psychologically painful the early life experience, the greater the investment in internal objects, the more an adult will engage in an unconscious effort to make all close relationships fit the internal role models.

Dicks (1967) expanded Fairbairn's object relations conceptualizations to include the interaction between husband and wife. He proposed that in a disturbed marriage each partner relates to the other in terms of unconscious needs; together they function as a joint personality. In this way each partner attempts to rediscover, through the other, the lost aspects of his or her primary object relations that had split off earlier in life. As Dicks (1967) states:

> The sense of belonging can be understood on the hypothesis that at deeper levels there are perceptions of the partner and consequent attitudes toward him or her *as if* the other was part of oneself. The partner is then treated according to how this aspect of oneself was valued; spoilt and cherished, or denigrated and persecuted. (p. 69)

Framo extends object relations theory even farther to include several generations of a single family. A person's current intimates, spouse and children, become shadowy stand-ins for old ghosts, the embodiments of old (parental) introjects (Framo, 1981). These introjects are reprojected onto current family members in the adult's effort to achieve satisfaction by compensating for unsatisfactory early object relations in childhood. As Framo illustrates, one major source of marital disharmony results from spouses who project disowned aspects of themselves onto their mates and then fight these characteristics in the mate. Similarly, he notes, children may be assigned inappropriate family roles based on parental introjects. In some cases, observes Framo, such roles may even be chosen for them before they are born (for example, conceiving a baby in the belief that the offspring will save a shaky marriage).

Framo, who now lives in San Diego, begins by treating the entire family, especially when the presenting problem involves the children. However, symptomatic behavior in a child may simply be a means of deflecting attention from a more basic marital conflict. In such cases, once the child's role as identified patient is made clear and the child **detriangulated** from the parents, Framo (1976) will dismiss the children and proceed to work with the marital dyad. Frequently working with a female cotherapist, Framo insists that couples be seen together. According to his reasoning (Framo, 1981), any advantage to individual meetings (disclosure of secrets, for example) is outweighed by the suspicions aroused in the absent partner or the conflicts of loyalty and confidentiality aroused in the therapist. Conjoint sessions help maintain the integrity of the marital unit.

Framo's unique contribution to family therapy technique is his process of guiding a couple through several treatment stages: conjoint therapy, couples group therapy, and, finally, family of origin (intergenerational) conferences.[2] The couples group, in which many couples participate soon after they begin treatment, allows Framo to use many of the positive aspects of group therapy (see discussion in Chapter 4). That is, he takes advantage of the group process, especially the therapeutic feedback from other couples, to assist his efforts as therapist. In many cases it is far more enlightening and potent for a couple to see its own interaction patterns acted out by another couple than to hear a therapist merely comment on the same behavior, with no one else present. The group experience has a secondary

2. For a detailed account of Framo's treatment of a couple, see "In-laws and Out-laws: A Marital Case of Kinship Confusion" in *Family Therapy: Full Length Case Studies*, edited by P. Papp. New York: Gardner Press, 1977.

function of reducing the individual's resistance to the next stage of treatment, which involves a number of family members meeting together.

In a daring therapeutic maneuver, Framo (1976) involves each individual (without the partner present) in sessions with his or her family of origin (parents, brothers, and sisters). Two major goals are involved—to discover what issues or agendas from the family of origin might be projected onto the current family and to have a corrective experience with parents and siblings. Framo (1976) reasons that if adults are able to go back and deal directly with both past and present issues with their original families—in a sense, to come to terms with parents before they die—then they are liberated to make reconstructive changes in their present marriage or family life. Usually held toward the end of therapy, family of origin conferences enable individuals to gain insight into the inappropriateness of old attachments, rid themselves of "ghosts," and respond to spouses and children as individuals in their own right—not as figures on whom they project unresolved issues and introjects from the past.

The Contextual Approach and the Family Ledger (Boszormenyi-Nagy)

Another increasingly influential family therapy approach that respects transgenerational legacies and influences is the work of Ivan Boszormenyi-Nagy. His **contextual** therapy, as elaborated in a recent collection of his papers spanning 30 years (Boszormenyi-Nagy, 1987), attempts to integrate psychoanalytic concepts, object relations theory, and general systems theory, while at the same time remaining deeply rooted in the reality of human relationships. One of the foremost original thinkers in the field, Boszormenyi-Nagy emphasizes that to truly grasp human existence it is essential to understand both individual and relational realities, particularly intergenerational issues that permeate every family's life.

To Boszormenyi-Nagy, the patterns of relating within a family that are passed on from generation to generation are keys to understanding individual as well as family functioning. Consistent with that view, he believes that effective family therapy must attend to family "context," especially to those dynamic and ethical interconnections—past, present, and future—that bind families together. "Context" implies the inescapability of intergenerational consequences; no one is exempt from the repercussions of good or bad family relationships. By the same token, "context" also implies intrinsic opportunities in significant relationships for transforming existing consequences by discovering new ways of relating or by making fresh inputs into stagnant relationships. Therapeutically, Boszormenyi-Nagy and Krasner (1986) view the realm of relationship subsumed under "context" as follows:

> An enabling whole, context recognizes the limiting aspects of thinking in terms of family "pathology." Instead, it emphasizes the existence of *resources* in significant relationships that, once actualized, can rechannel hatred into closeness, felt injustice into balances of fairness, and mistrust into trust. In this sense context is inductively defined by the process and flow of relational consequences (p. 9).

Boszormenyi-Nagy, a psychiatrist with psychoanalytic training who emigrated to the United States from Hungary in 1948, founded the Eastern Pennsylvania Psychiatric Institute in 1957 as a center for studying schizophrenia. (James Framo, along with Geraldine Spark, Gerald Zuk, and David Rubenstein were early associates at the institute.) After a long series of unsuccessful attempts to find biological clues to explain the etiology of the disorder, Boszormenyi-Nagy and his colleagues began to focus on the behavioral and psychological aspects of schizophrenia, ultimately turning to multigenerational issues within the family. Object relations theory, along with Erik Erikson's psychosocial notions of individual development (especially the key role of trust in personality formation) and Martin Buber's insistence on accountable human relating (responsible I-Thou dialogues) together helped establish the basis for a contextual view of family therapy.

Joining with Spark, a psychiatric social worker with an extensive psychoanalytic background and experience in child guidance centers, Boszormenyi-Nagy advanced a theory and set of therapeutic techniques that pertained to uncovering and resolving family "obligations" and "debts" incurred over time. They introduced such new (nonpsychoanalytic) terms as "legacy" and "loyalty" to emphasize that family members inevitably acquire a set of expectations and responsibilities toward each other. Figuratively speaking, each person has a sense of unsettled accounts, how much he or she has invested in relationships within the family, and whether there has been a fair balance between what has been given and received. While this is hardly a strict bookkeeping system and seldom if ever perfectly balanced, confronting and redressing imbalances is viewed as essential if a marriage is to be kept alive. Ulrich (1983) cites a temporary imbalance: a wife works at an unsatisfying job so her husband can finish law school—but with the expectation that what she has invested in the common fund will eventually be replaced, for their mutual enrichment. Boszormenyi-Nagy and Spark entitled their 1973 book *Invisible Loyalties: Reciprocity in Intergenerational Family Therapy* to emphasize that obligations rooted in past generations need not be explicity recognized or acknowledged to influence the behavior of family members in the present.

In a sense, every family maintains a "family ledger," a multigenerational accounting system of who, psychologically speaking, owes what to whom. Boszormenyi-Nagy and Krasner (1986) argue that traditional interventions, either individually or family focused, consistently ignore family balances due, either owed or deserved, especially intergenerational ones. Yet people, in or out of therapy, constantly raise such questions as: "What do I owe, and to whom?" "What do I deserve, and from whom?" "What relationships do I need and want?" "What relationships am I obliged to retain, whether or not I need or want them?"

Whenever injustices occur, there is the expectation of some later repayment or restitution. Problems in relationships develop when justice comes too slowly or in an amount too small to satisfy the other person. From this perspective, dysfunctional behavior in any individual cannot be fully understood without looking at the history of the problem, the family ledger, and examining unsettled or unredressed accounts. A symptom that develops might represent an accumulation of feelings of injustice that has grown too large.

Ivan Boszormenyi-Nagy, M.D.

The family legacy, then, dictates debts and entitlements. One son may be slated to be successful ("We expect you'll be good at anything you try"), another to become a failure ("We don't think you'll ever amount to much"). A son may be entitled to approval, the daughter only to shame. Because of such family imperatives, as Boszormenyi-Nagy and Ulrich (1981) point out, the children are ethically bound to accommodate their lives somehow to their legacies. Ulrich (1983) gives the following graphic example:

> *A son whose familial legacy is one of mistrust among family members, angrily confronts his wife every time she spends any money without his prior approval. He is convinced, and he tries to convince her, that her untrustworthy, spendthrift behavior is going to bankrupt them (p. 193).*

In fact, the wife, who works full-time as well as tending to their child, may temporarily unbalance the week's budget, but her overall efforts contribute to her husband's solvency. If her response to his anger is fear—a legacy she carries from her own family—she may hide her purchases. His discovery of such concealment reinforces his mistrust; his subsequent anger strengthens her fears. Together their legacies have had a corrosive effect on their marriage. In classical psychoanalytic terms, the husband may be labeled as having a penurious character disorder and the wife as a hysteric. In ledger terms, he is still making payment to his mother's injunction that a wife is not to be trusted. By "overpaying" his mother, he is robbing his wife. She, in turn, may be paying off similar debts. Contextual therapy would direct them to reassess all their relationships, pay off legitimate filial debts, and free themselves from oppressive obligations.

The ethical dimension gives contextual therapy its uniqueness. Insisting that they are not moralizing or taking a judgmental position, practitioners of this approach contend that they offer a realistic strategy for preventing individual and relational imbalance and eventual breakdown. They argue that effective therapeutic intervention must be grounded in the therapist's conviction that trustworthiness is a necessary condition for reworking legacy assessments and allowing family members to feel they are entitled to more satisfying relationships. Practitioners of contextual therapy maintain that families cannot be fully understood without an explicit awareness of family loyalty—who is bound to whom, what is expected of all family members, how loyalty is expressed, what happens when loyalty accounts are uneven ("We were there for you when you were growing up and now we, your aging parents, are entitled to help from you").

Contextual therapy helps rebalance the obligations kept in the invisible family ledger. Once these imbalances are identified, efforts can be directed at settling old family accounts (for example, mothers and daughters "stuck" in lifelong conflict), "exonerating" alleged culprits, transforming unproductive patterns of relating that may have existed throughout the family over many past generations. The major therapeutic thrust is to establish or restore trustworthiness in family relationships. Parental behavior may be reassessed (and forgiven) in light of its roots in the past.

In the following example, a therapist helps a family split by dissention and conflicting loyalties learn fairer and more ethically responsible ways of dealing with one another. In the process of overcoming a stagnating relationship with her mother, the woman gains a more trustworthy level of relating to her husband and daughter.

Mr. and Mrs. Jones were seeking help for their marriage. The presenting problem had to do with Mrs. Jones's angry outbursts at her husband and mother. An intelligent and compulsively neat person, Mrs. Jones was resentful of the fact that her mother had humiliated and frustrated her. Their relationship, she claimed, was characterized by mistrust and manipulation. She handled her rage through long-distance calls to her parents that inevitably resulted in tortuous arguments with her mother; or else she ignored them for prolonged periods of time.

His wife's hostile outbursts rendered Mr. Jones helpless. A hardworking, meticulously responsible salesman, he was deeply discouraged and never knew what he would face when he came home from work. On occasion, Mrs. Jones would try to ruin the garden equipment that he so highly prized. On other occasions, she would throw out his favorite books. On the other hand, there were times when their marriage seemed to be alright. For example, they could function as a team whenever members of their extended family were in real need. During their brief respite, they could enjoy each other and reported that their sexual relations were good.

However, the couple was often at war over their only child. Sheila, age 12, was chronically caught between them and lived in constant jeopardy of being split in her loyalties to them. Mrs. Jones would greet her husband at the door with complaints about their daughter. He resented being cast into the unfair role of referee and retaliated by forming a subversive alliance with Sheila. In therapy sessions, the couple finally consented to hear each other out. Together, the three of them began to work toward fairer ways of relating.

Mr. and Mrs. Jones and Sheila seemed comforted by the therapist's capacity to elicit the justifications of each of their sides (multidirected partiality). Yet, Mrs. Jones was openly annoyed at any attempts to offer fair consideration to her mother.

In the interim, things went better for the family. Until now Mrs. Jones had lacked the security to look for a job commensurate with her intelligence and ability. For a long time she had invested her energies in compulsive housekeeping. Suddenly she found a job that she liked. Immediately, tensions eased as her world widened and opened up. Mr. Jones learned to distance himself from his wife when she regressed into outbursts of anger. And Mrs. Jones began to exchange letters with her mother and managed some pleasant visits with both of her parents.

On occasion, some of the vindictiveness previously channeled toward her parents was now transferred to the therapist. At one point, Mrs. Jones refused to accompany her husband to their therapy session, arguing that the therapist "didn't care" about her. Two weeks later, though, she left an emergency message with the answering service: her mother had died suddenly, unexpectedly! Overcome by the intensity of her emotions, she expressed profound gratitude. What would have happened to her, she wondered, if the therapist had not enabled her to find a way to her mother? What if she had failed to repair their relationship before it was too late? (Boszormenyi-Nagy & Krasner, 1986, pp. 45–46).

Overall, each family member is viewed as someone who is a part of a multigenerational pattern. Each is guided to move in the direction of greater trust. Boszormenyi-Nagy and his coworkers believe it is the ethical dimension of trust within a family that is the invisible thread of both individual freedom and interindividual balance.

Redefining symptomatic behavior as evidence of family loyalty or as the sacrifice of self-development in the interest of the family led Boszormenyi-Nagy and Spark (1973) to describe how certain children in dysfunctional families are delegated to play such age-inappropriate, growth-retarding family roles as "parent," pet, scapegoat, or sexual object. Helm Stierlin, a German psychoanalyst and family therapist, has been particularly interested in how the processes of victimization and sacrifice and of exploitation and counterexploitation between generations are evident in the development of schizophrenia in a family member. Stierlin (1977) views all members as participating in a system of "invisible accounts" in which:

> massive guilt, an immense though thwarted need for repair work as well as revenge, a deeply felt sense of justice or injustice, and of loyalty confirmed or betrayed—all operating largely outside of awareness—become here formidable dynamic forces, influencing the members' every move. And the stakes in this "morality play" are high. On the one side, we find parents who, exploited and crippled by their own parents, attempt to survive by living through their children, crippling them in turn; and, on the other side, we find children who, as self-sacrificing, lifelong victims, gain the power to devastate their parents by inducing deep guilt. The power of loyalty-bound victims presents perhaps the most difficult single problem in the treatment of schizophrenia. (p. 228)

Stierlin's concept of the schizophrenic as a delegate, ostensibly permitted to move out of the parental orbit but remaining tied and beholden, bound to his or her parents through "invisible loyalties," meshes nicely with Boszormenyi-Nagy's outlook, particularly on the transgenerational influences on individual growth and development. More recently Stierlin has depicted anorectics as struggling with similar stultifying family bonds, their periodic "hunger strikes" representing efforts to withdraw from the family while at the same time remaining bound and united with them (Stierlin & Weber, 1989). Both theorists advocate a three-generational therapeutic effort, whenever possible, in which breaking through relationship deadlocks, gaining insight, balancing accounts, and a final reconciliation across generations are the goals.

The Open-Systems, Group-Analytic Approach (Skynner)

According to British psychoanalyst A. C. Robin Skynner (1981), trained in the Melanie Klein school of therapy, families evolving over several generations have important developmental milestones similar to the psychosexual stages in Freud's developmental scheme. A mother who lacked adequate mothering or a father who lacked satisfactory fathering is likely to behave inappropriately when called upon to play a role for which he or she has no internal model. When such a family faces stresses that correspond to repeated failures at parenting over several generations, they are likely to break down and decompensate in their functioning. Since poor relationship skills are likely to be passed along to children, developmental failures and deficits will probably occur over generations.

Offering an object relations approach, Skynner believes that adults with relationship difficulties (due to poor role models or other learning deficits) develop unrealistic attitudes toward others because they still carry expectations—Skynner calls them **projective systems**—left over from childhood deficiencies. When such persons select a spouse, they base the choice at least in part on the mutual "fit" of the potential partner's projective systems. That is, each partner comes equipped with projections corresponding to the stage at which some aspect of his or her development was blocked; each partner unconsciously seeks to create through marriage a situation in which the missing experience can be supplied. The danger, of course, is that since each wants the other to fulfill a parental role (and both wish to play the child), the partners are likely to manipulate, fight for control, and become frustrated. One consequence of this struggle between incompatible projective systems may be the diversion of some aspect of the projections onto the couple's offspring—saving the marriage at the expense of a child. In many cases, says Skynner, the child colludes in the process out of a deep, if unconscious, wish to preserve the marriage or the family.

As Skynner practices it, family therapy requires identification of the projective systems as well as removal of the projections from the symptomatic child, who is likely to be the identified patient. These projections are returned to the marriage, where more constructive resolutions are sought. Clarifying communication, gaining insight into inappropriate expectations, modifying the family structure, teaching new parenting skills are all part of Skynner's therapeutic efforts. In many cases, short-term tactics produce sufficient relief of discomfort and distress; in other situations, longer-term psychoanalytically oriented marital and family therapy (Skynner, 1976) is indicated for those families who can manage the conflict, pain, and disruption. In the latter cases, the goal is to facilitate differentiation of the marital partners to the point that they are separate, independent persons enjoying, but no longer simply needing, each other.

Skynner (1981) refers to his therapeutic technique as an "open-systems, group-analytic" approach. He genuinely engages with the family system through a "semipermeable interface" permitting the exchange of personal information between the family members and himself. To understand the family "from inside," Skynner believes he must open himself up to its projective system, internalize each member separately through identification, and experience personally the suffering and struggles of the family. For Skynner, the key requirement is that the therapist retain a deep awareness of his or her own identity, strong enough to sustain him or her in the face of the overwhelming (if transient) emotional arousal in the family as the result of the therapeutic encounter; arousal is particularly intense in therapy with profoundly disturbed families who seek to externalize their pathology.

To Skynner, the therapeutic encounter is an opportunity for growth for both the family and the therapist. (For more on the idea of the forces and counterforces at work in the interpersonal encounter between families and therapists, see Chapter 6). The therapist, by being receptive and responsive to the presenting problems of the family and its individual members, learns about their transactions and projective systems. In the process, the family is introduced to the family systems viewpoint and begins to look at symptomatic behavior within a family context. As Skynner becomes aware of emotional responses and fantasies in himself, he slowly responds to the family conflict. Gradually he discloses his own emotions; now he is putting his finger on the "real" family problem—what is *not* communicated, what is missing from the content of the session. In some cases, he may act upon his understanding of the family dynamic, even taking the role of scapegoat. In such instances, he consciously personifies the very emotions the family disowns. Although such a maneuver is carried out cautiously—and only after Skynner and the family have established a good therapeutic alliance—the effect may nevertheless be shocking to the family. As Skynner (1981) explains:

It is as if the family members have been fleeing from a monster and finally find refuge in the safety of the therapist's room only to discover, as they begin to feel secure and to trust him, that he turns into the monster himself! (p. 61)

By expressing the collusively denied or repressed emotions and by absorbing the projective system of a disturbed family, Skynner experiences its dilemma firsthand; by working out for himself a way of escape, he develops a route the family can follow. In his highly responsive approach to therapy, Skynner combines the principles and techniques of object relations theory, group analysis, and social learning (modeling) while retaining an overall view of the family as an ongoing system in need of restructuring.

FAMILY GROUP THERAPY

Related to the psychodynamic outlook is the view, particularly prevalent in the 1960s, that family therapy is a special subset of group therapy. Many of the early pioneers—practitioners and researchers alike—took the position that families are essentially natural groups and that the task of the therapist is to promote interaction, facilitate communication, clarify the group processes, and interpret interpersonal dynamics—much as any group therapy leader would do. John Bell, Lyman Wynne, and Christian Beels are probably the clinicians most closely identified with this psychodynamic group therapy orientation. Bell (1975, 1983) has written most extensively about his approach and we consider his contribution to be representative of the genre.

Social Psychology and Small-Group Behavior (Bell)

John Bell, one of the unsung founding fathers of family therapy, has continued to practice and refine his techniques for over thirty years. A California psychologist affiliated in recent years with the Palo Alto Veterans Administration Hospital and Stanford University, Bell calls his form of intervention **family group therapy** to emphasize that he is applying the social-psychological theories of small-group behavior to the natural group that is a family. His practical and simple purpose is to aid the family group (ultimately independent of the therapist) to function more effectively, with fewer constraints binding the members into nonfunctional activities and dysfunctional interactions, with less tension, with more skillful problem solving, and with more (and better) communications. To do this, Bell encourages the family to structure itself into a conference in which unsatisfactory relationships between members are confronted, family goals are clarified, methods of achieving those goals are agreed upon, and the proposed methods are tried until the outcome is mutually satisfactory. Bell remains the facilitator, the process leader, staying outside the family rather than joining it; he helps the family to determine its own goals and move toward them as a group.

To achieve his objectives, Bell (1976) works on process interventions that have the effect of engaging the family and moving it through the natural stages of small, task-oriented group development. Initially, the family group is helped to explore the expectations of its members as they begin to relate to the therapist, who carefully defines the rules of group participation. Even if members decide to proceed as a group, they inevitably test the limits of the rules and question the commitments each member has made and the ways in which each member will participate. Inevitably, a power struggle charged with hostility begins to develop as individuals and coalitions within the family fight to protect their own interests and compete for dominance. Rather than serving as an end in itself—exorcising family demons—the struggle is instrumental to group development and consolidation and to the ultimate emergence of consensus within the family about the problems on which to work. In Bell's view, the family members then constitute a group that has become functional.

In the next stage, the family group concentrates its energies on selecting a common task to undertake (for example, getting rid of a particular family annoyance or dealing with an acute family crisis). Bell keeps everyone engaged as they struggle toward a resolution that will accommodate the respective goals of each group member or family subgroup. This is the heart of the treatment: releasing the creativity of each member, overcoming lassitude or the urge to withdraw, resolving impasses, expanding communication, redefining expectations, and holding a splintering family together. The goals of therapy are reached when conciliation is achieved among the group participants, pressing problems are resolved, and the group separates from the therapist. In Bell's experience, family members then typically tighten the boundaries around their family "by accentuating the strengths and importance of family initiatives, communication, decisions, and other actions" (Bell, 1976, pp. 138–139). Throughout all stages of his work with a family, Bell continues to stress that the locus of the problems amenable to family therapy is in the family and not in the individual members; similarly, outcomes must be evaluated in terms of family well-being.

Bell as process leader provides a model of himself as a listener for others to emulate. He makes opportunities for family members to participate and mirrors back to them the behavior he is observing in the group. He confines the content to family-related subjects, refusing to allow a member to escape by introducing extraneous matters. He adapts to a particular family's pace of development as a group. He encourages exploring and trying out new ways of interacting. Bell insists that the entire family be present for each session, even postponing meetings if any one member cannot attend. After the initial contact he refuses to see or talk by telephone with any one member individually. His purpose is to emphasize that family members are dealing with a family problem and the group as a whole cannot resolve a family problem unless all work together.

Bell's leadership is gentle, sympathetic, respectful, and unemotional. He does not join in or intrude on a family but affirms the ability of its members to develop strategies to solve their own problems and attain their own goals. By remaining outside the family, Bell does not take over another person's role or authority (for example, play father to a child) or make decisions for the family on how it should function. Bell works with a family as a natural group, persons who have shared experiences in the past and who will continue to live together after family therapy is terminated. He sees the family group therapist as an agent of change whose role is to help initiate and monitor the process of change as the family transforms itself into a more perfectly functioning group.

Bell readily admits that his therapy cannot solve all family problems. More recently (Bell, 1983) he has concentrated his attention on developing methods to help families cope with problems that lie beyond the realm of family interaction. The targets of intervention might be families that include a hospitalized member; families affected adversely by unemployment and poverty, alienated from the mainstream of society, or deprived of adequate support networks; families disturbed by psychosis, character disorders, developmental problems, or physical or mental deterioration. In this work he is moving to create family-enhancing environments—a treatment program he calls **family context therapy**. Rather than treating the family directly, Bell attempts to modify the family's environment (for example, changing the circumstances of a patient's hospitalization so that the family is more closely involved, or reorganizing clinical and social services at a hospital or other large institution) toward the goal of improved family functioning.

Much as in the case of Ackerman, a fellow pioneer family therapist, there are few adherents per se to Bell's approach today. As Nichols (1984) observes, "unlike the other parents of family therapy, he had few offspring. He did not establish an important clinical center, develop a training program, or train well-known students" (p. 41). Nor has Bell particularly promulgated an original theoretical position, preferring to apply the ideas of group dynamics to families. He has, however, offered a workable, pragmatic approach to family intervention, contributing some basic therapeutic methods that have found their way into most forms of family therapy as practiced today.

SUMMARY

Approaches to family therapy can be divided into six groupings—psychodynamic, existential/humanistic, Bowenian, structural, communication/strategic, and behavioral. Among the major distinctions, in addition to theoretical orientation, are whether the emphasis in intervention is on the past or the present; the role unconscious processes play; whether insight or action is stressed; the primary functions of the therapist; the unit of analysis (individual, dyad, triad); and the goals of treatment.

The psychodynamic viewpoint, based largely on a psychoanalytic model, pays attention to the backgrounds and experiences of each family member as much as to the family unit itself. Psychodynamic therapists are concerned with the extent to which individuals are still attached to the past; in their model, a couple's marital distress is related to the pathogenic introjects each partner brings to the relationship.

Nathan Ackerman, a family therapy pioneer, attempted to integrate psychoanalytic theory (with its intrapsychic orientation) and systems theory (emphasizing interpersonal relationships). He viewed family dysfunction as a failure in role complementarity between members and as the product of persistent unresolved conflict (within and between individuals in a family) and prejudicial scapegoating. His therapeutic efforts were aimed at disentangling such interlocking pathologies. James Framo, another first-generation family therapist, believes that insoluble intrapsychic conflict, derived from the family of origin, is perpetuated in the form of projections onto current intimates such as a spouse or children. Using an object relations approach, Framo concerns himself with working through and ultimately removing these introjects; in the process he sees couples alone, then in a couples' group, and finally holds separate sessions with each partner and the members of his or her family of origin.

Ivan Boszormenyi-Nagy and his associates focus on transgenerational legacies and how influences from the past have a bearing on present-day functioning in all family members. In this view, families have invisible loyalties—obligations rooted in past generations—and unsettled accounts that must be balanced. Boszormenyi-Nagy's contextual therapeutic approach attempts to rebuild responsible, trustworthy behavior, taking into account the entitlements of all concerned. Helm Stierlin, in a related approach, is concerned with how families of schizophrenics as well as anorectics maintain such invisible accounts, delegating the identified patient to work out their underlying problems.

Robin Skynner contends that adults with relationship difficulties have developed unrealistic expectations of others in the form of projective systems related to childhood deficiencies. Marital partners, often with incompatible projective systems, attempt to create in the marriage a situation where the missing experience can be supplied, the deficiency remediated by the other partner. Inevitably frustrated, the couple may direct or transmit these projections onto a child, who becomes symptomatic. Skynner's therapeutic efforts, particularly the extended version, attempt to facilitate differentiation between marital partners so that each may become more separate and independent.

John Bell, a founder of family therapy, bases his approach on social-psychological theories of small-group behavior. His family group therapy approach promotes interaction; he facilitates communication, clarifies and interprets, much as any group therapy leader would do. In recent years, Bell has directed his attention to helping create family-enhancing environments by means of an intervention technique he calls family context therapy.

Chapter Six

Experiential/Humanistic Approaches to Theory and Practice

Experience, encounter, confrontation, intuition, process, growth, existence, spontaneity, action, the here-and-now moment—these are the concepts used by those family therapists who, in general, shun theory (and especially theorizing) as a hindrance, an artificial academic effort to make the unknowable knowable. They argue, instead, that therapeutic change resides in a growth experience and not merely intellectual reflection or insight into the origins of problems. It is the immediacy of the relationship between the family and an involved therapist and the process in which they engage together that catalyzes the growth of the individual family members as well as the family system as a whole.

Experiential/humanistic family therapy is an outgrowth of the phenomenological techniques (Gestalt therapy, psychodrama, client-centered therapy, the encounter group movement) so popular in the individual therapy approaches of the 1960s. Rather than endorsing a single technique, such therapeutic endeavors are, by definition, uniquely fitted to the individual client or family. Each of the therapists we will consider in this chapter works with families in different ways, although they share certain philosophical tenets in common.

All experiential/humanistic therapists emphasize choice, free will, and especially the human capacity for self-determination and self-fulfillment. Disordered or dysfunctional behavior is viewed as the result of a failure in the growth process, a deficiency in actualizing one's capabilities and possibilities. Because each person (and by extension, each family) is unique, each must be helped to become aware of and reach his, her, or their potential, discovering in the process the solutions to current problems. Psychotherapy, then, with individuals or with families, must be an interpersonal encounter in which therapist and client(s) strive to be real and authentic. Growth in sensitivity, in the expression of feelings, in spontaneity and creativity (nonrational experiencing), in authenticity are the typical goals of treatment. If the therapeutic intervention succeeds, the results should facilitate growth for all participants, clients and therapists alike.

The primacy of experience over rational thought and especially intellectualization is underscored by each of the therapists we are about to discuss. Consequently, each is active, often self-disclosing, and likely to make use of a variety of evocative procedures to help clients get closer to their feelings, sensations, fantasies, and inner experiences. Sensitivity to one's here-and-now, ongoing life experiences is encouraged throughout therapy; denying impulses and suppressing affect is viewed as dysfunctional and growth-retarding.

Experiential/humanistic family therapists are likely to behave as real, authentic people (rather than acting as blank screens or wearing therapeutic masks). By having direct encounters with clients, they attempt to expand their own experiences, often having to deal with their own vulnerabilities in the process. Their therapeutic interventions are likely to be spontaneous, challenging, and often idiosyncratic, as they attempt to help clients gain self-awareness, self-responsibility, and personal growth.

THE EXPERIENTIAL MODEL

As noted, experiential family practitioners tailor their approach to the unique conflicts and behavior patterns of each family with whom they work. There are probably as many ways to provide an experience for accelerating growth as there are variations in family dysfunction. The work of some experiential therapists such as Carl Whitaker (1976b) clearly reflects the psychodynamic orientation of their training and background, though they are careful, as far as possible, not to impose any preconceived theoretical suppositions upon families. Others such as Kempler (1981) show evidence of their training in Gestalt therapy under Fritz Perls. Many experiential therapists such as Kaplan and Kaplan (1978) attend to the "individual in context" in the manner of the systems theorists we discussed in Part I of this book. Client-centered therapists such as Levant (1986) apply many of Carl Rogers's ideas regarding therapeutic growth-producing experiences to families.

All experiential therapists deal with the present rather than the uncovering of the past. Their emphasis is on the here and now, the situation as it unfolds from moment to moment between an active and caring therapist and a family. The interactions among family members and with the therapist are confronted in an effort to help everyone involved in the encounter develop more growth-enhancing behavior. Rather than offer insight or interpretation, the therapist provides an experience—an opportunity for family members to open themselves to spontaneity, freedom of expression, and personal growth. The interpersonal experience is, in itself, the primary stimulus to growth in this approach to psychotherapy.

Symbolic-Experiential Family Therapy (Whitaker)

Carl Whitaker, unconventional and often provocative, is the epitome of an experiential family therapist. He first made his influence felt with his innovative (often radical) work in individual psychotherapy, especially his trailblazing efforts to redefine a schizophrenic's symptoms as signs that an individual was "stuck" in the process of growth and was attempting to apply "creative" solutions to vexing interpersonal problems. Coauthor of a landmark book, *The Roots of Psychotherapy* (Whitaker & Malone, 1953), Whitaker even then was beginning to be an active therapist providing an experience of growth and maturity for his patients and not simply offering insight to facilitate "adjustment" to society.

In his work with schizophrenics, Whitaker took the daring position, never before espoused, that each participant in therapy is, to some degree, simultaneously patient and therapist to the other. Both invest emotion in the process, both regress, both grow from the experience. The therapist must be committed to his own growth, personally as well as professionally, if he is to catalyze growth in others. As Neill and Kniskern (1982) have observed, the thesis that a therapist should avoid technique and somehow draw on his own pathology to effect a cure was particularly unsettling to most traditional practitioners at the time.

The Use of Cotherapy with Schizophrenics. Trained originally as an obstetrician/gynecologist with no formal background in psychoanalysis, Whitaker was called upon during World War II, after a brief hospital psychiatric residency, to treat patients in Oak Ridge Hospital in Tennessee, located where the secret U.S. atomic bomb was being built. Perhaps because of the heavy stress of the situation and the extraordinary demands on him, or perhaps because he believed he lacked sufficient experience, or perhaps because he wished to share his intense personal involvement in the therapeutic process, Whitaker began working with colleagues as part of a **cotherapy** team. In any event, following the war, he helped establish a psychiatry department at the medical school at Emory University in Atlanta, Georgia, where, together with associates such as psychologists John Warkentin and, later, Thomas Malone, he continued his earlier cotherapy treatment of schizophrenics.

As Whitaker pursued his unorthodox approach to treating schizophrenics, he became increasingly aware of the key role played by the family in the etiology of the disorder. Broadening his earlier perspective, he began to conceptualize schizophrenia as both an intrapsychic and interpersonal dilemma and to treat his schizophrenic patients along with their families. The multiple-therapist team—an extension of Whitaker's earlier reliance on cotherapy—was an innovation that helped to prevent a single therapist from becoming entangled in what Whitaker found to be a powerful, enmeshing family system. Two or more therapists working together afforded this protection and at the same time provided a model for desirable interpersonal behavior for the entire family.

The Symbolic Aspects of Family Therapy. By the mid-1960s Whitaker had moved from Emory University in Atlanta to the University of Wisconsin in Madison and had begun to elaborate his ideas about experiential therapy with families. In particular, he was starting to pay closer attention to what he personally was experiencing in the treatment process; he saw the potential for using that awareness to press for changes in his patients at the same time that he himself continued to benefit by investing in the therapeutic encounter. As Whitaker's students and colleagues Neill and Kniskern (1982) describe it, his thought processes over several decades evolved from the intrapsychic to the interpersonal, from the individual to the family, from "psyche to system."

Whitaker, recently retired from his university post, now refers to his therapeutic approach as symbolic-experiential family therapy (Whitaker & Bumberry, 1988). The basic assumption is that families are changed as a result of their experiences, not through education. Because most of our experiences occur outside of our awareness or consciousness, we can only gain access to them nonverbally or symbolically, through unstated but impactful processes occurring within the family. According to Whitaker, "While education can be immensely helpful, the covert process of the family is the one that contains the most power for potential changing" (Keith & Whitaker, 1982, p. 43).

Whitaker insists that both real and symbolic curative factors operate in therapy. He likens the symbolic aspect of therapy to the infrastructure of a city; while not apparent on the surface, what runs underneath the streets and buildings is what permits life on the surface to go on (Whitaker & Bumberry, 1988). Similarly, he believes our personal subterranean worlds are dominated by the flow of impulses and evolving symbols, even if not always conscious. According to Whitaker, it is these "emotional infrastructures" that ensure the flow of our impulse life. Since the meaning we give to external reality is determined by this internal reality, helping expand the symbolic inner worlds of families can aid in their leading fuller, richer lives.

As a therapist, Whitaker attempts to understand a family's complex world of impulses and symbols by looking for and giving voice to similar underlying impulses and symbols within himself. Not willing to settle for material from the surface world of thinking and reasoning, he probes into the covert world beneath the surface words, trying to sense the far more important symbolic meanings of what transpires between himself and the family. By showing ease with accepting and voicing his own impulses and fantasies, he helps family members become more comfortable in recognizing, expressing, and accepting theirs.

Throughout therapy, Whitaker listens, observes, stays in immediate touch with what he is experiencing, and actively intervenes to repair damage, without being concerned over why the breakdown occurred. He makes an effort to depathologize

Carl Whitaker, M.D.

human experience, as suggested earlier by his view of schizophrenia. Whitaker believes "psychopathology" arises from the same mechanisms that produce "normal" behavior. Consequently, he is not afraid to encourage "craziness" in family members (or, for that matter, in himself), believing that new outlooks and creative solutions typically follow, as the family is freed to stretch and grow. Through his sometimes quirky-appearing and irrepressible "right brain" style, Whitaker is thus helping sensitize the family to its own unconscious life.

For Whitaker, the focus of therapy is the process—what occurs during the family session—and how each participant (himself included) experiences feelings, exposes vulnerabilities, and shares uncensored thoughts. Whenever an individual or family system seeks to grow, the therapist (or cotherapists) can take advantage of this inherent drive toward fulfillment and maturity to engage that person or group in an existential encounter free from the usual social restraints and the role playing that customarily characterize doctor-patient or therapist-client relationships. The encounter is intended to shake up old ways of feeling and behaving and thus to provide an unsettling experience to reactivate the seemingly dormant but innate process of growth.

Whitaker, iconoclastic in view and creative—sometimes outrageous—in dealing with families, has been described by Minuchin (1982) as using "humor, indirection, seduction, indignation, primary process, boredom, and even falling asleep as equally powerful instruments of contact and challenge" (p. ix). Though they may appear to be chosen at random and though Whitaker himself may not always consciously know why he did or said something (he claims his therapy is controlled by his unconscious), his interventions consistently challenge the symbolic meaning that people give to events. In response to such challenges, creative solutions to problems and new arrangements among family members may arise.

Establishing Therapeutic Goals. The family therapist's mission, as Whitaker sees it, is to help the three-generational family to simultaneously maintain healthy separation and autonomy. Family roles, while largely determined by generation, should nevertheless remain flexible, Whitaker maintains, and members should be encouraged to explore, and on occasion even exchange, family roles. Healthy families, according to Whitaker and Keith (1981), develop an "as if" structure that permits latitude in role playing, often allowing each family member to try on new roles and gain new perspectives:

> For example, the 6-year-old son says to daddy, "Can I serve the meat tonight?" and daddy says, "Sure, you sit over on this chair and serve the meat and potatoes and I'll sit over in your place and complain." (p. 190)

For Whitaker, this exchange is an opportunity to develop a healthy, straight-talking communication, in which all family members are able to look at themselves and grow both as individuals and as a family. Consistent with his experiential perspective, Whitaker views family health as an ongoing process of becoming, in which each member is encouraged to explore a full range of family roles in order to develop maximum autonomy.

Earlier in his career, Whitaker (1975) labeled his often playful and deliberately irrational therapeutic style "the psychotherapy of the absurd." Intentionally provocative, it is intended to shock, mystify, confuse, and induce chaos; in system terms, the therapist is using positive feedback to activate a stalled system and accelerate disruption, believing that in the reconstitution the symptoms will disappear. In a certain sense, Whitaker is the Zen master offering *koans*—riddles or puzzles for the novice to contemplate—and in the process stimulating a nonlinear and nonlogical way of thinking that will bring enlightenment.

Whitaker (1975) has likened the use of the absurd to the Leaning Tower of Pisa. If someone comes in offering an absurd statement, he will accept it, build on it, escalate it until the tower becomes so high and so tilted that it crashes. If a woman tells Whitaker "I can't stand my husband," he will agree that men are difficult but then ask "Why haven't you divorced him?" or "Why not try an interim boyfriend?" If she answers that she loves her husband, Whitaker will respond "Of course, that's why you'd have an affair—to prove your love and to stimulate his love until it equals yours." Should she respond with "But I love my kids," Whitaker will say "Well, if you do, then you should make a sacrifice by leaving them so they'll learn that father also loves them." Her answer "He'll neglect them" is met with the rejoinder "Then you can prove your love of them by suing him for child neglect." Ultimately the tower of deliberate absurdity comes crashing down, frequently with the woman saying something like "Carl, you're crazy, but I think I see what you're talking about. I really couldn't stand my husband, the rat. I would have left him long ago, but there must be something about him that makes me go on loving him." In this manner Whitaker provides an enlightenment experience; the patient develops a deeper awareness of the absurdity of certain aspects of her view of the marriage. To Whitaker, one indicator of a family's growth is their increased tolerance for the absurdities of life.

Symbolic-experiential family therapy sets itself the goal of helping the family members evolve a greater sense of family belonging, at the same time as it encourages individuation by all family members. Rather than attend to symptoms in an identified patient, Whitaker immediately engages the entire family, forcing all of them as a group to examine the basis of their existence as a family unit.

The Therapeutic Process. In Whitaker's colorful description, "the journey of family therapy begins with a blind date and ends with an empty nest" (Whitaker & Bumberry, 1988, p. 53). Initially, the therapist must deal with the inevitable *battle for structure*, as the family sizes up the therapist and his or her intentions and attempts to impose its own definition of the upcoming relationship: what's wrong with the family, who's to blame, who requires treatment, how the therapist should proceed. Whitaker insists that the therapist control the ensuing structure, from the first telephone contact onward, so therapy can begin on a productive note and the therapist not to compromise his or her own needs, beliefs, or standards. If the therapist loses this initial foray, the family will then bring into therapy the identical behavioral patterns that are likely creating their current problems in the first place.

In the process, Whitaker is establishing an "I" position with the family, stimulating them, ultimately, to piece together an identifiable "we" position as a family. By insisting on his own autonomy, he is telling them that he is interested in his own growth as a result of their experience together, and that they need not be concerned about protecting him. Real caring, for Whitaker, requires distance, partially achieved by caring for himself and not only for his client family. Whitaker (Whitaker & Bumberry, 1988) emphasizes dealing with the family on a symbolic level in a "metaposition"—establishing what each can expect from the other. Whitaker, who frequently uses baseball metaphors, sees himself as a coach, not interested in playing on the team, only in helping them play more effectively. By stepping in to play first base, he argues, he would be indicating he did not think much of the first baseman they already have, a destructive message. Instead, as coach, he is encouraging them to develop their own resources.

If the therapist must win the battle for structure, the family must be victorious in the *battle for initiative* (Napier & Whitaker, 1978). That is, any initiative for change must not only come from the family, but also be actively supported by its members. Whitaker shuns responsibility for changing a family, and especially for seeking family leadership.

Whitaker insists the family convene as a group with all members present, underscoring their sense of a family unit as well as acknowledging that the family itself is the client. Together they are encouraged to probe their relationships—in Whitaker's words "to ante up"—despite efforts to identify specific members as the problem. In the following case, a mother, father, and 6-year-old girl attend the first session. The daughter is described as school phobic, the mother obese, the father a hard-driving executive. Mother and father deny relationship struggles, despite his working nearly 75 hours a week and frequently staying out late.

Carl: You mean he's totally lost interest in you?

Mom: Well, no, it's not that. It's just that his way of contributing to the family is to make sure that we have everything we need.

Carl: Except a husband and father.

Mom: No. He's a good father.

Carl: (turning to the daughter) Sarah, do you think that Mommy worries that Daddy might be kissing the secretary? You know, he's gone at work so much. Maybe he gets lonely too.

Sarah: No. Daddies don't get lonely. Just Mommies, but since Mommy has me, she doesn't have to be lonely either.

Carl: Well, I'm sure glad you take such good care of your Mommy but I still worry about Daddies. It's very hard to tell when they're lonely.

Here Whitaker is beginning to get them to think about family relationships, without specifically suggesting that Sarah's dedication to Mom may be related to her refusal to go to school, or that she may be expressing through remaining at home her desire to help Mom hide from her depression. Later in the same session, Mom begins to complain about her inability to play tennis with her high-powered husband because of her weight.

Carl: (turning to Dad) Do you worry about her weight, too, or do you prefer playing with other partners?

Dad: Of course I'd love her to pick up the sport, but it's just not possible. It would be dangerous for her to exert herself with so much excess weight.

Carl: So you don't want to feel like you killed her by pushing tennis. I suppose I can understand that. How is it that you manage to live with the knowledge that she's slowly committing suicide via her obesity? (Whitaker & Bumberry, 1988, pp. 62–64)

Note how Whitaker has started them thinking beyond the presenting symptoms of separate individuals, expanding the symptom framework to now include possible extramarital affairs, self-destructive overeating, and a relationship gap between the parents. Each member's participation in the lives of the other members is in the process of becoming clarified under Whitaker's provocative comments. While they may not yet make the necessary connections, they leave the session with new ideas to consider, all within a relationship or interpersonal perspective. In future sessions, having set the therapeutic structure, Whitaker must be careful to get the family to take responsibility for facing themselves, winning the battle for initiative, and, through an experiential exchange with him, come alive and cease playacting.

In Whitaker's view (1977), then, family therapy occurs in stages: (1) a pretreatment phase in which the entire nuclear family is expected to participate; the therapist or cotherapists establish that they are in charge during the sessions but that the family must make its own life decisions outside of these office visits (the latter is intended to convey the message that a therapist does not have better ideas for how family members should run their lives than they themselves do); (2) a middle phase in which increased involvement between both therapists and the family develops; care is taken by the therapist not to be absorbed by the family system; symptoms are relabeled as efforts toward growth; and the family is incited to change by means of confrontation, exaggeration, anecdote, or absurdity; (3) a late phase in which increased flexibility in the family necessitates only minimal intervention from the therapist or therapy team; and (4) a separation phase in which the therapists and family part, but with the acknowledgment of mutual interdependence and loss. In the final phase, the family uses more and more of its own resources, and assumes increased responsibility for its way of living. With separation—the "empty nest"—there is joy mingled with a sense of loss. [1]

Whitaker's change-producing interventions have a covert, implicit quality. Symptoms are rarely attacked directly. Insight seems to follow changes in feelings and behavior, not precede such changes. History taking is occasionally important but not carried out routinely; in any case, it must not be allowed to impede Whitaker's major therapeutic thrust—forming a close and personal alliance with the family as a whole and providing an experience that is symbolic to the family but does not reinforce its distress (Keith & Whitaker, 1982). What the family therapist has most to offer, believes Whitaker, is his or her personal maturity; the stage of the therapist's personal development has an influence on the kind of support or assistance provided to the family. Whitaker maintains that the therapist who does not derive benefit, therapeutically, from his or her work has little to give, therapeutically speaking, to client families. The use of cotherapists adds another dimension; the ability of both therapists to join together, have fun together, disagree, or even fight with each other, and perhaps to go off on different tangents—one acting "crazy" and the other providing stability—is a model for spontaneous and productive interaction.

Increasingly, Whitaker has included grandparents or other extended family members in his therapeutic endeavors with families. In part an effort to help a family come to grips with its continuity over time, in part an effort by Whitaker to expand his own personal growth, the participation of members of three generations may be especially effective when family therapy has reached an impasse. In such situations grandparents may be invited as assistants to the therapist, not as patients. Whitaker may even say to the family, "We want your grandparents in to help us; we are failing" (Whitaker, 1976a). Typically a part of the middle phase of treatment, this maneuver is used by Whitaker to overcome an "impotence impasse" in which the therapist feels stymied and in need of outside help. Symbolically, grandparents

1. Napier and Whitaker provide an intriguing full account of family therapy with the Brice family (two parents, a suicidal, runaway, teenage daughter, an adolescent son, and a 6-year-old daughter) in their book *The Family Crucible* (New York: Harper & Row, 1978).

are apt to be seen more as real people than as threatening authority figures. Their acknowledgment that their children are in fact adults may have therapeutic value for the members of all generations. Similarly, the discovery that elderly parents are capable of running their own lives may have many liberating consequences for their children.

The Person of the Therapist. Throughout his work with individuals and families, Whitaker has stressed his personal need to "stay alive" as a human being and as a therapist. He frequently asserts that "nothing worth knowing can be taught," insisting that the therapist must uncover his or her own belief system and symbolic world, and then use that self (rather than specific therapeutic techniques) to grow and help families do the same. He has offered the following set of rules for therapists (Whitaker, 1976b, p. 164):

1. Relegate every significant other to second place.
2. Learn how to love. Flirt with any infant available. Unconditional positive regard probably isn't present after the baby is three years old.
3. Develop a reverence for your own impulses, and be suspicious of your behavior sequences.
4. Enjoy your mate more than your kids, and be childish with your mate.
5. Fracture role structures at will and repeatedly.
6. Learn to retreat and advance from every position that you take.
7. Guard your impotence as one of your most valuable weapons.
8. Build long-term relations so you can be free to hate safely.
9. Face the fact that you must grow until you die. Develop a sense of the benign absurdity of life—yours and those around you—and thus learn to transcend the world of experience. If we can abandon our missionary zeal we have less chance of being eaten by cannibals.
10. Develop your primary process living. Evolve a joint craziness with someone you are safe with. Structure a professional cuddle group so you won't abuse your mate with the garbage left over from the day's work.
11. As Plato said, "practice dying."

Gestalt Family Therapy (Kempler)

All of the family therapy approaches we are considering in this chapter are, to a greater or lesser extent, existential in character. More an orientation to understanding human behavior than a formal school of psychotherapy, existentially influenced therapies are concerned with entering and comprehending the world as it is being experienced by the individual family members as well as the family as a functioning whole. The therapies have in common an emphasis on the meaning the patient gives to existence, to being. Because people define themselves through their current choices and decisions, action in the present, not reflection on the past, is the key to understanding for the existentialist. Even the future—what people choose to become—is charged with more influence than the past and the conflicts associated with the past. In existential therapies, patients examine and take responsibility for

Walter Kempler, M.D.

their lives. Unconscious material may be brought forth but is not automatically assumed to be any more meaningful than the conscious data of life.

Psychotherapy in this framework is an encounter between two or more persons who are constantly developing, evolving, and fulfilling their inner potential. Technique is deemphasized to preclude one person seeing the other as an object to be analyzed. In contrast to the common therapeutic belief that understanding stems from technique, existentialist therapists believe that technique follows understanding. Formal and conventional doctor-patient roles are replaced by a more egalitarian and open arrangement in which each participant opens his or her world to the other as an existential partner. The emphasis is on presence; in a real, immediate, ongoing relationship between two or more persons, each tries to understand and experience as far as possible the being of the other(s).

If existentialism is concerned with how humans experience their immediate existence, Gestalt psychology focuses on how they perceive it. Having accepted the therapeutic implications of existentialism along with much of the rhetoric of Gestalt psychology, Frederick (Fritz) Perls is generally credited with launching the Gestalt-therapy movement in the United States.

An earthy and charismatic person, Perls spent the last decade of his life holding numerous demonstration workshops throughout the country in addition to making tape recordings and films demonstrating his Gestalt techniques; he died in 1970 at age 77. His book *Gestalt Therapy Verbatim* (Perls, 1969) is an edited version of his seminars at Esalen, a growth center in the Big Sur region of California. Although the practice of Gestalt therapy is for most students synonymous with the techniques developed by Perls, this is not always the case. As a matter of fact, the approach assumes that each therapist will discover his or her own unique style and uses his or her "I"-ness as an essential part of the working relationship. According to the Gestalt approach, the organized whole of a person—his or her Gestalt—must be maintained in an integrated rather than fragmented state. In the process of attaining this wholeness, aspects of the personality that once were disowned are identified and reclaimed. Self-awareness is the means by which change is accomplished. Self-defeating tendencies must be recognized; emotional blocks to self-understanding removed; moment-to-moment feelings expressed. As self-awareness increases, so does a sense of self-direction. The Gestalt approach holds that through life experiences and observations of others a person internalizes the values by which he or she wants to live. Once a person's inner resources are mobilized, they are assumed to be more than adequate for coping with life's problems.

The Therapeutic Encounter. The therapist's role in Gestalt therapy is to help clients become aware of how they use their resources ineffectively and to point out what they do to block achievement of their goals, not to tell clients why they act in certain ways. Explanations and interpretations of self-defeating behavior based on the recovery of past memories or on historical reports are considered irrelevant to learning to change ineffective behavior patterns. As the California psychiatrist Walter Kempler (1982) insists, the focus must remain on the immediate moment: "What people say, how they say it, what happens when it is said, how it corresponds with what they are doing, and what they are attempting to achieve" (p. 141). Therapeutic intervention, addressed to current conflict, consists of bringing discordant elements into the open and confronting the incongruence.

Gestalt therapy, historically speaking, has dealt primarily with intrapersonal issues and responsibilities. In recent years a number of Gestaltists such as Hatcher (1978), Kaplan and Kaplan (1978), and especially Kempler (1974, 1981, 1982) have urged that more attention be paid to interpersonal processing. Kempler (1982) has gone so far as to declare that in a dynamic sense there is no such thing as an "individual"—our existence and survival are derived from and wholly dependent upon our mutual connections and relations.

Gestalt family therapy represents an effort to blend some of the principles and procedures of family and Gestalt therapies in order to help people reach beyond their customary self-deceptive games, defenses, and facades. The goal here is to guide them, frequently by the therapist's own forthright behavior, to become aware of and release feelings; ideally, family members become aware of their reciprocal influence on each other, the identified patient's symptoms are ameliorated, and the family learns new ways of working and living together.

Kempler's (1981) therapeutic efforts are provocative, highly personal, uncompromisingly honest, and powerful. Kempler presses for self-disclosure by family members, expecting that the wish or need to resolve their problems or improve relationships will give them the courage to expose their vulnerabilities. He actively and directly insists that everyone, therapist included, become more intensely aware of what they are doing or saying or feeling. Like the mechanic who would rather listen to a troublesome engine than hear a description of it, Kempler first starts up a family conversation:

Transcript	*Comments*
Mother: Our 15-year-old son Jim has been making a lot of trouble for us lately.	The healthier the family, the more readily they talk to each other. For instance, should Jim respond immediately to his mother's charge with "That's not true!" it would indicate that he has both self-confidence and the hope of being heard. Let's assume Jim doesn't leap in.
Therapist (to Jim evocatively): Do you agree that the number one problem in this family is that you are a troublemaker?	
Jim: Not really.	
Therapist: Tell her what you think it is.	
Jim: It's no use.	
Therapist (to Mother): Do you have anything to say to his hopelessness?	
Mother: I think we've said all there is to say.	Family members are often reluctant to engage one another, particularly initially. The therapist perseveres by offering himself, if necessary.
Therapist (to Jim): I'd like to know what you think is the problem, Jim.	
Jim: They're too rigid.	The battlelines often have both parents on one side. It is better when it is a free-for-all.
Therapist: Both of them identical?	
Jim: Mother more than Father.	
Therapist: Then, maybe you can get some help from him.	
Jim: He's too weak. He always gives in to her.	

(continued)

Transcript	*Comments*
Therapist (to Father): Do you agree with him?	
Father: Of course not.	
Therapist: You didn't tell him.	

(Source: Kempler, 1974, pp. 27--28)

Kempler is interested in what each person wants and from whom, expressed in the most specific terms possible. Participants are forced to talk to each other. If a wife complains to Kempler that her husband lacks understanding or sensitivity, Kempler directs her to tell that to her husband, not the therapist, and to be specific in her complaint. If she argues that it will do no good, Kempler insists she tell that to her husband. If she then breaks down, admits her feelings of hopelessness, and begins to cry—all without provoking a response from her husband—Kempler will point out his silence and invite him to answer her. From the initial interview through the subsequent sessions, the focus remains the immediate present. Self-disclosure and open, honest exchanges with others are basic ground rules for family members to follow if they are to untangle a family problem or overcome an impasse.

Viewing the individual within his or her functional context—the family—Gestalt family therapists attempt to help each family member achieve maximum individuation at the same time as they promote more vital relationships among the various members. Thus, the traditional goals of the Gestalt therapist working with an individual client (growth of the individual and the development of a distinct sense of self) are combined with objectives for the family group as a whole. First helping family members to explore how their awareness is blocked, the therapist then channels the increased awareness so that they may engage in more productive and fulfilling processes with one another (Kaplan & Kaplan, 1978).

The Gestalt therapist facilitates self-exploration, risk taking, spontaneity. Since such undertakings are all but impossible if an individual or family fears that self-discovery could be harmful, it is essential that the therapist provide an unchecked and unequivocal model for self-disclosure. To strike the familiar pose as a benevolent and accepting therapist only plays into the client's fantasies that disapproval is dangerous, according to Kempler (1982). By contrast, Kempler is emotionally intense, assertive, genuine, challenging, sometimes brutally (if refreshingly) frank; in short, he expresses whatever he is feeling at the moment in the hope of making an impact on the family. As the following excerpt from a couple's therapy session begins, Kempler has just completed a moving exchange with the wife, during which the husband remained silent. Kempler now turns to the husband because he wants his participation.

Transcript	*Comments*
Therapist: Where are you?	
He: I don't know. (pause) I was thinking of something else. (pause) I don't understand what is going on. I guess that's it (pause) partly thinking what I had to do today.	He was always inarticulate, always speaking haltingly and tentatively. His eyes blinked nervously as if he were being buffeted. I had mentioned this before. On past occasions I had confronted him with his inarticulateness and his blinking, but we had made no progress with it. It seemed that I had tried everything I knew to no avail.
Therapist: Damn, that makes me angry. You're a clod. That's the word I want to buffet you with. Damn you. So insensitive. No wonder you've got problems in your marriage. (Then, cooling down enough to make an "I" statement instead of the "you" accusations, I continued) I want you to hear; I want you to join in; I want you to at least acknowledge our presence some way other than leaving. At best, I'd want you to appreciate us in what happened, at worst, to tell us you don't like us for being inane, but not just to abandon us.	
He: (Thoughtful) Earlier I was aware of something like envy (pause) resentment (pause) I don't know.	
Therapist: (Still angry) You never know. That's your standard answer. Now I don't know. I don't know what the hell to do with you to get in touch with you.	
He: I'm sorry. (pause) I always say I'm sorry. I guess I'm sorry. I was envious. (pause) I felt angry 'cause I was envious.	He was trying to be with me now, and I wanted to try harder myself. I decided to try clarifying and/or intensifying his statement.

(continued)

Transcript	*Comments*
Therapist: Try on: "I long to be close to both of you, but I never learned how."	I felt my own sadness when I said that and knew I was on target—or else I would not have been so angry with him. His tears were confirmation as he choked up trying to say the sentence.
Therapist: You don't have to, but I wish you could talk to us now.	
He: I can't. It's too sad.	
Therapist: It?	
He: The sentence . . .	
Therapist: Then try to include all the words "I'm so sad when I think of how I long to be close and can't because I never learned."	I kept wanting to return to this key phrase and yet I did not want my urging to become more central for him than his experiencing his longing. He sat thoughtfully, still tearing and saying nothing. Several minutes passed.
Therapist: I'm suddenly aware of my own difficulty in speaking about longing. I could debate with you more easily than I can speak of feeling the longing to be close. I realize I still haven't spoken of mine and can only hesitantly speak about yours. This feels better than debating or idly chatting but it sure is sad. I feel closer to you in our sadness.	I began to cry. He was now trying harder to look at me through his tears. I found myself smiling through my tears. "It," I thought. How clever. He nodded, still unable to speak.
He: (Finally) I can do it with my car—feeling close by racing people . . . I'm so safe that way. I can't just be close.	
Therapist: (I seemed finished with me for the moment and was free to turn once again to him. I offered the sentence again—modified.) "I long to be close but never learned how, but now I'm learning finally."	

He began to cry more heavily as he nodded his head and turned inward again, looking down. His wife reached out warmly, "This reminds me of the time that you . . ." I interrupted her, "Leave him alone now. You can talk to him later." She grasped, or at least readily accepted, my command. I wanted him to be wherever he was with his feelings, not diverted to some other time and place. Her comment sounded like an "aha" announcement and I felt no compunction to honor it. She could keep it to and for herself.

I left them and was visiting my father, fluttering through historical scenes like a hummingbird. His lovingly tousling my hair—the only times he ever touched me that I could recall. His angrily shouting at me. His intellectual lectures to teach me something. I became painfully aware of his absent touch and never being spoken to affectionately by him. He never told me he loved me or even that he liked me. I recalled the surprise I once felt when I overheard him admiring me to one of his friends. I am sad. Of course, I long.

I came back to our session and was aware of this couple once again. They were both looking at me. I shared my thoughts. Then he related clearly, articulately his own longings, recalling, smiling through his fresh tears, his father teaching him to drive, the only closeness he knew with his father. To intensify his experience, I suggested that he envision his father. He couldn't. He just cried. "Tell him," I suggested, "how you longed to be close to him but just didn't know how because you never learned." After a long pause, he replied: "I used to feel angry and frustrated. I realize now he never learned either."

He was integrating and I was pleased. I became vacant, and we all sat silently, alone and close. (Kempler, 1981, pp. 11–13)

Kempler's demand for a complete and honest encounter with and between family members reflects his Gestalt heritage. No holds are barred, no feelings stifled. The therapist is a real flesh-and-blood person who knows who he is, what his needs are, and what he is experiencing from moment to moment during the shared therapeutic encounter with the family. At the same time, he expects—nay, insists—that all participants search for, uncover, and express what they are experiencing *now*, since to Gestaltists, *nothing exists except in the now.* He urges clients to stay with the experience as it is happening and until they recognize and "own" what they are feeling from moment to moment. All efforts to avoid this awareness are counteracted by Kempler as soon as they occur; it is in the now, say Gestaltists, that people are or are not growing, are or are not enhancing their coping abilities, are or are not in touch with themselves and with reality.

By offering himself as a model of genuineness, Kempler attempts to draw the same from family members, and in the process of their shared intimate experience, all engage in growth-producing behavior. The therapeutic goal, for Kempler (1981), is the integration of each family member within the family, each learning to recognize, appreciate, and express his or her personal sense of being.

THE HUMANISTIC MODEL

Humanistically oriented clinicians, like their experiential counterparts, conceptualize dysfunctional behavior as the result of a deficit in growth. They point to an arrest in self-development (or somewhat more specifically, in self-awareness or self-direction) or to a failure to actualize one's inherent potential, as the explanation for all current psychological problems. In general, they define a mature person as a rational being (rather than one driven by irrational forces) who is capable of making conscious choices on the basis of his or her intentions (rather than being directed by unresolved unconscious conflicts) and who is able to plan for the future (and not simply fall victim, as an adult, to problems from the past). From the humanistic viewpoint, growth is a natural and spontaneous process occurring in all human beings, given an environment that encourages it; psychological disorders represent a failure to fulfill potential for growth.

As noted earlier, the theories presented in this section may be considered phenomenological. The philosophy of phenomenology contends that understanding another person requires an understanding of that individual's perception of a situation, not simply the physical reality of the situation. Phenomenologists insist that behavior is determined by personal experience and by individual perception rather than by external reality. Thus, behavior that appears irrational and confused to an outside observer may seem reasonable and purposeful to the person experiencing the situation; the action may seem to the actor to be the most appropriate and effective behavior he or she can muster under the circumstances, although it seems to others to be based on faulty perceptions. With such an orientation, all behavior makes sense; it reflects the client's perception of reality, the only reality he or she can know. The humanistic family therapist takes on the task of enriching a family's experiences and enlarging the possibilities for each family member to realize his or her unique and extraordinary potential.

The Process/Communication Approach (Satir)

Virginia Satir's central place in the history of the family therapy movement has been noted several times earlier in this book. In the 1950s, among the founding parents of the family therapy movement, Satir was in the unique position of being both the only woman and a social worker among primarily male psychiatrists. Actually, she probably preceded most of her male counterparts in working with families, reportedly having seen her first family in therapy in 1951 and having offered the first training program ever in family therapy in 1955 at the Illinois State Psychiatric Institute (Luepnitz, 1988). It was several years later that she learned of a group engaging in family research efforts in Palo Alto, California (Bateson, Jackson, Haley, & Weakland, 1956); having contacted them, she was invited by Jackson to help him start what became the Mental Research Institute. The institute's major purpose initially was to study the relationship between family interaction and the development of health and illness in its members (Yapko, 1988). More interested in training than in research, Satir soon set about demonstrating her techniques with families, culminating in the first published description of

Virginia Satir, M.S.W.

conjoint family therapy (Satir, 1964), truly a ground-breaking text for therapists and students alike. For many people, even today, the text is the vehicle of their initial acquaintance with family therapy.

Along with Ackerman, Satir is usually named as one of the earliest and most charismatic leaders of the field (Beels & Ferber, 1969). Over a 30-year span, until her death in 1988, she continued to be a prolific writer and is especially celebrated for her inspiring family therapy demonstrations (said to number between 400 and 500) around the world. Although linked to the communication approach because of her early MRI affiliation, Satir's work at Esalen, a growth center, during the 1960s, encouraged her to adopt a humanistic framework and emphasize a number of growth-enhancing techniques (sensory awareness, dance, massage, group encounter techniques) to evoke feelings and clarify family communication patterns. In her more recent writing, Satir (1982) identified her approach as a "process model" in which the therapist and family join forces to stimulate an inherent health-promoting process in the family.

Symptoms and Family Balance

Satir concerned herself with the family as a balanced system. In particular, she wanted to determine the "price" each part of the system "pays" to keep the overall unit balanced. That is, she viewed any symptom in an individual member as signaling a blockage in growth, and as having a homeostatic connection to a family system that requires blockage and distortion of growth in some form in all of its members to keep its balance. To Satir (1982), the rules that govern a family system are related to how the parents go about achieving and maintaining their own self-esteem; these rules, in turn, shape the context within which the children grow and develop their own sense of self-esteem.

A presenting symptom in a family member gave Satir (1982) the initial clues for "unraveling the net of distorted, ignored, denied, projected, unnourished, and untapped parts of each person so that they can connect with their ability to cope functionally, healthily, and joyously" (p. 41). What she offered, instead, was acceptance and a nonjudgmental attitude, believing that as a consequence family members would begin to explore their patterns and change the destructive transactions that left no one happy or satisfied.

Individual Growth and Development. Satir believed that all humans strive toward growth and development, and that each of us possesses all the resources we need for fulfilling our potential, if only we can gain access to these resources and learn to nourish them. More specifically, she pointed to three types of factors influencing human development: (1) unchangeable genetic endowment, determining our physical, emotional, and temperamental potential; (2) longitudinal influences, the result of learning acquired in the process of growth; and (3) the constant mind-body interaction.

Longitudinal influences—the sum of learning since birth—are especially significant. Here Satir emphasized the child's experiences of the *primary triad* (father, mother, child) as the essential source of self-identity. Adult self-worth or self-esteem evolves from the relative proportion of constructive to destructive interaction experiences arising from this triad. To Satir, positive self-worth is the cornerstone of individual and family mental health (Satir & Baldwin, 1983). From the primary triad, the child also learns to decipher parental messages; discrepancies between words, tone, touch, and looks help shape future adult communication patterns.

Another important factor in individual growth is the *mind, body triad*. Body parts may often take on metaphoric meaning; each part usually has a positive or negative value attached to it by its owner. Some are liked, others disliked, some need awakening. In what Satir called a therapeutic *parts party*, clients are encouraged to become aware of these parts and learn to use them "in an harmonious and integrated manner" (Satir & Baldwin, 1983, p. 258).

Satir contended that the self—the core of every person—consists of eight separate but interacting elements or levels, which together exert a constant influence on a person's well-being. To tap the individual's nourishing potentials, Satir claimed to work at one or more of the following levels: physical (the body), intellectual (thoughts, facts, left-brain activity), emotional (feelings, intuition, right-brain activity), sensual (sound, sight, touch, taste, smell), interactional (I-Thou communication between oneself and others), contextual (colors, sound, light, temperature, movement, space, time), nutritional (solids and fluids ingested), and spiritual (one's relationship to life's meaning, the soul, life force). Each approach is important, she insisted, from the tactile contact with one needy family member to the spiritual experience required by another.

As noted, Satir believed all persons possess all the resources they need for positive growth, if she could help them harness their potential to nourish themselves. Building self-esteem, promoting self-worth, exposing and correcting discrepancies in how the family communicates—these were the issues Satir tackled as she attempted to help each member of the family develop "wellness" and become as "whole" as possible. The humanistic influence of the human potential movement on these goals, aimed at achieving more healthy living patterns rather than offering "treatment," is unmistakable.

Family Roles and Communication Styles. Satir contended that the way the family communicates reflects the feelings of self-worth of its members. Dysfunctional communication (indirect, unclear, incomplete, unclarified, inaccurate, distorted, inappropriate) characterizes a dysfunctional family system. One of Satir's lasting contributions is her simple, but far from simplistic, classification of styles of communication. She argued that under stress, a person in a relationship with another person communicates in one of five ways (Satir, 1972). These styles are expressed through body position and body language as much as through verbal behavior. The *placater* acts weak, tentative, self-effacing; always agrees, apologizes, tries to please. The *blamer* dominates, invariably finds fault with others, and self-righteously accuses. The *super-reasonable* person adopts a rigid stance, remains detached, calm, cool, maintaining intellectual control while making certain not to become emotionally involved. The *irrelevant* person distracts others and seems unable to relate to anything going on. Only the *congruent communicator* seems real, genuinely expressive, responsible for sending straight (not double-binding or other confusing) messages in their appropriate context.

Various combinations of these styles exist in most families. For example, take the case of a blaming wife, a blaming husband, and a placating child triad: "It's the school, they don't teach anything anymore"; "It's the child down the street, that's where she's learned those bad words"; "It's the way you've raised her, she's just like you"; "I'll try to do better, Daddy, you're absolutely right. I'll stop watching TV tomorrow, go to the library . . . leave the dishes and I'll do them tomorrow after school." In a blamer/super-reasonable couple, the wife might complain bitterly, "We hardly ever make love anymore; don't you have any feelings for me?" The husband might respond coldly, "Of course I do or I wouldn't be married to you. Perhaps we define the word *love* differently." In the case of a conversation between a super-reasonable parent ("Let's discuss precisely why you seem to be having difficulties with your math problems tonight") and the irrelevant child ("It's time for my shower now"), nothing gets settled or resolved and the tension is maintained if not increased. Table 6.1 on the following page illustrates Satir's four-stance model of dysfunctional family communication.

Satir maintained that these roles are essentially poses that keep distressed people from exposing their true feelings because they lack the self-esteem that would allow them to be themselves. Placaters are afraid to risk disapproval if they speak up or disagree or act in any way independent of a parent or spouse. Blamers also feel endangered and react by attacking in order to cover up feeling empty and unloved themselves. Super-reasonable people only feel safe at a distance and rely

Table 6.1 Four Dysfunctional Communication Stances Adopted under Stress (Satir)

Category	*Caricature*	*Typical verbal expression*	*Body posture*	*Inner feeling*
Placater	Service	"Whatever you want is okay. I'm just here to make you happy."	Grateful, bootlicking, begging, self-flagellating	"I am like a nothing. Without you I am dead. I am worthless."
Blamer	Power	"You never do anything right. What is the matter with you?"	Finger pointing, loud, tyrannical, enraged	"I am lonely and unsuccessful."
Super-reasonable	Intellect	"If one were to observe carefully, one might notice the workworn hands of someone present here."	Monotone voice, stiff, machinelike, computerlike	"I feel vulnerable."
Irrelevant	Sponteneity	Words unrelated to what others are saying. For example, in midst of family dispute: "What are we having for dinner?"	In constant movement, constant chatter, distracting	"Nobody cares. There is no place for me."

(Adapted from Bandler, Grinder, & Satir, 1976)

on their intellect to keep from acknowledging that they too have feelings and are vulnerable. Irrelevant people (often a youngest child in a family or a family pet) gain approval only by acting cute and harmless. Satir, a warm, caring, nurturing person, but also capable of being fearlessly direct, inevitably tried to facilitate straight talk between family members, encouraging them to be congruent in their communications, matching words to feelings to body stance, without qualification.

The "Seed" Model. In her workshops, Satir often presented two contrasting views of the world, which she labeled the "Threat and Reward" model and the "Seed" model. Relationships in the former suppose a hierarchy in which some people define rules for others to follow without question. The hierarchy is based on roles that powerful individuals hold onto for life. While those on top are not necessarily malevolent, their behavior helps create individuals who feel weak and have low self-esteem. Conformity is expected in the "Threat and Reward" model, whether based on gender or lower-status positions in society. The cost of nonconformity is guilt, fear, or rejection. Resentment and hostile feelings also are common, and, for some people, feelings of hopelessness may be present.

In the "Seed" model, personhood rather than role determines identity, and every person is born with a potential that may be fulfilled. While roles and status differences exist (parent-child, doctor-patient), they define relationships only within certain contexts, and are not based on permanent status or role differences outside of that context. In the "Seed" model, change is viewed as an ongoing life process, and as an opportunity for growth. Satir was a strong advocate of the "Seed" model, insisting that given the proper conditions of nurture, children, like seedlings, can develop into healthy adults.

Family Assessment and Intervention. Satir tried to help people feel good about themselves, often as a result of her own boundless, optimistic approach to life. She tended to work with families in terms of their members' day-to-day functioning and their emotional experiences with each other. She taught people congruent ways of communicating by helping to restore the use of their senses and the ability to get in touch with and accept what they were really feeling. Thus, she helped individuals (and families) build their sense of self-worth; she opened up possibilities for making choices and bringing about changes in relationships (Bandler, Grinder, & Satir, 1976).

Because Satir believed human beings have within them all the resources that they need in order to flourish, she directed her interventions at helping families gain access to their nourishing potentials—and then learn to use them. This is a growth-producing approach in which she encouraged people to take whatever risks were necessary in order to take charge of their own lives. Early in the treatment process, Satir would present herself as a teacher introducing the family to a new language, helping them to understand their communication "discrepancies," blocking the kinds of repetitive sequences that end with members falling into the incongruent family communication styles discussed earlier.

Satir's primary talent was as a therapist and trainer rather than a theory builder or researcher. She aimed at accessibility in her writing style, consistent with her desire for clear and direct communication, although her concepts (self-esteem;

family pain; family health) often lacked precision. She was a vigorous, down-to-earth, massively perceptive person who engaged a family authoritatively from the first session onward. She spoke simply and directly, kept up a running account of what she was doing with the family, tried to pass along her communication skills to family members, then arranged encounters between members according to the rules she had taught them. In the following example from her early work (Satir, 1967), the parents and their children, Johnny (age 10) and Patty (age 7), are being seen together; Johnny, the identified patient, is having behavior problems at school. Satir wants to clarify what ideas each member has about what to expect from therapy and why each is there. Note how she tries to help the family members (1) recognize individual differences among them by having each member speak for himself or herself; (2) accept disagreements and differing perceptions of the same situation; and most important, (3) say what they see, think, and feel in order to bring disagreements out into the open.

Patty:	Mother said we were going to talk about family problems.
Therapist:	What about Dad? Did he tell you the same thing?
Patty:	No.
Therapist:	What did Dad say?
Patty:	He said we were going for a ride.
Therapist:	I see. So you got some information from Mother and some information from Dad. What about you, Johnny. Where did you get your information?
Johnny:	I don't remember.
Therapist:	You don't remember who told you?
Mother:	I don't think I said anything to him, come to think of it. He wasn't around at the time, I guess.
Therapist:	How about you, Dad? Did you say anything to Johnny?
Father:	No, I thought Mary had told him.
Therapist:	(to Johnny) Well, then, how could you remember if nothing was said?
Johnny:	Patty said we were going to see a lady about the family.
Therapist:	I see. So you got your information from your sister, whereas Patty got a clear message from both Mother and Dad. (Shortly, she asks the parents what they remember saying.)
Therapist:	How about that, Mother? Were you and Dad able to work this out together—what you would tell the children?
Mother:	Well, you know, I think this is one of our problems. He does things with them and I do another.
Father:	I think this is a pretty unimportant thing to worry about.

Therapist: Of course it is, in one sense. But then we can use it, you know, to see how messages get across in the family. One of the things we work on in families is how family members communicate—how clearly they get their message across. We will have to see how Mother and Dad can get together so that Johnny and Patty can get a clear message. (Later, she explains to the children why the family is there.)

Therapist: Well, then. I'll tell you why Mother and Dad have come here. They have come here because they were unhappy about how things were going in the family and they want to work out ways so that everyone can get more pleasure from family life.

(Source: Satir, 1967, pp. 143–145)[2]

In this brief excerpt we also see Satir's effort to build self-esteem in each family member and to emphasize that each person is unique and has the right to express his or her own views without another person (for example, a parent) answering for him or her. Warm and caring herself, with a strong set of humanistic values, Satir stressed the role of intimacy in family relationships as a vehicle for growth among all family members. A healthy family, to Satir, is a place where members can ask for what they need, a place where needs are met and individuality is allowed to flourish. Dysfunctional families do not permit individuality and members fail to develop a sense of self-worth. If parental messages to one another or to their children are incongruent or confusing, then family communication across generations tends to be similarly unclear or confounded. Parents with low self-esteem communicate poorly and contribute to feelings of low self-esteem in their children.

In some cases, Satir initiated a family's treatment by compiling a **family life chronology** to understand the history of the family's development. As outlined in Table 6.2 and as described in greater detail by Satir (1967), the family life chronology goes beyond the simple gathering of historical facts. Rather, Satir attempted to force family members to think about the relevant concepts that had formed the basis for their developing relationships, how the family's ideology, values, and commitments had emerged and changed over time, and, in general, what the impact of the past had been on the family as a whole as it functioned in the present. In the process, she carefully commented on possible trends and introduced ideas to which she intended to return in later sessions.

In her work with families, Satir gathered information to ascertain the way the family members themselves wanted their family experience to be. What did they seek and what resources had they already developed to achieve it? For the therapist, this information is a key to the process of opening up the family system to the possibilities of growth and change and preparing the members for active participation in creating a new state of existence. As the work progresses, the information

2. A more recent and far more detailed description and analysis of Satir's work with a family can be found in Satir and Baldwin (1983). The major portion of the book is devoted to a transcript of one of Satir's family therapy demonstrations, including a step-by-step explanation of her techniques and interventions.

gathered early in therapy is discussed openly so that the members understand more clearly the process that brought them to where they are now and what steps are in order to make the changes they desire. As they learn to understand and trust each other, past miscommunications can be uncovered and corrected. The verbal communication among family members begins to match the nonverbal behavior. In this respect, the therapist's chief role is to be a model for the desired change. The therapist's messages must be congruent; gestures and tone of voice must match the words.

Table 6.2 Main Flow of Family Life Chronology to Family as a Whole

Therapist asks about the problem.

TO MATES:
Asks about how they met, when they decided to marry, and so on.

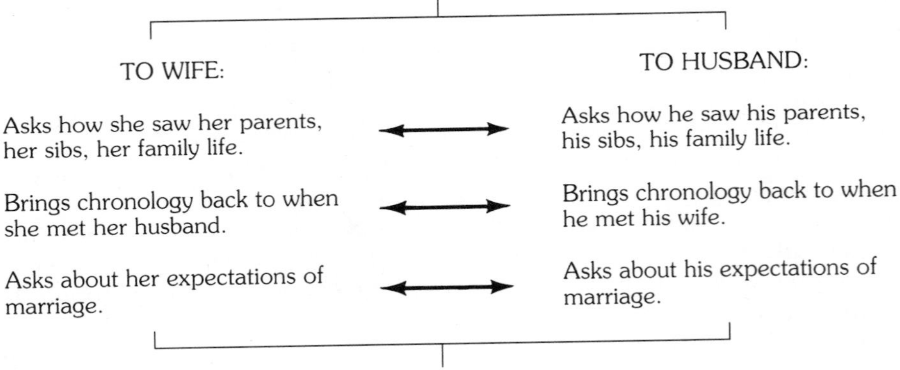

TO MATES:
Asks about early married life. Comments on influence of past.

TO MATES AS PARENTS:
Asks about their expectations of parenting. Comments on the influence of the past.

TO CHILD:
Asks about his views of his parents, how he sees them having fun, disagreeing, and so on.

TO FAMILY AS A WHOLE:
Reassures family that it is safe to comment.
Stresses need for clear communication.
Gives closure, points to next meeting, gives hope.

(Source: Satir, 1967, p. 135)

If parents are models of confused and ambiguous communication, Satir believed the therapist must show them how to change, how to get in touch with their own feelings, how to listen to others, how to ask for clarification if they do not understand another person's message, and so on. Through her gentle, matter-of-fact questioning, Satir enabled parents to listen to their children's statements and opinions for the first time and the children to understand their parents' views and behavior. In time, with the feedback process flowing in both directions, congruent communication replaces the blaming, placating, super-reasonable, even irrelevant family communication styles described earlier.

In the final phase of treatment, the therapist assists the family to solidify its changes and gains. In effect, a new family history gives the family the confidence to take further risks toward growth.

Family Reconstruction. **Family reconstruction**, a therapeutic innovation developed by Satir in the late 1960s, attempts to guide clients to unlock dysfunctional patterns stemming from their families of origin. Blending elements of Gestalt therapy, guided fantasy, hypnosis, psychodrama, role playing, and **family sculpting** (physically molding family members into characteristic poses representing one family member's view of family relationships), the idea is to shed outgrown family rules and dislodge early misconceptions. Used with families as well as in group therapy settings (Nerin, 1986), family reconstruction is a process that takes family members through certain fixed stages of their lives. By reenacting their family's multigenerational drama, members have an opportunity to reclaim their roots, and in the process perhaps view old perceptions in a new light, thereby changing entrenched perceptions, feelings, and beliefs (Nerin, 1989).

Generally speaking, family reconstruction has three goals: (1) to reveal to family members the source of their old learning; (2) to enable them to develop a more realistic picture of the personhood of their parents; and (3) to pave the way for members to find their own personhood.

Within a group setting, usually with enough members so that separate actors can portray each family member, the client (here called the Explorer) elicits the aid of others to play key family roles in the history of the Explorer's extended family across at least three generations. With the therapist acting as the Guide, the Explorer works through lingering family conflicts (for example, "healing" a relationship between him and his mother) in an effort to reconstruct the past mysteries of his or her life, come away with a new understanding of past events, and as a result become free to maximize his or her potential.

The Guide leads the Explorer through the reconstruction, asking questions based on a chronological account of the family history extending over several generations. A trusting relationship between Guide, Explorer, and auxiliary members is essential if the Explorer is to maximize learning from the process.

Satir is quoted (Nerin, 1989) as saying:

> When one views human life as sacred, as I do, family reconstruction becomes a spiritual as well as a cognitive experience to free human energy from the shackles of the past, thus paving the way for the evolvement of being more fully human. (p. 55)

The Avanta Network. For the last decade of her life, Satir moved away from the mainstream of the family therapy movement. While continuing to travel around the world as a kind of roving emissary of humanistic family therapy, Satir was persuaded to try to supply a systematic rationale for her interventions. With two colleagues who have analyzed and devised a model of Satir's linguistic style with families (Bandler, Grinder, & Satir, 1976), she began to identify the key elements in her therapeutic approach: challenging the built-in expectations in the family's existing communication patterns; helping the family members work together to understand what they want in terms of change; preparing the family for a new growth experience; helping the members learn a new family process for coping; and providing the tools they will need to continue the change process after therapy. Most important, their linguistic analysis indicated she taught the actual skills necessary to communicate differently as a family. Having learned these skills, family members presumably would be able to cope more creatively and effectively with any new problem or crisis using the strategies they themselves developed during family therapy.

Having developed a worldwide following, Satir turned her attention to larger systems. In 1977, as an outgrowth of her humanistic orientation, she formed the Avanta Network (*avanti* is Italian for "moving ahead"; thus, Avanta referred to "going beyond"), a nonprofit organization to train others in her therapeutic outlook and procedures. Beginning in 1980 and up to the time of her death in 1988, she conducted annual month-long training experiences throughout the world, offering other therapists an opportunity to combine personal growth with skills acquisition. Sensory and body awareness, learning congruent communication patterns, resolving residual problems of one's triad of origin, family reconstructions, and parts parties were all included in what Satir referred to as a Process Community.

Throughout her career, Satir concerned herself with individual health as well as personal and social responsibility. To that end, she spent her last years putting into practice her concern for helping others achieve positive self-worth. As one of her final projects, she spent a month in the Soviet Union, demonstrating her techniques, offering training, and working for world peace.

SUMMARY

Experiential/humanistic family therapists use the immediacy of the therapeutic encounter with family members to help catalyze the family's natural drive toward growth and the fulfillment of the individuals' potentials. Essentially nontheoretical and nonhistorical, the approach stresses action over insight or interpretation, primarily by providing a growth-enhancing experience through family-therapist interactions.

Major practitioners of the experiential approach are Carl Whitaker and Walter Kempler. Whitaker, who some 30 years ago began redefining a schizophrenic's symptoms as signs of arrested growth, has continued in his work with families to stress both intrapsychic and interpersonal barriers to development and maturity. His family therapy approach, often involving a cotherapist, is designed to capitalize on both the real and symbolic experiences that arise from the therapeutic process, and is aimed at bringing enlightenment. Claiming that his interventions are largely controlled by his unconscious, Whitaker promotes a "psychotherapy of the absurd" designed to shock, confuse, and ultimately activate a stalled or disrupted family system. In the process he seeks a growth-producing experience for himself, believing that a therapist who does not personally benefit, therapeutically speaking, from the encounter has little to give to client families.

Kempler, a practitioner of Gestalt family therapy, is adamant in dealing only with the *now*—the moment-to-moment immediacy shared by the therapist and the family members. Like most Gestalt therapists, Kempler guides individuals to reach beyond their customary self-deceptive games, defenses, and facades. Uncompromisingly honest himself, he confronts and challenges all family members to explore how their self-awareness is blocked and to channel their increased awareness into more productive and fulfilling relationships with each other.

The most celebrated humanistically oriented family therapist is Virginia Satir. Over a thirty-year period, until her death in 1988, Satir was at the forefront of the family therapy movement. Her demonstrations with families were known around the world. Her approach to families combined her early interest in clarifying communication "discrepancies" between family members with humanistically oriented efforts to build self-esteem and self-worth in all the members. Believing that human beings have within themselves the resources they need in order to flourish, Satir viewed her task as one of helping people gain access to their nourishing potentials and teaching people to use them effectively. The Avanta Network represents her last effort to help others around the world to "become more fully human."

Chapter Seven

Bowen's Approach to Theory and Practice

By turning to Murray Bowen, one of the foremost original thinkers in the field, we intend to expound on a theory that represents the foundation from which much of mainstream family therapy has sprung. Bowen, the developer of **family systems theory**, conceptualizes the family as an emotional unit, a network of interlocking relationships, best understood when analyzed within a multigenerational or historical framework. His theoretical contributions, along with their accompanying therapeutic efforts, represent a bridge between psychodynamically oriented approaches that emphasize self-development, intergenerational issues, and the significance of the past, and the systems approaches that restrict their attention to the family unit as it is presently constituted and currently interacting.

A key figure in the development of family therapy, Murray Bowen remains today its major theoretician. Since his early clinical work with schizophrenics and their families at the Menninger Clinic, as well as at NIMH, Bowen has stressed the importance of theory for research, for teaching purposes, and as a blueprint for guiding a clinician's actions during psychotherapy. He is concerned with what he considers the field's lack of a coherent and comprehensive theory of either family development or therapeutic intervention and its all-too-tenuous connections between theory and practice. In particular, Bowen (1978) decries efforts to dismiss theory in favor of an intuitive "seat of the pants" approach, which he considers to be especially stressful for a novice therapist coping with an intensely emotional, problem-laden family. The contrast between Bowen's cerebral, deliberate, theoretical approach and Satir's or Whitaker's spontaneous, emotional, nontheoretical way of working with families will surely not be lost on the reader.

By educational background and training, Bowen was imbued with the individual focus of psychoanalysis, a fact reflected in some of his early (1957–1963) theoretical formulations (Bowen, 1976). His professional interest in the family, however, began early in his career, when he was a psychiatrist at the Menninger Clinic in the late 1940s. Intrigued, from a research perspective, by the family relationships of inpatients, especially schizophrenics (Kerr & Bowen, 1988), Bowen became particularly interested in the impact of a mother-child **symbiosis**, consistent with his then psychoanalytic viewpoint, in the development of schizophrenia. Assuming schizophrenia to be the result of an unresolved symbiotic attachment to the mother, herself immature and in need of the child to fulfill her own emotional needs, Bowen began working with mother and child together. In 1951, he organized a research project in which mothers and their schizophrenic children resided together in cottages on the clinic grounds for several months at a time.

In 1954, Bowen, eager to put his new ideas into clinical practice but stifled by what he saw as the prevailing emphasis on conventional individual psychiatry at the Menninger Clinic, moved his professional activities to the National Institute of Mental Health in Maryland. Soon he had entire families with schizophrenic members living on the research wards for months at a time, where he and his associates were better able to observe ongoing family interaction. Here Bowen discovered that the emotional intensity of the mother-child interaction was even more powerful than he had suspected. More important, the emotional intensity seemed to characterize relationships throughout the family, not merely those between mother and child. Fathers and siblings were found to play key roles in fostering and perpetuating family problems. The reciprocal functioning of all the individual members within the family became so apparent that Bowen began to expand his earlier mother-child symbiosis concepts to now viewing the entire family as an emotional unit. Although he did not adopt a cybernetic epistemology per se, Bowen had moved from concentrating on the separate parts that make up the whole to a focus on the whole itself, what he called the family emotional system. The conceptual shift was to prove to be a turning point in his thinking, as Bowen increasingly viewed human emotional functioning as part of a natural system, following the same laws that govern other systems in nature, no less valid than the laws of gravity.

When the NIMH project ended in 1959, Bowen moved to Georgetown University in Washington, D.C., where he remains today. Working in an outpatient setting, and with families many of whom had less severe problems than schizophrenia, he began to formulate a comprehensive family systems theory that could be applied to processes occurring in all families, functional as well as dysfunctional ones. At the same time, Bowen proposed a method of therapy based on a solid theoretical foundation (in contrast to those techniques that have evolved on an empirical or experiential basis). Developing a training program in family therapy while continually refining the concepts he first developed in the 1960s, he published *Family Therapy in Clinical Practice* in 1978, detailing his theoretical formulations and offering therapeutic techniques consistent with that theory. An updated explication of Bowen's ideas has been offered more recently by Michael Kerr (Kerr & Bowen, 1988), a longtime associate of Bowen's at the Georgetown University Family Center.

FAMILY SYSTEMS THEORY

As Bowen moved toward developing the theory that emotional disturbance in an individual arises from, and is maintained by, relational binds with others, he adopted the language of systems science and its broader view of human functioning. Departing from previous theories of psychopathology, in which mental disturbances were viewed as rooted within the person, Bowen emphasized the role of the *family as an emotional unit* in the etiology of individual dysfunction. He conceptualized interlocking relationships within the family as being governed by the same counterbalancing life forces that operate in all natural systems (Kerr & Bowen, 1988).

Rather than functioning as autonomous psychological entities, individual family members are inextricably tied in thinking, feeling, and behavior to the family relationship system. Moreover, according to Bowen, multigenerational trends in functioning require the clinician's attention, since he hypothesized an orderly and predictable relationship process connecting the functioning of family members across generations.

Bowen's theory, which we are about to present, is derived from the view of the human family as one type of natural system. It has only passing acquaintance with general systems theory. In an attempt to distinguish the two, once the notion of family systems came into widespread use among therapists, Bowen decided to change the name of his theory from family systems theory to Bowen theory. While general systems theory developed from assumptions that grew out of studies of feedback mechanisms and self-regulating systems, as we have elaborated in Chapter 3, Bowen's work offers a natural systems theory in which the human family is seen as appearing as the result of an evolutionary process in nature. Thus, like all living systems (ant colonies, the tides, the solar system), humans and the human family are guided by processes common in nature. In particular, Bowen has concerned himself with a special kind of natural system—the family's emotional system (Kerr & Bowen, 1988).

Bowen's theories have attracted many family therapists, and over the years Bowen has become a leading trainer of family therapists, numbering among his students and colleagues such currently well-known family therapists as Philip Guerin, Elizabeth Carter, Monica McGoldrick, Thomas Fogarty, and Michael Kerr. In 1977, Bowen became the first president of the newly formed American Family Therapy Association.

BOWEN'S EIGHT INTERLOCKING THEORETICAL CONCEPTS

In its present state of refinement, Bowen's theory of the family as an emotional relationship system consists of eight interlocking concepts. Six of the concepts, formulated before 1963, address emotional processes taking place in the nuclear and extended families. Two later concepts, emotional cutoff and societal regression, added in 1975, speak to the emotional process across generations in a family and in society (Papero, 1983). According to Bowen, then, the eight forces shaping family functioning are

1. Differentiation of self
2. Triangles
3. Nuclear family emotional system
4. Family projection process
5. Emotional cutoff
6. Multigenerational transmission process
7. Sibling position
8. Societal regression

Differentiation of Self

The cornerstone of Bowen's carefully worked out theory is his notion of the forces within the family that make for togetherness and the opposing forces that lead to individuality. To Bowen, the degree to which a **differentiation of self** occurs in an individual reflects the extent to which that person is able to distinguish between the intellectual process and the feeling process he or she is experiencing. Thus, differentiation of self is related to the degree to which one is able to choose between having his or her functions guided by feelings or thoughts.[1]

Those individuals with the greatest **fusion** between the two function most poorly; they are likely to be at the mercy of involuntary emotional reactions and tend to become dysfunctional even under low levels of stress. Just as they are unable to differentiate thought from feeling, such persons have trouble differentiating themselves from others and thus fuse easily with whatever emotions dominate the family.

Bowen (1966) introduced the concept of **undifferentiated family ego mass**, derived from psychoanalysis, to convey the idea of a family emotionally

1. A number of feminists, such as Hare-Mustin (1978) and Lerner (1986), dispute this distinction, arguing that what seems to be valued here are qualities for which men are socialized, while simultaneously devaluated are those qualities for which women are socialized.

"stuck together," one where "a conglomerate emotional oneness . . . exists in all levels of intensity" (p. 171). For example, the symbiotic relationship of interdependency between mother and child may represent the most intense version of this concept; a father's detachment may be the least intense. The degree to which any one member is involved in the family from moment to moment depends on that person's basic level of involvement in the family ego mass. Sometimes the emotional closeness can be so intense that family members know each other's feelings, thoughts, fantasies, and dreams. This intimacy may lead to uncomfortable "overcloseness," according to Bowen, and ultimately to a phase of mutual rejection between two members. In other words, within a family system, emotional tensions shift over time (sometimes slowly, sometimes rapidly) in a series of alliances and rejections. What Bowen had initially characterized in psychoanalytic terms—*undifferentiated family ego mass*—he later recast in systems language as *fusion-differentiation.* Both sets of terms underscore Bowen's insistence that maturity and self-actualization demand that an individual become free of unresolved emotional attachments to his or her family of origin.

For illustrative purposes, Bowen (1966) proposed a theoretical scale (not an actual psychometric instrument) for evaluating an individual's differentiation level. As noted in Figure 7.1, the greater the degree of undifferentiation (no sense of self or a weak or unstable personal identity), the greater the emotional fusion into a common self with others (the undifferentiated family ego mass). A person with a strong sense of self ("These are my opinions . . . This is who I am . . . This is what I will do, but not this . . .") expresses convictions and clearly defined beliefs. Such a person is said by Bowen to be expressing a *solid self.* He or she does not compromise that self for the sake of marital bliss or to please parents or achieve family harmony, or through coercion.

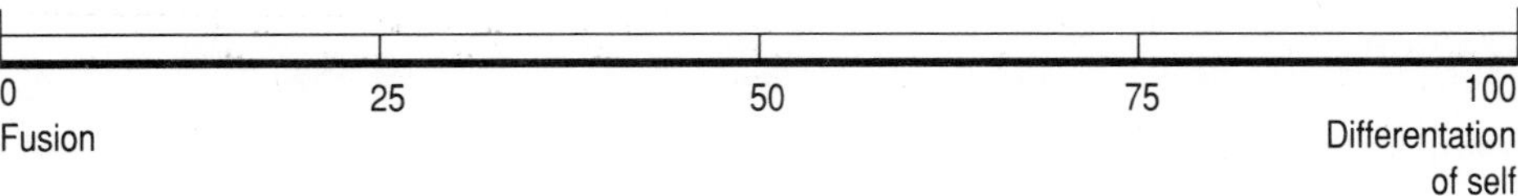

Figure 7.1 The theoretical differentiation-of-self scale, according to Bowen's conception, distinguishing people according to the degree of fusion or differentiation between their emotional and intellectual functioning. Those at the lowest level (0–25) are emotionally fused to the family and others and lead lives in which their thinking is submerged and their feelings dominate. The lives of those in the 25–50 range are still guided by their emotional system and the reactions of others; goal-directed behavior is present but carried out in order to seek the approval of others. In the 50–75 range, thinking is sufficiently developed so as not to be dominated by feeling when stress occurs, and there is a reasonably developed sense of self. Those rare people functioning between 75–100 routinely separate their thinking from their feelings; they base decisions on the former but are free to lose themselves in the intimacy of a close relationship. Bowen (1978) considers someone at 75 to have a very high level of differentiation and all those over 60 to constitute a small percentage of society.

People at the low extreme are those whose emotions and intellect are so fused that their lives are dominated by the feelings of those around them. As a consequence, they are easily stressed into dysfunction. Bowen considers them to be expressing a *pseudo self*, which they may deceive themselves into thinking is real, but which is composed of the opinions and values of others. Those far fewer individuals at the high end are emotionally mature; because their intellectual or rational functioning remains relatively (although not completely) dominant during stressful periods, they can take action independent of the emotionality around them. In the midrange are persons with relative degrees of fusion or differentiation. Note that *the scale eliminates the need for the concept of normality*. It is entirely possible for people at the low end of the scale to keep their lives in emotional equilibrium and stay free of symptoms, thus appearing to satisfy the popular criteria for being "normal." However, these people are not only more vulnerable to stress than those higher on the scale, but also, under stress, are apt to develop symptoms from which they recover far more slowly than those at the high end of the scale. According to Bowen, any person's level of differentiation reflects that individual's level of differentiation from the family as well as from others outside the family group. A moderate-to-high level of differentiation permits interaction with others without fear of fusion (losing one's sense of self in the relationship). While all relationships ranging from poorly to well-differentiated ones are in a state of dynamic equilibrium, the flexibility in that balance decreases as differentiation decreases. Figure 7.2 illustrates the varying degrees to which a person's functioning can be influenced by the relationship process.

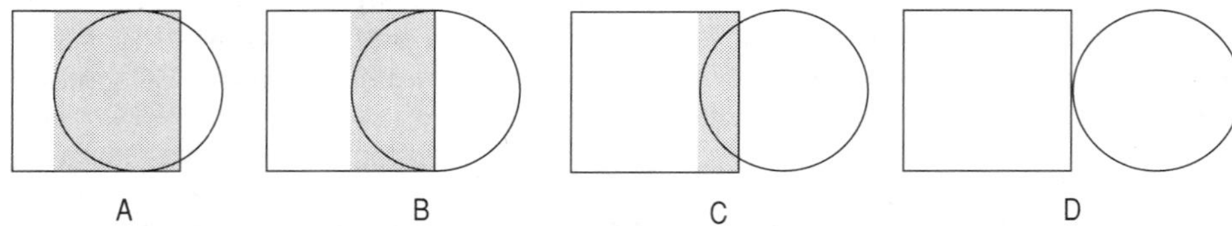

Figure 7.2 Relationship A is one where the functioning of each person is almost completely determined by the relationship process. The degree to which individual functioning is either enhanced or undermined by the relationship is indicated by the shaded area. The clear area indicates the capacity for self-determined functioning while in a relationship. Relationships B and C are progressively better differentiated. Individual functioning, therefore, is less likely to be enhanced or undermined by the relationship process. Relationship D is theoretical for the human. It represents two people who can be actively involved in a relationship yet remain self-determined. (Source: Kerr & Bowen, 1988, p. 71)

Bowen's theory assumes that an instinctively rooted life force in every human propels the developing child to grow up to be an emotionally separate person, able to think, feel, and act as an individual. At the same time, Bowen proposes that a corresponding life force, also instinctively rooted, propels the child and family to remain emotionally connected. As a result of these counterbalancing forces, argues Bowen, no one ever achieves complete emotional separation from the family of origin. However, there are considerable differences in the amount of separation each of us accomplishes, as well as differences in the degree to which children from the same set of parents emotionally separate from the family. The latter is due to characteristics of the different parental relationships established with each child, as we intend to elaborate later in this section.

Triangles

In addition to its interest in the degree of integration of self, Bowen's theory also emphasizes anxiety or emotional tension within the individual or in that person's relationships. Stress between husband and wife may arise, for example, as they attempt to balance their needs for closeness with their needs for individuation. The greater their fusion, the more difficult the task of finding a stable balance satisfying to both. One way to resolve such two-person stress within a family, according to Bowen (1978), is to triangulate—bring in another family member to form a three-person interaction.

The basic building block in a family's emotional system is the *triangle*, according to Bowen. During periods when anxiety is low and external conditions are calm, two persons may engage in a comfortable back-and-forth exchange of feelings. However, the stability of this situation is threatened if one or both participants gets upset or anxious, either because of internal stress or from stress external to the twosome. When a certain intensity level is reached, one or both partners will involve a vulnerable third person. According to Bowen (1978), the twosome may "reach out" and pull in the other person, the emotions may "overflow" to the third person, or that person may be emotionally "programmed" to initiate involvement. This triangle dilutes the anxiety; it is both more stable and more flexible than the twosome and has a higher tolerance for dealing with stress. When anxiety in the triangle subsides, the emotional configuration returns to the peaceful twosome plus the lone outsider. However, should anxiety in the triangle increase, one person in the triangle may involve another outsider, and so forth. Sometimes such triangulation can reach beyond the family, involving social agencies or the courts.

Generally speaking, the higher the degree of family fusion, the more intense and insistent the triangulating efforts will be; the least well-differentiated person is particularly vulnerable to being drawn in to reduce tension. Beyond seeking relief of discomfort, the family relies on triangles to help maintain an optimum level of closeness and distance between members while permitting them the greatest freedom from anxiety (Papero, 1983).

Bowen (1976) refers to the triangle as the smallest stable relationship system. By definition, a two-person system is unstable (Bowen, 1975) and forms itself into a three-person system or triad under stress, as each partner attempts to create a triangle in order to reduce the increasing tension of their relationship. As more people become involved, the system may become a series of interlocking triangles, in some cases heightening the very problem the multiple triangulations sought to resolve. For example, a distraught mother's request for help from her husband in dealing with their son is met with withdrawal from the father. As the mother-son conflict escalates, she communicates her distress to another son, who proceeds to get into conflict with his brother for upsetting their mother. What began as a mother-son conflict has now erupted into interlocking conflicts—between mother and son, brother and brother, and mother and father.

Thus, triangulation does not always reduce tension. Kerr & Bowen (1988) point out that triangulation has at least four possible outcomes: (1) a stable twosome can be destabilized by the addition of a third person (for example, the birth of a child brings conflict to a harmonious marriage); (2) a stable twosome can be destabilized by the removal of a third person (marital conflict follows after a child leaves home, and thus is no longer available to be triangulated into their conflict); (3) an unstable twosome can be stabilized by the addition of a third person (a conflictful marriage becomes more harmonious after the birth of a child); and (4) an unstable twosome can be stabilized by the removal of a third person (conflict is reduced by avoiding a third person who has consistently taken sides).

To give another familiar example, note that conflict between siblings quickly attracts a parent's attention. Let us assume that the parent has positive feelings toward both children who, at the moment, are in conflict with each other. If the parent can control his or her emotional responsiveness and manage not to take sides while staying in contact with both children, the emotional intensity between the original twosome, the siblings, will diminish. (A parallel situation exists when parents quarrel and a child is drawn into the triangle in an attempt to dilute and thus reduce the strain between the combatants.) Generally speaking, the probability of triangulation within a family is heightened by poor differentiation of family members; conversely, the reliance on triangulation to solve problems helps maintain the poor differentiation of certain family members.

As we discuss later in this chapter when we describe Bowen's therapeutic technique, a similar situation exists when a couple visits a marital/family therapist. Following from this theory, Bowen contends that if the therapist—the third person in the system—can remain involved with both spouses without siding with one or the other, the spouses may learn to view themselves as individual, differentiated selves as well as marital partners. However, if the third person loses emotional contact with the spouses, the twosome will proceed to triangulate with someone else.

Nuclear Family Emotional System

Bowen (1978) contends that people choose mates with equivalent levels of differentiation to their own. Not surprisingly, then, the relatively undifferentiated person will select a spouse who is equally fused to his or her family of origin. It is probable, moreover, that these poorly differentiated people, now a marital couple, will themselves become highly fused and will produce a family with the same characteristics. According to Bowen, the resulting **nuclear family emotional system** will be unstable and will seek various ways to reduce tension and maintain stability. The greater the nuclear family's fusion, the greater will be the likelihood of anxiety and potential instability, and the greater will be the family's propensity to seek resolution through fighting, distancing, the impaired or compromised

functioning of one partner, or banding together over concern for a child (Kerr, 1981).

More specifically, Kerr & Bowen (1988) regard three possible symptomatic patterns in a nuclear family as the product of the intense fusion between partners. Each pattern is intensified by anxiety and, when the intensity reaches a sufficient level, results in a particular form of symptom development. The person (or the relationship) who manifests the specific symptom is largely determined by the patterns of emotional functioning that predominate in that family system. The three patterns are as follows:

1. Physical or emotional dysfunction in a spouse, sometimes becoming chronic, as an alternative to dealing directly with family conflict; the anxiety generated by the undifferentiated functioning of every family member is being absorbed disproportionately by a symptomatic parent.
2. Overt, chronic, unresolved marital conflict, in which cycles of emotional distance and emotional overcloseness occur; both the negative feelings during conflict and the positive feelings for one another during close periods are likely to be equally intense in roller-coaster fashion; the family anxiety is being absorbed by the husband and wife.
3. Psychological impairment in a child, enabling the parents to focus attention on the child and ignore or deny their own lack of differentiation; as the child becomes the focal point of the family problem, the intensity of the parental relationship is diminished, thus the family anxiety is being absorbed in the child's impaired functioning; the lower a child's level of differentiation, the greater will be his or her vulnerability to increases in family anxiety and thus to dysfunction.

Dysfunction in one spouse may take the form of an **overadequate-underadequate reciprocity**, in which one partner takes on most or even all family responsibilities (earning a living, caring for the children, cooking, shopping, and so on) while the other plays the counterpart role of being underresponsible. Fused together, the two pseudo selves develop an arrangement in which one partner increasingly underfunctions while the other takes up the slack by assuming responsibility for them both. When the tilt gets too great, according to Singleton (1982), the one giving up more pseudo self for the sake of family harmony becomes vulnerable to physical or emotional dysfunction.

In some cases, this pattern intertwines with marital conflict, the underadequate one complaining of dominance, inconsiderateness, and so forth from the spouse. The overadequate one is more comfortable with the arrangement until the underadequate one complains or becomes so inadequate as to cause difficulties for the overadequate one. When this occurs, the problem is likely to be seen as belonging to the unhappy underadequate spouse, rather than as a relationship problem for which both need help.

Almost every family has one child who is more vulnerable to fusion than the others, and thus likely to be triangulated into parental conflict. Any significant increase in parental anxiety triggers the child's dysfunctional behavior (in school, at home, or both), leading to even greater anxieties in the parent. In turn, the child's behavior becomes increasingly impaired, sometimes turning into a lifelong pattern of poor functioning.

The nuclear family emotional system is a multigenerational phenomenon. Individuals tend to repeat in their marital choices and other significant relationships the style of relating learned in their families of origin, and to pass along similar patterns to their children. To Bowen, the only effective way to resolve current family problems is to change the interactions with the families of origin. Only then can differentiation proceed and the individuals involved become less overreactive to the emotional forces sweeping through the family.

Family Projection Process

As we have just observed, parents do not respond in the same way to each child in a family, despite their claims to the contrary. Differences in parental behavior make for significant differences in how each child functions. Children who are the object of parental focus tend in general to develop greater fusion to the family than their siblings and consequently remain more vulnerable to emotional stresses within the family (Papero, 1983). The fusion-prone, focused-on child is the one most sensitive to disturbances and incipient signs of instability within the family. Bowen (1976) believes that the parents, themselves immature, select as the object of their attention the most infantile of all their children, regardless of his or her birth order in the family; Bowen calls this the **family projection process**.

The projection process operates within the mother-father-child triangle; the transmission of undifferentiation occurs through the triangulation of the most vulnerable child into the parental relationship. Bowen stresses the sibling positions of the parents in their families of origin as possible clues to which child will be chosen in the next generation. As the child most emotionally attached to the parents of all the children within a family, he or she will have the lowest level of differentiation of self and the most difficulty in separating from the family. Moreover, Kerr (1981) believes that the greater the level of undifferentiation of the parents and the more they rely on the projection process to stabilize the system, the more likely it is that several children will be emotionally impaired. This process of projecting or transmitting parental undifferentiation may begin as early as the initial mother-infant bonding.

The intensity of the family projection process is related to two factors: the degree of immaturity or undifferentiation of the parents and the level of stress or anxiety the family experiences. In one triangulating scenario described by Singleton (1982), the child responds anxiously to the mother's anxiety, she being the principal caretaker; the mother becomes alarmed at what she perceives as the child's problem, and becomes overprotective. Thus a cycle is established in which the mother infantilizes the child, who in turn becomes demanding and impaired. The third leg of the triangle is supplied by the father, who is sensitive to his wife's anxiety and, by attempting to calm her, plays a supporting role to her in dealing with the child. As collaborators, the parents have now stabilized their relationship around a "disturbed" child, and in the process perpetuated the family triangle.

Murray Bowen, M.D.

Emotional Cutoff

Children less involved in the projection process are apt to emerge with a greater ability to withstand fusion, to separate thinking and feeling. Those who are more involved try various strategies upon reaching adulthood, or even before. They may attempt to insulate themselves from the family by geographic separation, through the use of psychological barriers, or by the self-deception that they are free of family ties because actual contact has been broken off. Bowen (1976) considers such supposed freedom an **emotional cutoff**, a flight from unresolved emotional ties, not true emancipation. Avoidance of attachments may simply represent denial of unresolved conflicts and mask unexamined fusion. Kerr (1981) contends that emotional cutoff *reflects* a problem (underlying fusion between generations), *solves* a problem (reducing anxiety associated with making contact), and *creates* a problem (isolating people who might benefit from closer contact).

Cutoffs occur most often in families in which there is a high level of anxiety and emotional dependence (Bowen, 1978). As both increase and greater family cohesiveness is expected, conflicts between family members may be disguised and hidden. Should the fusion-demanding situation reach an unbearable stage, some members may seek greater distance, emotionally, socially, perhaps physically, for self-preservation. When communication is demanded, it is apt to be superficial, inauthentic, and brief. Bowen has suggested that when emotional cutoffs exist between parents and grandparents, then a cutoff between parents and children of the subsequent generation increases in likelihood.

Bowen insists that adults must resolve their emotional attachments to their families of origin. In a very revealing paper about his own family Bowen delivered in 1967 to a national conference of family researchers and therapists ("Towards," 1972), he openly described his personal struggles to achieve a differentiation of self from his own family of origin. Without this differentiation, Bowen argues, family therapists may unknowingly be triangulated into conflicts in their client families (much as they were as children in their own families), perhaps overidentifying with one family member or projecting onto another their own unresolved difficulties. In general, the therapist is vulnerable to the client family's effort to resist change and retain homeostasis. Family therapists need to get in touch with and be free of their own internalized family so that unfinished business from the past does not intrude on current dealings with client families.

Multigenerational Transmission Process

In perhaps his most intriguing formulation, Bowen (1976) proposed the concept of **multigenerational transmission process**, in which severe dysfunction is conceptualized as the result of the operation of the family's emotional system over several generations. Two earlier concepts are crucial here—the selection of a spouse with a similar differentiation level and the family projection process that results in lower levels of self-differentiation for certain offspring.

Assume for a moment that the least well-differentiated members of two families marry—as Bowen's theory would predict—and that at least one of their children, as the result of the projection process, will have an even lower differentiation level. The eventual marriage of this person—again, to someone with a similarly poor differentiation of self—passes along the increasingly lowered level of differentiation to the members of the next generation, who in turn pass it along to the next, and so forth. As each generation produces individuals with progressively poorer differentiation ("weak links"), those people are increasingly vulnerable to anxiety and fusion. Although the process may slow down or remain static over a generation or two, ultimately—it may take as many as eight or ten generations—a level of impairment is reached that is consistent with schizophrenia. If the family encounters severe stress and anxiety, however, schizophrenia may develop in an earlier generation. In some less-stressful cases or under favorable life circumstances, Bowen believes poorly differentiated people may keep their relationship system in relatively symptom-free equilibrium for several generations longer. This process may be reversed, of course, should someone in this lineage marry a person considerably higher on the differentiation-of-self scale. However, as noted earlier, Bowen observes that most persons choose mates at more or less their own level of differentiation.

Sibling Position

Bowen credits Toman's (1961) work on the relationship between birth order and personality with clarifying his own thinking regarding the influence of **sibling position** in the nuclear family emotional process. Toman hypothesized that children develop certain fixed personality characteristics on the basis of their birth order in the family. He offered ten basic personality sibling profiles (such as older brother, younger sister; younger brother, older sister; only child; twins), suggesting that the more closely a marriage duplicates one's sibling place in childhood, the better will be its chance of success. Thus, a firstborn would do well to marry a secondborn, the youngest should marry an older child. He maintained further that, in general, the chances for a successful marriage are increased for persons who grew up with siblings of the opposite sex rather than with same-sex siblings only.

Bowen realized that interactive patterns between marital partners may be related to the position of each partner in his or her family of origin, since birth order frequently predicts certain roles and functions within one's family emotional system. Thus, an oldest child who marries a youngest may expect to take responsibility, make decisions, and so on; this behavior is also expected by the mate on the basis of his or her experiences as the youngest in the family. Two youngest children who marry may both feel overburdened by responsibility and decision making; the marriage of two oldest children may be overly competitive because each spouse is accustomed to being in charge (Kerr, 1981). Note, however, that it is a person's functional position in the family system, not necessarily the actual order of birth, that shapes future expectations and behavior.

Societal Regression

In a final concept, **societal regression**, Bowen extended his thinking to society's emotional functioning. In the least well developed of his theoretical formulations, Bowen argues that society, like the family, contains within it opposing forces toward undifferentiation and toward individuation. Under conditions of chronic stress (population growth, depletion of natural resources) and thus continual anxiety, there is likely to be an erosion of the forces intent on achieving individuation. It is Bowen's (1977) pessimistic view that society's functional level of differentiation has decreased over the last several decades. He calls for better differentiation between intellect and emotion in order for society to make more rational decisions rather than act on the basis of feelings and opt for short-term "band-aid" solutions.

BOWEN'S SYSTEM OF FAMILY THERAPY

Family therapy in the Bowen system occurs in stages. Adopting a neutral and objective role, the therapist first attempts to assess the family's emotional system, past and present, through a series of evaluation interviews and measurement techniques, before intervening therapeutically with the family.

The Evaluation Interview

The appraisal of a symptomatic family begins with the initial telephone contact. Kerr & Bowen (1988) caution the therapist against being drawn into the family emotional system by overresponding to the caller's forceful, charming, or theatrical presentation of the family's problem. Throughout the subsequent therapy, they warn, the therapist must guard against becoming incorporated into the family's problem, taking sides in disputes, or becoming overly sympathetic with one member or angry at another. A therapist who thus becomes fused with the family's emotional system, or allows himself or herself to be triangulated into their conflicts, or becomes engulfed by their anxiety, can have a divisive influence on family functioning and fail to promote further differentiation among family members. While the family must become convinced that the therapist cares and remains interested in them, the therapist must resist their efforts to get him or her emotionally involved.

Objectivity and neutrality, then, should characterize the therapist's behavior in Bowen's system of family therapy. Consistent with his views of the importance of remaining outside the system in order to keep from becoming too subjectively involved, Bowen believes that the more a therapist has worked on becoming differentiated from his or her own family of origin, the more the therapist can remain detached, unswayed, and objective.

Family evaluation interviews are carried out with any combination of family members: a parent, husband and wife, the nuclear family, perhaps including extended family members. Since Bowen views family therapy as a way of conceptualizing a problem rather than as a process that requires a certain number of people to attend the sessions, he is content to work with one family member, especially if that person is motivated to work on self-differentiation from his or her family of origin. In fact, according to Kerr & Bowen (1988), while conjoint sessions are generally useful, at times seeing people together may impede the progress of one or the other. Instead, they argue, if one parent can increase his or her basic level of differentiation, the functioning of the other parent as well as the children will inevitably improve.

Family evaluation interviews begin with a history of the presenting problem, focusing especially on the symptoms (physical, emotional, social) and their impact on the symptomatic person or relationship. If more than one person is present, the therapist is interested in each member's perception of what created and what sustains the problem for which they seek relief, why they seek such help now, and what each hopes to get from the experience. Through a series of such questions, the therapist attempts to assess the pattern of emotional functioning as well as the intensity of the emotional process in the nuclear family of the symptomatic person. What is the relationship system like in this family? What are the current stressors? How well differentiated are the family members? What is the family adaptive level? How stable is the family and how (and how successfully) does it handle anxiety? Are emotional cutoffs operating? The initial interview, which may extend over several sessions, seeks information on all of these issues in assessing the degree of family dysfunction associated with the presenting symptoms, which may appear in one or more family members.

Bowen is particularly interested in the historical pattern of their emotional functioning, their anxiety levels at varying stages of their family life, and the amount of stress experienced in the past compared to current functioning. Of special interest too is whether one spouse's functioning has improved significantly and the other spouse's has declined significantly over the course of their relationship. By probing the history of the symptoms in each family member, he searches for clues as to where the various pressures on the family have been expressed and how effectively the family has adapted to stress since its inception. At this point in the evaluation, the focus has begun to expand beyond the symptomatic person to an examination of the relationship network of the nuclear family.

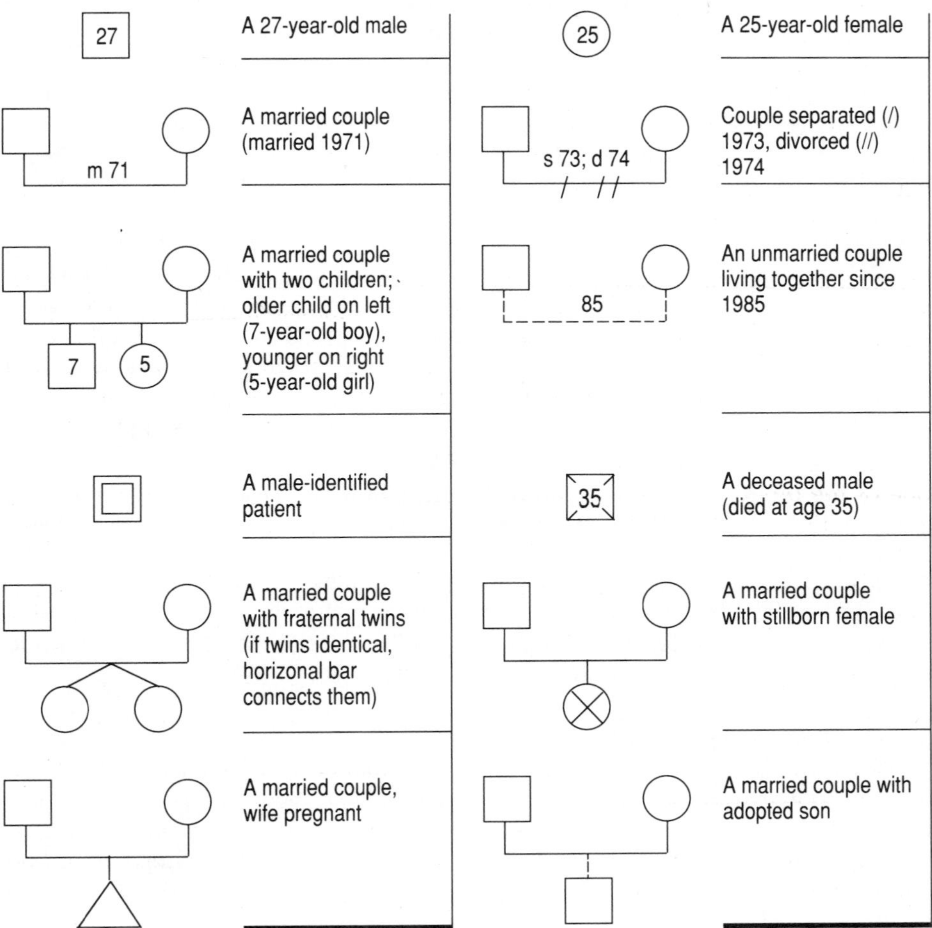

Figure 7.3 A partial set of commonly agreed-upon genogram symbols. (Based on McGoldrick & Gerson, 1985)

The final part of the evaluation interview attempts to understand the nuclear family in the context of the maternal and paternal extended family systems. Bowen is interested in multigenerational patterns of fusion, the nature of the nuclear family's relationship with the extended families, the degree of emotional cutoff of each spouse. Parallels in relationship patterns between the husband and wife and his or her parents may offer important clues of poor differentiation from the families of origin.

The Genogram

Since Bowen believes multigenerational patterns and influences are crucial determinants of nuclear family functioning, he has developed a graphic way of investigating the genesis of the presenting problem by diagramming the family over at least three generations. To aid in the process and to keep the record in pictorial form in front of him, he constructs a family **genogram** in which each partner's family background is laid out. Worked out with the family, it provides a useful tool for allowing therapist and family members alike to examine the ebb and flow of the family's emotional processes in their intergenerational context.

Figure 7.3 on the previous page offers a partial set of commonly used genogram symbols. Together, the symbols provide a visual picture of a family tree: who the members are, what their names are, ages, sibling positions, marital status, divorces, and so on, typically extending back at least three generations for both parents. When relevant, such additional items of information as religious affiliation, occupations, ethnic origins, geographic locations, socioeconomic status, and perhaps significant life events may be included. More than providing a concise pictorial depiction of the nuclear family, the genogram may suggest certain emotional patterns in each partner's family of origin, thus providing data for assessing each spouse's degree of fusion to extended families and to one another. As McGoldrick & Gerson (1985) suggest, family patterns tend to repeat themselves; what happens in one generation will often occur in the next, as the same unresolved emotional issues are replayed from generation to generation.

Genograms often provide families with their first inkling of intergenerational family relationship patterns. Goldenberg & Goldenberg (1990) offer the following example of just such a situation (see Figure 7.4):

A family . . . contacted a counselor because their son, Ivan, was having school difficulties, disrupting class activity and generally being inattentive. The genogram revealed that his mother, Loretta, had been adopted, after her adoptive parents had tried unsuccessfully to have a daughter after three sons. She married early, at 20, soon after the death of her mother. Steve, a middle child whose parents had divorced when he was a preteenager, lived in a single-parent household with his mother, sister, and brother until he married Loretta. Steve and Loretta started their own family before either was 25, perhaps in an effort to create some stability in contrast to what either had known growing up.

The fact that they now have four children (one died in childbirth) suggests a strong involvement in family life, especially because the children's ages are spread over ten years or more. Are the parents being overprotective, perhaps to compensate for what they felt deprived of as youngsters? What was the effect of Loretta's pregnancies over the last several years on the other children? To what extent does Ivan feel he is being displaced as the youngest child by the birth of Bianca? (p. 69)

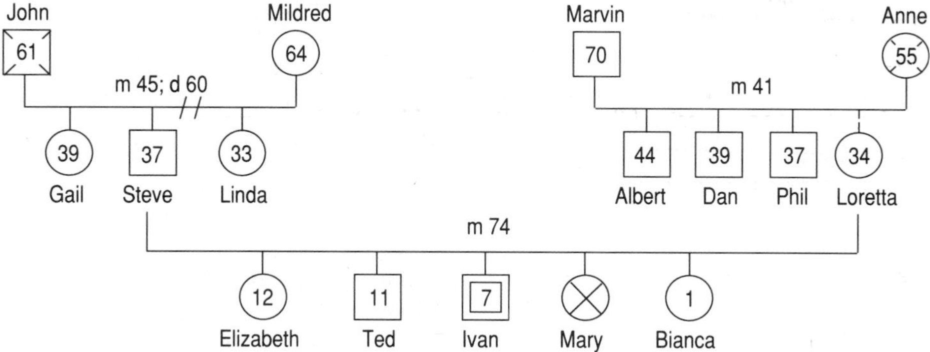

Figure 7.4 Genogram of a three-generation family. (Source: Goldenberg & Goldenberg, 1990, p. 69)

Note how many hypotheses spring from the genogram, to be explored with the family subsequently. Fusion-differentiation issues in the family of origin, the nuclear family emotional system, emotional cutoffs by the parents, sibling positions, and many other of Bowen's concepts appear as possibly relevant to Ivan's presenting symptoms. When evaluation interview data are put into schematic form in a family genogram, therapist and family together are better able to comprehend the underlying emotional processes connecting generations.

Family Intervention Techniques

Therapy based on Bowen's theory, no matter what the nature of the presenting clinical problem is, is always governed by two basic goals: (1) reduction of anxiety and relief from symptoms; and (2) an increase in each participant's level of differentiation in order to improve adaptiveness (Kerr & Bowen, 1988). Generally speaking, the family needs to accomplish the former goal first, before the latter can be undertaken. Ultimately, however, overreactive emotional interactions with the extended family must be changed, leading to greater self-differentiation among nuclear family members.

Bowen's standard method of conducting family therapy is to work with a system consisting of two adults and himself. Even when the identified patient is a symptomatic child, Bowen asks the parents to accept the premise that the basic problem is between the two of them—the family's emotional system—and that the identified patient is not the source of the problem. In such a situation, Bowen may never see the child at all. As Kerr (1981), one of Bowen's associates, explains, "A theoretical system that thinks in terms of family, with a therapeutic method that works toward improvement of the family system, is 'family' regardless of the number of people in the sessions" (p. 232).

Bowen presents himself as a researcher helping the family members become researchers into their own ways of functioning. The term he prefers is coach (having moved during his career, in his own words, "from 'couch' to 'coach' ")—an active expert who helps individuals change the nature of their relationships with parents, siblings, and other extended family members. When the coach has taught them successfully, the individual family members are responsible for the actual work of changing. Their self-differentiation, the basic goal of the therapy, must come from them and not the therapist, on the basis of a rational understanding of the family emotional networks and transmission processes.

Bowen (1976) takes the position that the successful addition of a significant other person (a friend, teacher, clergyman) to an anxious or disturbed relationship system can modify all relationships within the family. The family therapist can play this role as long as he or she manages to stay in emotional contact with the two most significant family members (usually the parents) but remain uninvested in (or detriangulated from) the family conflict. Bowen's insistence that the therapist not engage with the family system is dramatically different from the "total immersion" approach of family therapists such as Ackerman, Satir, Kempler, or Whitaker. In the Bowen approach, the therapist remains unsusceptible, calm, detriangulated from the emotional entanglements between the spouses. If the therapist can maintain that kind of stance—despite pressures to be triangulated into the conflict—tension between the couple will subside, the fusion between them will slowly resolve, and other family members will feel the positive repercussions in terms of changes in their own lives. Bowen's overall objective is for each family member to maximize his or her self-differentiation.

Bowen frequently chooses one partner, usually the one who is more mature and better differentiated, and works with that individual for a period of time. This person is assumed to be the member of the family most capable of breaking through the old emotionally entangling patterns of interaction. When that person succeeds in taking an "I"-stand, the others will shortly be motivated to do the same, subsequently moving off in their own directions. A stormy period may follow before a new equilibrium is reached, but the former pathological ties are broken and each person has achieved a greater sense of individuality.

Family therapy sessions as directed by Bowen (1975) are controlled and cerebral. Each partner talks to the therapist rather than talking directly to the other. Confrontation between the partners is avoided to minimize the tensions between them. Instead, what each partner is thinking is externalized in the presence of the other. Interpretations are avoided. Calm questioning defuses emotion and forces the partners to think about the issues causing their difficulties. Rather than allowing partners to blame each other or ignore their differences in a rush of intimacy, Bowen insists that each partner focus on the part he or she plays in the relationship problems.

In Bowen's experience, some families need as few as 5 to 10 sessions to achieve good results. Other families may require 20 to 40 sessions until symptoms subside. Bowen (1975) claims that no other approach to family therapy has been as effective in producing good long-term changes in family functioning.

Because Bowen is particularly concerned that his clients develop the ability to differentiate themselves from their families of origin, the focus of much of his work is on extended families. In this respect Bowen resembles Framo (1981)[2], although Bowen sends clients home for frequent visits (and self-observations) after coaching them in their differentiating efforts, while Framo brings origin family members into the final phases of therapy with his clients (see Chapter 5). Going home again, for Bowen, is directed at greater understanding of one another—not at confrontation, the settlements of old scores, or the reconciliation of longstanding differences. Reestablishing contact with the family of origin is a critical step in reducing a client's residual anxiety due to emotional cutoff, in detriangulating from members of that family, and in ultimately achieving self-differentiation, free of crippling entanglements from the past or present.

SUMMARY

Murray Bowen's approach, called family systems theory, may be considered a bridge between psychodynamically oriented views and more strictly systems perspectives. The major theoretician in the family therapy field, Bowen conceptualizes the family as an emotional relationship system and offers eight interlocking concepts to explain the emotional processes taking place in the nuclear and extended families.

The cornerstone of Bowen's theory is the concept of the differentiation of self, the extent to which a family member can discriminate his or her intellectual and emotional functioning and thus avoid fusion with whatever emotions dominate the family. Under stress, participants in a two-person relationship have a tendency to recruit or triangulate with a third member in order to lower the intensity and regain stability. The nuclear family emotional system is usually founded by marital partners with similar differentiation levels; if the system is unstable, the partners seek ways to reduce tension and preserve equilibrium, sometimes at the expense of particu-

2. A number of other family therapists, notably Norman Paul and Donald Williamson, endorse the transgenerational viewpoint that certain unfinished issues with one's family of origin must be addressed directly before family therapy is terminated. Paul (1974) is particularly concerned that unresolved issues over grief be dealt with therapeutically, arguing that a family's rigid or otherwise dysfunctional behavior patterns are often tied to an earlier inappropriately expressed grief over the death of a loved one. He advocates uncovering the loss and helping family members complete the unresolved mourning process together. Williamson (1981, 1982) believes that by the fourth decade of their lives, individuals should have terminated the earlier hierarchical power structure with their older parents, and begun to redistribute power on a more equitable basis between the generations. Failure to do so, he hypothesizes, leads to marital and family behavior in the second generation that becomes dysfunctional and symptomatic. He contends that the renegotiation is essential if one is to differentiate from one's parents, gain a sense of "personal authority," and resolve current interpersonal difficulties. After careful preparation with selected clients (writing an autobiograpy, audiotaping of phone conversations with each parent, informal conversations with parents, and so on), Williamson arranges several office sessions extending over three days between the adult child and the parents, aimed at shifting power and achieving peerhood between generations.

larly vulnerable, fusion-prone offspring. The sibling position of the parents in their families of origin offers clues as to which child will be chosen in this family projection process.

Bowen uses the concept of emotional cutoff to describe how some family members, usually upon reaching adulthood, attempt to break off contact with their families in the mistaken notion that they can insulate themselves from fusion. However, as progressively lower levels of differentiation of self occur over several generations, symptoms of severe dysfunction may eventually appear as a result of a multigenerational transmission process. The sibling position of each of the marital partners influences their interaction. In extending his theory to society at large, Bowen believes that chronic external pressures and stresses lower society's functional level of differentiation, resulting in societal regression.

As part of Bowen's system of family therapy, family evaluation interviews stress objectivity and neutrality, in an effort to remain outside the family's emotional network. Genograms offer helpful pictorial depictions of the family's relationship system over at least three generations.

Therapeutically, Bowen works with marital partners in a calm and carefully detriangulated way, attempting to resolve the fusion between them; his goals are to reduce anxiety and resolve symptoms, and ultimately to maximize each person's self-differentiation within the nuclear family system—and from the family of origin.

Chapter Eight

The Structural Approach to Theory and Practice

Many of the basic concepts of the structural approach to family therapy are already familiar to the reader: family rules, roles, coalitions, subsystems, boundaries, wholeness, organization. The very fact that these constructs are part of the everyday vocabulary of family therapy—and so readily come to mind in thinking of family relationships and interactional patterns—underscores the prominence of this model. In particular, the theory of family organization, along with its substantiating research, and the specific intervention approaches offered by Salvador Minuchin (Minuchin, 1974; Minuchin, 1984; Minuchin & Fishman, 1981; Minuchin, Rosman, & Baker, 1978) have helped ensure that a legion of systems-oriented family therapists would adopt the structural viewpoint.

The model's major thesis—that an individual's symptoms are best understood as rooted in the context of family transaction patterns, and that a change in family organization or structure must take place before the symptoms are relieved—has also had great impact on the current practices of many family therapists.

Structural theorists emphasize the influence of the family's hierarchical organization, the wholeness of the family system, and the interdependent functioning of its subsystems as three important determinants of the well-being of its individual members. It is the family's underlying organizational structure (that is, its enduring and regulating interactional patterns) and its flexibility in responding to changing conditions throughout the family life cycle that helps govern the appearance of functional or dysfunctional patterns.

Structural therapists strive for organizational changes in the family as their primary goal, assuming that individual behavioral changes as well as symptom reduction will follow as the context for the family's transactions changes. That is, when the family's structure is transformed, the positions of its members are altered, and as a result each person experiences change. It is the therapist's task, from this framework, to actively engage the family as a whole, in the present, in order to facilitate the restructuring process.

More strictly systems-oriented than Bowen's theory, the structural approach is primarily (although not exclusively) associated with Salvador Minuchin and his colleagues (at one time or another including such notable family therapists as Edgar Auerswald, Braulio Montalvo, Harry Aponte, Jay Haley, Lynn Hoffman, and Charles Fishman). Born in Argentina, Minuchin received his medical training there and set out to practice pediatrics. When Israel declared itself a state in 1948, Minuchin volunteered his services as an army doctor in the war with the Arab nations. After subsequent training as a child psychiatrist in the United States, a good part of which was under the tutelage of Nathan Ackerman, he returned to Israel to work with displaced children from the Holocaust and then with Jewish immigrants from the Arab countries.

Back in the United States, Minuchin began psychoanalytic training, eventually becoming intake psychiatrist at a residential school for delinquent adolescents outside New York City, the Wiltwyck School. Inspired by an article by Don Jackson in 1959, Minuchin began observing the children, primarily black and Puerto Rican youngsters from New York's inner city, along with their families. Perhaps because these families often had multiple problems and poor structure, Minuchin started developing a theory and set of special intervention techniques for working with these urgently needy, underorganized poor families. Finding both his earlier traditional child psychiatric as well as psychoanalytic techniques ineffective with this population, Minuchin and his associates devised many brief, direct, action-oriented intervention procedures for restructuring the family. The results of his eight years at Wiltwyck, during which he developed many techniques for working with poor families, were described in *Families of the Slums* (Minuchin, Montalvo, Guerney, Rosman, & Schumer, 1967) and earned Minuchin widespread recognition (Simon, 1984).

Minuchin, desirous of testing his techniques with a wider cross section of families, took on the directorship of the Philadelphia Child Guidance Center in 1965. Originally a small clinic with a staff of ten located in the heart of the black ghetto, the Philadelphia Child Guidance Clinic blossomed under Minuchin's boldly imaginative leadership until it grew into the largest facility of its kind ever established. The clinic soon occupied an elaborate modern complex, had close to 300 people on its staff, and became affiliated with Children's Hospital on the campus of the University of Pennsylvania. It remains today one of the few clinics in the United States where ghetto families represent a majority of the clients served. In 1974, Minuchin published *Families and Family Therapy*, an elaboration of ideas concerning change in families through structural family therapy.

Minuchin soon turned his attention to psychosomatic conditions; as Colapinto (1982) observes, the urgent problems of a social nature Minuchin encountered at Wiltwyck were replaced by urgent medical problems in Philadelphia. More specifically, no medical explanations could be found for the unusually large number of diabetic children who required emergency hospitalization for acidosis, nor would they respond to individual psychotherapy directed at helping them deal with stress. As Minuchin and his coworkers began to accumulate research and clinical data and to redefine the problem in family terms, successful interventions became possible. Later expanded to include asthmatic children with severe, recurrent attacks as well as anorectic children, the additional data confirmed for Minuchin that the locus of pathology was in the context of the family and not simply in the afflicted individual.

As proposed in *Psychosomatic Families* (Minuchin et al., 1978), families of children who manifest severe psychosomatic symptoms are characterized by certain transactional problems that encourage somatization. **Enmeshment** is common, subsystems function poorly, boundaries between family members are too diffuse to allow for individual autonomy. A psychosomatic family was found to be overprotective, inhibiting the child from developing a sense of independence, competence, or interest in activities outside the safety of the family. The physiologically vulnerable child, in turn, feels great responsibility for protecting the family. The manifestation of symptoms typically occurs when stress overloads the family's already dysfunctional coping mechanisms. Thus the symptoms are regarded as having a regulating effect on the family system, the sick child acting as a family conflict defuser by diverting family attention away from more basic, but less easily resolved, family conflicts. Therapeutic intervention is directed at changing the structure of relationships within the family, helping the family develop clearer boundaries, increase their flexibility in dealing with family transactions, and deal more directly with hidden, underlying conflicts.

Since stepping down as director of the Philadelphia Child Guidance Center in 1975, and as director of training there in 1981, Minuchin has spent most of his professional time teaching, consulting, supervising, writing, and demonstrating his dramatic techniques in front of professional audiences around the world. His most recent book, *Family Kaleidoscope* (Minuchin, 1984) represents an effort to bring family systems thinking to a general readership.

STRUCTURAL FAMILY THEORY

As Minuchin (1974) describes his viewpoint:

> In essence, the structural approach to families is based on the concept that a family is more than the individual biopsychodynamics of its members. Family members relate according to certain arrangements, which govern their transactions. These arrangements, though usually not explicitly stated or even recognized, form a whole—the structure of the family. The reality of the structure is of a different order from the reality of the individual members. (p. 89)

Like most systems theorists, the structuralists are interested in how the components of a system interact, how balance or homeostasis is achieved, how family feedback mechanisms operate, how dysfunctional communication patterns develop, and so forth. Beyond that, they are especially attentive to family transactional patterns because these offer clues to the family's structure, the permeability of the family's subsystem boundaries, and the existence of alignments or coalitions—all of which ultimately affect the family's ability to achieve a delicate balance between stability and change.

Family Structure

A family's structure is the invisible set of functional demands that organizes the way family members relate to one another (Minuchin, 1974). In essence, the structure represents the sum of the rules the family has evolved for carrying out transactional patterns between its members, governing how, when, with whom, and in what manner family members interact. These patterns serve to arrange or organize the family's component subunits into more or less constant relationships (Umbarger, 1983) and thus regulate the family's day-to-day functioning. However, structure (for example, a father-son coalition) should not necessarily be thought of as static or fixed. On the contrary, structure may not persist beyond a brief arrangement, and thus must be considered to be dynamic. It can only be discerned by observing a family in action over time.

A family's transactional patterns regulate the behavior of its members, and are maintained by two sets of constraints: *generic* or universal rules, and *idiosyncratic* or individualized rules (Minuchin, 1974). With regard to the former, structuralists contend that all well-functioning families should be hierarchically organized, the parents exercising more power than the children, the older children having more responsibilities as well as more privileges than their younger siblings. In addition, there must be *complementarity* of functions—the husband and wife, for example, operating as a team and accepting their interdependency. The degree to which the needs and abilities of both spouses dovetail and reciprocal role relations provide satisfaction, are key factors in harmonious family functioning. In some cases, family balance is achieved by different family members' being assigned complementary roles or functions (good child–bad child; tender mother–tough father). Thus, complementarity or reciprocity between family roles provides a generic restraint on family structure, allowing the family to carry out its tasks while maintaining family equilibrium.

Idiosyncratic constraints apply to specific families, and involve the mutual presumptions of particular family members regarding their behavior toward one another. While the origin of certain expectations may no longer be clear to the persons involved, buried in years of implicit and explicit negotiations, their pattern of mutual accommodation, and thus functional effectiveness, is maintained (Minuchin, 1974). The evolved rules and subsequent behavioral patterns of a particular family's game become a part of the family's structure, ensuring that the system will maintain itself.

Thus, a family will try to maintain preferred patterns—its present structure—as long as possible. While alternate patterns may be considered, any deviation from established rules that goes too far too fast will be met with resistance, as the family seeks to reestablish equilibrium. On the other hand, the family must be able to adapt to changing circumstances (a child grows into a young adult; mother goes to work outside the home; grandmother comes to live with them). It must have a sufficient range of patterns (including alternatives to call upon whenever necessary) and must be flexible enough to mobilize these new patterns in the face of impending change, if members are to continue to exist as a family unit. According to Minuchin (1974), the family must be able to transform itself in ways that meet new circumstances, while at the same time taking care not to lose the continuity that provides a frame of reference for its members.

Family Subsystems

As we pointed out in Chapter Three, families carry out their basic functions in part by organizing themselves into coexisting subsystems, often arranged in hierarchical order. Typically, family subsystem divisions are made according to gender (male/female), generation (parents/children), common interests (intellectual/social), or function (who is responsible for what chores).

Subsystems, then, are components of a family's structure; they exist to carry out various family tasks necessary for the functioning of the overall family system. Each member may belong to several subgroups at the same time, and families are capable of organizing themselves into a limitless number of such units. As we noted in Chapter Three, each person may have a differing level of power within different subgroups, may play different roles, may exercise different skills, and may engage in different interactions with members of other subsystems within the family. Complementarity of roles is a key here—as Minuchin (1974) points out, a child has to act like a son so his father can act like a father, but he may take on executive powers when he is alone with his younger brother.

Subsystems are defined by boundaries and rules for membership. Such boundaries determine who participates and what roles those participants will have in dealing with one another and with outsiders who are not included in the subsystem. They may be based on temporary alliances (mother and daughter go shopping together on Saturday afternoon) and may have rules concerning exclusion (fathers and brothers are unwelcome). Or they may be more enduring (based on generational differences in roles and interests between parents and children) with clearly defined boundaries separating the two generations. Minuchin (1974) argues that subsystem organization within a family provides valuable training in developing a sense of self, in the process of honing interpersonal skills at different levels.

As previously noted in Chapter Three, the spousal, parental, and sibling subsystems are the most prominent and important subsystems in the family. In a well-functioning family, all operate in an integrated way to protect the differentiation, and thus the integrity, of the family system.

Boundary Permeability

The membership of a subsystem is not nearly as important as the clarity of its boundaries. Put another way, boundaries within a family vary in their flexibility or **permeability**, and that degree of accessibility helps determine the nature and frequency of contact between family members. Clearly defined boundaries between the subsystems within a family help maintain separateness and at the same time emphasize belongingness to the overall family system. An ideal arrangement, the clarity enhances the family's overall well-being by providing support and easy access for communication and negotiation between subsystems whenever needed, while simultaneously encouraging independence and the freedom to experiment by the members of the separate subsystems. The autonomy of members is not sacrificed, but at the same time the boundaries remain flexible enough so that care, support, and involvement are available as needed. An important benefit of such clarity becomes apparent whenever the family attempts to make structural changes over time to accommodate changing life circumstances.

Excessively rigid or inflexible boundaries lead to impermeable barriers between subsystems. In this case, the worlds of parents and children—the generational hierarchy—are separate and distinct; the members of neither subsystem are willing or able to enter into the other's world. With parents and children unable to alter or cross subsystem boundaries when necessary, autonomy may be maintained, but nurturance, involvement, and the easy exchange of affection with one another are typically missing.

Diffuse boundaries are excessively blurred and indistinct, thus easily intruded upon by other family members. Here, parents are too accessible and contact with their children may take the form of hovering and the invasion of privacy. Children run the risk of becoming too involved with their parents, and in the process failing to develop independent thinking and behaving or to learn the necessary skills for developing relationships outside the family. Because there is no clear generational hierarchy, adults and children may exchange roles easily, and a member's sense of self or personal identity becomes hard to establish for later adulthood.

In a well-functioning family, clear boundaries give each member a sense of "I"-ness along with a group sense of "we" or "us." That is, each member retains his or her individuality but not at the expense of losing the feeling of belonging to a family. Most family systems fall somewhere along the continuum between enmeshment (diffuse boundaries) and **disengagement** (rigid boundaries) (Minuchin et al., 1967). Most families are neither totally enmeshed nor totally disengaged, although they may contain enmeshed or disengaged subsystems.

Enmeshment refers to an extreme form of proximity and intensity in family interactions in which members are overconcerned and overinvolved in each other's lives. In extreme cases, the family's lack of differentiation between subsystems makes separation from the family an act of betrayal. Belonging to the family dominates all experiences at the expense of each member's self-development. Whatever is happening to one family member reverberates throughout the system. A child sneezes, his sister runs for the tissues, his mother reaches for the thermometer, and his father becomes anxious about sickness in the family.

Subsystem boundaries in enmeshed families are poorly differentiated, weak, and easily crossed. Children may act like parents and parental control may be ineffective. Excessive togetherness and sharing leads to a lack of separateness; members, overly alert and responsive to signs of distress, intrude on each other's thoughts and feelings. Members of enmeshed families place too high a value on family cohesiveness, to the extent that they yield autonomy and have little inclination to explore and master problems outside the safety of the family. As we indicated earlier in this chapter, enmeshment is common in psychosomatic families.

At the other extreme, members of disengaged families may function separately and autonomously but with little sense of family loyalty. Interpersonal distance is great, the members frequently lacking the capacity for interdependence or to request support from others when needed. Communication in such families is strained and guarded, and the family's protective functions are limited. When an individual family member is under stress, the enmeshed family responds with excessive speed and intensity while the disengaged family hardly seems to look up, offer emotional support, or even respond at all. As Minuchin (1974) illustrates, the parents in an enmeshed family may become enormously upset if a child does not eat dessert, while in a disengaged family they may feel unconcerned about the child's hatred of school.

Alignments, Power, and Coalitions

While boundaries are defined by how a family is organized, **alignments** are defined by the way family members join together or oppose one another in carrying out a family activity. **Power** within a family has to do both with authority (who is the decision maker) and responsibility (who carries out the decision). Thus, alignments refer to the emotional or psychological connections family members make with one another. Power, on the other hand, speaks to the relative influence of each family member on an operation's outcome.

Aponte and Van Deusin (1981) believe that every stroke of a family transaction makes a statement about boundaries, alignments, and power. As we have noted, the boundaries of a subsystem are the rules defining who participates and what roles they will play in the transactions or operations necessary to carry out a particular function. (For example, should the sex education of young children be carried out by father, mother, older siblings, or be a shared responsibility? Or should the task be left to the schools?) Alignments refer to how supportive or unsupportive of one another the players are in carrying out an operation. (For example, does father agree or disagree with his wife's disciplinary actions with the children?) Power is seldom absolute but is related to the context or situation. (For example, the mother may have considerable influence on her adolescent daughter's behavior at home but minimal influence over the daughter's social contacts outside the home.) Power is also related to the way family members actively or passively combine forces. (For example, the mother's authority depends on her husband's support and backing as well as on the acquiescence of her children.)

Figure 8.1 According to Minuchin, family coalitions frequently introduce stress into a family system, handicapping the functioning of individual members as well as the family as a whole. In this simulated family scene, the mother and younger daughter sit separately from the father and older daughter, suggesting a division within the family. Mother's whispered secret further strengthens her alliance with one child, while the other members appear to be out of touch with what is going on. Successful structural family therapy may produce role changes, clearer communication patterns, and a restructuring of the family organization.

Certain alignments are considered by structuralists to be dysfunctional. In what Minuchin (1974) calls **triangulation**, each parent demands the child ally with him or her against the other parent. Whenever the child does side with one parent, however, the other views the alignment as an attack or betrayal and, in such a dysfunctional structure, the child is in a no-win situation. Every movement the child makes causes one or the other parent to feel ganged up on and assailed. Because the problems fail to be worked out between the parents, a third person is brought in (similar to Bowen's concept of triangles) and becomes part of the process taking place.

Salvador Minuchin, M.D.

Coalitions (Minuchin et al., 1978) are alliances between specific family members against a third member (see Figure 8.1). A **stable coalition** is a fixed and inflexible union (such as mother and son) that becomes a dominant part of the family's everyday functioning. A **detouring coalition** is one in which the pair hold a third family member responsible for their difficulties or conflicts with one another, thus decreasing the stress on themselves or their relationship.

Alignments, power, boundaries, and coalitions are interrelated phenomena within a family system. Power often results from alignments between members, and can be an important determinant of functional or dysfunctional living. Structuralists believe that power resulting from a strong parental alignment is often beneficial to child rearing and limit setting. On the other hand, coalitions between a parent and a child against the other parent can have an undermining effect on family functioning. Detouring, while it may give others the impression of family harmony, may often be destructive to maintaining clear boundaries.

Structuralists believe that for parents to achieve a desired outcome in the family, there must be (1) clearly defined generational boundaries so that parents together form a subsystem with executive power; (2) alignments between the parents on key issues, such as discipline; and (3) rules related to power and authority, indicating which of the parents will prevail if they disagree and whether the parents are capable of carrying out their wishes when they do agree. Note that strong generational boundaries also prohibit interference from grandparents as much as they prevent children from taking over parenting functions. In addition, alignments must function properly or individuals will cross generational boundaries—go to Father for permission if Mother says no—to get what they want.

Family Dysfunction

Rosenberg (1983) summarizes the structural position succinctly when he concludes that "when a family runs into difficulty, one can assume that it is operating within a dysfunctional structure" (p. 160). Perhaps the family, functioning along normal developmental lines, has hit a snag in entering a new developmental stage or in negotiating a particular life cycle crisis such as the birth of another child, children leaving for college, or retirement. Perhaps the family members have become overinvolved or enmeshed with each other (parental behavior that seems supportive and loving to a preadolescent is experienced as suffocating and intrusive by a teenager). Or, at the other end of the continuum, perhaps we are dealing with the dilemma of disengagement (parents' detachment permits growth and encourages children's resourcefulness, but at the same time represents parents' unavailability and lack of support in time of crisis). Dysfunction suggests that the covert rules that govern family transactions have become (perhaps temporarily) inoperative or inappropriate and require renegotiation.

Minuchin (1974) reserves the label of *pathological* for those families who, when faced with a stressful situation, increase the rigidity of their transactional patterns and boundaries, thus preventing any further exploration of alternatives. Normal families, by way of contrast, adapt to life's inevitable stresses by preserving family continuity while remaining flexible enough to permit family restructuring.

STRUCTURAL FAMILY THERAPY

Minuchin attempts to assess a family by attending primarily to its structure and ongoing transaction patterns. His major concerns are the family's hierarchical organization, the ability of its subsystems to carry out their functions, the family's possible alignments and coalitions, the permeability of its current boundaries. He is interested in how the family adapts to developmental changes as well as unexpected situational crises. Generally speaking, Minuchin is less concerned than Bowen (Chapter 7) with transgenerational issues; instead, his attention is directed at the family's current structure, which he is likely to sketch in symbolic form to map out the changing relationships within the family.

After describing some of Minuchin's mapping techniques, we offer examples of typical therapeutic interventions used by structural family therapists.

Family Mapping

Like Bowen, Minuchin uses family diagramming to depict family patterns related to current functional difficulties. However, while Bowen uses the genogram to gain clues regarding the family's intergenerational influences, Minuchin concerns himself with conveying information, through lines and spatial arrangements, about the family's current structure. He makes use of a simple pictorial device called a structural map to formulate hypotheses about those areas where the family functions well and other areas where dysfunction may be occurring. Used as a diagnostic device, family mapping often helps set therapeutic goals.

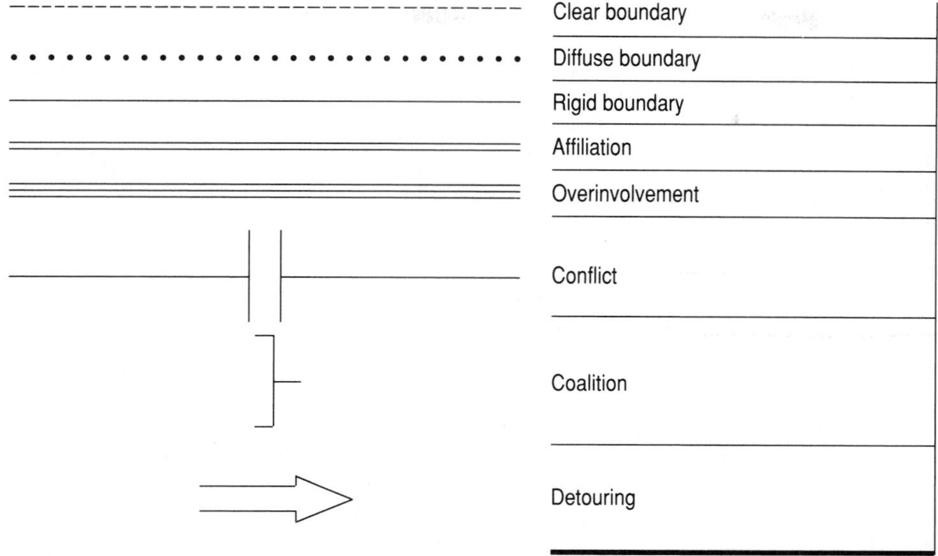

Figure 8.2 Minuchin's symbols for family mapping. (Source: Minuchin, 1974, p. 53)

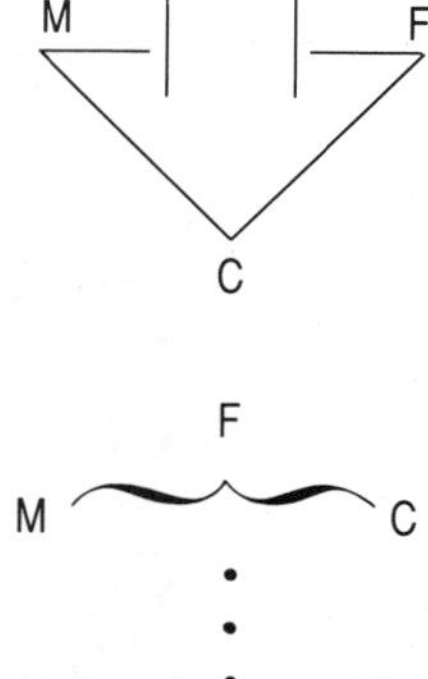

Figure 8.3 The effect of stress on the subsystem boundaries of a family. In the top diagram, a father (F) and mother (M), both stressed at work, come home and criticize each other, but then detour their conflict by attacking a child. This results in less danger to the spouse subsystem, but stresses the child (C). In the lower figure, the husband criticizes the wife, who seeks a coalition with the child against the father. Note the rigid cross-generational subsystem of mother and child; both have the effect of excluding the father. Minuchin refers to this as a cross-generational dysfunctional pattern. (Source: Minuchin, 1974, p. 61)

Figure 8.2 illustrates some common symbols used by structuralists to delineate the clarity of family boundaries (clear, diffuse, rigid), subsystem operations, and family transactional styles. Figure 8.3 offers two examples of the use of structural mapping in depicting family conflict. The upper figure exemplifies a familiar detouring coalition within a family in which parents cope with direct conflict with one another by directing the problem they are having onto their child. The lower figure, again familiar, is a simple notation by a structural therapist of an intergenerational coalition in a family with diffuse mother-child boundaries.

Minuchin's schema offer an almost endless number of possible combinations for picturing family boundaries, alliances, affiliations, coalitions, detouring strategies, and so on. For example, family enmeshment may be illustrated by the symbol of overinvolvement; a coalition of several members against another can be shown by brackets. Family mapping, although a simple shorthand device, has two useful diagnostic purposes: it describes how the family is organized, and also shows what particular subsystem is most directly involved in a problem (Umbarger, 1983). Figure 8.4 diagrams an overinvolved parent-child bond as well as a family coalition against the other parent.

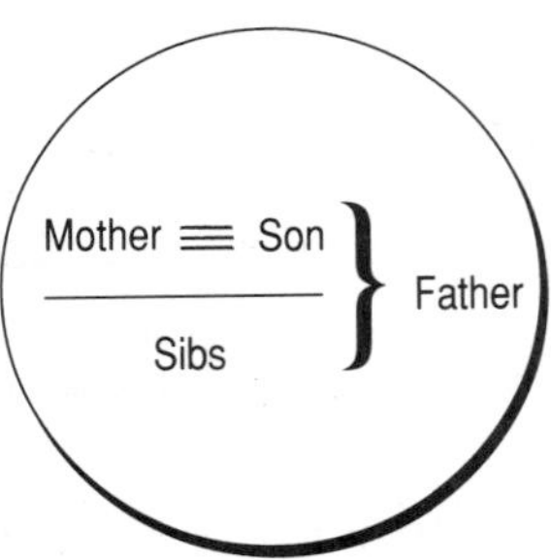

Figure 8.4 This diagram shows a closed-family-unit boundary with an overinvolved mother and son comprising the parental subsystem. Between them and the other children is a rigid boundary, yet apparently under enough control so that all are in a coalition against the father. (Source: Umbarger, 1983, p. 36)

General Therapeutic Considerations

Therapeutically, structuralists actively challenge the rigid, repetitive transactional patterns by which some families attempt to organize themselves and cope with stress, and then, by deliberately "unfreezing" these patterns, create an opportunity for the family to structurally reorganize. Generally, this therapeutic effort involves a push for clearer boundaries, increased flexibility in family interactions, particularly at transition points in family life, and most important, modification of the dysfunctional structure.

Any dysfunctional hierarchical issues within the family also are explored, since structuralists insist that functional families require parents to be in charge of their children and require differentiation between subsystems. Parents together must form and maintain an executive coalition, a parental subsystem; they have the responsibility to care for and protect and help socialize their children. They also have rights to make decisions (selection of schools, relocation) they believe are best for the survival of the overall family system. However, as the children grow and their needs change, the parental subsystem must change accordingly, sharing opportunities for decision making and self-direction with the children.

Siblings too must develop a working subsystem of peers; within the sibling system they learn to negotiate, cooperate, compete, make friends, deal with enemies, develop a sense of belonging. Spouses, aside from being parents, must also receive support from one another and together develop a subsystem that serves as a model for expressing affection, helping each other deal with stress, and dealing with conflict as equals. If there is a major dysfunction within the spousal subsystem, it will likely reverberate throughout the family (Minuchin & Fishman, 1981).

Minuchin (1974) conceives of family pathology as resulting from the development of dysfunctional sets. Dysfunctional sets are the family reactions, developed in response to stress, that are repeated without modification whenever there is family conflict. A husband experiencing stress at work comes home and shouts at the wife. The wife counterattacks, escalating the conflict that continues without change until one partner abandons the field. Both parties experience a sense of nonresolution. In another example, a mother verbally attacks an adolescent son, the father takes his side, and the younger children seize the opportunity to join in and pick on their older brother. All family members become involved and various coalitions develop but the family organization remains the same and the dysfunctional sets will be repeated in the next trying situation.

Minuchin assumes that any family seeking treatment is experiencing some stress that has overloaded the system's adaptive and coping mechanisms, handicapping the optimum functioning of its members in the process. Consequently, he sets himself the task of rearranging the family organization—restructuring the system that governs its transactions—so that the family will function more effectively and the growth potential of each member will be maximized. Restructuring involves changes in family rules and realignments, changes in the patterns that support certain undesirable behaviors, changes in the sequences of interaction.

Structural Intervention Techniques

Minuchin's therapeutic efforts are geared to the present and are based on the principle of action preceding understanding. That is, action leads to new experiences, to insight and understanding, to rearranged structures. (The sequence is reversed for Bowen.) Minuchin's approach is to challenge the family's patterns of interaction, forcing the members to look beyond the symptoms of the identified patient in order to view all of their behavior within the context of family structures (the covert rules that govern the family's transactional patterns).

He offers the family leadership, direction, and encouragement to examine and discard rigid structures that no longer are functional. For example, changes in the relative positions of family members may be in order, such as more proximity between husband and wife or more distance between mother and son. Hierarchical relationships in which the parents customarily exercise authority may be redefined and made more flexible in some cases and reinforced in others. Alignments and coalitions may be explored, embedded conflicts acknowledged, alternative rules considered. To use an example offered by Colapinto (1982), a mother may be urged to abstain from intervening automatically whenever the interaction between her husband and son reaches a certain pitch, while father and son may be encouraged not to automatically abort an argument just because it upsets Mom. For Minuchin and his colleagues, the most effective way to alter dysfunctional behavior and eliminate symptoms is to change the family's transactional patterns that maintain them.

Minuchin himself is a compelling presence, a colorful and somehow larger-than-life therapist who enters a family, adapts to the family organization, refuses to be ignored, and forces the family members to accommodate to him in the ways he chooses to facilitate movement toward the goals of treatment. He adopts the family's affective style: in a constricted family he is undemonstrative, in an expansive family he is jovial and uses expressive movements. He quickly assimilates the family's language patterns and commonly used terms. He tells anecdotes about his own experiences when he feels they are relevant to the family discussion. As a therapist, he describes himself (Minuchin, 1974) as acting like a distant relative, **joining** a family system and **accommodating** to its style. As Minuchin blends into the family and begins to understand family themes and family myths, to sense a member's pain at being excluded or scapegoated, to distinguish which persons have open communication pathways between them and which closed, he intuitively obtains a picture of the family structure in operation.

Joining, then, lets the family know the therapist understands and is working with and for them. In the process, the structural therapist is encouraging the family to feel secure enough to explore alternative ways of interacting and solving problems together. Acknowledging their areas of pain or stress, the therapist lets them know it is safe to confront the distressing—and thus previously avoided—issues. For example, in a close family, if a family member has an obviously negative characteristic, the structural therapist will confirm its existence while at the same time "absolving" the individual of responsibility for the behavior. Minuchin and Fishman (1981) give the following illustrations:

> To a child, the therapist might say: "You seem to be quite childish. How did your parents manage to keep you so young?" To an adult, the therapist could say: "You act very dependent on your spouse. What does she do to keep you incompetent?" (p. 34)

Through this technique, the person feels recognized in a problem area without feeling criticized or guilty or to blame about it. As a result, the behavior is more readily acknowledged by the person, rather than being denied or the individual becoming defensive.

Minuchin's therapeutic approach is innovative and deliberately manipulative, following a carefully calculated set of plans and intervention procedures. Minuchin generally advises that the therapist begin by affiliating with the family to experience firsthand the pressures of the family system. Once Minuchin has gained entrance, he begins to probe the family structure, looking for areas of flexibility and possible change. For example, a family has come to him for therapy because the teenage daughter is shy, withdrawn, and has difficulties in her social life. He may observe for diagnostic purposes how the family enters the therapy room: the girl sits next to her mother and they move their two chairs close together. When the therapist asks what the problem is, the mother answers, ignoring her daughter's attempts to add her thoughts on the matter. The mother makes comments that suggest she has too intimate a knowledge of her adolescent daughter's personal life, more knowledge than is usual. Within a few minutes after starting, Minuchin makes his first intervention, asking the mother and father to change chairs. Structural therapy has begun: as the father is brought into the picture, the family flexibility is being tested; with the implication of pathology in the mother-daughter dyad, the family's reason for seeking therapy for the teenager is already being reframed or relabeled as a problem with a larger focus.

Several other therapeutic tactics that are simple, practical, and calculated to have certain effects deserve special note. **Mimesis** (Greek for "copy") refers to the process of joining the family by imitating the manner, style, affective range, or content of its communications. The therapist might tell of personal experiences ("I have an uncle like that") or mimic a family member's behavior (taking off his coat, sitting in a particular position, playing with the baby). These efforts may or may not be contrived; in either case they often have the effect of increasing kinship with the family.

Through **tracking**, the structural therapist adopts symbols of the family's life gathered from members' communication (such as life themes, values, significant family events) and deliberately uses them in conversation with the family. This effort to confirm that the therapist values what family members say, without soliciting the information, is also a way of influencing their later transactional patterns; Minuchin (1974) calls this "leading by following." Tracking a particular family theme may also provide clues as to family structure. For example, in working with an enmeshed family, Minuchin noted the father's statement that he disliked closed doors. Tracking the door issue, Minuchin discovered that the children were not permitted to close the doors of their rooms, that a brother slept in his older sister's room, and that the sex lives of the parents were curtailed because their own bedroom door remained open. Later, Minuchin was able to use the metaphor of the doors to help the family clarify their boundaries. Thus, tracking can be used as a restructuring strategy.

An **enactment** is an effort by the therapist to bring an outside family conflict into the session so that the family members can demonstrate how they deal with it and the therapist can begin to map out a way to modify their interaction and create structural changes. Using this technique, the therapist constructs a scenario during a session in which the players act out their dysfunctional transactions. To use an example offered by Rosenberg (1983), a mother complained that her 2-1/2-year-old daughter had tantrums and embarrassed her in front of grandparents, on buses, and in other situations. The daughter remained well behaved during the early sessions despite (or maybe because of) her mother's insistence that she engaged in this awful behavior away from the therapist. During the third or fourth session, when the child asked for gum, Rosenberg saw his chance: he asked the mother not to give her the gum because lunchtime was approaching. As the child's whimper turned to crying, to begging, and finally to falling on the floor and undressing herself—and as the mother considered giving in—Rosenberg encouraged the mother to hold firm, despite the by-now deafening noise. More than a half-hour later, the child came to a whimpering stop; she seemed fine, although both mother and therapist were exhausted! However, the mother had asserted her control as a result of the enactment. In structural terms, the generational boundaries were reestablished, effective alternative transactional patterns were introduced, the proper hierarchical order was put into place (mother was again in charge), and the daughter, whose tantrums at home ceased shortly thereafter, was comfortable in knowing that her mother could handle her.

Another useful technique, **reframing**, changes the original meaning of an event or situation, placing it in a new context in which an equally plausible explanation is possible. The idea is to relabel what occurs in order to provide a more constructive perspective, thereby altering the way the event or situation is viewed. As used by structuralists, reframing is directed toward relabeling the problem as a function of the family structure. Typically, within the context of an enactment, the therapist first redefines a presenting problem. For example, in the case of an adolescent daughter's self-starvation, the anorectic girl is labeled as "stubborn" and not "sick," forcing the family members to reconsider their earlier view that she is not responsible for what is occurring. Giving new meaning to her behavior creates a new context that can ultimately change their transactional patterns. The fact of the daughter's not eating has not changed, only the meaning attributed to that behavior. Not intended to deliberately deceive, reframing rather is used by many family therapists (especially the communication/strategic approach advocates described in the following chapter) to change family perspectives and ultimately to change family behavior patterns on the basis of the new options and alternatives.

Minuchin's interventions very likely increase the stress on the family system—perhaps even create a family crisis that unbalances family homeostasis—but they also open the way for transformation of the family structure. Minuchin recognizes that in an enmeshed family system, for example, members often believe the family as a whole can neither withstand change nor adapt to it; as a consequence, the system demands that certain members change (develop symptoms) in order to maintain the dysfunctional homeostasis. When the danger level of family stress is approached, the symptom bearer is activated as part of a conflict avoidance maneuver; the family system reinforces the continuance of the symptoms that help maintain the system's balance and status quo. It is the therapist's job to make everyone aware, often through reframing, that the problem belongs and pertains to the family, not an individual; that the implementation of new functional sets must replace the habitual repetition of the dysfunctional ones.

The therapeutic tactics employed by Minuchin are often dramatic and at times theatrical. Like a stage director, he enjoys setting up a situation, creating a scenario, assigning a task to the family, and requiring the members to function according to the new sets he has imposed. For example, in treating an anorectic adolescent, self-starving and refusing to eat, Minuchin arranges to meet the family at lunch for the first session (Minuchin, et al., 1978). He creates such an enactment deliberately, to foster a crisis around eating and to experience what the family members are experiencing. He observes the parents pleading, demanding, cajoling, becoming desperate, and feeling defeat. He watches the adolescent girl demonstrate hopelessness and helplessness, pathetically asserting through her refusal to eat that she has always given in to her parents at the expense of her self, but will do so no longer. While the daughter has been labeled as the problem, Minuchin, reframing, helps the family see that anorexia nervosa is a diagnosis of a family system, not simply the adolescent's symptomatic behavior. All the family members are locked into a futile pattern of interaction that has become the center of their lives; each member has a stake in maintaining the disorder. In turn, the syndrome plays an important role in maintaining family homeostasis. Structural family therapy helps each person in the family to recognize the syndrome and take responsibility for contributing to it. By creating a family crisis, Minuchin forces the family to change the system, substituting more functional interactions.

Typical of Minuchin's manipulative, unyielding, crisis-provoking approach is his insistence in this case that the parents force the emaciated girl to eat. They coax, cajole, threaten, yell, and finally stuff food down her throat until their daughter collapses in tears. Minuchin believes she will now eat. As he later explains it:

> The anorectic is obsessed with her hopelessness, inadequacy, wickedness, ugliness. I incite an interpersonal conflict that makes her stop thinking about how terrible she is and start thinking about what bastards her parents are. At that demonstration, I said to the parents, "Make her eat," and when they did she had to deal with them as people. Previously, the parents had been saying "We control you because we love you." In the position I put them in, they were finally saying "God damn it, you eat!" That freed her. She could then eat or not eat; she could be angry at them as clearly delineated figures. (Malcolm, 1978, p. 78)

With this approach, Minuchin has been able to show that the anorectic symptom is embedded in the faulty family organization. Changing that organization eliminates the potentially fatal symptom.

Therapeutic Goals

Generally speaking, structuralists strive to restructure the family's system of transactional rules, so that members learn alternate and more satisfying ways of dealing with one another and are better able to cope with future conflict and stress. Appropriate boundaries between subsystems need to be (re)established, the family's hierarchical order strengthened, outgrown rules replaced by those more related to the family's current realities. With enmeshed families, greater differentiation between subsystems is sought through more clear boundary separations. In the case of disengaged families, the goal is to increase interaction between members by making rigid subsystem boundaries more permeable.

The emergence of new structures is intended to aid the identified patient along with the family as a whole. From this viewpoint, a symptomatic person's presenting problem is embedded in the family's dysfunctional rules; as inappropriate or constricting rules are replaced, and family members are released from stereotyped positions and functions, there no longer is need for the symptom to maintain family homeostasis, and it becomes unnecessary (Colapinto, 1982). As a result of family reorganization, future symptom development should become less likely as the opportunity is increased for all members, and the family as a whole, to enhance their growth potential.

SUMMARY

The structural approach in family therapy is primarily associated with Salvador Minuchin and his colleagues at the Philadelphia Child Guidance Center. Systems-based, structural family theory focuses on the active, organized wholeness of the family unit and the ways in which the family organizes itself through its transactional patterns. In particular, the family's subsystems, boundaries, alignments, and coalitions are studied in an effort to understand its structure. Dysfunctional structures point to the covert rules governing family transactions that have become inoperative or in need of renegotiation.

Structural family therapy is geared to present-day transactions and gives higher priority to action than to insight or understanding. All behavior, including symptoms in the identified patient, is viewed within the context of family structure. Family mapping provides a simple observational technique for charting the family's transactional patterns. Minuchin's interventions are active, carefully calculated, even manipulative efforts to alter rigid, outmoded, or unworkable structures. By joining the family and accommodating to its style, he gains an understanding of the members' way of dealing with problems and with each other, ultimately helping them to change dysfunctional sets and rearrange or realign the family organization.

Enactments (having the family demonstrate typical conflict situations in the therapy session) and reframing (the therapist's relabeling or redefining a problem as a function of the family's structure) are therapeutic techniques frequently used to bring about a transformation of the family structure. The ultimate goal is to restructure the family's transactional rules by developing more appropriate boundaries between subsystems and strengthening the family's hierarchical order.

Chapter Nine

The Communication/ Strategic Approach to Theory and Practice

Enormously influential in the founding of the family therapy movement, communication theory as it first took form in the late 1950s offered an intriguing alternative to the established ways of conceptualizing psychopathology. For example, the traditional psychoanalytic or psychodynamic view of conflict between a mother and adolescent daughter holds that the mother is overidentifying with her child and perhaps projecting unresolved problems from her own adolescence onto her. The daughter, rebellious and with an incompletely formed sense of personal identity, may be introjecting many of her mother's characteristics but undergoing an "identity crisis" at the same time. However, it is entirely possible, argued people like Gregory Bateson, Don Jackson, Jay Haley, John Weakland, and, later, Paul Watzlawick, to understand this conflict not in terms of the separate problems of two persons, but as a dysfunctional relationship that manifests itself, among other ways, in faulty communication.

If we adopt the latter view, notice how the emphasis has shifted—from the past to the here and now, from analyzing the inner dynamics of each individual to studying their recursive pattern of interaction and communication, from seeing pathology in one or both members of a family to understanding how a dysfunctional relationship has been established. Their recurring struggle becomes circular: "I nag because you defy me." "No, Mom, it's the other way around; I defy you because you nag." In this way of conceptualizing a problem, attention is paid to the question of *what* rather than *why*—to the ongoing process between and among people and the ways in which they interact, define, and redefine their relationships. Communication patterns—the manner in which information is exchanged within a family, the clarity of the transmission, and the behavioral or pragmatic effect of the communication—as much as the content of what is communicated, help determine those relationships.

The major impact of this new epistemology, as we have discussed earlier in this book, was to recast human problems as interactional and situational (specific to a particular time and place). In shifting the locus of pathology from the individual to the social context and the interchange between individuals, Jackson and his coworkers were not denying that intrapsychic mechanisms influence individual functioning. Rather, they were giving greater credence to the power of family rules to govern interactive behavior; to them, a breakdown in individual or family functioning follows from a breakdown in rules. This paradigmatic shift in thinking led inevitably to redefining the appropriate unit of study for the therapist; the observation of exchanges between people became more relevant than the process of drawing difficult-to-validate inferences regarding the character or personality deficits of an individual (Greenberg, 1977).

In the mother-daughter situation just described, according to communication theorists, the attempt to determine cause and effect is irrelevant and, indeed, incorrect. The mother is not the cause of her daughter's behavior, nor is the daughter causing her mother's behavior. Both are caught up in a reverberating system, a chain reaction that feeds back on itself. Communication theorists argue that this circular interaction continues because each participant imposes her own **punctuation**; each arbitrarily believes that what she says is caused by what the other person says. In a sense, such serial punctuations between family members resemble the dialogue of children quarreling: "You started it!" ("I'm only reacting to what you did.") "No, you started it first!" and so on. As Weakland (1976) contends, it is meaningless to search for a starting point in a conflict between two people because it is a complex repetitive interaction, not a simple, linear, cause-and-effect situation with a clear beginning and end.

Once considered iconoclastic if not radical, this view of redundant patterns of communication within the family as providing clues to family rules and possible family dysfunction has now been adopted by all systems-oriented therapists. The communication perspective itself has undergone considerable revision as it has evolved over three decades, and its current proponents also can be considered to represent the strategic approach. For clarity of presentation, however, we have separated three outlooks: the original Mental Research Institute (MRI) interactional view, the strategic therapy refinements advanced primarily by Jay Haley and Cloe Madanes, and the systemic outlook as advocated by Selvini-Palazzoli, Prata, Boscolo, and Cecchin in Milan, Italy. One final reminder: there is much overlap among the three, each borrowing freely from the theory and therapeutic techniques of the others.

MRI INTERACTIONAL FAMILY THERAPY

We have already noted the role played by the prestigious Mental Research Institute (MRI) in Palo Alto in originating many of the ideas regarding family communication patterns now considered axiomatic to the field. Gregory Bateson, Don Jackson, Jay Haley, Virginia Satir, John Weakland, Jules Riskin, Paul Watzlawick, Arthur Bodin, and Richard Fisch are just some of the prominent family therapy figures who have been closely affiliated with the institute at one time or another over the years. In the decade ending not long after Jackson's death in 1968, the theoretical foundation for a communication/interaction approach to the family was laid, based largely on ideas derived from general systems theory, cybernetics, and information theory. The concepts of family rules, family homeostasis, marital quid pro quo, the redundancy principle (according to which a family interacts within a limited range of repetitive behavioral sequences), punctuation, **symmetrical** and **complementary** relationships, and circular causality, in addition to prototypic work on the double bind in schizophrenia, are all attributable to the seminal thinking of MRI researchers.

All Behavior Is Communication

To communication/interaction theorists, all behavior is communication at some level (Watzlawick, Beavin, & Jackson, 1967). Just as one cannot not behave, so one cannot not communicate. The wife who complains in utter frustration that her husband "refuses to communicate" with her but instead stares at the television set all evening is responding too literally to his failure to talk to her. On a nonverbal level, she is receiving a loud and clear message that he is rejecting her, withdrawing from her, may be angry or bored with her, wants distance from her, and so on. Communication thus may occur at many levels—gesture, body language, tone of voice, posture, intensity—in addition to the content of what is said.

Not infrequently, the receiver can become confused when contradictions appear between what is said and what is expressed in tone or gesture. A double-bind message is a particularly destructive form of such **paradoxical communication**. As we described it in Chapter Four, a double-bind message is communicated when one person issues a statement to another that simultaneously contains two messages or demands that are logically inconsistent and contradictory, as in the following:

IGNORE THESE INSTRUCTIONS

To follow the instructions, one must not follow these instructions, which becomes very confusing. The receiver is being called upon to make a response but is doomed to failure with whatever response he or she makes.

There is, of course, no such thing as a simple message. People continually send and receive a multiplicity of messages by both verbal and nonverbal channels, and every message is qualified and modified by another message on another level of abstraction (Weakland, 1976). People can say one thing and mean another, modifying, reinforcing, or contradicting what they have just said. In other words, they are both communicating ("How are you?") and communicating about their communications ("I do not really expect you to answer, nor do I especially want to know the answer, unless you say you are fine"). All communication takes place at two levels—the surface or content level and a second level called **metacommunication** that qualifies what is said on the first level (Watzlawick, Beavin, & Jackson, 1967). Problems may arise when a message at the first level ("Nice to see you") is contradicted by a facial expression or voice tone that communicates another message ("How can I make a quick getaway from this boring person?") that communicates at the second level. As we noted earlier, communication theorists, following the original research of Bateson and his coworkers, propose that such contradictions are common in families that produce schizophrenic children: "We love you (hate you)," "We want you close by (go away)," and so on. In effect, the parent is saying "I order you to disobey me" to a confused child to whom the relationship is important; the child cannot escape but must respond to the incongruent messages. In that situation he or she may develop a similarly incongruent way of communicating back, sometimes in a schizophrenic manner.

Report and Command Functions

Every communication has a content (report) and a relationship (command) aspect. That is, every communication does more than convey information; it also defines the relationship between communicants. For example, the husband who announces "I'm hungry" is offering information but also, more important, is telling his wife that he expects her to do something about it by preparing dinner. He is thus making a statement of his perceived rights in the relationship; he expects his wife to take action based on his statement. The way his wife responds tells him whether she is willing to go along with his definition of the relationship or wants to engage in what could be a struggle to redefine it ("Why don't you make the dinner tonight?" or "I'd like to go out to a restaurant tonight," or "I'm not hungry yet").

Relationships are defined by command messages. These messages constitute regulating patterns for stabilizing relationships and defining family rules. In operation, the rules preserve family homeostasis. The notion of the family attempting to maintain a homeostatic balance is central to the viewpoint of communication theorists. You will recall from Chapter Three that Jackson (1965b) likened the family's operations to those of a home heating system, in which a sudden change in temperature initiates a number of events designed to reestablish the equilibrium. In a family, when a teenager announces she is pregnant, or parents decide to get a divorce, or a handicapped child is born, or a family member becomes schizophrenic, it has an effect similar to flinging open a window when the house has been warmed to the desired temperature. The family goes to work to reestablish its balance; ironically, a family that was disintegrating and disunited has a sudden impetus to become functional again in order to cope with the crisis.

Symmetrical and Complementary Relationships

In a family, a communication pattern reveals much about the sender's and receiver's relationship. If it is a relationship based on equality, the pattern is symmetrical; if not, the pattern is complementary. In the former, partipants mirror each other's behavior; if A boasts, B boasts more grandly, causing A to boast still further, and so on in this one-upmanship game. Symmetrical communication can be a simple open exchange of views or it can be highly competitive, but it takes place between peers and each person assumes equal control and authority.

Complementary communication inevitably involves one person who assumes a superior position and another who assumes an inferior one. One partner's behavior complements the other; if A is assertive, B becomes submissive, encouraging A to greater assertiveness, demanding still more submissiveness from B, and so on. Bateson's (1958) original description of these phenomena was adapted by Jackson and his associates to characterize specific family interaction patterns.

While a symmetrical relationship may be characterized by equality and the minimization of differences between participants, it also runs the risk of becoming competitive. In this case, each partner's actions influence the reactions of his or her partner in a spiraling effect called **symmetrical escalation**. Quarrels may get out of hand and become increasingly vicious as a nasty jibe is met with a nastier retort, which prompts the first person to become even more mean and ill-tempered, and so on. Squabbling partners may continually vie for ascendance over one another, neither willing to back down or concede a point. (In one Woody Allen movie, an exchange between a bickering couple goes something like this: "The Atlantic is the best ocean"; "You're crazy—the Pacific is a much better ocean"; "You're the one who's crazy and doesn't know what he's talking about"; and so on.) The process of the exchange rather than its content is of interest in defining the relationship.

By definition, complementary relationships are based on inequality and the maximization of differences. In this form of reciprocal interaction, one partner (traditionally the male) takes the "one-up" position and the other (traditionally the female) assumes the submissive "one-down" position. However, despite appearances, these positions need not be taken as an indication of their relative strength or weakness or power to influence the relationship. Each partner behaves in a manner that presupposes—and at the same time provides a rationale for—the other's behavior. In a complementary relationship, dissimilar but apt responses evoke in each other an interlocking pattern (Watzlawick, Beavin, & Jackson, 1967).

While at the MRI, Haley (1963) underscored the struggle for power and control in every relationship that is inherent in the messages that sender and receiver exchange. Who will define the relationship? Will that person attempt to turn it into a symmetrical or complementary one? Who decides who decides? Observe a couple discussing how to allocate expenditures, or what television program to watch, or who will answer the telephone, balance the checkbook, go to the refrigerator to get a snack, or pick up the dirty socks and underwear from the bedroom floor, and see if you do not learn a great deal about how the partners define their relationship.

Therapeutic Assumptions

Led primarily by the innovative thinking of Watzlawick (Watzlawick, 1978; Watzlawick, 1984; Watzlawick, Weakland, & Fisch, 1974), the MRI therapeutic model emphasizes that, ironically, the solutions people sometimes attempt to alleviate a problem often contribute to the problem's maintenance or even its exacerbation. In this view, problems may arise from some ordinary life difficulty, perhaps coping with a transition such as the birth of a child or going off to school for the first time. Most families handle such transitions with relative ease, although occasionally the difficulty turns into a problem, particulary when the difficulty is mishandled or it remains unresolved and the family persists in applying the same "solution" despite its previous failure to eliminate the difficulty. Eventually, the original difficulty escalates, by a vicious cycle process, into a problem "whose eventual size and nature may have little apparent similarity to the original difficulty" (Fisch, Weakland, & Segal, 1982, p. 14).

The task for the therapist in such situations is to break into the repetitive but self-perpetuating cycle. According to Watzlawick (1978), therapy must accomplish second-order changes (a change in viewpoint, often as the result of a therapist's reframing of a situation) rather than mere first-order changes (a conscious decision by clients to behave differently). He argues that the two cerebral hemispheres have different functions, and each has its own language. The language of change, analogic language, is the language of the right hemisphere; it deals with imagery, symbols, synthesis. Digital language, corresponding to left-brain activity, is the language of logic, reason, explanation—to Watzlawick, the language of most psychotherapy. Watzlawick urges gaining access to the right hemisphere, using paradoxes, puns, ambiguities, imagery, and such to facilitate second-order changes. In the process, the left hemisphere—the logical watchdog—must be bypassed, often through reframing techniques or through the use of the **therapeutic double bind**.

The Therapeutic Double Bind

Interactionists assume that the therapist, as an outsider, is the one to provide the family with an experience that will enable the members to change their rules and metarules concerning their relationships with one another and with the outside world. They need to learn how each punctuates an interaction, and how conflict often follows differences in such interpretations. Families must examine their patterns of communication (including report and command functions) and especially the context in which communication occurs. More specifically, faulty but persistent solutions to everyday difficulties must be examined to learn if the family

(1) ignores a problem when some action is called for; (2) overreacts, taking more action than is necessary or developing unrealistic expectations from actions taken; or (3) takes action at the wrong level (making cosmetic first-order changes when second-order changes are necessary). (We'll return to these issues in Chapter Eleven when we consider the MRI brief therapy approach.)

While focusing on the presenting problem and helping the family develop clear and concise goals, interactionists often try to induce change by offering directives to the family that appear to fly in the face of common sense. The purpose of such paradoxical approaches is often to jar the family's established (if unsuccessful) pattern of interaction by powerful indirect means. Since second-order change is the goal, the therapist is attempting to circumvent family resistance to altering the interactive patterns that maintain the problematic behavior.

One direct outgrowth of the MRI research on the pathological double bind has been the notion of the therapeutic double bind, a general term that describes a variety of paradoxical techniques used to change entrenched family patterns. A paradox can be defined as a "contradiction that follows correct deduction from consistent premises" (Watzlawick, Beavin, & Jackson, 1967, p. 188). In a pathogenic double-bind situation, the recipient is placed in a position where no solution is possible. A double bind is applied therapeutically when a symptomatic person is told not to change (for example, a depressed person is told not to be in such a hurry to give up the depression) in a context where the individual has come expecting to be helped to change. The person thus is caught in a trap: if the directive is defied and the individual tries to lift the depression, this constitutes therapeutic change; if the person complies and does not attempt to change, he or she acknowledges a choice and the exercise of control. Since symptoms, by definition, are beyond control, the person can no longer claim to be behaving symptomatically.

Technically, Watzlawick, Beavin, and Jackson (1967) outline the structure of the therapeutic double bind as follows:

> 1. It presupposes an intense relationship, in this case the psychotherapeutic situation, which has a high degree of survival value and of expectation for the patient.
> 2. In this context, an injunction is given which is so structured that it:
>   a) reinforces the behavior the patient expects to be changed;
>   b) implies that this reinforcement is the vehicle of change; and
>   c) thereby creates paradox because the patient is told to change by remaining unchanged. He is put in an untenable situation with regard to his pathology. If he complies, he no longer "can't help it"; he does "it," and this, as we have tried to show, makes "it" impossible, which is the purpose of therapy. If he resists the injunction, he can do so only by not behaving symptomatically, which is the purpose of therapy. If in a pathogenic double-bind the patient is "damned if he does and damned if he doesn't," in a therapeutic double-bind he is "changed if he does and changed if he doesn't."
> 3. The therapeutic situation prevents the patient from withdrawing or otherwise dissolving the paradox by commenting on it. Therefore, even

> though the injunction is logically absurd, it is a pragmatic reality: the patient cannot not react to it, but neither can he react to it in his usual, symptomatic way. (p. 241)

In a form of therapeutic double bind called **prescribing the symptom**, interactionists try to produce a runaway system (positive feedback) by urging or even coaching the client to engage in or practice his or her symptoms, at least for the present time. A family is instructed to continue or even to exaggerate what it is already doing (for example, the mother and daughter described at the beginning of this chapter might be directed to have a fight on a regular basis, every evening immediately after dinner). Since the family has come for help from the therapist (who does not seem to be stupid, crazy, or incompetent) and since the directive is easy to follow because the symptomatic behavior is occurring anyway, the family complies.

The therapist, asked to help them change, appears to be asking for no change at all! Such an assignment, however, undermines family members' resistance to change by rendering it unnecessary. At the same time, the therapist is challenging the function or purpose of the symptom, which probably serves to maintain family balance. In our example, confronted with the repugnant idea of fighting on a regular basis, the mother and daughter begin to interact in a different manner. The unstated rules by which they operated before become more obvious to them, as does the notion that their previous quarreling did not "just happen" involuntarily but can be brought under voluntary control.[1] Since their interactive pattern no longer serves the family function of providing balance, the entire family must seek new ways of interacting with one another.

Another form of therapeutic bind, **relabeling** (similar to what was described in Chapter Eight as reframing), attempts to alter the meaning of a situation by altering its conceptual and/or emotional context in such a way that the entire situation is perceived differently. That is, language is used to alter the interpretation of what has occurred, and thus invites the possibility of a new response to the behavior. The situation remains unchanged, but the meaning attributed to it, and thus its consequences, is altered. The classic example comes from Tom Sawyer, who relabeled as pleasurable the drudgery of whitewashing a fence and thus was in a position to ask other boys to pay for the privilege of helping him. Relabeling typically emphasizes the positive ("Mother's not being overprotective; she merely is trying to be helpful") and helps the family redefine disturbing behavior in more sympathetic or optimistic terms. Relabeling provides a new framework for looking at interaction; as the rules by which the family operates become more explicit, the family members become aware that old patterns are not necessarily unchangeable.

1. Maurizio Andolfi (1979), director of the Family Therapy Institute in Rome, is particularly adept at unbalancing rigid family systems, often through effective use of "prescribing the symptom." In a family in which an anorectic adolescent girl controls family communication and defines all relations, including the relationship between her parents, Andolfi will forbid the girl from eating during a lunch session when the therapist and family eat together normally. Since her symptom (non-eating) is now involuntary, it no longer serves as a means of controlling family interactions. At the same time, the family can no longer use its typical incongruent message, "Eat, but don't eat." The prescription interrupts the family game based on the daughter's eating problems and helps expose the rules of the anorectic system.

The goal of relabeling, like the other double-bind techniques, is to change the structure of family relationships and interactions.

STRATEGIC FAMILY THERAPY

If the communication/interaction approach, the MRI model, drew the greatest attention from professionals in the 1960s, and Minuchin's structural model was the most consistently studied and emulated in the 1970s, then it is fair to say that the strategic approach took center stage in the 1980s. As its leading advocates Madanes and Haley (1977) contend, the main characteristic of this therapeutic approach is that the therapist devises a strategy for solving the client's presenting problems. Goals are clearly set; therapy is carefully planned, in stages, to achieve these goals; problems are defined as involving at least two and usually three people. The thrust of the intervention is to shift the family organization so that the presenting problem no longer serves a function. To the strategic therapist, change occurs not through insight and understanding but through the process of the family carrying out directives issued by the therapist.

The career of Jay Haley plays an important part in the development of the strategic approach to family therapy. Haley was a member of Bateson's schizophrenia research project in the 1950s, playing a significant role in developing the double-bind concept to account for the effect of a family's pathological communication patterns on the development of schizophrenia in a family member (Bateson, Jackson, Haley, & Weakland, 1956). In the process of that investigation, Haley became interested in issues around power and control in human relationships, and in 1963 published his classic work *Strategies of Psychotherapy*, in which he contended that implicit in every interpersonal transaction is a struggle for control of the definition of the relationship. He viewed symptomatic behavior in one partner as a pathological control strategy, warning that the therapist must maintain control of the therapy relationship, lest the client gain control and perpetuate his or her difficulties in order to "continue to govern by symptomatic methods" (Haley, 1963, p. 19).

While at MRI, Haley became a student and interpreter of Milton Erickson, whose hypnotic techniques typically required the therapist to assume full charge of the treatment and to issue directives (however subtle) as a way of gaining leverage with patients and, ultimately, manipulating them to change. Erickson argued that an effective therapist needs to be a strategist who approaches each new client with a specific therapeutic plan tailored to that individual. Erickson's extraordinary feats of observation and seemingly uncanny ability to tap unrecognized resources in his clients (usually individuals rather than families) have been chronicled by Haley (1973) as well as by Zeig (1980).

Erickson, noted for a number of creative and unconventional hypnotic techniques, was particularly skilled at "encouraging resistance" through the use of paradoxical directives. That is, he was able to encourage patients to maintain a symptom (by not fighting it or insisting the client work at giving it up) and then

Milton Erickson, M.D.

subtly introduce directions to induce change. Thus, he was able to avoid direct confrontation with the symptom, a tactic likely to have been met with resistance, and to use the client's own momentum to force symptom abandonment. This technique, developed so that the hypnotic subject would not experience a loss of control to the hypnotist, became the later basis for some of Haley's techniques in working with families. That is, the family's unwillingness to relinquish control to the therapist often makes them resistant to change. Not directly confronting the resistance lessens their fear that they will be required to do things against their will.

Haley was also influenced by his long association as trainer and theory-builder with Salvador Minuchin and Braulio Montalvo at the Philadelphia Child Guidance Center. Hoffman (1981) actually classifies Haley's position as a structural-strategic approach; Minuchin himself points out that there are obvious similarities between the structural and strategic outlooks (Simon, 1984). Haley's concern with family hierarchy and coalitions and other family structure issues places him in the former group, while his interest in paradoxical directives and other unobtrusive ways of managing resistance identifies him with the latter.

By 1974 Haley and his wife Cloe Madanes had formed the Family Therapy Institute (renamed the Haley-Madanes Institute in 1989) in Washington, D.C., a highly respected training program for family therapists. Haley, a prolific writer, described his strategies for changing the way a family is organized in *Problem-Solving Therapy* (1976); more recently, he published *Ordeal Therapy* (1984), an account of treatment based on the premise that if a client is maneuvered into a position where he or she finds it more distressful to maintain a symptom than to give it up, the client will abandon the symptom. Madanes has presented recent innovations in the field in *Behind the One-Way Mirror: Advances in the Practice of Strategic Therapy* (1984). Haley and Madanes, separately and together, have demonstrated their active, directive, highly focused therapeutic techniques around the world.

The Meaning of Symptoms

Haley (1963) believes a symptom, rather than representing behavior beyond one's control, to be a strategy for controlling a relationship when all other strategies have failed; moreover, the symptomatic person denies any intent to control by claiming the symptom is involuntary. As an example, Haley cites the case of a woman who insists her husband be home every night because she suffers anxiety attacks if left alone. However, she refuses to acknowledge her demand as a means of controlling his behavior, but blames it on the anxiety attacks over which she presumably has no control. The husband faces a dilemma; he cannot acknowledge that she is controlling his behavior (the anxiety attacks are at fault for that) but he cannot refuse to let her control his behavior (after all, she has anxiety attacks). He is in a double-bind situation.

Haley, therefore, focuses on the power and control struggles within a family and how each family member constantly seeks to define or redefine his or her relationships. ("You can't boss me around anymore; I'm not a baby" is a familiar taunt heard from a teenager trying to change old family rules.) Jockeying for control, according to Haley, occurs in all families and in every relationship between two or more people. Most couples develop suitable up-front means of dealing with issues of control; people who present symptoms are resorting to subtle, indirect methods. It is Haley's contention that control struggles in a relationship are inevitable; one cannot not try to define a relationship or attempt to control an outcome. Haley considers the maneuver pathological only if one or both participants denies trying to control the other's behavior and/or exhibits symptomatic behavior in the process of doing so.

Strategic therapists concern themselves with here-and-now family communication patterns as well as repetitive sequences of behavior between and among family members. Like the communication/interactionists, they believe that communication defines the nature of the relationship between partners. If a husband is willing to discuss only the weather when he and his wife are together in the evening, he may be defining the relationship as one where they talk only about conventional matters. If the wife refuses to comment on tomorrow's forecast but instead expresses the idea that they seem distant from each other this evening, she is attempting to redefine the relationship on more personal and intimate terms. Their conflict is not a struggle to control another person, according to Haley, but a struggle to control the definition of the relationship. As we have noted, in some marriages a partner's symptoms (for example, anxiety attacks, phobias, depressions, heavy drinking) control what takes place between the partners—where they go, what they do together, whether one can leave the other's side for any length of time, and so on. Traditionally, such symptoms have been explained as expressions of intrapsychic conflict and therefore as involuntary aspects of one person's "illness." Haley, strongly opposed to intrapsychic explanations, defines symptoms as interpersonal events, as tactics used by one person to deal with another. In his view, the therapist's goal is to maneuver the patient into developing other ways of defining relationships so that the symptomatic methods will be abandoned.

Developing Therapeutic Strategies

Strategic family therapists tailor their interventions to a specific set of presenting problems, deal with the present rather than the past, and devise novel strategies for helping the family prevent the repetition of destructive behavior. Rather than offer interpretation or provide insight—the family may actually resolve a problem without ever knowing why or how—strategic therapists attempt to change only those aspects of the family system that are maintaining the problematic or symptomatic behavior. The emphasis in strategic therapy, according to Madanes (1981), is not on devising a therapeutic method applicable to all cases, but rather on designing a strategy for each specific problem. The focus throughout is on alleviating the presenting problem, not exploring its roots or buried meanings.

Haley (1963) points out that therapists and patients continually maneuver with each other in the process of treatment. Elements of a power struggle exist in psychoanalysis, hypnosis, behavior therapy, family therapy, and other forms of treatment. Family members may try to manipulate, deceive, exclude, or subdue a therapist in order to maintain the homeostatic balance they have achieved, even if it is at the expense of symptomatic behavior in one of their members. The therapist, therefore, must take an authoritative stance. Haley (1976) sees his task as taking responsibility for changing the family organization and resolving the problem that brought the family to see him. He is highly directive, giving the family members precise instructions or directives and insisting that they be followed. Thus, he is highly manipulative in his procedures. For example, Haley cites the case (1976) of a grandmother siding with her grandchild (age 10) against the mother. He saw the mother and child together, instructing the child to irritate the grandmother and instructing the mother to defend her daughter against the grandmother. This task forced a collaboration between mother and daughter and helped detach the daughter from her grandmother.

As we can see from this example, Haley is an active, take-charge family therapist. Eschewing the use of a cotherapist because working alone permits the strategic therapist to move more quickly and decisively, Haley nevertheless frequently has associates observe from behind a one-way mirror so that the therapist may benefit from their feedback later. The therapist, however, is in charge of the session. Artfully gaining the position of family change-maker, he intervenes when he chooses (rather than when the family requests his participation), comments openly about the family's efforts to influence or control him, gives directions and assigns tasks, and assumes temporary leadership of the family group. He avoids getting enticed into coalitions within the family; adroitly, he takes sides to overcome an impasse but quickly disengages before becoming allied with one or another family faction.[2]

Another Haley tactic is to emphasize the positive, usually by relabeling seemingly dysfunctional behavior as reasonable and understandable. In one often quoted example, Haley boldly (and at first glance, outrageously) told a wife whose husband had chased after her with an ax that the man was simply trying to get close to her! Here, Haley was simply following a principle of communication theory described earlier; namely, that all communication occurs at two levels and that the message at the second level (metacommunication) qualifies what takes place on the surface level. What Haley was communicating by the relabel, and what the wife also sensed, was that the husband indeed did want to connect with her, but his rage got in the way of doing so in any constructive manner. (In everyday exchanges, a remark made by a sender in normal conversation can be taken as a joke or an attack, as praise or as blame, depending on the context in which the receiver places it.) By addressing the metamessage—he wanted to get close—Haley changed the context, freeing the participants to behave differently in the new context.

The Initial Interview

Haley (1976) contends that the first interview, which he insists the whole family attend, sets the stage for the entire course of therapy. Proceeding systematically, through stages, he negotiates with the family to decide what problem(s) require attention, then formulates a plan of action to change the family's dysfunctional behavior patterns in order to eliminate the problem(s). In the opening brief *social stage*, he observes family interaction and tries to get all members to participate, indicating all are involved and should have a voice in the therapy. Next he shifts to the *problem stage*, getting down to the business of why the family is there. He poses such questions as "Why do you seek help now?"; "What would each of you like to change?"; "Quickly or slowly?"; "Do you wish to realize what is happening or just to change?"; "Are you willing to make sacrifices to change?" (Haley, 1988). In this information-gathering phase, conversation is directed at the therapist, who displays an interest without rushing to interpret the thoughts and feelings being expressed. The *interaction stage*, during which the family discusses the problem aloud with one another in the presence of the therapist, permits Haley to observe any dysfunctional communication sequences, coalitions, power hierarchies, and such, thereby offering clues about future therapeutic interventions. The final segment of the initial interview, the *goal-setting stage*, provides an opportunity for therapist and family together to determine precisely the presenting problem

2. Another noteworthy side-taker is Gerald Zuk (1981). Although Madanes and Haley (1977) classify him as a strategic therapist, Zuk does not use the term himself. Nevertheless, as Stanton (1981) notes, Zuk often displays the kind of planning and forethought exercised by strategists. A systems-oriented psychologist long affiliated with the Eastern Pennsylvania Psychiatric Institute in Philadelphia, Zuk offers a **triadic-based therapy** in which the therapist acts as go-between in working with a couple, setting the rules for communicating, in order to shift the balance of "pathogenic relating" among family members. As go-between and as side-taker, Zuk may select an issue to be negotiated, with himself as mediator, deliberately siding with one and then the other family member. By taking control and setting limits, Zuk structures and directs the therapy process.

they wish to solve or eliminate. In a sense, the last phase results in a contract that clearly defines goals, allowing all participants to measure change or gauge the success of their efforts as therapy progresses. In many cases, Haley ends the initial session with his first set of assignments or directives for change (Haley, 1976).

The Use of Directives

Directives, or assignments of tasks to be performed outside of the therapeutic session, play a key role in strategic family therapy, and are given for several reasons: (1) to get people to behave differently so they will have different subjective experiences; (2) to intensify the therapeutic relationship by involving the therapist in the family's actions during the time between sessions; and (3) to gather information, by their reactions, as to how the family members will respond to the suggested changes. Advice, direct suggestions, coaching, even assignments of ordeal-like behavior to be followed if a symptom appears, are examples of straightforward directives by the therapist aimed at achieving problem solution.

In most cases, Haley issues a directive to family members (for example, instructing a mother to stop intruding when the father and son try to talk to each other) because he wants or expects them to follow it in order for them to change their behavior toward one another. However, asking someone to stop engaging in certain behavior is a difficult directive to enforce; its success depends upon the status of the therapist giving the instruction, the severity or chronicity of the behavior, how often the directive is repeated, whether the family members are willing to cooperate with the therapist in accomplishing the task, and so forth. In short, a key factor determining whether the therapist will succeed in this direct approach is the motivation of all the family members.

Frequently, the direct approach is unsuccessful. Another kind of task assignment, more indirect, is one by which the therapist hopes to provoke the family to resist him or her so that it will change. Assignment of paradoxical tasks can be directed at individual family members, pairs of people, or at the family system (Weeks & L'Abate, 1982). It can take one of two forms—prescriptive or descriptive. Prescriptive paradoxes ask the client(s) to do something, while descriptive paradoxes relabel something already being done by giving it a positive meaning or connotation. As Wachtel and Wachtel (1986) illustrate the former, a patient seeking help for his procrastination is asked not to try to accomplish more in the coming week between sessions, but rather to record the various ways he wastes time each day and how long each takes. The changing set, or perhaps the unpleasant task, often leads to a reduction of procrastination. The client may report that there was little to write down the previous week because he got his work done. Or in the case in which a list is made, the client will often gain greater awareness of his self-defeating behavior or perhaps learn that he is less a procrastinator than overdemanding or expecting too much from himself. We offered an example of a descriptive paradox earlier in this section in Haley's relabeling the ax-wielding husband as performing a loving act.

As used by Haley, a paradox is a restraint of change, and is designed to provoke defiance in the recipient. The client is told to continue to do what he or she came to therapy to get over doing. The therapist, on the other hand, is trying to get the client or family to decide that they won't do what they have now been directed to do. Confused, the family members perceive that through the assignment of such a task the therapist is asking them not to change at the same time that the therapist has declared the intention of helping them change.

Paradoxical intervention[3], as Haley uses it, represents a particularly ingenious way of forcing a person or family to abandon old dysfunctional behavior. Similar to "prescribing the symptom," this technique is particularly appropriate for Haley (1976), the strategist, because he assumes that families who come for help are also resistant to any help being offered. The result may be a standoff, a power struggle with the therapist trying to help family members change but in doing so destabilizing their previous homeostatic balance, and the family trying to get the therapist to fail but to go on trying because they realize something is wrong. Andolfi (1979), also considered a structural/strategic therapist, describes such an encounter as a game into which the therapist is drawn, and in which every effort on the part of the therapist to act as an agent of change is nullified by the family group. If not careful, Andolfi warns, the therapist can easily get entangled in the family's contradictory logic of "help me to change, but without changing anything."

Haley's paradoxical approach encompasses several stages. First, he attempts to set up a relationship with the family in which change is expected. Second, the problem to be corrected is clearly defined; third, the goals are clearly stated. In the fourth stage, the therapist must offer a plan; it is helpful if a rationale can be included that makes the paradoxical task seem reasonable. In the fifth stage, the current authority on the problem (such as a physician or a parent) is disqualified as not handling the situation the right way; in the sixth stage, the therapist issues the directive. In the seventh and last stage, the therapist observes the response and continues to encourage the usual problem behavior.

It is of utmost importance that the therapist using paradoxical intervention carefully encourage the member(s) with the behavior to be changed to continue that behavior unchanged—a domineering wife to continue to run everything in the family; a daughter refusing to attend school to stay home; an adolescent boy

3. By now the reader is aware that this approach is employed by many family therapists, especially in dealing with defiant or resistant families. We particularly underline its use in our discussion of those therapeutic approaches that emphasize clear communication, because a paradoxical injunction (for example, "Be spontaneous") is a prototype of a double-bind situation. To command someone to be spontaneous is to demand behavior that cannot be spontaneous because it is commanded! Thus, with seeming innocence, the sender is trapping the receiver into a situation where rule compliance entails rule violation (Watzlawick, Weakland, & Fisch, 1974). The receiver is faced with two conflicting levels of messages, is bewildered, and cannot make an effective response. As Haley, Watzlawick, Erickson, and others use the paradox therapeutically, the family is directed, in effect, "disobey me." As in the case of commanding someone to be spontaneous, instructing the person to disobey what you are saying is to create a paradox. Thus, the family told not to change in effect defies the therapist's injunction; the family begins to change to prove the therapist wrong in assuming it cannot change. If the therapist allows himself or herself to be put down as wrong and even suggests that the change is very likely to be temporary and a relapse probable, the family will resist relapse and continue to change to prove the therapist wrong again. It is essential that the therapist never claim credit for helping the family—indeed, the therapist remains puzzled by the change—in order to preclude the family's need to be disobedient in the form of a relapse.

masturbating in public to continue doing so but to keep a chart of how often, what days he enjoyed it most, and so on. Haley might tell a couple who always fight unproductively to go home and fight for three hours. The issue becomes one of control. The domineering wife no longer runs everything if the therapist is telling her what to do, and if she resists his directive she will become less domineering in relation to her husband. Similarly, Haley assumes in the other cases that the symptom presented, originally a way of gaining an advantage, will resolve if the symptom now places the person at a disadvantage. In the case of the couple, Haley expects them to stop fighting; people do not like to make themselves miserable because someone else tells them to do so.

Haley is a master at bringing about change through the use of therapeutic paradox. By the use of this technique he forces the symptom bearer into a win-win situation: should the individual or family follow his instruction and continue the problematic or symptomatic behavior, Haley has been given the power and control to make the symptom occur at his direction. Should the individual or family resist the paradoxical intervention, the symptomatic behavior is, in the process, given up (and, again, the therapist retains power and control). Strategic therapists devote a great deal of time to devising a nonharmful, if often absurd, paradoxical task appropriate to the problem of the person desiring to change or get rid of a disturbing symptom. For example, in prescribing ordeals, Haley (1984) will direct a client to carry out an unpleasant chore if the symptom appears during the day, thus making the distress of the consequences possibly more unpleasant than the distress of the original symptom. By selecting a task consistent with a client's desires (say, keeping a spotless house) yet like an ordeal in its execution, Haley again tries to make it more difficult for the client to have the problem or symptom than to give it up. Straightforward or paradoxical, ordeal therapy calls for a clear statement of the problem or symptom to be addressed, a commitment to change on the part of the client even if suffering is required, as well as a willingness to follow a therapist's directive regardless of its logic or relevance to the presenting problem.

There are three major steps in designing a paradox, according to Papp (1984): *redefining*, *prescribing*, and *restraining*. Before a therapist can "prescribe the symptom," the behavior to be maintained must be redefined as a loving gesture in the service of preserving family stability. Thus, anger may be relabeled as love, suffering as self-sacrifice, distancing as a way of reinforcing closeness. Next, the wording of the prescription ("Practice being depressed," "Continue being rebellious against your parents") must be brief, concise, and unacceptable (in order for the family to recoil at the instruction) but the therapist must appear to be sincere by offering a convincing rationale for the prescription. Later, when the family members show signs of changing, the therapist must restrain them.

Restraining strategies ("go slow") are efforts to emphasize that the system's homeostatic balance is in danger if improvement occurs too fast; there is danger of relapse before solid gains can be made. Haley (1976) inquired, in a case of a young, middle-class couple concerned that their young child soiled his pants, what the consequences would be if he began to go to the toilet normally. (This move suggested that Haley could help them with the problem but would rather not until he was sure of the consequences to the entire family.) When they returned the next week and indicated that they could think of no adverse consequences, the therapist suggested some possibilities: for example, could the mother tolerate being successful with her child? This effort to restrain the mother from changing her overinvolved but exasperated behavior contained messages at several levels: (1) Haley thought she could tolerate success; (2) he was benevolently concerned so he wanted to make sure she could tolerate it; and (3) the mother would find the suggestion of not tolerating success to be unacceptable. No mother is likely to think she cannot be successful with her own child, as Haley well knew. Thus provoked (the father was similarly confronted), both parents became highly motivated to solve their problem to prove they could tolerate being normal; the boy's problematic behavior ceased.

Some critics have argued that Haley's methods are too manipulative and authoritarian, a charge he dismisses as baseless since he claims all therapies, whether they acknowledge it or not, rely to some extent on interpersonal influence, challenge, and therapist expertise to resolve family problems. Nevertheless, detractors charge that paradoxical intervention need not be so blatantly reliant on power and provocation.

Madanes (1981, 1984) has developed a number of **pretend techniques** that are less confrontational, less apt to invite defiance and rebelliousness, but still helpful in overcoming family resistance. Based on playfulness, humor, and fantasy, these gentler approaches would have a therapist suggest, for example, that a symptomatic child "pretend" to have a symptom and that the parents "pretend" to help. By manipulating the family through this kind of paradoxical intervention, Madanes manages to work out in make-believe what once produced an actual symptom. In many cases, if the family is pretending, then the actual symptom cannot be real and can be abandoned at will. As does Haley, Madanes searches for the underlying family conflict for which the presenting problem or symptom is the metaphor. Then, by strategically helping families abandon symptomatic metaphors, she helps open up the possibility of attempting more adaptive ones.

MILAN SYSTEMIC FAMILY THERAPY

Three major related approaches to family therapy emerged from the work of the Bateson research project of 1952–62: the MRI communication/interactional model; the strategic model developed by Haley and Madanes; and the model put forth by a group of family therapists in Milan, Italy, led by Mara Selvini-Palazzoli. Of the three, the Milan group's model is the most consistent, conceptually and methodologically, with Bateson's circular epistemology (MacKinnon, 1983). That is, this approach focuses on information, much like Bateson (1972) did—as exemplified in his famous definition of information as "a difference that makes a difference." Characterized by a systematic search for differences—in behavior, in relationships, in how different family members perceive and construe an event—and by efforts to uncover the connections that link family members and keep the

Mara Selvini-Palazzoli, M.D.

system in balance, the approach has come to be known as **systemic family therapy**.

Trained as a child psychoanalyst, Selvini-Palazzoli in the late 1960s set about organizing a team of psychiatrists to treat severely disturbed children along with their families. However, their initial efforts to apply psychoanalytic concepts to the family soon proved to be very time-consuming and to produce limited results. By 1972, having become intrigued by published accounts of the works of Bateson, Jackson, Watzlawick, and others at the MRI, especially their emphasis on the relationship context in which the troubled behavior occurs, she, along with Giuliana Prata, Luigi Boscolo, and Gianfranco Cecchin split off from the original group. Together the four began to adopt a family systems perspective and formed the Center for the Study of the Family in Milan.

While Watzlawick was their major consultant in these early years, the group gradually developed their own theory and set of strategic techniques over the next decade (Boscolo, Cecchin, Hoffman, & Penn, 1987). Working with families with a wide range of the most severe emotional problems, they reported particular success in treating anorectic children as well as schizophrenics with their systemic approach. The first comprehensive exposition of their work in book form can be found in *Paradox and Counterparadox: A New Model in the Therapy of the Family in Schizophrenic Transaction* (Selvini-Palazzoli, Boscolo, Cecchin, & Prata, 1978).

The four colleagues separated into two autonomous groups (Boscolo and Cecchin; Selvini-Palazzoli and Prata) in 1980, although they continue to retain

Luigi Boscolo, M.D.

much similarity in therapeutic outlook. Boscolo and Cecchin, calling themselves the Milan Associates, have focused their recent efforts on training in various parts of the world, while Selvini-Palazzoli and Prata (separately since 1982) have pursued family systems research. In the United States, the systemic outlook has found a particularly receptive audience among some members of the Ackerman Institute for Family Therapy in New York, especially Peggy Papp, Peggy Penn, Joel Bergman, and Lynn Hoffman (Hoffman has since founded her own family institute in Amherst, Massachusetts). In Canada, Karl Tomm of the University of Calgary is a leading advocate of the Milan systemic approach. An updated description of the work of Boscolo and Cecchin can be found in *Milan Systemic Family Therapy* (Boscolo, Cecchin, Hoffman, & Penn, 1987). Selvini-Palazzoli's new work, carried out in collaboration with a new group of colleagues, is called *Family Games* (Selvini-Palazzoli, Cirillo, Selvini, & Sorrentino, 1989); in it she proposes an **invariant prescription** for all families with disturbed adolescents or young adults (see following).

Long Brief Therapy

The distinguishing characteristics of Milan systemic family therapy have been its spacing of therapeutic sessions and its use of a team of therapists who work together on a case. The original Milan team method has been described as "long brief therapy" (Tomm, 1984a), since relatively few sessions (generally about ten) were held approximately once a month and thus treatment might extend up to a year or so. Initially, this unusual spacing of sessions was instituted because so many of the families seen at the Center in Milan had to travel hundreds of miles by train for treatment. Later, however, the therapy team realized that their interventions—often in the form of paradoxical prescriptions aimed at changing the way an entire family system functioned—took time to incubate and finally take effect. Once the frequency was determined, the therapists did not grant an extra session or move up a session to shorten the agreed-upon interval. Such requests by families are seen as efforts to disqualify or undo the effects of a previous intervention (Selvini-Palazzoli, 1980). Systemicists are adamant in their determination that the therapist not submit to the family's "game" or become subjugated to its rules for maintaining sameness and controlling the therapeutic relationship. Even in a dire emergency, these therapists remain unavailable in the belief that a request for an exceptional meeting actually means the family is experiencing rapid change and needs time to integrate any subsequent changes in family rules.

During most of the 1970s, the Milan group worked in an unconventional but fairly set way developed from their research. The entire family was seen together by one or sometimes two therapists (typically, a man and a woman), while the remainder of the team watched from behind a one-way mirror. From time to time during the session, the observers would summon one of the therapists out of the room in order to change therapeutic direction; while conferring with the therapist, they would make suggestions, share opinions, provide their own observations, and often issue directives to be shared with the family. Following this strategy conference, the therapist rejoined the family group, discussed what had transpired with the other team members, and assigned the family members a task, usually a paradoxical prescription. Sometimes such a prescription took the form of a letter, a copy of which was given to every member. In the rare event that a key member missed a session, a copy of the letter would be sent by mail, frequently with comments (again, often paradoxically stated) regarding his or her absence. Prescriptions took the form of opinions ("We believe Father and Mother, by working hard to be good parents, are nevertheless . . . "), or requests that certain behavioral changes be attempted by means of rituals carried out between sessions ("The immediate family, without any other relatives or outsiders, should meet weekly for one hour, with each person allowed fifteen minutes to . . . "). By addressing the behavior of all the members, the therapists underscored the connections in the family patterns. Prescriptions usually were stated in such a way that the family was directed not to change for the time being.

The Milan therapeutic interview format thus is divided into five segments: the presession, the session, the intersession, the intervention, and the postsession discussion. Family therapy begins with the initial telephone call from the family. The team member who takes the call talks to the caller at length, recording the information on a fact sheet. Who calls? Who referred the family? What is the problem? How disturbed is the caller's communication? What tone of voice is used? What is the caller's attitude regarding the forthcoming treatment? What special conditions, if any, does the caller attempt to impose (specific date or time)? These intake issues are then taken up with the entire team in the presession, prior to the first interview, in a lengthy and detailed way, and tentative hypotheses regarding the family's presenting problem are proposed by the various team members. The referring person or agency is kept involved throughout treatment, remaining part of the larger system.

In a similar fashion, such team conferences occur before each session, as the group meets to review the previous session, and, together, plan strategies for the upcoming one. All of these tactics affirm the Milan therapists' belief that the family and therapist(s) are part of one system. During the session itself, a major break in the family interview (the intersession) occurs as the observer team has an active discussion with the therapist outside of the hearing of the family, during which hypotheses are validated or modified; the therapist then returns to offer the team's intervention (usually a prescription or ritual) to the family. The team postsession discussion focuses on an analysis of the family's reaction to the intervention as well as providing a chance to plan for the following session (Boscolo, Cecchin, Hoffman, & Penn, 1987).

In this earlier version of the Milan model there is more concern with process than family structure. Members of dysfunctional families are seen as engaging in unacknowledged destructive, repetitive sequences of interaction. No one seems able to extricate himself or herself from the family's self-perpetuating "games" in which members try to control each other's behavior. Systemicists argue that to attempt to change an individual player is to doom the intervention to failure. Even the identified problem is seen as serving the system in the best way possible at the moment. Why, then, can the family not find a better way to survive and function, one that does not involve sacrificing one of its (symptomatic) members? Perhaps the rules governing the system are too rigid, tolerating an extremely narrow range of behavior. Since the family members, through their communication patterns, maintain the system's rules and thus perpetuate the transactions in which the symptomatic behavior is embedded, the therapist must try to change the rules in order to change that behavior (Selvini-Palazzoli, Boscolo, Cecchin, & Prata, 1978).

Put more succinctly, systemic therapy tries to discover, interrupt, and thus change the rules of the game before the behavior of the players (the symptomatic member as well as other family members) can change. For example, the therapist working with a family with an anorectic daughter must break the code inherent in the following family game, as each parent both insists upon and denies family leadership (Selvini-Palazzoli, 1978):

Mother:	I don't let her wear miniskirts because I know her father doesn't like them.
Father:	I have always backed my wife up. I feel it would be wrong to contradict her. (p. 208)

Note the trap the therapist is drawn into if he or she tries to change such confusing and disqualifying statements. Direct interventions are likely to bring forth countermoves, as the family members fight off any challenge to their rules. Following Bateson's earlier work, Selvini-Palazzoli and her colleagues contend that a family double-bind message, a paradox, can only be undone by a therapeutic double-bind, which they call a **counterparadox**.

Milan Interviewing Techniques

Central to the Milan approach and thus the first act of this type of therapy is **hypothesizing**. Systemicists believe that unless the therapist comes to the family session prepared with hypotheses to be checked out, there is the risk that the family may impose its own definition of the problem and its resolution, which is likely to be faulty and perpetuating of the presenting problem. Hypothesizing refers to the active efforts the team makes during the presession to formulate in advance of the family session what they believe might be responsible for maintaining the family's problems. Diagnostically useful in formulating a "map" of the family's problems, hypothesizing also serves to orient the therapist to ask the kinds of questions that will elicit answers that confirm, necessitate revision of, or refute the suppositions.

Hypothesizing helps the team organize forthcoming information from the family and begin to comprehend why the symptomatic behavior manifested itself in this family at this time. The construction of hypotheses, a continuous process throughout therapy, is based on cybernetic feedback loops; how the family responds to hypothesis-based questions alters the hypothesis, which again may require modification as a result of family response. Hypotheses are carefully constructed to elicit a picture of how the family is organized around the symptom or presenting problem. Circularity throughout the family system is stressed. Asked for a description of the problem at the start of the first interview, the family might point to the symptom bearer as the one with the problem. The Milan therapist will ask, "Who noticed the problem first?" This redefines the problem as interpersonal—it does not exist without a "noticer" and thus it does not belong to one person alone. Moreover, the problem is depicted as an event between two or more family members, thus involving the wider family system (Boscolo, Cecchin, Hoffman, & Penn, 1987).

Circular questioning by the therapist reflects the systemic hypothesizing generated by the Milan team. The technique focuses attention on family connections rather than individual symptomatology, by framing every question so that it addresses differences in perception by different family members about events or relationships. Asking a child to compare his mother's and father's reactions to his sister's refusal to eat, or to rate each one's anger on a ten-point scale, or to hypothesize what would happen if they divorced—these are all subtle and relatively benign ways to compel people to focus on differences. By asking several people the same question about their attitude toward the same relationship, the therapist is able to probe more and more deeply without being directly confrontational or interrogating the participants in the relationship (Selvini-Palazzoli, Boscolo, Cecchin, & Prata, 1980). Here again we see the influence of Bateson's thinking, with its stress on information, differences, and circularity.

Family members reveal their connections through the communication of information, expressed in verbal as well as nonverbal fashion. Information about the family lies in differences in meaning each participant gives an event. Such differences in turn reflect family relationships. Circular questioning aims at eliciting and clarifying confused ideas about family relationships and introducing information about such differences back to the family in the form of new questions.

Such triadic questioning (addressing a third person about the relationship between another two) often produces change in the family in and of itself, as well as providing information to the therapist. Families learn in the process to think in circular rather than linear terms, and to become closer observers of family processes. Another member's perspective may prove enlightening when compared to one's own view of an event or relationship. Circular questioning, a Milan trademark, always addresses significant family issues and not trivial or irrelevant differences. Such questions need to be guided by hypotheses, since hypotheses are what give order and coherence to the therapist's pattern of circular questioning (Tomm, 1984b).

Neutrality refers to the therapist's efforts to remain allied with all family members, avoiding getting caught up in family coalitions or alliances. Such a position, typically low-key and nonreactive, gives the therapist maximum leverage in achieving change by not being drawn into family "games" or appearing to side with one family member against another. More concerned with understanding how the family system works than with attempting to change it, the neutral therapist assumes that the system the family has constructed makes sense; the family could not be any other way than they are at the moment. By not offering suggestions as to how the family should be, the therapist activates the family's capacity to generate its own solutions (Boscolo, Cecchin, Hoffman, & Penn, 1987).

Being neutral does not imply being inactive or indifferent. Actually, the therapist might display neutrality by listening without prejudice to what is being said, but at the same time asking challenging circular questions. A report that the family argues a lot might be accepted by the neutral therapist as interesting information. Without joining the family in assuming arguing is bad, the therapist might inquire, "Who enjoys fighting the most?" or "What would be missing if all the arguing suddenly stopped?" (Tomm, 1984b). Nor should the therapist become too committed to the family's changing. As Selvini-Palazzoli has observed, "If you wish to be a good therapist it is dangerous to have too much of a desire to help other people" (quoted in Simon, 1987, p. 28). The therapist's goal should be to help the family achieve the ability to change. They also have the right not to change. Neutrality precludes taking a position for or against any specific behavioral goals from therapy. (Here the contrast with fellow strategist Haley is great, perhaps reflecting in part the psychoanalytic background of many of the Milan therapists.)

Positive connotation is a form of reframing in which symptomatic behavior is seen as positive or good because it helps maintain the system's balance and thus facilitates family cohesion and well-being. By suggesting a good motive for negative behavior ("The reason your child refuses to go to school is that he wants to provide companionship for his lonely mother"), the systemic therapist is indicating to the family that the symptomatic behavior formerly looked upon negatively may actually be desirable. Instead of being considered "bad" or "sick" or "out of control," the symptomatic child is considered to be well intentioned and to be behaving volitionally. Note that it is not the symptomatic behavior (school refusal) that is connoted to be positive, but rather the intent behind that behavior (family cohesion or harmony).

All members are considered to be motivated by the same positive desire for family cohesion and thus all are linked as participants in the family system. Because the positive connotation is presented as an approval rather than a reproach, the family does not resist such explicit confirmation and accepts the statement. As a result of reframing, the symptomatic behavior can now be viewed as voluntary, greatly enhancing the possibilities for change. However, the positive connotation has implicitly put the family in a paradox: why must such a good thing as family cohesion require the presence of symptomatic behavior in a member?

One other important function of positive connotation deserves mention: it prepares the family for forthcoming paradoxical prescriptions. That is, when each member's behavior is connoted as positive, all view one another as cooperative and thus are more willing to join in complying with any tasks they may be assigned by the therapist, reducing family resistance to future change. If the therapist adds a no-change prescription ("And because you have decided to help the family in this way, we think that you should continue in this work for the time being") (Tomm, 1984b, p. 266), an additional paradox of "no change in the context of change" further increases the impact of the intervention. The seemingly innocuous phrase "for the time being" implies that the current family pattern need not always occur in the current manner, leaving open the possibility of future spontaneous change. The family is left to resolve the paradoxical absurdities on their own.

Family **rituals,** such as weddings, birthday parties, baptisms, bar mitzvahs, graduations, funerals, and so forth, often play a central role in a family's life. Such transitions are designed to mark and facilitate family developmental transitions and changes. Therapeutically, they may be designed to intervene in established family patterns, promoting new ways of doing things, which in turn may alter thoughts, beliefs, and relationship options (Imber-Black, 1988).[4] Rituals may be assigned in paradoxical prescriptions describing in detail what is to be done, by whom, when, and in what sequence. Typically, carrying out the ritual calls for the performance of a task that challenges some rigid, covert family rule.

Rituals are often designed during the intersession, based on how the team views the family's current difficulty. Generally, they are proposed by the therapist in a tentative way as suggestions or family experiments, and are not expected to become a permanent part of family life. The therapist does not insist the ritual be carried out, only indicates that he or she believes the gesture to be useful.

Generally speaking, the purpose of a ritual is to provide clarity where there might be confusion in family relationships; the clarity is gained by the family's

4. Strategic therapists make frequent use of assigned rituals in working with individuals as well as families to help them break out of rigid behavior patterns. Fisch, Weakland, & Segal (1982) of the MRI report the case of a perfectionist who was given the task of making one deliberate mistake a day. In this case, a woman potter who expressed various complaints about her performance was directed to create imperfect pottery for one hour on an agreed-upon day. Similarly, instructing a rigid or compulsive person to fail purposely (say something inappropriate or stupid, behave in clumsy or gauche ways) often has a liberating effect.

enactment of the directive (Tomm, 1984b). Take the case of parents who are inconsistent or competitive with one another in attempting to maintain behavioral control of a disruptive child. An odd day–even day ritual might be suggested in which Mother takes full charge of discipline on odd days (with father observing and taking exact notes on the ensuing mother-child interaction) and Father takes charge on even days (with mother playing the counterrole). Each is directed to carry out the asssigned roles for a certain number of days, and to behave "spontaneously" for the remaining days of the week. Carrying out the ritual clarifies differences in approach for the parents and provides greater awareness of how their differences can cause confusion in their child. It also highlights the importance of consistency, a comfort to the child when only one parent is present.

Drawing attention to crucial distinctions is thus an important aspect of a ritual. In some cases the message the therapists wish to convey is sufficiently critical that they prepare a written statement for the family to read before carrying out the task. As Tomm (1984b) observes, rituals often enable the family to clarify chaotic patterns and confront inherent but previously unrecognized contradictions.

Principles of Therapeutic Intervention

Systemic therapeutic techniques in the earlier Milan version were typically based on the paradox-counterparadox phenomenon. Dysfunctional families, presumably seeking change, themselves seem to behave in a paradoxical manner—the moves each member of the system makes seek to keep change from occurring. As Tomm (1984a) describes it, in effect their common message is that they have a problematic or symptomatic member who needs to change, but as a family the rest of the members are fine and do not intend to change. Recognizing from a systems perspective that it is impossible for a part to change without a complementary change in the whole, the Milan group began to design interventions in the form of counterparadoxes directed at breaking up such contradictory patterns, thus freeing up the family to change. One common counterparadox was to declare that although they are change agents, they do not wish to upset what appears to be a workable family homeostatic balance and therefore prescribe no change for now (Selvini-Palazzoli, Boscolo, Cecchin, & Prata, 1978).

In a later revision (the Milan approach is ever-evolving), influenced by Bateson, they began to think of systems as evolving rather than seeking homeostasis. Extrapolating from Bateson's (1972) work, the Milan group theorized that dysfunctional families are making an "epistemological error"—they are following an outdated or erroneous set of beliefs or "maps" of their reality; that is why they appear to be "stuck" or in homeostatic balance. In point of fact, their beliefs about themselves are not the same as their actual behavior patterns. In reality their behavior is changing continuously. The Milan group decided they needed to help families differentiate between two levels—meaning and action. Therapeutically, they began to introduce new information, new distinctions in thought and action, in an effort to activate a process in which the family creates new belief patterns and new patterns of behavior consistent with those beliefs (Tomm, 1984a). New information was given the family explicitly through reframing or implicitly through the prescription of a family ritual.

By uncovering connecting patterns, by revealing family "games," by introducing new information into the system through opinions or requests that certain family rituals be carried out between sessions, Milan therapists try to bring about a transformation in family rules and relationships. Note that, unlike Haley, they do not issue prescriptions to arouse defiance and resistance. Rather, they offer "information" about family connectedness and the interrelatedness of members' behavior. By deliberately trying not to provoke resistance to change, they help the family discover its own solutions (MacKinnon, 1983).

The Invariant Prescription

In the latest therapeutic modification, developed from research begun with Prata, Selvini-Palazzoli (1986) has focused on the impact of a single sustained intervention to unhinge collusive parent-child patterns. As a result of their work with chronically psychotic adolescents and adults, the Milan researchers began to conceptualize severely dysfunctional behavior as linked to a specific "game" within the family. To break up the game, they made the dramatic if controversial proposal that therapists offer a solitary prescription or task for the parents. Later, Selvini-Palazzoli proposed that this universal or invariant prescription be applied to all families with schizophrenic or anorectic children.

Selvini-Palazzoli contends that a single process takes place in all schizophrenic and anorectic families, beginning with a child's attempt to take sides in a stalemated relationship between the parents (Simon, 1987). Eventually drawn into the family game, the child erroneously considers the actively provoking parent to be the winner over the passive parent, and sides with the "loser." The subsequent development of disturbed behavior, requiring parental attention, represents, according to Selvini-Palazzoli, a demonstration to the passive parent of how to defeat the "winner." Instead of joining the child, however, the passive parent sides with the other parent in disapproving of the child's behavior. The child, in this scenario, feels betrayed and abandoned and responds by escalating the disturbed behavior, determined to bring down the "winning" parent and show the "loser" what can be done. Ultimately the family system stabilizes around the symptomatic behavior, all participants resorting to "psychotic family games" as each tries to turn the situation to his or her advantage (Selvini-Palazzoli, 1986).

Selvini-Palazzoli's provocative therapeutic strategy in such a situation is to offer the parents an invariant prescription—a fixed sequence of directives they must follow to break up the game. After an initial family interview, the therapist sees the parents separately and gives them the following prescription intended to introduce a clear and stable boundary between generations (Selvini-Palazzoli, 1986):

> Keep everything about this session absolutely secret at home. Every now and then, start going out in the evenings before dinner. Nobody must be forewarned. Just leave a written note saying, "We'll not be home tonight." If, when you come back, one of your (daughters) inquires where you have

> been, just answer calmly, "These things concern only the two of us." Moreover, each of you will keep a notebook, carefully hidden and out of the children's reach. In these notebooks each of you, separately, will register the date and describe the verbal and nonverbal behavior of each child, or other family member, which seemed to be connected with the prescription you have followed. We recommend diligence in keeping these records because it's extremely important that nothing be forgotten or omitted. Next time you will again come alone, with your notebooks, and read aloud what has happened in the meantime. (pp. 341–342)

The parental alliance, reinforced by joint action and by secretiveness, is strengthened by the prescription, according to Selvini-Palazzoli, and previously existing alliances and family coalitions are broken. Parental disappearance exposes and blocks family games, over which none of the players had complete control but which nevertheless perpetuated psychotic behavior.

Although Selvini-Palazzoli (1986) claims a high success rate for the invariant prescription, there remains considerable skepticism regarding the universality of her latest therapeutic proposals. The therapeutic power of the single prescription for all disturbed families still remains to be established, as does its potential applicability to troubled families with less serious dysfunction.

SUMMARY

Communication theories, emerging from the research at the Mental Research Institute in Palo Alto in the 1950s, have had a major impact on the family therapy field by recasting human problems as interactional and situational (tied to a set of circumstances that maintains them). The introduction of this epistemology by Bateson, Jackson, and others laid the foundation for the therapeutic efforts of the MRI (interactional view), strategic family therapy as developed by Haley and Madanes, and the systemic approach of Selvini-Palazzoli and her Milan team. Particularly characteristic of these approaches is the use of therapeutic double binds or paradoxical techniques for changing family rules and relationship patterns.

Paradoxes—contradictions that follow correct deductions from consistent premises—are used therapeutically to direct an individual or family not to change in a context that carries with it the expectation of change. The procedure promotes change no matter which action, compliance or resistance, is undertaken. "Prescribing the symptom," as used by Jackson, Watzlawick, and other strategists is a paradoxical technique for undermining resistance to change by rendering it unnecessary.

The strategic family therapy approach is characterized by carefully planned tactics and the issuance of directives for solving a family's presenting problems. Haley, its most influential practitioner, uses directives or task assignments as well as indirect paradoxical interventions; the latter force the willing abandonment of dysfunctional behavior by means of the family defying the directive not to change. Madanes, another strategic family therapist, uses "pretend" techniques, nonconfrontational interventions directed at achieving change without inviting resistance.

The Milan group practices systemic family therapy, a technique based on Bateson's circular epistemology. The technique has undergone a number of changes over the years, and continues to present new techniques. According to a "long brief therapy" procedure in which sessions are spaced at more or less monthly intervals, the family is seen by a team of therapists who plan strategy together; one or two therapists work directly with the family, while the others observe from behind a one-way mirror. Families are assigned tasks between sessions, usually based on paradoxical prescriptions. The goal of the Milan model is to offer "information" in order to influence families to change the rules—the destructive repetitive sequences—of their self-perpetuating, self-defeating "games." The Milan approach contends that a family's paradoxical or double bind messages can only be countered by a therapeutic double bind or counterparadox. The Milan group has introduced a number of interviewing techniques: hypothesizing, circular questioning, neutrality, positive connotation, and family rituals. The latest therapeutic innovation, the invariant prescription, remains controversial.

Chapter Ten

Behavioral Approaches to Theory and Practice

Behavioral models of family therapy are relatively recent additions to the field, since it is only within the last twenty years or so that the application of behavioral concepts has been extended to the family unit. The use of clinical behavioral methods with individuals goes back to the early 1960s when, as a reaction against psychodynamic theory and technique, a movement began to bring the scientific method to bear upon the psychotherapeutic process. Today, although many behavioral therapists attend less exclusively to observable behavior and also try to modify a client's **cognitive** processes, they continue to "place great value on meticulous observation, careful testing of hypotheses, and continual self-correction on the basis of empirically derived data" (Lazarus, 1977, p. 550). The unique contribution of the behavioral approach, then, lies not in its conceptualizations of psychopathology or adherence to a particular theory or underlying set of principles, but in its insistence on a rigorous, data-based set of procedures and a regularly monitored scientific methodology.

Despite their relatively recent entrance into the marital and family field, behavioral family therapists have made a significant and lasting impact on current practices. Indirectly, we see their influence on therapists such as Haley and Minuchin, who use distinct interventions to manipulate environments and attempt to change specific maladaptive patterns of interactive behavior. More directly, the behavioral approach is best illustrated by several areas of treatment that we describe in this chapter: (1) **behavioral marital therapy** for intervention in troubled couple relationships; (2) **behavioral parent-skills training** to teach greater facility at child management; (3) **functional family therapy** aimed at achieving cognitive as well as behavioral changes in the family system; and (4) **conjoint sex therapy** to ameliorate various dyadic forms of sexual dysfunction.

The behavioral methods in family therapy apply principles of human learning derived from the psychological laboratory to changing or modifying the maladaptive, problematic, or dysfunctional behavior in which family members are engaged. For behavioral family therapists, theory precedes practice. That is, intervention procedures follow logically from behavioral theory; in most other approaches to family therapy, successful therapeutic techniques are developed first, and only afterward is a theory constructed to explain their success.

Increasingly in recent years, behaviorists have recognized the place of cognitions as events mediating family interactions. Particularly significant has been the willingness of many behavioral therapists to deal with an individual's imagery, mental activities, and thought patterns as frequently being key factors in the development, maintenance, and modification of dysfunctional behavior in individuals. Less determinedly antimentalistic than in the past, behaviorists today are likely to view people as neither exclusively driven by inner forces nor helplessly buffeted by outside forces. Instead, they are likely to understand personal functioning to be the result of continuous, reciprocal interaction between behavior and its controlling social conditions. They recognize that cognitive functioning—the ability to think and make choices—must also be taken into account. While once behaviorists sought exclusively to change the environmental conditions that maintain undesired behavior, many now also emphasize the importance of self-regulation and self-direction in altering behavior. **Cognitive behavior therapy** attempts to modify thoughts and actions by influencing an individual's conscious patterns of thoughts (Meichenbaum, 1977).

Although the behavioral viewpoint for the most part continues to focus on the identified patient as the person having the problem, and in that sense remains largely linear in approach, there are efforts by some (for example, Alexander & Parsons, 1982) to accommodate a systems/behavioral/cognitive perspective. Most behavioral family therapists today are apt to view family interactions as maintained by environmental events preceding and following each member's behavior. These events or contingencies, together with mediating cognitions, are what determine the form as well as the frequency of each family member's behavior. The important role of cognitive factors, both in determining relationship distress and in mediating behavior change, increasingly has been emphasized (Epstein, Schlesinger, & Dryden, 1988).

SOME BASIC BEHAVIORAL CONCEPTS

Before we consider some of the current forms of behavioral family therapy, we present some underlying theoretical assumptions (see Table 10.1) and define important terms. Behaviorists strive for precision in identifying a problem, employ quantification to measure change, and conduct further research to validate their results. They design programs that emphasize assessment (the **behavioral analysis** of the family's difficulties) along with a number of direct and pragmatic treatment techniques to alleviate symptoms and teach the family to improve its skills in communication and self-management. A behavioral analysis might include an objective recording of discrete acts exchanged by family members, along with the behaviors of others that serve as antecedent stimuli, as well as the interactional consequences of the problematic behavior (Epstein, Schlesinger, & Dryden, 1988).

Table 10.1 Ten Underlying Assumptions of Behavioral Therapy

1. All behavior, normal and abnormal, is acquired and maintained in identical ways (that is, according to the same principles of learning).
2. Behavior disorders represent learned maladaptive patterns that need not presume some inferred underlying cause or unseen motive.
3. Maladaptive behavior, such as symptoms, is itself the disorder, rather than a manifestation of a more basic underlying disorder or disease process.
4. It is not essential to discover the exact situation or set of circumstances in which the disorder was learned; these circumstances are usually irretrievable anyway. Rather, the focus should be on assessing the current determinants that support and maintain the undesired behavior.
5. Maladaptive behavior, having been learned, can be extinguished (that is, unlearned) and replaced by new learned behavior patterns.
6. Treatment involves the application of the experimental findings of scientific psychology, with an emphasis on developing a methodology that is precisely specified, objectively evaluated, and easily replicated.
7. Assessment is an ongoing part of treatment, as the effectiveness of treatment is continuously evaluated and specific intervention techniques are individually tailored to specific problems.
8. Behavioral therapy concentrates on "here-and-now" problems, rather than uncovering or attempting to reconstruct the past. The therapist is interested in helping the client identify and change current environmental stimuli that reinforce the undesired behavior, in order to alter the client's behavior.
9. Treatment outcomes are evaluated in terms of measurable behavioral changes.
10. Research on specific therapeutic techniques is continuously carried out by behavioral therapists.

(Source: Goldenberg, 1983, p. 221)

The behavioral therapist is interested in increasing positive interaction between family members, altering the environmental conditions that oppose or impede such interaction, and training family members to maintain the improved behavior. No effort is made to infer motives, uncover unconscious conflicts, hypothesize needs or drives, or diagnose inner pathological conditions producing the undesired behavior; the individual or family is not necessarily helped to gain insight into the origin of current problems. Instead, emphasis is placed on the environmental, situational, and social determinants that influence behavior (Kazdin, 1984). Since almost all behavior is learned rather than innate, behavior can be altered by new learning. Thus, behavioral therapists attempt to train a person's behavior rather than probe those dimensions of personality that, according to other models, underlie behavior.

Classical conditioning is a form of learning first investigated by Ivan Pavlov in studying the physiology of digestion in dogs. In effect, the concept refers to the fact that a neutral stimulus, paired repeatedly with a stimulus that ordinarily elicits a response, eventually elicits the response by itself. As applied to human beings by John Watson (Watson & Rayner, 1920), an American psychologist, and later elaborated by Joseph Wolpe, then a South African psychiatrist, the concept seemed particularly relevant to clinical work because it suggested that certain responses, such as phobias, might simply (and perhaps accidentally) be learned responses. Even more important, they could be unlearned or overcome through experimental **extinction** or various counterconditioning techniques. This last idea is especially germane to the removal or reduction of symptoms of sexual dysfunction, as we shall see later in this chapter.

An even more cogent concept for behavioral therapists is Skinner's (1953) notion of **operant conditioning**, the process of strengthening a particular kind of responsive behavior in a particular situation by selectively rewarding, or reinforcing, that behavior so that it will occur more frequently than other responses that are not being rewarded. For example, what some voluntary, everyday actions (such as answering a doorbell, opening a refrigerator door, choosing a particular flavor of ice cream cone, or buying a ticket to a movie or concert) have in common is that they have usually led to pleasurable consequences in the past and are therefore more likely to occur again than is behavior that has not been so rewarded (such as making an appointment with the dentist).

The point is that much of our behavior, especially that which is voluntarily emitted, is controlled and maintained primarily by its consequences. Behavioral therapists believe that altering the consequences that follow from undesired behavior may make this behavior amenable to modification and control. In family terms, a behavioral therapist might focus on teaching marital partners to exchange positive or pleasing behavior, on the assumption that a person is more likely to exhibit pleasing behavior to someone who pleases him or her, and less motivated to do so if the other's behavior is seen as unrewarding (Stuart, 1969).

Reinforcement refers to the use of certain consequences immediately following and contingent upon a behavior in order to increase the frequency of that behavior. Another way of looking at it is to say that a contingent event that increases the frequency of any behavior can be considered a reinforcer. **Positive reinforcement** aims to increase the frequency of a response by following it with a favorable event (a reward or positive reinforcer). Thus, a student studying for an examination who receives an "A" is likely to increase study activity because of having achieved the desired payoff. By the same token, an infant who cries before going to sleep and is picked up by his or her parents is likely to increase the frequency of crying before sleeping, since the attention and physical contact provided by the parents are probably positive reinforcers (Kazdin, 1984). In interpersonal terms, a smile, a kiss, a gift, a show of attention and affection are all positive reinforcements that lead to increases in the occurrence of behavior that gives rise to these consequences.

Negative reinforcement aims to increase the frequency of a response by removing or terminating an ongoing painful, unpleasant, or aversive stimulus or event immediately after the desired response is made. For example, a mother says to her teenager, "When your room is straightened up to my satisfaction, you will no longer be grounded." Having experienced the removal of the negative reinforcer, presumably the teenager is more likely to repeat the (room-cleaning) response in the future.

Note that in operant conditioning, reinforcement is always contingent on the emission of a response; the response, whether positive or negative, leads to an increase in the targeted behavior. Unlike classical conditioning, operant conditioning usually concerns behavior we consider voluntary. It derives its name from the fact that some voluntary action, or "operation," must be carried out by the individual in relation to the environment. The concept has particular applicability to managing young children who manifest acting out, aggressive behavior (especially when parents are able to exercise control over the reinforcers, both positive and negative). Gerald Patterson (Patterson, Reid, Jones, & Conger, 1975) has been especially effective in developing programs for increasing parenting skills.

Another operant technique useful in achieving behavioral changes is called **shaping**. Developed by Skinner, shaping involves the reinforcement of successive approximations of a targeted behavior until the desired behavior is achieved. In many cases, the behavioral therapist hopes to produce an outcome that is so complex, or involves elements so unlike those in the individual's or family's current repertoire, that it cannot be reached simply by reinforcing existing responses. Under such circumstances, the therapist may employ shaping—achieving the desired behavior by gradually reinforcing small steps along the way instead of reserving reinforcement for the final response itself. For example, parents might be taught to induce the performance of new behaviors in a child by initially reinforcing responses from the child that show some similarity to the ultimately desirable behavior. Gradually, reinforcements are withdrawn from the less similar behaviors and concentrated on the more similar ones, which progressively become more and more similar to the desired behavior until they are one and the same (Masters, Burish, Hollon, & Rimm, 1987).

Contingency contracting refers to the process of arriving at a written agreement or signed contract between parties (for example, parents and children; teachers and students) specifying the circumstances under which one is to do something for another; in effect, the contracting parties exchange positively rewarding behavior with each other. In behavioral terms, the contract specifies the relationship between certain kinds of behavior and their consequences. As an instrument that is easy to understand, straightforward, simple to devise, and noncoercive, the contract has proven to be useful in negotiating parent-child differences. By specifying contingencies, the family members together can agree on the explicit rules for their interaction and determine the consequences of compliance with those rules.

Social learning theory represents an effort to integrate the basic principles of learning with an appreciation of the social conditions under which that learning takes place. In this view, people are capable of learning vicariously, by observing the behavior of others as well as its consequences and by imitating that behavior; children in particular learn a great many behavioral patterns in this way (Bandura, 1977).

Social learning theory, then, offers a broader perspective than the classical or operant conditioning theories of learning, since it views behavior as more than the product of directly experienced response consequences. Moreover, it enables many behavioral therapists to recognize the role of cognition and feelings in influencing behavior. Social learning theorists focus their attention on the contribution of faulty thought patterns (self-defeating, anxiety-engendering statements a person consciously makes to himself or herself) to producing dysfunctional or maladaptive behavior and on the acquisition of new behavior through observing a model of that behavior. Social learning theory is highly applicable to problematic family behavior. A therapist or family member, through **modeling** the desired behavior, provides an example for an observer to imitate; the imitation eventually becomes part of the observer's own behavioral repertoire. For example, parents may watch and then reproduce a therapist's child-management strategies in their own home; a child learns to attend to cues, emulate the behavior of a parent, and finally make that behavior his or her own response to a given situation.

VARIETIES OF BEHAVIORAL FAMILY THERAPY

The Association for the Advancement of Behavior Therapy broadly defines behavioral therapy as involving "the application of principles derived from research in experimental and social psychology for the alleviation of human suffering and the enhancement of human functioning" (Franks & Wilson, 1975, p. 2).

The application of research principles suggests that assessment and evaluation play a key role, not merely in treatment planning but throughout therapy as the behavioral therapist continues to appraise, modify, and even change interventions as behavioral data direct. The treatment approach is tailored to fit the family's specific needs. To begin, the behavioral therapist makes a careful, systematic behavioral analysis of the family's maladaptive behavior patterns, often using reliable questionnaires, pinpointing exactly which behavior needs to be altered and what events precede and follow manifestation of the behavior. For instance, working with a distraught family in which the presenting problem is a 4-year-old boy's "temper tantrums," the behavioral therapist might want to know exactly what the family means by "tantrums," the frequency and duration of such behavior, the specific responses to the behavior by various family members, and especially the antecedent and consequent events associated with these outbursts. By means of this inquiry, the behavioral therapist attempts to gauge the extent of the problem and the environmental factors (such as the presence of a particular family member, a particular cue such as parents announcing bedtime, a particular time and place such as dinnertime at home) that maintain the problematic behavior. The assessment of environmental circumstances is especially crucial, since the behavioral therapist believes that all behavior (desirable and undesirable) is maintained by its consequences.

Generally speaking, the work of behavioral family therapists has a number of characteristics that distinguish it from the approaches taken by the systems-oriented family therapists we have considered: (1) a direct focus on observable behavior, such as symptoms, rather than an effort to establish causality intrapsychically or interpersonally; (2) a careful, ongoing assessment of the specific, usually overt, behavior to be altered; (3) a concern with either increasing (accelerating) or decreasing (decelerating) targeted behavior by directly manipulating external contingencies of reinforcement; (4) an effort to train families to monitor and modify their own reinforcement contingencies; and (5) an interest in empirically evaluating the effects of therapeutic interventions.

The behavioral family therapist is more likely than most systems-based family therapists to use distinct clinical procedures (such as skills training) and not to be insistent on the participation of the entire family. Sometimes the family is brought in when individual procedures fail or when behavioral observation suggests that family members are helping maintain the individual's symptomatic behavior; they are excused after that phase of therapy is completed, the therapist continuing with individually oriented procedures. Extended family members are far less likely to be involved in behavioral therapy. In general, behavioral family therapists view the family as burdened by the patient, or perhaps as unwittingly responding in ways that support and maintain his or her problem behavior, while systems-oriented family therapists assume that family involvement is always present and plays an active part in symptom maintenance (Todd, 1988).

Moreover, as noted earlier, behavioral family therapists, with few exceptions, adopt a linear rather than a circular outlook on causality. For instance, a parent's inappropriate, inconsistent, or otherwise flawed response to a temper tantrum is believed to cause as well as maintain a child's behavioral problem (contrary to the more commonly held view among family therapists that the tantrum constitutes an interaction, including an exchange of feedback information, occurring within the family system). Predictably, the behavioral family therapist is likely to aim his or her therapeutic efforts at changing dyadic interactions (for example, a mother's way of dealing with her child's having a tantrum) rather than adopting the triadic view more characteristic of systems-oriented family therapists, in which the participants in any exchange are simultaneously reacting to other family transactions (for example, a mother who feels neglected by her husband and who attends too closely to the slightest whims of her child; a father who resents his wife taking so much attention away from him in order to interact with their son).

While some of the leading behavioral family therapists such as Gerald Patterson, Robert Liberman, Richard Stuart, and James Alexander do view the family as

Robert Liberman, M.D.

a social system (whose members exercise mutual control over one another's social reinforcement schedules), others remain far from convinced. Gordon and Davidson (1981), for example, acknowledge that in some cases a strained marital relationship may contribute to the development and/or maintenance of deviant child behavior (or vice versa), but they argue that systems theorists have exaggerated the prevalence of the phenomenon. Their experiences lead them to conclude that deviant child behavior may occur in families with and without marital discord; they state that "the simple presence of marital discord in these families may or may not be causally related to the child's problems" (p. 522).

Behavioral Marital Therapy

Not long after the behavioral approach in psychology began to be applied to clinical problems in individuals, interest grew in adapting this perspective to problems of marital discord. By the end of the 1960s, Robert Liberman, a psychiatrist, and Richard Stuart, a social worker, separately had published their early efforts in this regard, each offering a straightforward, step-by-step set of intervention procedures in which some basic learning principles were applied to distressed marital relationships.

The Application of Behavioral Principles. Liberman (1970) introduced an operant conditioning framework to alleviate a variety of family problems, including marital discord. Assuming the role of trainer or educator, he saw marital therapy as an opportunity to induce significant behavioral changes in both partners by restructuring their interpersonal environments. After creating a positive therapeutic alliance with the couple, he began his assessment (or behavioral analysis) of their problems. What behavior is adaptive or maladaptive (that is, should be increased or decreased) in each partner? What specific behavioral changes would they like to see in themselves and in the other family members? What interpersonal contingencies currently support the problematic behavior? Answers to questions such as these force the therapist to specify the behavioral goals of the treatment, a step that behaviorists argue is conspicuously lacking in other therapeutic approaches. The ultimate choice of specific behavioral goals, however, remains the therapist's prerogative.

In one early example of behavioral marital therapy, Liberman (1970) first conducted a behavioral analysis, primarily through interviews with husband and wife, including having the couple collect data on their problems in order to discover what triggered the undesirable behavior and what consequences maintained it. He then applied such basic principles of learning as positive reinforcement, shaping, modeling, and the contingency management of mutual reinforcers of deviant behavior in an effort to restructure the reciprocal exchange of rewards between the marital partners, as described in the following excerpt:

> *My behavioral analysis pointed to a lack of reinforcement from Mrs. S's husband for her adaptive strivings. Consequently her depressions, with their large hypochondriacal components, represented her desperate attempt to elicit her husband's attention and concern. Although her somatic complaints and self-depreciating accusations were aversive for her husband, the only way he knew how to "turn her off" was to offer sympathy, reassure her of his devotion to her, and occasionally stay home from work. Naturally, his nurturing her in this manner had the effect of reinforcing the very behavior he was trying to terminate.*
>
> *During five half-hour sessions, I focused primarily on Mr. S, who was the mediating agent of reinforcement for his wife and hence the person who could potentially modify her behavior. I actively redirected his attention from his wife "the unhappy, depressed woman" to his wife "the coping woman." I forthrightly recommended to him that he drop his extra job, at least for the time being, in order to be at home in the evening to converse with his wife about the day's events, especially her approximations at successful homemaking. I showed by my own example (modeling) how to support his wife in her efforts to assert herself reasonably with her intrusive mother-in-law and an obnoxious neighbor. (p. 113)*

A decade later, Liberman and his colleagues (Liberman, Wheeler, deVisser, Kuehnel & Kuehnel, 1980) prepared a *Handbook of Marital Therapy* in which they described a variety of more sophisticated behavioral techniques, including the contributions of social learning theory as well as the communication approach to marital therapy. In general, the techniques are directed at (1) increasing the couple's recognition, initiation, and acknowledgment of pleasing interactions; (2) decreasing the couple's aversive interactions; (3) training the partners in the use of effective problem-solving communications skills; and (4) teaching them to use contingency contracting in order to negotiate the resolution of persistent problems.

At about the same time as Liberman presented his historically pivotal paper, helping inaugurate the field of behavioral marital therapy, Stuart (1969) also used such behavioral principles as contingency contracting in an effort to get couples to maximize their exchange of positive behaviors. Terming his approach **operant interpersonal therapy**, Stuart assumed from the beginning that the pattern of interaction between spouses at any point in time is the most rewarding of all available alternatives—and that is precisely why they choose it. (For example, a wife who complains that her husband spends too much time with his friends and not enough with her should not simply be angry at him but should face up to the fact that his friends offer greater relative rewards for him than she does.) Stuart assumed further that successful marriages involve a quid pro quo ("something for something") arrangement; here he is in agreement with proposals made earlier by communication theorist Don Jackson. In behavioral terms, according to Stuart, successful marriages can be differentiated from unsuccessful ones by the frequency and range of reciprocal positive reinforcements the partners exchange ("I'll be glad to entertain your parents this weekend if you accompany me to that baseball game [or ballet performance] next month"). In unsuccessful marriages, coercion, withdrawal, and retaliatory behavior are more common. Presumably, the rejected wife in the example above must take the "positive risk" of changing her behavior (that is, making a positive move toward her mate before expecting one from him). In behavioral terms she must be willing to give reinforcement before receiving it. The consequences of her behavioral change increase the likelihood of a "positive risk" from her spouse. The new social exchange reshapes and redefines their relationship.

In a troubled relationship, according to Stuart, the couple is "locked into" a problematic pattern of interaction, each requiring a change in the other before changing his or her own behavior. Stuart proposed that the couple make explicit reinforcement contracts with each other, negotiating exchanges of desired behavior. Negative statements and complaints are restated in terms of specifically desired positive behavior (Wife: "I would like you to talk to me for at least 30 minutes each night after dinner"; Husband: "I would like you to read the newspaper every day so we can spend at least ten minutes of that time talking about the news"). Next, each person records the frequency with which the other completes the desired behavior. Stuart even suggested a token system, somewhat in the style of hospital **token economy** programs, to facilitate behavioral change. The husband may earn tokens for conversing with his wife, and vice versa (these criteria can be negotiated depending on circumstances). Conversation tokens accumulated by the couple can later be redeemed for increased physical affection and sexual activity.

The Contribution of Social Exchange Theory. In perhaps an oversimplified and incomplete approach to a complex marital exchange, Stuart was beginning to blend Skinner's operant learning principles with social exchange theory (Thibaut

& Kelley, 1959). The contribution of the operant model—which posits that the key determinants of behavior are to be found in the external environment—and the contribution of the social exchange model—which holds that ongoing behavioral exchanges influence long-range outcomes in relationships—are quite compatible. As Jacobson (1981) points out, relationship satisfaction in marriage can be appraised according to long-term reward-cost ratios. If missing but potentially rewarding events can be identified and maximized and displeasing events occurring in excess can be identified and minimized, then the reward-cost ratio should increase greatly and each partner should not only feel more satisfied but also more willing to provide more rewards for the other partner. This is in contrast to unsuccessful marriages, where each partner, out of self-protection, acts to minimize costs of the relationship but makes no effort to exchange rewards.

The use of behavioral exchange procedures characterized the approach of other behavioral marital therapists during the 1970s, particularly Jacobson and Margolin (1979). Contingency contracting remained the focal point of the approach, both to enhance the quality and quantity of mutually pleasing interactions and to diminish the frequency of arguments, provocations, and generally negative communication sequences (Falloon & Lillie, 1988).

Stuart (1976, 1980) has since refined his techniques for working with maritally troubled couples. He begins by noting that every dimension of a marriage is subject to continued fluctuation, ranging from issues such as who is to provide what kind of new and stimulating activities to how old and new responsibilities should be allocated and reallocated over time. In the same way, Stuart recognizes that each spouse's commitment to the marriage varies over time, depending on his or her experience within the marriage or outside of that relationship. Stuart makes the further assumption that at least one of the spouses has doubts about remaining married, and that is why the couple has sought treatment or counseling. Therefore, he views the therapists's task as helping both spouses to create the best relationship possible at this point in time. Then, he reasons, if even at its current best it is not good enough (that is, in behavioral terms, the marriage offers insufficient reinforcements relative to the rewards each partner expects to earn living alone or with someone else), the partners can decide to end their marriage. On the other hand, if the husband and wife—having changed their behavior toward each other—evaluate the changes positively, they can recommit themselves to maintaining the marriage.

Orderly and precise in his approach, Stuart (1976) presents an eight-step model (see Figure 10.1) with the central theme of accelerating positive behavioral change. After each spouse independently completes a Marital Precounseling Inventory (detailing daily activities, general goals, current satisfactions and targets for change, and level of commitment to the marriage), the therapist can plan an intervention program in an organized and efficient manner. The couple is asked to agree by telephone to a treatment contract stipulating joint sessions, permission for the therapist to reveal to both partners the information each has already provided, and a commitment to participate in six sessions, after which a decision about further treatment can be made. In the process of contracting, Stuart has made it clear that he will not enter into collusion with one spouse (for example, by

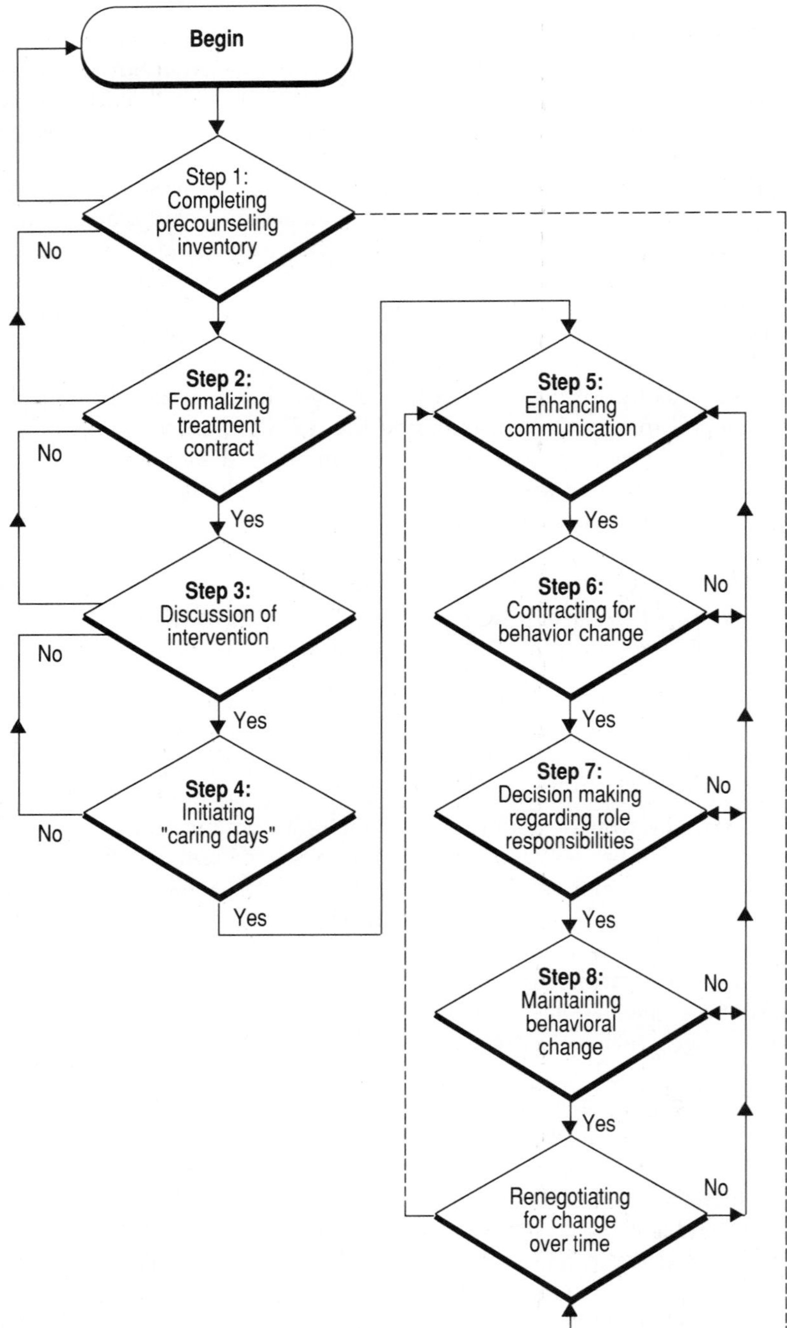

Figure 10.1 Flowchart of a behavioral treatment process for marital discord. (Source: Stuart, 1976)

keeping a secret) against the other, that he expects both of them to become involved in the process, and that he expects them to initiate change within a finite period.

During the first conjoint session (step 3), in which Stuart discusses the rationale of this therapeutic approach, he attempts to indoctrinate the partners with the idea that the most effective way to initiate change in a troubled marriage is to increase the rate at which they exchange positive behavior. Step 4, creating "caring days," is consistent with the notion of motivating both partners to achieve their treatment objectives. As exemplified in Table 10.2, each person defines the specifics of the behavior he or she desires on the part of the other and is asked to carry out from eight to twenty of the requests made by the partner, on a daily basis. Each partner is to exhibit caring behavior independently of the other's actions, as a demonstration of commitment that is consistent with Stuart's idea of "positive risks" described earlier. Each partner records the number of instances and the type of caring behavior he or she offers each day (a "commitment index") and experiences each day (a "pleasure index").[1]

The remaining four steps in Stuart's approach are tailored to the unique needs of each couple. Step 5 is devoted to training the partners to accurately communicate honest, timely, and constructive messages without subterfuge, misinterpretation, or superfluous innuendo. A behavioral contract can then be negotiated (step 6). At this point, for example, efforts might be made to modify ritualized role expectations, a wife asking her husband to babysit so that she might attend an evening class or a husband asking his wife to take over responsibility for balancing a checkbook. They might work on developing specific strategies for dealing with arguments, perhaps even arranging signals to alert one person to the other's willingness to end the argument. Changes oriented toward producing greater trust between the partners are also negotiated. A behavioral contract, implicit and explicit, is established based on the quid pro quo exchange of desirable behaviors.

In step 7, the couple learns more effective decision-making strategies (that is, formulating a goal and problem-solving set, assembling facts, and so on), particularly regarding who will take major responsibilities for what areas of life. In step 8, the partners are helped to maintain the changes they have made by learning specific "relationship rules"; the rules summarize what they have agreed on as the best methods for continuing to make communicational, behavioral, and decision-making changes. Stuart insists that the couple evaluate the relationship at four-month intervals using the Marital Precounseling Inventory, in order to gauge progress and choose new objectives for further change.

1. *In Helping Couples Change* (1980), Stuart spells out in greater detail his "caring days" technique for building commitment in a faltering marriage. All requests must meet the following criteria: (1) they must be positive ("Please ask how I spent my day" rather than "Don't ignore me so much"); (2) they must be specific ("Come home at 6 p.m. for dinner" rather than "Show more consideration for your family"); (3) they must be "small" instances of behavior that can be demonstrated at least once daily ("Please line up the children's bikes along the back wall of the garage when you come home" rather than "Please train the children to keep their bikes in the proper place"); and (4) they must not have been the subject of recent sharp conflict (since neither spouse is likely to concede major points at this stage of treatment).

Table 10.2 A Sample Request List for Caring Days

Wife's Requests	*Husband's Requests*
1. Greet me with a kiss and a hug in the morning before we get out of bed.	1. Wash my back.
2. Bring me pussywillows (or some such).	2. Smile and say you're glad to see me when you wake up.
3. Ask me what record I would like to hear and put it on.	3. Fix the orange juice.
4. Reach over and touch me when we're riding in the car.	4. Call me at work.
5. Make breakfast and serve it to me.	5. Acknowledge my affectionate advances.
6. Tell me you love me.	6. Invite me to expose the details of my work.
7. Put your things away when you come in.	7. Massage my shoulders and back.
8. If you're going to stop at the store for something, ask me if there is anything that I want or need.	8. Touch me while I drive.
9. Rub my body or some part of me before going to sleep, with full concentration.	9. Hold me when you see that I'm down.
10. Look at me intently sometimes when I'm telling you something.	10. Tell me about your experiences at work every day.
11. Engage actively in fantasy trips with me—e.g., to Costa Rica, Sunshine Coast.	11. Tell me that you care.
12. Ask my opinion about things you write and let me know which suggestions you follow.	12. Tell me that I'm nice to be around.
13. Tell me when I look attractive.	
14. Ask me what I'd like to do for a weekend or a day with the desire to do what I suggest.	

(Source: Stuart, 1976)

Learning Marital Skills. Stuart (1980), like Liberman and associates (1980), also has moved in the direction of helping couples improve their communication skills. Specifically, Stuart proposes these exercises as part of a five-skill training sequence: listening to one's partner more effectively (and, as far as possible, without preconceived notions of the other's motives); learning self-expression (making self-statements for which one takes responsibility); learning to make requests (framed and timed properly); exchanging appropriate feedback information with each other; and using clarification (to check out the meaning of one person's message until mutual meaning is achieved).

Marital skills training—teaching couples strategies for improving their communication patterns—is an important feature of the behavioral marital therapy approach. As developed by Gerald Patterson and his colleagues at the Oregon Marital Studies Program (Patterson, Weiss, & Hops, 1976), a ten-session assessment/intervention package is now available for helping couples track, self-monitor, and then self-report their home behavior, rating pleasing and displeasing interactions on a checklist containing categories such as companionship, spouse independence, and so on. These ratings (based on a family interaction coding system that records, for example, the number of positive or negative responses; extent of communication-facilitating and communication-impeding behavior) are then used for assessment purposes. Intervention, based on such an assessment, provides training in such areas as conflict resolution, communication skills, negotiation, and contracting.

Contracts, used by Stuart, Jacobson, and other practitioners of behavioral marital therapy, are written agreements between spouses stipulating specific behavioral changes. Each spouse explicitly states what behavior he or she wants increased, thus avoiding the all-too-familiar marital plea for mind reading, "If you really loved me, you'd know what I want." Note how the agreement developed by Stuart (1980) in Table 10.3 offers each partner a range of constructive choices, any one of which can satisfy their reciprocal obligations. By not creating the expectation that reciprocation should be forthcoming immediately ("I'll do this if you do that"), a contract can increase the likelihood of spontaneous reciprocation.

Table 10.3 A Holistic Therapeutic Marital Contract

It is understood that Jane would like Sam to:	*It is also understood that Sam would like Jane to:*
wash the dishes; mow the lawn; initiate lovemaking; take responsibility for balancing their checkbooks; invite his business partners for dinner once every six or eight weeks; meet her at his store for lunch at least once a week.	have dinner ready by 6:30 nightly; weed the rose garden; bathe every night and come to bed by 10:30; call him at the office daily; plan an evening out alone for both of them at least once every two weeks; offer to drive the children to their soccer practice and swim meets; accompany him on occasional fishing trips.
It is expected that Sam and Jane will each do as many of the things requested by the other as is comfortably manageable, ideally at least three or four times weekly.	

(Source: Stuart, 1980, p. 248)

Behavioral marital therapy, as a treatment model, has gone through a number of transitions in the last decade, although its basic premises and methods, as outlined by Liberman and Stuart, remain tied to basic behavioral principles. Some of its earlier assumptions were too simplistic: that both partners, as rational adults, will not resist change but will follow the therapist's suggestions; that a focus on overt behavior change is sufficient, without attending to underlying perceptual processes; that marital disharmony derives from the same sources, such as insufficient reciprocity, throughout the marital life cycle; that displeasing behavior, such as anger, should be extinguished without exploring the covert reasons for conflict; that the couple-therapist relationship can be ignored (Gurman & Knudson, 1978).

Although still largely based on social learning and behavior-exchange principles, the approach is becoming less technological and more flexible as it attempts to incorporate other theoretical perspectives. Increasingly, attention is being paid to such "internal" processes as thoughts, attitudes, the expression of feelings, and the role of cognitions in marital dysfunction (for example, unrealistic expectations of marriage, faulty attributions for relationship problems). In addition to encouraging the increased exchange of pleasing behavior, behavioral marital therapists such as Jacobson and Margolin (1979) also aim at problem reduction through teaching couples more effective problem-solving skills. Such problem solving is broken down into two separate phases: *problem definition* (learning to state problems in clear, specific, nonblaming ways; learning to acknowledge one's own role in creating or perpetuating the problem; attempting to paraphrase the other's view, even if inconsistent with one's own) and *problem resolution*. Brainstorming solutions together and negotiating compromises (which later may be put in writing) often facilitate problem resolution. Rather than the accusatory "You don't love me anymore," the therapists suggest the more concrete, less provocative, more self-revealing "When you let a week go by without initiating sex, I feel rejected" (Jacobson & Margolin, 1979, p. 230). These therapists consider contingency contracting as the last phase of developing viable problem-solving skills, for which the partners share responsibility.

As currently practiced (Hahlweg, Baucom, & Markman, 1988), behavioral marital therapy typically includes four basic components: (1) a behavioral analysis of the couple's marital distress based on interviewing, self-report questionnaires, and behavioral observations; (2) the establishment of positive reciprocity through techniques such as "caring days"; (3) comunication skills training (using "I" messages to express one's own feelings; sticking to here-and-now problems rather than dwelling on the past; describing the other's specific behavior rather than applying a label such as "lazy" or "cold"; providing positive feedback to the other person in response to similar behavior from that person); and (4) training in problem solving, including specifying, negotiating, and contracting.

Behavioral Parent-Skills Training

Much behavioral work, generally following a social learning model, has been directed at problems of child management within the family. While nonbehavioral family therapists might question whether such efforts should be considered methods of family therapy, in actual practice clinicians representing a variety of theoretical approaches are frequently called upon to help parents cope with various behavior problems in their children. In the last two decades or so, increased attention has been paid to training parents themselves in behavioral principles and techniques, so that they might apply these at home—using their daily contact with the child to act as change agents in bringing about a modification of the child's undesirable behavior (Berkowitz & Graziano, 1972).

Gerald Patterson, Ph.D.

Learning Child Management Techniques. Most behavioral parent training (BPT) advocates have had as their goal the alteration of the undesirable behavior in the child, accepting the parents' view that the child is the problem. By changing parental responses, the behavioral therapist hopes to produce a corresponding change in the child's behavior. Psychologists at the Oregon Social Learning Center, under the direction of Gerald Patterson and John Reid, in particular have led the way in developing a series of treatment programs for parents aimed at reducing and controlling disruptive behavior in children (Patterson, Reid, Jones, & Conger, 1975). Initially focused on helping parents control the acting-out child's environment, their recent efforts tended to deal with parent-child conflicts more directly.

This is consistent with social learning theory as outlined by Bandura (1977), in which cognitive, behavioral, and environmental determinants are seen as being in continuous reciprocal interaction. The targeted child is viewed, from this perspective, as behaving in a deviant way in response to the behaviors of others in the family; they in turn behave in ways that reinforce the deviancy; that deviancy in turn supports and reinforces their behaviors, and so on in a perpetual loop. The deviant behavior, then, is seen as a response to the reinforcement contingencies within the family (similar in view if not in language to the systems ideas advanced by Bateson, Jackson, and Haley). The therapist's job, after analyzing the behaviors, antecedents in the environment, and consequences of the behavior, is to help the family develop a new set of reinforcement contingencies in order for them to begin to learn new behaviors.

Parent training has many practical features to recommend it. It minimizes the family's reliance on qualified professional therapists, who may be in short supply. Without diminishing parental authority, the training process, if successful, builds competence in parents. Intervention generally begins early, thus reducing costs and the difficulties inherent in correcting an established problem; parent training thus has a preventive aspect. Perhaps most important, parents possess the greatest potential for generating behavior change because they have the greatest control over the significant aspects of the child's natural environment (Gordon & Davidson, 1981). The use of parents as trainers makes it easier for children to actually use the new behavior they learn, since they do not have to go through the process of transferring what they have acquired from a therapist to their home situation.

The initial request for treatment rarely comes from the child. It is likely to be the parents who are concerned about their child's disturbed behavior (see Table 10.4) or failure to behave in ways appropriate to his or her age or sex. According to Patterson and Reid (1970), a faulty parent (usually mother)-child interaction pattern has probably developed and been maintained through *reciprocity* (a child responding negatively to a negative parental input) and *coercion* (parents influencing behavior through the use of punishment). BPT intervention aims to change this mutually destructive pattern of interaction, usually by training parents to observe and measure the child's problematic behavior and then to apply behavioral techniques for accelerating desirable behavior, decelerating undesirable behavior, and maintaining the consequent behavioral changes.

Table 10.4 Behavior Problems Described as "Severe" by Over 4000 Parents During 10 Years of BPT Workshops

Behavior Problem	*Percentage Rating as "Severe"*
Disobedience; difficulty in disciplinary control	52
Disruptiveness; tendency to annoy and bother others	49
Fighting	45
Talking back	43
Short attention span	42
Restlessness; inability to sit still	40
Irritability; easily aroused to intense anger	37
Temper tantrums	35
Attention seeking; "show-off" behavior	35
Crying over minor annoyances	33
Lack of self-confidence	33
Hyperactivity; "always on the go"	33
Distractibility	33
Specific fears; phobias	17
Bed wetting	16

(Source: Falloon & Liberman, 1982, p. 123)

In teaching parenting skills, the behavioral therapist relies on behavioral interviews, checklists, and naturalistic observations of parent-child interactions in order to identify the specific problem behavior along with its antecedent and consequent events. Through such a behavioral analysis, the therapist is able to pinpoint the problem more exactly; evaluate the form, frequency, and extent of its impact on the family; and systematically train parents to use social learning principles to replace the targeted behavior with more positive, mutually reinforcing interaction.

The actual training of parents in behavioral techniques may be as simple as instructing them in how, when, and under what circumstances to enforce rules or act consistent, or as sophisticated as the use of behavioral deceleration procedures such as **time out** from positive reinforcement, or acceleration procedures such as token economy techniques (Gordon & Davidson, 1981). Most training programs include verbal or written instructions, often in the form of lectures, books, or instructional guides that illustrate social learning theory. Applied to family life, the theory emphasizes that parents control many of the contingencies that influence the child to acquire and maintain certain behavior patterns; parents are therefore in a logical position to change that behavior, if properly taught to do so.

In *Families*, Patterson (1971) outlined procedures for parents to acquire "behavior management skills" toward more effective child management. Presumably, many adults come by these skills "naturally," that is, without deliberately following a prescribed program. For less well-equipped parents, Patterson spelled out a plan for observing a child's behavior to establish a **baseline**, pinpointing the specific behavior the parents wish to change, observing and graphing their own behavior, negotiating a contract with the child, and so on. Figure 10.2 represents a checklist constructed for a boy who displayed a wide range of out-of-control behavior. The parent-child contract, jointly negotiated, stipulated that the parent would check with the teachers daily to get the necessary information and would regulate the consequences for the child's behavior. These consequences included mild but fair punishment for continued problem behavior in addition to "payoffs" (such as no dishwashing chores, permission to watch TV) for adaptive behavior. In establishing the contract, the child helps set the "price" in points for each item, sees the results daily (the program is posted in a conspicuous place at home, such as the refrigerator door), and negotiates the backup reinforcers (for example, TV programs) for the accumulated points. The parents are rehearsed and then supervised in the use of these procedures; additional performance training, such as demonstrations by the therapists, may be provided for those having difficulties in carrying out the program. Gordon and Davidson (1981), surveying the literature on the usefulness of the procedure, concluded that "it is an effective intervention for discrete, well-specified behavior problems. In cases of more complex deviant behavior syndromes, the research is encouraging but not conclusive" (p. 547). A major concern, of course, is how long therapeutic changes are maintained after treatment ceases; longer range follow-up studies are indicated.

The behavioral therapist may also work through the parents when the target for intervention is an adolescent's behavior. By observing the natural interaction between family members (sometimes in a home visit), the behavioral therapist performs a **functional analysis** of the problem behavior, determining what elicits it, what reinforces and maintains it, and how the family members' interaction reflects their efforts to deal with it (passive acceptance, resignation, anger, bribes, encouragement, and so forth). Such an analysis calls for systematic observation of family behavior, typically recording concrete instances of which behaviors were displayed by which family members in response to which other bits of behavior. Behavioral intervention strategies chosen by the therapist are apt to be specific and directed at helping to resolve or eliminate the problem.

Dave's Program

	M	T	W	T	F	S
Gets to school on time (2)	2					
Does not roam around the room (1)	0					
Does what the teacher tells him (5)	3					
Gets along well with other kids(5)	1					
Completes his homework (5)	2					
Does homework accurately (5)	3					
Behaves OK on the schoolbus (2)	2					
Gets along well with brothers and sisters in evening (3)	0					
Total	13					

1. If Dave gets 25 points, he doesn't have to do any chores that night and he gets to pick all the TV shows for the family to watch.
2. If Dave gets only 15 points, he does not get to watch TV that night.
3. If Dave gets only 10 points, he gets no TV and he also has to do the dishes.
4. If Dave gets only 5 points or less, then he gets no TV, washes the dishes, and is grounded for the next two days (home from school at 4:00 and stays in yard).

Figure 10.2 A parent-child negotiated contract checklist indicating specific duties to be performed and a point system based on the degree of goal achievement. (Source: Patterson, 1971)

Constructing Contingency Contracts. Contingency contracting may be a particularly useful technique in reducing parent-adolescent problems. As we defined the management process earlier in this chapter, the technique is simple and straightforward, usually involving a formally written agreement spelling out in advance the exchange of positively rewarding behaviors between the teenager and his or her parents. A number of prominent BPT advocates (Patterson & Reid, 1970; Stuart & Lott, 1972; Weathers & Liberman, 1975) have applied such a reciprocity concept to family conflict where the previous excessive use of aversive controls by parents (nagging, demanding, threatening) has been met by equally unpleasant responses from the adolescent. The goal is to reverse this persistent negative exchange by means of a mutual exchange of pleasurable behavior.

A contract is negotiated wherein each participant specifies who is to do what for whom, under which circumstances, times, and places. Negotiations are open and free from coercion; the terms of the contract are expressed in clear and explicit statements. For example, a contract negotiated between parents and an adolescent with poor grades specifies that she will "earn a grade of 'C' or better on her weekly quiz" rather than "do better in school." The latter is too vague and open to different interpretations by the participants; by that kind of definition the adolescent may believe she has done better and fulfilled her part of the agreement, while the parents believe the gain is insignificant, and the conflict between them over school performance remains unresolved. By the same token, the rewards must be specific ("We will give you $10 toward the purchase of new clothes for each week your quiz grade is 'C' or better") and not general or ambiguous ("We'll be more generous about buying you clothing if you get good grades"). The point here is that each participant must know exactly what is expected of him or her and what may be gained in return.

A contract (Figure 10.3) is an opportunity for success, accomplishment, and reward. However, the desired behavior, such as a "C" grade, must be realistic and within the grasp of the contractor. In addition, each member must accept the idea that privileges are rewards made contingent on the performance of responsibilities. Behavioral therapists believe that a family member will exchange maladaptive behavior for adaptive behavior in anticipation of a positive consequence, a desired change in the behavior of the other. The teenager's responsibility (that is, better grades) is the parents' reinforcer, and the parents' responsibility (money) is the teenager's reinforcer. BPT helps a family set up a monitoring or record-keeping system that enables the contractors and the therapist to assess the reciprocal fulfillment of the terms of the contract. Bonuses are given for consistent fulfillment of the terms, and penalties imposed for failure to adhere to them. Note that as in all behavioral procedures, the success of treatment can be measured by the extent to which the contract works for all parties.

Contingency contracting is not an end in itself but merely one motivating and structuring device among a variety of family intervention techniques (for example, modeling, shaping, time out, use of tokens, and other operant reinforcement strategies) used in the BPT approach. Contracting may open up communication within a family and help members express for the first time what each would like from the others. In some cases, the contracting process even makes family members aware of wishes or desires they had not previously recognized within themselves. Finally, an important aspect of this approach is its focus on goals and accomplishments. Liberman (1970) contends that contingency contracting formalizes the family's natural expectations into concrete actions. By giving recognition for achievement, the family becomes more positive in its interactions. By improving specific interactions between certain family members, the behavioral therapist is teaching a way of negotiating that may serve as a model for conflict resolution in other areas of family life.

Functional Family Therapy

Based on a clearly stated set of principles, and strongly supported by research findings, functional family therapy (Alexander & Parsons, 1982; Barton & Alexander, 1981) is designed to bring about both cognitive and behavioral changes in

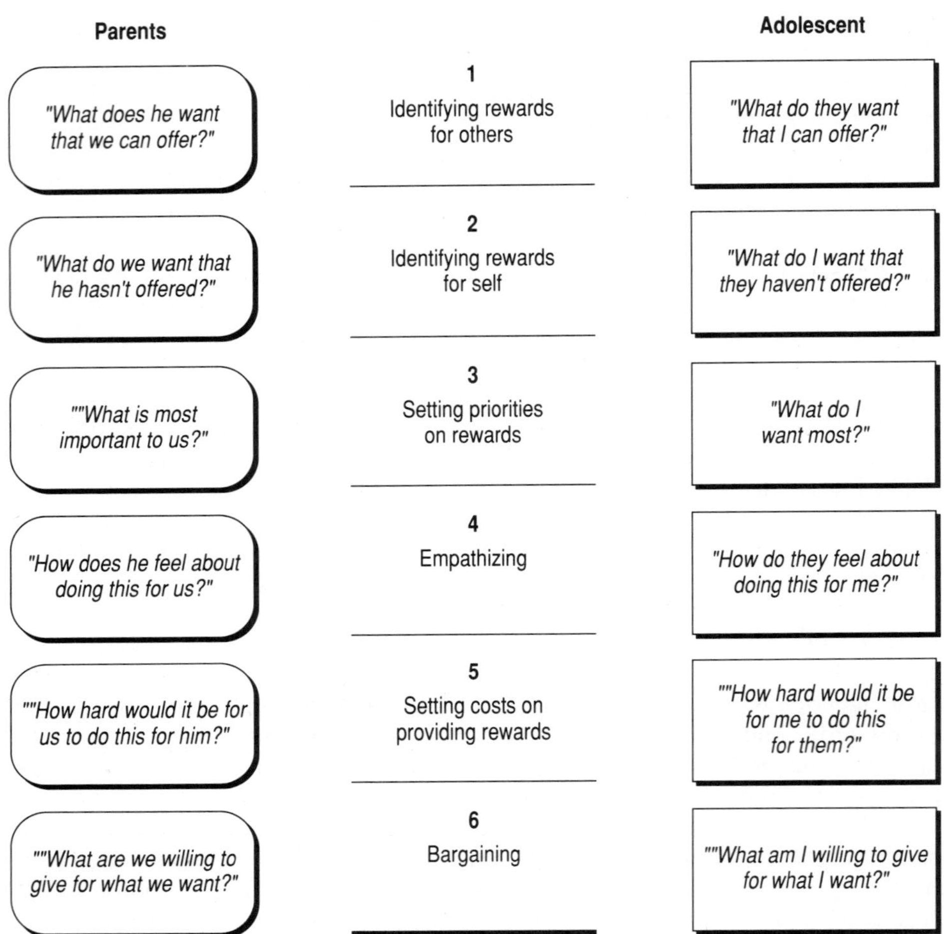

Figure 10.3 Steps in negotiating a contingency contract between parents and an adolescent. The family contracting exercise is a structured learning experience conducted by the behaviorally oriented family therapist to help family members, stepwise, to identify their needs and desires (rewards) for themselves and each other, to set priorities for rewards for self, to empathize with the other, to set costs of providing rewards to others, and finally to bargain and compromise. (Source: Weathers & Liberman, 1975)

individuals and their families. The model, which purports to integrate systems theory, cognitive theory, and behaviorism, goes beyond most behavioral models by attempting to do more than change behavior; it posits that clients need help first in understanding and changing the function the behavior plays in regulating relationships.

To the functional family therapist, all behavior is adaptive. Rather than being thought of as "good" or "bad," behavior is viewed as always serving a function, as representing an effort to create a specific outcome in interpersonal relationships. While the interpersonal payoffs or functions for individual members may appear to take a variety of forms (a child elicits parental attention by having a tantrum; a teenager creates independence by having himself thrown out of the house; a husband avoids arguments by busying himself at work for long hours into the evening), they are seen, ultimately, as efforts to achieve one of three interpersonal states: contact/closeness (merging), distance/independence (separating), or a combination of the two (midpointing) (Alexander & Parsons, 1982).

Without placing a prior value on the usefulness of the behavior, the functional therapist makes an effort to comprehend why the behavior exists and how and why it is maintained by others within the family. Alexander & Parsons (1982) offer the following illustration of the function of behaviors within the family context:

> *Mother reports that Debbie, 14 years old, has been receiving increasingly poor grades for 18 months. Within the past 12 months she has begun smoking dope; has been having sexual relations with her 19-year-old boyfriend; has almost stopped going to school; and rarely comes home except late at night. At home she is sullen, argumentative, occasionally hysterical, and rarely truthful. (p. 14)*

Looking at the family context, the functional family therapist might speculate on the interpersonal payoffs Debbie's behavior offers each of the family members. One guess is that a function of Debbie's behavior for her is creating justification for running away. What's in it for Debbie's mother that might prompt her to go along with her daughter's behavior, while at the same time protesting that it makes her miserable? The authors perceive a number of possible functions for the mother: (1) it enables her to justify coercing her withdrawn husband into becoming more involved with what is happening at home, thus joining her more actively in parenting; (2) it removes her from responsibility because the father is brought in as final authority; (3) it arouses a response from the father, which the mother does not ordinarily receive if she handles the situation herself; and (4) it keeps her in the mothering role, despite her adolescent daughter's becoming more self-sufficient.

Thus, whatever the misery, interpersonal payoffs may exist for the mother (as well as the father), perpetuating Debbie's behavior. The functional family therapist, having attempted to understand what interpersonal functions are served for whom by the problem behavior (for instance, increased closeness between the spouses) might then offer help to the family in finding more effective ways to accomplish the same end result. Note that the therapist does not try to change the functions but rather the specific behaviors used to maintain these functions. Table 10.5 illustrates how the same interpersonal functions are retained as a result of intervention, but their behavioral manifestation is altered.

Functional family therapy proceeds in stages. In the initial assessment stage, the therapist is interested in determining the functions served by the behavioral sequences of various family members. Are they creating greater distance, or are they becoming closer through their interpersonal patterns? How do they use merging/separating to enhance or retard or in general to regulate their interactions? The second stage, instituting change in the family system, aims at modifying attitudes, expectations, cognitive sets, and affective reactions. Family members typically enter therapy with a punitive, blaming explanation for their problems ("My mother bugs me; she still thinks I'm a baby"; "My daughter is a chronic liar; she creates all the tension in the house"). The therapist's task during this phase of treatment is to change the focus from an individualistic, blaming outlook to one in which all participants understand that together they form a system and share responsibility for family behavior sequences.

Table 10.5 Selected Functions in Debbie's Family and Their Behavioral Manifestations Before and During Successful Intervention.

		Behavioral manifestations	
Relationship	*Interpersonal function*	*Preintervention*	*During intervention*
Debbie-Mother	Separating	Is truant, is never home, runs away.	Is not truant, has Mother's permission to be away from home, brings reports and calls.
Mother-Debbie	Midpointing	Makes contact via arguing and monitoring, distance via slapping and nagging.	Makes contact via reports and calls, distance via approved absence from home for specified times.
Mother-Father	Merging	Complains about Debbie, coerces Father into responding to her.	Holds daily discussion about family chart.
Father-Mother	Separating	Avoids home, refuses to respond.	Is allowed to fill Father role via family chart rather than direct interaction.
Mother-Good Son	Merging	Elicits and praises information about others' transgressions.	Elicits and praises information about others' accomplishments.
Good Son-Mother	Merging	Snoops and reports to Mother.	Reports positive accomplishments of others to Mother.
Debbie-Boyfriend Boyfriend-Debbie	Merging	Avoid school together and have evening contact.	Go to and from school together and have evening contact.

(continued)

Table 10.5 *(continued)*

Relationship	Interpersonal function	Behavioral manifestations: Preintervention	Behavioral manifestations: During intervention
Debbie-Father Father-Debbie	Separating	Have almost no contact except for occasional intense arguing and hitting.	Have almost no contact; information is channeled through Mother.

(Source: Alexander & Parsons, 1982, p. 28)

Functional family therapists employ some familiar systems and behavioral principles in their interventions. Relabeling ("Father is uninvolved because he wants to protect the others from the unpleasant emotions he's experiencing") is a primary method used (Morris, Alexander, & Waldron, 1988). By providing reattributions for the causes of family members' behavior, functional family therapists believe they can reduce family members' use of pejorative trait labels for one another, and as a consequence correspondingly lower their resistance to change. Like the strategists we considered in the last chapter, functionalists contend that giving an event a new and more benign or benevolent meaning will lead to changed perceptions and subsequent behavioral change. Recast in behavioral language, relabeling interrupts the virtually automatic eliciting of thoughts, emotions, and behavior, which in the past have led to predictable outcomes. Alternate explanations provide an opportunity to activate different repertoires of thoughts, emotions, or behaviors, in some cases forcing the learning of new repertoires entirely.

Therapy helps people become receptive to learning new skills; however, a third stage, education, is necessary in order to provide a context in which to learn specific skills needed to maintain positive change. In this essential and innovative part of the intervention process, functional family therapists use a variety of behavioral/cognitive technology (contingency management, modeling, communication training) to stamp in new behaviors. This phase is vital if the family is to learn new skills for future problem resolution. Positive change is more likely to be produced or reliably maintained if the educational technologies used by functional family therapists are fitted to the values and functions of the family members (Morris, Alexander, & Waldron, 1988).

Conjoint Sex Therapy

Sexual dysfunction can be seen as a symptom of a troubled relationship or as a problem itself that requires remediation. Conjoint sex therapists make the assumption that some marriages founder primarily because of sexual difficulties or incompatibilities per se, and thus focus their behavioral interventions specifically on a couple's sexual problems. Probably the most promising therapeutic work in this field has been done at the Masters and Johnson Institute in St. Louis under the direction of physician William Masters and psychologist Virginia Johnson; the procedures pioneered there have been incorporated into the programs of numerous sex therapy clinics throughout the United States. The institute offers a treatment program that relies heavily on behavioral therapy techniques. It is distinguished by its brevity (generally two weeks) and its proven high rate of success for certain types of sexual dysfunction.

A basic assumption in the Masters and Johnson (1970) approach, and what puts it into a systems framework, is that there is no such thing as an uninvolved partner in a relationship in which some form of sexual inadequacy exists. Consequently, husband and wife are always treated conjointly to emphasize that any dysfunction is a problem for the marital couple rather than one that belongs to only one partner. Each couple is seen by a male-female cotherapy team; ideally, one member is trained in the biological sciences and the other in a behavioral discipline. The dual-sex team is designed to avoid potential misinterpretation due to a therapist's male or female bias, consistent with Masters's and Johnson's belief that neither sex can ever fully understand the other's sexual experiences. The two-week program of daily sessions begins with an extensive assessment; a detailed sexual history is taken from each partner, not only in regard to chronological sexual experiences but, more important, in respect to sexually oriented values, attitudes, feelings, and expectations. Next, a medical history is taken and each partner is given a thorough physical examination. On the third day, the cotherapists and the marital partners meet to review the accrued clinical material and to begin to relate individual and marital histories to current sexual difficulties. During the next several days, the therapists concentrate on giving the couple instruction in "sensate focus"—that is, learning to touch and explore each other's bodies and to discover more about each other's sensate areas, but without feeling any pressure for sexual performance or orgasm. During this period, regular round-table meetings that include both therapists and both marital partners are held to deal with either partner's discomfort, guilt feelings, or apprehensions. In the time remaining, the therapists use procedures aimed at teaching both partners to work together on their specific sexual dysfunction.

According to Masters and Johnson, a primary reason for sexual dysfunction is that the participant is critically watching (they refer to it as "spectatoring") his or her own sexual performance instead of abandoning himself or herself to the giving and receiving of erotic pleasure with a partner. Masters and Johnson point out that in order to enjoy fully what is occurring, partners must suspend all such distracting thoughts or anxieties about being evaluated (or evaluating oneself) for sexual performance.

Psychiatrist Helen Singer Kaplan (1974) distinguishes a variety of immediate causes of sexual dysfunction in a couple attempting intercourse (sexual ignorance, fear of failure, demand for performance, excessive need to please one's partner, failure to communicate openly about sexual feelings and experiences). In addition, she points out that there may be various intrapsychic conflicts (such as early sexual trauma, guilt and shame, repressed sexual thoughts and feelings) within one or both partners that impede satisfying sexual activity. Finally, Kaplan cites a third set of psychological determinants of sexual dysfunction—namely, factors arising from the relationship such as various forms of marital discord, lack of trust, power struggles between partners, and efforts to sabotage any pleasure being derived from the sexual experience. In combination or singly, any of these problems or conflicts can lead to distressing sexual symptoms (for example, impotence or premature ejaculation in a male, nonorgasmic response in a female) that threaten a marriage by heightening tensions and that can even lead to its dissolution.

Unlike Masters and Johnson, who require participating couples to spend two weeks in residential treatment, Kaplan treats couples on an outpatient basis once or twice a week. No time limit is place on treatment; the program terminates when the couple achieves good sexual functioning (that is, when the presenting symptom is eliminated) and there are indications that the changes are more or less permanent. Rather than the dual-sex team used in Masters's and Johnson's approach, one therapist treats the couple. Kaplan uses a combination of psychoanalytic and behavioral theories and techniques and assigns couples various sexual tasks (for example, taking turns stimulating or "pleasuring" each other's erotic areas, free of the demand for orgasm or coitus) to practice at home. Six to 15 visits are generally required for successful treatment.

Unlike psychotherapeutic undertakings that have loose or vague criteria for defining their effectiveness (for example, "patient is happier," "more productive," "feels more fulfilled"), sex therapy is considered successful only if the presenting symptom in the marital unit is eliminated. Masters and Johnson have reported a remarkably high overall success rate despite their stringent criterion of success—no recurrence of the symptom within five years. Their greatest success (97.8 percent) has come in treating premature ejaculation in men; for secondary impotence (losing the capacity to achieve or maintain an erection long enough to engage in intercourse) the success rate, while lower (73.7 percent), is nevertheless extraordinarily high compared to that of other therapeutic interventions having to do with secondary impotence. Similarly, a success rate of 83.4 percent for treating primary orgasmic dysfunction in women (never having reached a climax) is very impressive. Kaplan reports similar results for rapidly relieving a wide variety of sexual dysfunctions. However, as she points out, although sex therapy may represent a major advance in our understanding and treatment of a couple's sexual difficulties, it is no panacea for a marriage that has already failed.

The use of explicitly behavioral sex therapy techniques has been widely reported (LoPiccolo & LoPiccolo, 1978) with about the same levels of success as those recorded by the Masters and Johnson program, especially for procedures treating premature ejaculation and primary orgasmic dysfunction (Kinder & Blakeney, 1977). In a review of treatment programs for sexual dysfunction in heterosexual couples, Heiman, LoPiccolo, and LoPiccolo (1981) concluded that the various behavioral approaches have the following elements in common: the reduction of performance anxiety, sex education, skill training in communication as well as in sexual technique, and attitude change procedures. As currently practiced, sex therapy appears to offer a combined cognitive behavioral therapy/reeducation program to couples with sexual problems.

SUMMARY

Behavioral family therapy, the latest entrant in the family therapy field, attempts to bring the scientific method to bear upon the therapeutic process by developing regularly monitored, data-based intervention procedures. Drawing on established principles of human learning—such as classical and operant conditioning, positive and negative reinforcement, shaping, extinction, and social learning—the behavioral approach emphasizes the environmental, situational, and social determinants of behavior. In recent years, the influence of cognitive factors as events mediating family interactions also has been recognized by most behaviorists. The behaviorally oriented therapist attempts to increase positive interaction between family members, alter the environmental conditions that oppose such interactions, and train people to maintain their newly acquired positive behavioral changes.

Currently, the approach is having a significant impact in four distinct areas: behavioral marital therapy, behavioral parent-skills training, functional family therapy, and the treatment of sexual dysfunction. Behavioral marital therapy blends principles of social learning theory and social exchange theory, teaching couples how to achieve positive reciprocity so that their relationship will have more pleasing consequences for both partners.

Behavioral parent-skills training, also largely based on social learning theory, represents an effort to train parents in behavioral principles of child management. Patterson has been particularly influential in focusing attention on the parent (usually mother)-child dyad by stressing that the child's behavior has probably developed and been maintained by means of the reciprocity and coercion inherent in their interaction. Intervention typically attempts to help families develop a new set of reinforcement contingencies in order to begin to learn new behaviors.

Functional family therapy attempts to integrate systems, behavioral, and cognitive theories in working with families. Viewing all behavior as serving the interpersonal function of creating specific outcomes in behavior sequences, functional family therapists do not try to change these functions but rather to change the behaviors used to maintain the functions.

Conjoint sex therapy is a time-limited program involving both marital partners in an effort to alleviate problems of sexual dysfunction; the treatment may strengthen a marriage by correcting a disharmonious (thus potentially destructive) aspect of the relationship. First developed by Masters and Johnson and elaborated by Kaplan, the treatment of sexual dysfunction now uses a variety of explicitly behavioral techniques; conjoint sex therapy in its present form may be conceptualized as a type of cognitive behavioral therapy/reeducation program applied to couples with sexual problems.

Chapter Eleven

Variant Forms of Therapeutic Intervention

While most of the therapeutic techniques we have considered up to this point are tied to the distinct theories we have described, there remain a number of intervention procedures that are not theory-specific. By and large these have developed on a trial-and-error basis, based on clinical expediency emerging from work with specific populations, but without benefit of following from a set of theoretical formulations. Many no longer have more than historical importance; others have found a theoretical home and have been taken up in particular by practitioners of specific persuasions.

Ideally, therapists select a particular technique out of the theoretical framework from which they operate, in a situation where it can achieve a specified purpose or some desired goal. The therapist should have a rationale for using a specific intervention, with some sense of what consequences to expect with this particular family system. In their everyday clinical work, family therapists often are called upon to design their own techniques, tailored to a particular set of family interactive sequences, and directed at maximizing behavioral change. In practice, there is considerable overlap among the techniques used by practitioners from different approaches.

Techniques are simply tools for achieving therapeutic goals. In practice, some emerge out of a theoretical framework, others in answer to a practical need or perhaps accidentally, borrowing from another modality. Thus there is considerable flexibility in choosing a specific therapeutic procedure, depending on the clinical judgment of the therapist as to its applicability to a particular family. For example, as described in Chapter Eight, Minuchin provided both a new technique and an important theoretical idea by inviting a family with an anorectic child to join him for lunch, in order to provoke an enactment of the family problem. In some cases, therapists may develop interventions based on pragmatic considerations, such as lengthening the time between sessions, as in the Milan approach discussed in Chapter Nine, in an effort to allow the family sufficient time to carry out prescribed rituals. The technique may later prove to be effective and have broader applicability than first envisioned. Out of his experience with hypnosis, Haley (Chapter Nine) developed a number of paradoxical techniques especially useful with resistant families. Therapists of any particular viewpoint might use a technique originated by another (for example, the use of relabeling, a strategic tactic, by functional family therapists) to accomplish a specific therapeutic goal.

In this chapter, we plan to expand on several variations in technique tailored to particular populations or extrapolated from existing theoretical models. More specifically, we intend to elaborate four sets of intervention practices: (1) nonverbal procedures; (2) time-limited procedures; (3) crisis-oriented procedures; and (4) large-group procedures.

NONVERBAL TREATMENT PROCEDURES

Two related therapeutic techniques, both intended to make implicit dysfunctional family patterns more open to direct expression—and ultimate change—are considered first.

Family Sculpture

Described by Sherman and Fredman (1986) as a sociometric technique—a method for observing, measuring, and modifying social interactions—family sculpting often provides a useful supplementary intervention procedure for restructuring roles and functions within a family system. The emphasis here is on revealing how each member perceives his or her place in the family as well as that person's perception of what is being done to whom, by whom, and in what manner. Just as a genogram pictorially charts a family's history and constellation, a family sculpture provides a method of physically positioning members in space to express a view of their relationships. The latter is especially appealing to those therapists who feel comfortable using physical movement to facilitate changes in the family's interpersonal relationships.

Family sculpture involves the metaphoric use of space and movement for understanding a family's relationships through the eyes of one of the family's members. Developed by Duhl, Kantor, and Duhl (1973) at the Boston Family Institute, the technique attempts to translate systems theory into physical form by creating an arrangement of people placed in various physical positions in space that represent their relationships to each other at a particular moment in time. While it may be very difficult for an individual to verbalize his or her perceptions of how family members relate—how intimate or distant they are, how loving or indifferent—sculpting allows the person to reveal his or her private view of invisible but meaningful boundaries, alliances, subsystems, roles, and so on. When each member has created a sculpture, conflicts are removed from the verbal arena and given a graphic, more active but nonverbal mode of expression. The entire family and the therapist are able to grasp each member's experiences and perceptions more easily and immediately. In this manner, the family is prepared for choosing new options—taking new actions—to change relationships. Making use of this form of feedback may in and of itself prompt major changes in a family's relationships (Constantine, 1986).

The sculpting technique is particularly suited to the experiential approach of Satir (1972) since it provides a nonintellectualized way for each family member to put his or her feelings into action. In recent years, as we noted briefly in Chapter Six, Satir (1982) used sculpting to place people in certain postures herself, saying that she "activated the right brain experience so people could feel their experience with minimal threat. They were *experiencing* themselves, instead of only hearing about themselves" (p. 18). Constantine (1978) observes that the act of externalizing one's perception of relationships between family members often provides insights about those relationships for all family members and the therapist alike. Bandler and Grinder (1975) contend that these visual, spatial, metaphorical representations reveal in compact form each person's map of the world—the way each person perceives his or her complex interpersonal landscape.

The family therapist may use sculpting at any point in the assessment or therapeutic process. Preferably at least three or four persons should be present, although at times a movable piece of furniture can pinch-hit for an absent member. The request for a member to make a sculpture is often timed to cut through excessive verbalizations or, on the other hand, when a member (often an adolescent) sits silently through a session or cannot easily express his or her thoughts verbally. According to Simon (1972), adolescents usually make excellent sculptors because of their awareness of family truths and their relish in manipulating their parents. Younger children, by contrast, typically lack comprehension of what is really taking place in the family; and parents are often too anxious about losing their dignity to participate fully themselves. Once the ice has been broken by the first presentation, however, all family members are likely to want a turn at sculpting in order to present their points of view. Family sculpting can be repeated at various points during the course of family therapy, revealing to all participants how their individual perceptions of their relationships are undergoing change.

The procedure calls for each member to arrange the bodies of all the other family members in a defined space, according to his or her perception of their relationships either at present or at a specific point in the past. Who the sculptor designates as domineering, meek and submissive, loving and touching, belligerent, benevolent, clinging, and so on, and how those people relate to each other becomes apparent to all who witness the tableau. The sculptor is invited to explain the creation, and a lively debate between members may follow. The adolescent boy who places his parents at opposite ends of the family group while he and his brothers and sisters are huddled together in the center conveys a great deal more about his views of the workings of the family system than he would probably be able to state in words. By the same token, his father's sculpture—placing himself apart from all others, including his wife—may reveal his sense of loneliness, isolation, and rejection by his family. The mother may present herself as a confidante of her daughter but ignored by the males in the family, and so forth. Nonverbally—without emotional outburst or intellectualization—the members have openly portrayed their various views of the family's difficulties. Their actions have indeed spoken louder than words, often revealing to others for the first time what each has felt but never expressed before.

Family Choreography

Family choreography, an outgrowth of family sculpture, was developed by Peggy Papp (1976) (*see* Figure 11.1) at the Ackerman Institute and was so named because the sculpture moves to show the dynamic, shifting transactional patterns within the family. Choreography is a method for actively intervening in the family, realigning relationships, creating new patterns, and changing the system. While family members seldom surprise each other by what they say—in most families the pattern of verbal exchange is all too predictable—they may be surprised by what they choreograph. Alliances, triangles, and shifting emotional currents are all represented by the family movement. Choreography may help a family to physically retrace old interactive patterns and create new ones. An entrenched vicious cycle of behavior within a family, dramatized in the therapist's office, may be replayed using alternative ways of reacting and relating. With the old pattern experienced differently by the entire family, under the direction of the therapist, the newly enacted changes may be easier to recreate at home. Action-oriented, family choreography has as its goal to change the family system by exploring alternate transactional patterns through physical movement and changing positioning.

TIME-LIMITED TREATMENT PROCEDURES

Brief therapy is not just less of the same. Rather, the approach calls for finding alternative ways of facilitating beneficial changes that are relatively quick and inexpensive, and that are especially suited at symptomatic junctures in the life cycle of individuals and families (Peake, Borduin, & Archer, 1988). The two examples

Figure 11.1 In this simulation of a family choreography session, therapist Papp (rear) observes as a mother creates a tableau to illustrate her perception of her family's relationship to her. (Bernard Gotfryd—*Newsweek*)

we offer represent specific strategies that are pragmatic, method oriented, and focused on the presenting problem.

The MRI Brief Family Therapy

The Brief Therapy Project at the Mental Research Institute in Palo Alto, in operation since 1967, has developed a number of ingenious systems-based tactics for treating a wide assortment of clinical problems, including anxiety, depression, marital discord, sexual dysfunction, family conflict, psychosomatic illness, and drug and alcohol dependence (Fisch, Weakland, & Segal, 1982; Watzlawick, Weakland, & Fisch, 1974). These interventions represent the clinical application of some of the communication/interaction theories and techniques of Bateson, Jackson, Haley, and especially Erickson to families seeking immediate resolution of problems and relief from symptoms.

Brief family therapy is a time-limited (no more than ten sessions), pragmatic, nonhistorical, step-by-step strategic family therapy approach based on the notion that most human problems develop through the mishandling of normal difficulties in life. In such cases, the attempted "solutions" themselves become the problem, as people persist in self-perpetuating and self-defeating "more of the same" attempts at problem resolution. The patient (or, correspondingly, the family) is like a person caught in quicksand: the more struggling, the more sinking; the more sinking, the more struggling (Segal, 1982). In other words, wrong attempts persist, and now the "solution" itself only makes matters worse. According to advocates of this approach, it is only by giving up solutions that perpetuate the problem and attempting new solutions that are different in kind that changes can occur in behavior and/or the view of the problem.

According to Watzlawick, Weakland, and Fisch (1974), the kinds of problems presented in psychotherapy persist because people maintain them through their own behavior and that of others with whom they interact. (Note the influence of behavioral therapy as well as the concepts of feedback and circular causality from cybernetics and systems theory.) If, however, the current system of interaction is changed, then the problem will be resolved regardless of its history and etiology. Accordingly, the strategically oriented brief therapist tries to obtain a clear picture of the specific problem as well as the current behavior that maintains it, then devises a plan for changing those aspects of the system that perpetuate the problem (Segal, 1987). By restraining people from repeating old unworkable solutions (and by altering the system to promote change) the therapist can help them break out of their destructive or dysfunctional cycle of behavior.

Brief therapy advocates argue that most therapists, in attempting to help a distressed person, encourage that person to do the opposite of what he or she has been doing—an insomniac to fall asleep, a depressed person to cheer up, a withdrawn person to make friends. These approaches, by emphasizing opposites or negative feedback, only lead to internal reshuffling; they do not change the system. Watzlawick and associates (1974) call such moves superficial first-order changes (effecting change within the existing system without changing the structure of the system itself). In the example of feedback loops we used in Chapter Three, such a therapeutic effort is equivalent to the thermostat that regulates room temperature, activating the heating system to cool down when the room gets too hot. Real change, however, necessitates an alteration of the system itself; it calls for a second-order change to make the system operate in a different manner. To continue the analogy, the thermostat on the wall must be reset. First-order changes, according to Watzlawick, Beavin, and Jackson (1967), are "games without end"; they are wrong attempts at changing ordinary difficulties that eventually come to a stalemate by continuing to force a solution despite available evidence that it is precisely what is *not* working (Bodin, 1981).

Clinicians report three ways in which a family mishandles solutions so that they lead to bigger problems: (1) some action is necessary but not taken (for example, the family attempts a solution by denying there is a problem—the roof is not leaking, sister is not pregnant, money is no problem even though father has lost his job); (2) an action is taken when it is unnecessary (for example, newlyweds separate because their marriage is not as ideal as each partner fantasized it would be); (3) action is taken at the wrong level (for example, marital conflicts or parent-child conflicts are dealt with by "common sense" or first-order changes, such as each party agreeing to try harder next time, when revisions in the family system—second-order changes—are necessary). The third type is probably most common, since people with problems attempt to deal with them in a manner consistent with their existing frame of reference. Repeated failures only lead to bewilderment and "more of the same" responses.

The MRI version of brief therapy focuses on resolving problems that result from prior attempts to solve an ordinary difficulty. Paradoxical interventions, especially reframing, are emphasized in order to redefine the family's frame of reference so that members conceptualize the problem differently and change their efforts to resolve it. As we saw in our earlier discussions of the structural (Chapter Eight) and strategic (Chapter Nine) approaches to therapy, reframing involves a relabeling process in which a situation remains unchanged but the meaning attributed to it is revised. Reframing allows the situation to be viewed differently and thus facilitates new responses to it.

As practiced at the MRI, brief therapy with its short-term duration sets up a powerful expectation of change. At the same time, the therapists tend to "think small," to be satisfied with minor but progressive changes. They also urge their clients to "go slow" and to be skeptical of dramatic, sudden progress; this paradoxical technique is actually designed to promote rapid change as the family is provoked to prove the therapist wrong in his or her caution and pessimism. In general, the therapists "go with the resistance," neither confronting the family *nor* offering interpretations to which the members might react negatively or defensively. Brief therapy aims to avoid power struggles with the family while it reshapes the members' perspectives on current problems and on their previous attempts to overcome difficulties.

The brief therapy program is a team effort. Although each family is assigned a primary therapist who conducts the interviews, other team members watch from behind the one-way mirror and may telephone the therapist with suggestions while treatment is in progress; in special cases (for example, a therapist-family impasse) one of the team members may enter the room and address the primary therapist or the clients, perhaps siding with the client to increase the likelihood that forthcoming directives from the observer will be implemented. Families are not screened prior to treatment and are taken into the program on a first-come, first-served basis. Team discussions precede and follow each session after the initial family contact. A follow-up evaluation of each family receiving treatment at the center takes place 3 months and 12 months after the last interview. Although the treatment is not conducted under ideal research conditions, overall results indicate that this technique is cost-effective and has a positive impact on family systems—sometimes a significant one—in a relatively short period of time (Segal, 1982).

The reader will recognize the similarity of the Brief Therapy Project model to the work of Haley and even more to the work of the Milan group discussed in Chapter Nine. All three approaches have as their focus, at least initially, a presenting problem that is thought to occur within, and be maintained by, a repetitive sequence of behavior. All three pay attention to the family's developmental stage and deliberately design interventions (most likely, paradoxical strategies) to fit the particular problems of that stage (MacKinnon, 1983). However, the brief therapy approach differs from Haley's efforts in being less concerned with power issues or family structures (such as hierarchies or coalitions). Also, it is more likely to be active, practical, and problem-focused, and to offer suggestions that activate the family system, in contrast to the Milan associates, who emphasize neutrality and view the therapist and family as one large system.

The following example (Segal, 1982) illustrates the effectiveness of the brief therapy approach. The therapy team helps a concerned wife to revise her earlier self-defeating solutions to a problem and thus to institute second-order changes in her interactions with a resistant husband.

> *The author and Dr. Fritz Hoebel studied and treated 10 families in which the husbands had suffered a major heart attack but were still continuing to engage in high risk behaviors: poor diet, smoking, lack of exercise, and excessive consumption of alcohol. All of these families were referred by cardiologists, or by the staff of a cardiac rehabilitation program, who had given up on these individuals, fearing they were on a suicide course. In all 10 cases the identified heart patient would have nothing to do with any further treatment or rehabilitation efforts.*
>
> *Rather than wasting a lot of time and energy trying to convince the patient to come for treatment, we worked with their spouses. Using a five-session limit, we focused our attention on the way the wives had attempted to reduce their husbands' high-risk behavior—our aim was to change the system, that is, the husband's behavior, by getting the wives to change their attempted solutions. In most cases the wives struggled, argued, and nagged their men to change, so our primary effort was getting the wives to back off from this position. In one case that worked particularly well, on our instructions the wife returned home and told her husband that she had been doing a lot of thinking about him. She said she had decided that he had a right to live out the rest of his life in his own style, no matter how short that might be. Her primary concern now was herself and the children and how they would be provided for when he died. She then insisted that her husband go over all the life insurance and estate planning, instructing her how to handle things after his death. She also called life insurance agencies and asked whether there was any way her husband's life insurance could be increased. As instructed, she told them to call back at times she knew she would not be home but her husband would be there to take the calls. Within 2 weeks after she had begun to deal with him this way, the husband had resumed his participation in the cardiac rehabilitation exercise program and was watching his diet. (pp. 286–287)*

Solution-Focused Brief Therapy

Another innovative approach to brief therapy based on systems theory comes from the work of Steve deShazer and his associates at the Brief Family Therapy Center in Milwaukee, established in 1978. DeShazer (1985) shares with other strategists, such as the MRI group just described, the notion that dysfunction essentially arises from faulty attempts at problem solution; the family system is simply stuck, having run out of ways of dealing with the problem. Rather than focus on why or how the particular presenting problem initially arose, deShazer attempts to aid the family in discovering their own creative solutions for becoming "unstuck."

The assumption here is that clients already know what they need to do to solve their complaints; the therapist's task is help them construct a new use for knowledge they already have. The overall aim of this approach, then, is to help clients start the solution process. To deShazer, the solution does not need to be matched to the specific problem to be effective. Actually, he believes, the solution process is more similar from one case to another than the problems each intervention is meant to solve. In describing his approach, deShazer uses a simple metaphor: the complaints clients bring to the therapist are like locks on doors that could open to a more satisfactory life, if only they could find the key. Often time is wasted and frustration heightened in trying to discover why the lock is in the way or why the door won't open, when the family should be looking for the key. DeShazer's contribution is to provide the family with "skeleton keys"—interventions that work for a variety of locks. Such keys do not necessarily fit a complex lock perfectly; they only need to fit sufficiently well so that a solution evolves. That is, in constructing a solution, the therapist does not need to know about the history of the problem or what maintains the complaint. Nor is the therapist particularly interested in the details of the complaint, preferring to attend instead to developing with the family expectations of change and solution. By limiting the number of sessions (typically five to ten), the therapist helps create the expectation of change. Similarities in viewpoint to Erickson as well as to the Milan group are apparent here.

One theoretical view that sets deShazer and his colleagues at the Brief Family Therapy Center apart from other strategists is the rejection of the idea that clients who come asking for change at the same time resist change. DeShazer argues that clients really do want to be cooperative and to change; they resist interpretations or other interventions from the therapist only if these do not seem to them to fit. To promote cooperation, he compliments clients on what they are already doing that is useful for problem solving and, once they become convinced the therapist is on their side, he is in a position to make suggestions that they try something new that might also make them feel better. Typically, deShazer offers suggestions for initiating small changes, which, once achieved, lead to further changes in the system generated by the clients.

Observe how the therapist sets up an expectation of change in the following situation (deShazer, 1985), helping create in the client a corresponding sense of what to expect after the problem or presenting complaint is gone:

Mrs. Baker came to therapy complaining about her approach to her children. She thought she should completely stop yelling at them because the yelling did not achieve its aim and just left them frustrated. Trying to find a minimal goal, the therapist asked her, "What sort of thing do you think will happen when you start to, Joan, take a more calm and reasonable approach to your children?" (p. 35)

Several key features are noteworthy in this therapeutic intervention that resembles an Ericksonian directive in hypnosis. The phrasing recasts the goal (a more calm and reasonable approach) as small and thus more reachable than stopping yelling completely. There is not only the implied therapist suggestion that Joan should take a more calm and reasonable approach, but also that she will (the use of "when" rather than "if"). Moreover, there exists the further expectation that taking a more calm and reasonable approach will make a difference, and that that difference will be sufficient for Joan to notice (things will happen).

By turning the goal into a small start, the therapist is encouraging the client to proceed with changes she is likely to view as self-generating, minimizing further therapeutic interference. In fact, as a result of Joan's randomizing her approach and permitting herself the solution of yelling or being calm, depending on the circumstances, the children no longer found her behavior so predictable (and thus able to be ignored) and therefore the "causes" of her yelling diminished in both frequency and intensity. Soon her occasional yelling took on a new meaning, signaling to the children that she meant business this time. Joan did not have to stop yelling completely, as she thought she would at the start of therapy, since she now had a solution—she could choose to do so or not according to the situation and the response of others. DeShazer's technique fully accepts her (as a yeller), and does not scold her for yelling nor tell her to change by eliminating the yelling. Any continued yelling, when appropriate, is not seen as a sign of resistance, but rather as cooperation with the therapy.

DeShazer, again using an Ericksonian ploy, takes the position with clients that change is inevitable; the only issue is when it will occur. In this way he creates expectations of change as soon as the "key" is found. As just seen in our example, he might wonder aloud what the client expects to be different after the presenting complaint is gone. As this new framework gets established, the therapist and client are then likely to set to work finding a solution to resolve the problem. Just expecting to get somewhere different, somewhere more satisfactory, according to deShazer, creates the expectation of beneficial change in the client, and makes it easier to get there.

As do other strategists, the Milwaukee group uses one-way mirrors and intercom systems; it is common for the therapist to take a consultation break for ten minutes or so while the team develops an intervention message. The first part of that message is likely to compliment what the client(s) is doing already that is useful. Subsequent parts might offer clues about possible solutions, give behavioral homework assignments, or issue team-constructed directives that will lead to solutions.

Similar to Selvini-Palazzoli's invariant prescription, deShazer's "skeleton keys" aim at initiating new behavior patterns without focusing on the details of the presenting complaint. He offers formula tasks ("Do something different"; "Pay attention to what you do when you overcome the temptation or urge to overeat"), implying that the client can change while simultaneously focusing attention on the future triumphant moment when success is achieved. Rather than argue with the overeater who complains of *never* being able to control herself, deShazer simply instructs her to watch for when she does control her urge to eat, thus learning for herself that *never* was a gross overstatement.

Similarly, a client who complains of *always* being depressed might be directed to pay attention to an "up day" and later to describe what he did differently that day. Later, when a depressing day is expected, the therapist directs the client to do something normally done on an "up day" in order to find a solution. Clients who report vague complaints might be told to observe and report back next time what happens in their lives that they want to continue to have happen. In the following session, they might be asked what they think they need to do to get those satisfying experiences to continue to happen. As in most of deShazer's techniques, the therapist does not teach the client what to do differently or teach her or him new tactics for accomplishing behavioral change. His interventions tend to be simple and minimal, and in most cases often are effective in opening doors.

CRISIS-ORIENTED TREATMENT PROCEDURES

Crises may overload a family's coping skills, making its customary problem-solving strategies unworkable or ineffective. A prolonged crisis is likely to upset existing homeostatic balances and ultimately, if unresolved, provoke family disorganization. Crises then, by definintion, are dangerous times for families; however, they may also represent an opportunity, during a time of turmoil and transition, to bring about a major change in the life of the family system.

We offer in this section two examples of research or demonstration projects aimed at therapeutically exploiting the crisis situation in order to achieve long-term benefits for the family.

Multiple Impact Therapy

As part of a research project treating troubled adolescents referred from correctional agencies, psychologist Robert MacGregor and his associates (MacGregor, Ritchie, Serrano, & Schuster, 1964) at the University of Texas Medical Branch in Galveston developed a unique, maximum-impact, crisis-focused approach to family therapy. Because the team needed to create a technique for helping families in crises, but at the same time needed to accommodate families who lived a considerable distance away, they developed a therapeutic plan of intense interaction with the family called multiple impact therapy (MIT). Operating as a clinic team, the group devoted a full two days or so to the study and brief treatment of a single family.

This highly focused procedure is based on two assumptions: (1) that individuals and families facing a crisis are motivated to mobilize family resources to meet it, and thus are more likely to be receptive to professional help than at other times, and (2) that psychotherapy is likely to produce faster results in the early stages of treatment, so rapid intervention is highly desirable (Ritchie, 1971).

Essentially an expanded intake procedure focused on adolescents with behavior problems, MIT involved an entire family in a series of continuing interactions with a multidisciplinary team of mental health professionals (psychologists, psychiatric residents, social workers, and trainees) over the two-day period. Beginning with a diagnostic team-family conference, the team started to gather information about the family's role in the social development of the adolescent in crisis. Following this first collective conference, private individual interviews were arranged, each family member meeting with a different therapist. The venting of grievances, the presentation of each person's viewpoint, and attempts at self-justification were common at this point. Later, various combinations of team members and family members might hold joint sessions, such as when the teenager and his or her interviewer joined with one or both parents and their interviewer(s). Therapists might overlap in working with different individuals or combinations; multiple therapists might work with the same individual or same pair of family members; occasionally two family members (for example, father and son) were left alone to work on their problems themselves. After the team had had an opportunity to discuss their findings at lunch—the family was also encouraged to talk together at this time—individual interviews resumed but with a switch in interviewers (that is, the husband's interviewer in the morning might become the wife's interviewer in the afternoon, and vice versa). While the adolescent was being given psychological tests, joint sessions between the parents and their interviewers were held, as the team began to close in on the dysfunctional aspects of the family's functioning that were being revealed. At the end of the first day, the team and family reassembled for a group discussion of what they had learned.

The second day accelerated many of the first day's interviewing procedures, with family members likely to produce more emotionally charged responses to what was taking place. The overlapping material from interviews was used more freely; insights gained from one interview were shared in the next one. Factors interfering with family communication in general and intimate communication between the parents in particular were likely to become the focus of interest. A final team-family conference was held, findings were reviewed, and specific recommendations made for dealing with "back-home problems." In some cases, an additional half day was needed. Before the family left, arrangements were made for follow-up sessions to be held several months later in order to evaluate the extent to which any gains made during the intensive treatment period were sustained (MacGregor, 1971).

During the course of two days, the team had examined the marital relationship closely and taken initial steps toward strengthening it. Parent-adolescent transactions had been investigated, with the objective of clarifying lines of authority. All members had undergone a powerful emotional experience, and as a result of the team's efforts, were oriented to the future rather than the past. The treatment team's solidarity, its prior experience with families, and the sheer number of mental health professionals involved had had a positive impact on the family and its value system. More than simply providing insights, MIT aimed to change the family from a relatively closed system to an open system conducive to growth. MIT encouraged more open communication between members, greater mutual acceptance, clearer role differentiation, and increased flexibility in attempting new ways of relating—especially to and by the disturbed adolescent—so that family members could give up old and unsatisfying roles and begin to explore new ways of growth.

Early published results from work with 62 families indicated somewhat more success than that obtained by traditional therapeutic approaches (MacGregor et al., 1964). In addition, it should be noted that the team dealt with families not likely to remain involved in weekly child guidance clinic sessions; brief, direct, action-oriented, problem-solving procedures were a matter of necessity, not choice. Nevertheless, MIT is not practiced much today, largely due to the considerable time, expense, and number of professional staff members needed, as well as its overall lack of empirical support. Conceptually, too, many therapists challenge the maximum-input approach, arguing that families often require time between sessions to assimilate what they have learned and to transfer gains to real-life situations (Piercy, Sprenkle, & Associates, 1986). MIT does have historical significance, however, and many of its systems assumptions and procedures appear in current practices of family therapy.

Family Crisis Therapy

Crises of varying magnitude, duration, and frequency occur in all families throughout their life cycles. The family's usual functioning may become temporarily disrupted as the members try unsuccessfully to impose their customary problem-solving strategies in a situation where such strategies are inappropriate or inadequate. Since the crisis period is a time of increased vulnerability as well as an opportunity for growth and change, prompt, action-oriented intervention focused on resolving the urgent problem may have great benefits for all concerned. A landmark research project offering family crisis therapy designed for such emergency situations sought to help the family resolve the crisis through a process of systems change and to restore its functioning to its previous adaptational level.

Family crisis therapy aims to help a distressed individual and his or her family to actively define the crisis in terms of the family system and then use the family's combined coping skills to deal with the existing, as yet unresolved, situation. It is time-limited (typically no more than six sessions) and highly focused on the management of the current crisis and the prevention of future crises.

The first extensive and systematic treatment of families in crisis came with the establishment of the Family Treatment Unit at the Colorado Psychiatric Hospital in 1964 (Langsley & Kaplan, 1968). This research unit was set up to offer brief, crisis-focused outpatient therapy to families in which one member, usually diagnosed as acutely schizophrenic, would ordinarily be hospitalized. Part of the rationale for the unit was the belief that removing a disturbed young person from the home and placing him or her in a hospital has two drawbacks: it scapegoats that person as the cause of all family problems, and it thereby helps the family to avoid those very problems that may have precipitated the crisis that led to the person's disturbed behavior. In this alternative approach, the family in an acute crisis situation remains together, receiving intensive family therapy on an outpatient basis. Family crisis therapy typically lasts about three weeks and includes five office visits and one home visit. The home visit is especially valuable for observing family interaction and functioning in a natural environment, in addition to strengthening the family's commitment, involvement, and belief that the hospital team cares (Langsley, Pittman, Machotka, & Flomenhaft, 1968).

As practiced by the Colorado group, the process consists of seven overlapping steps: (1) immediate aid is offered at any hour of the day or night; (2) the crisis is defined as a family problem and all relevant family members are involved in the treatment from the outset; (3) the focus remains on the current crisis, placing immediate responsibility for change on all the family members; (4) a nonspecific treatment program (discouraging regression, offering reassurance and hope, lowering the family's tension level, prescribing medication for the identified patient for symptom relief) is begun; (5) specific tasks are assigned to each family member in an effort to resolve the crisis; (6) resistances to change are negotiated, as are role conflicts that have hindered the members' ability to deal with the crisis; and (7) therapy is terminated, with the understanding that further treatment is available in the event of a future crisis. If necessary, referral for long-term family therapy may be made during this step.

In a carefully designed experiment on the effectiveness of family crisis therapy (FCT) in averting the need for mental hospital admission, Langsley and associates (1968) responded to requests for immediate hospitalization of a family member by assigning alternate applicants to the outpatient Family Treatment Unit or to the university psychiatric hospital. In the former group, the patient and his or her family were seen together for crisis therapy for six visits over a three-week period. The latter group of matched patients received the customary hospital treatment—individual and group psychotherapy, medication, participation in the hospital's therapeutic community—for an average stay of slightly less than a month. In addition, their families were seen separately from them by the hospital's psychiatric social worker. A follow-up study showed that the FCT patients were less likely to be hospitalized within six months following treatment than the hospitalized patients were to be rehospitalized. A later study (Langsley, Machotka, & Flomenhaft, 1971), comparing 150 FCT patients and 150 hospitalized patients 18 months after treatment, showed similar benefits for FCT patients, although the differences in hospitalization rates between the groups tended to decrease with time. If hospitalization became necessary by the 6-month or 18-month checkpoint, the FCT patients were likely to spend considerably less time in the hospital than did their previously hospitalized counterparts.

Hospital treatment apparently encourages further hospitalization. Family crisis therapy has demonstrated itself to be a cost-effective preventive measure in averting hospitalization, returning patients and families to a functional level, and helping them manage hazardous events in the future. Nevertheless, once the Colorado research project ended, few if any hospitals carried on the crisis-oriented approach. One of the original researchers, Pittman (1987), does continue to use a family crisis intervention approach, especially in dealing with families who are currently in transition or who face other crisis situations. It is possible that the national trend toward ambulatory outpatient care as opposed to hospitalization may resurrect a version of this technique.

LARGE-GROUP TREATMENT PROCEDURES

Many of the positive aspects of group therapy (see Chapter Four), along with the advantages of clinical intervention at the family level, are evident in the two large scale approaches described below.

Multiple Family Therapy

Developed from work with hospitalized schizophrenic patients and their families, multiple family therapy (MFT) is an adaptation of group therapy techniques to the treatment of whole families. During the 1950s, Laqueur, then a psychiatrist at Creedmore State Hospital in New York, made the observation that many patients improved steadily while receiving treatment in the hospital, only to return in worse condition after weekend visits with their families. Laqueur originally invited large numbers of patients and their family members to joint informational meetings, but later decided it was more workable to deal with groups of four or five families. Not only did this prove expedient, saving time and personnel, but the interaction between families seemed to bring about desired behavior changes more quickly than working with the individual patient alone or with individual families. The approach also proved useful in helping the patient adjust later from a structured hospital milieu to an unstructured home situation (Laqueur, 1976).

Since its introduction in the early 1950s, MFT has progressed to the point where it is now used with a wide variety of dysfunctional families and in a great number of clinical settings (Strelnick, 1977). Recent efforts to serve heterogeneous outpatient populations (single-parent families, divorced-family groups, groups for families with learning disabled children) generally comprising less seriously disturbed individuals have been described by Gritzer and Okun (1983). Unlike Laqueur's work with groups requiring hospitalization, outpatient treatment usually entails a broader client selection potential, each family voluntarily seeking help for its own particular stresses and crises.

Whether as an inpatient or outpatient treatment, MFT usually involves four to six families (sometimes randomly selected and sometimes screened in advance) who meet with a therapist and cotherapist weekly for 60–75 minute sessions. The members share problems and help each other in the problem-solving process. In recent years, especially in outpatient facilities, families go through a four- or five-session screening process to prepare them for the larger group, reduce their anxieties, and help build a trusting alliance with the therapist (Gritzer & Okun, 1983). The therapist(s) acts as facilitator, guiding the discussion, pointing out transactional patterns, and reviewing at the close of the session what has taken place. Group members do not necessarily sit clustered as individual families; shifts in seating are common as mothers may join together temporarily at one point or perhaps children group together as they learn of their common problems. Groups are open-ended, so that a family leaving the group for whatever reason is replaced by a newly referred family.

Apparently, the benefits of such an approach accrue from the combined effects of family and group therapy. The group members particularly value group identification and support, the easy recognition of—and quick involvement with—each other's problems, seeing their own family's communication problems portrayed by another family, and learning how other families solve their relationship problems (Goldenberg & Goldenberg, 1975). It is possible to learn new patterns for resolving conflict from observing another family dealing with an analogous conflict situation more successfully. For some children (often, the identified patients), new experiences with parents other than their own may be less threatening and may prove enlightening and therapeutic. A therapist may use the less-disturbed families to reach the more-disturbed families; the former understand the latter's problems as not totally different from their own, but can offer suggestions or serve as models, through their family interaction, of better methods of conflict resolution. This is particularly true in open-ended groups where families new to the group may be helped by other families closer to successful termination.

What are the mechanisms of change in multiple family therapy? Laqueur (1973, 1976), adopting a general systems theory outlook, views each individual as a subsystem of a higher system, the family, which in turn represents a subsystem of the MFT group. The MFT group, then, receives input from its various subsystems, processes the information, and through its feedback loops provides output in the form of feedback information to the distressed family and its individual members. Through the circular interaction between the therapist and all group members, such insights may reverberate throughout the entire MFT system, speeding up progress for all the participating families. The secret codes of a disturbed family's internal verbal and nonverbal communication may be broken by other families. A signal from the therapist may be picked up by a sensitive family member who amplifies it throughout his or her family and into the entire MFT system. Because so many authority figures—therapist, fathers, mothers—are present, the young identified patient may feel encouraged to work out conflicts over independence through the comparatively nonthreatening mechanisms of analogy and identification. Role playing a father-son relationship with a father from another family not only helps the son learn new ways of coping with such a situation with his own father, but also provides similar insights to all the sons and fathers present.

Over a 25-year period, Laqueur (1976) and his colleagues treated over 1500 families in MFT groups, largely families with hospitalized schizophrenic members. According to Laqueur, only a handful were considered unsuited to this form of family therapy, primarily because exposure of some vital secret might have explosive consequences. Even in these cases, Laqueur acknowledged that such secrets are usually common knowledge within the family despite conspiracies of silence; rather than true secrets, they are more accurately described as barriers to communication and the free sharing of experiences.

An interesting variation of multiple family therapy involves multiple marital-couple therapy, usually in groups consisting of three to five couples. Even when the identified patient is a child, the course of family therapy frequently evolves to the identification and consideration of parental conflict, as we have noted earlier. In such cases, family therapy becomes marital-couple therapy. Bringing together a number of couples to deal with common problems of marriage seems the next logical and efficient step. Framo (1973), Alger (1976b), and Liberman, Wheeler, and Sanders (1976) have all described their work with multiple-couple groups. In some instances, cotherapists who themselves are husband and wife (Low & Low, 1975) add greater personal involvement and authenticity to the group; their ongoing demonstration of problem solving as a couple serves as a model.

A couples group seems the ideal context for marriage partners to recognize that their problems are not unique, that some conflict is an inevitable part of a marital relationship, that all marital pairs have to work out accommodations in a number of areas (children, sex, money, and so on). Couples may teach each other how to negotiate differences and how to avoid the escalation of conflict. In one sense, a couples group provides a forum where each person can express his or her expectations of marriage and of his or her mate, with feedback from others providing reality testing. Based on his work with over 200 couples, Framo (1973) considers such an approach the most effective therapy for marital couples. A positive support system of peers—other couples contributing as much or more than the therapist—is a significant therapeutic advantage of couples groups (Alger, 1976b). Liberman, Wheeler, and Sanders (1976), adopting a behavioral approach, train couples in communication skills and in learning to recognize, initiate, and acknowledge pleasing interactions. Their goal is to increase the range and frequency of positively experienced interaction between spouses, aided by the support and cohesiveness of the couples group. They contend that as a couple's exchange of positive reinforcements is more equally balanced, marital satisfaction greatly increases.

Social Network Intervention

Some family therapists choose to work in a troubled person's home, assembling that person's entire social network, including his or her nuclear family as well as friends, neighbors, work associates, significant persons from school, church, various social agencies and institutions—in short, the sum total of human relationships that are meaningful in his or her life. Brought together and led by a team of therapists called "network intervenors," such a group of interrelated people has within itself the resources to develop creative solutions to the distressed individual's current predicament, according to Speck and Attneave (1973). Moreover, these therapists contend that much of the behavior traditionally associated with mental illness is instead derived from the individual's feelings of alienation from just such relationships and resources.

Social network intervention (sometimes referred to as network therapy), in which 40 to 50 people who are willing to come together in a crisis are mobilized as a potent therapeutic force, is particularly appealing in an age of increasing depersonalization. Originally developed from work with schizophrenics in their homes, network therapy is based on the assumption that there is significant disturbance in the schizophrenic's communication with all members of his or her social network, not just within the nuclear family. Consequently, this approach works at intensifying the person's network of relationships, intimately involving the entire group as much as possible in each other's lives. Rueveni (1979) sees such networks as analogous to clans or tribal units; they offer support, reassurance, and solidarity to their members. No longer limited to schizophrenics and their families, this technique may be used with any kind of dysfunctional behavior (for example, drug abuse, depression following a suicide attempt) labeled as "sick" by society (Pattison, 1981). In each case, social network intervention attempts to foster an emotional climate of trust and openness as a prelude to constructive encounters between the participants.

In such an assembly, tribal-like bonds can be created or revived not only to cope with the current crisis but also to sustain and continue the process long after formal meetings with a team of therapists have been terminated. According to Speck and Attneave (1973), the benefits derive from the "network effect"—a spirited and euphoric group phenomenon seen in peace marches, revival meetings, tribal healing ceremonies, and massive rock concerts, and even the seemingly dissimilar group singing at the Lions Club. In such situations, the group takes on an affiliative life of its own and achieves a sense of union and oneness that is somehow larger than what each participant contributes. In the case of social network intervention, the participants, under the influence of the "network effect," focus more energy, more attention, and bring more reality to bear on the tasks to be carried out than could any therapist acting alone during the same brief period of time.

Therapeutic intervention usually gets under way when the network intervention team redefines the troubled person's "symptoms" as a natural reaction to an inadequate social structure, rather than a sign of mental illness. As presented to his or her nuclear family and those people who are daily intimates, the person's present predicament is further defined in terms of two or three specific issues (for example, the need to find employment, to make more and better friends, to move out of the house) that are potentially resolvable. Next, this close group assembles its social network to meet with the intervention team (usually, two to five professionals possibly joined by nonprofessional "network activists" who can help mobilize and organize group action). Those who are invited are told that they are coming together to help the nuclear family in its crisis and that a team of intervenors will provide leadership, at least at the start. Although the number and length of meetings varies, it is common to hold six evening sessions, each four hours in duration, at one- to four-week intervals. In rare cases, the network intervenors have only one meeting in which to produce the therapeutic "network effect." More commonly, several sessions take place and the team of intervenors can meet regularly between sessions to plan their strategy.

The goal of network intervention is to capitalize on the power of the assembled network to shake up an overly rigid family unit in order to allow changes in the family system. It is hoped that some new bonds will be strengthened and that others, too constricting, will be weakened. Other goals include changing the members' perceptions of each other, opening clearer channels of communication, and releasing latent positive forces within the family and its larger social network.

Each session typically proceeds through several distinct phases. After some informal milling around with the intervenors scattered throughout the group, a number of encounter-group exercises (holding hands, vigorously jumping up and down, screaming out in unison) are employed as warm-up exercises, knitting the group together as a network. Called **retribalization** by Speck and Attneave (1973), this experience enhances the creation or revival of tribal-like bonds so that the network can sustain the process of seeking solutions to the current family crisis. As they reach the point of perceiving themselves as a connected, functioning organic unit, the participants (with the team's help) start to formulate what needs to be done and how to go about doing it. Conflicting viewpoints become apparent as the network becomes polarized (for example, between generations). Subgroups may form inner and outer circles, each in turn listening to the other and presenting its own position (in respect, for instance, to the use of drugs). The point here is to increase tension, generating greater interpersonal involvement and tribal commitment. As the energy developed by polarization starts to become focused, each subgroup trying hard to change the other, the team moves in to mobilize the energy and emotion and channel them constructively. The team conductor, aided by other team members and activists, introduces the task to be dealt with by the network. It is common at this time for the participants to become temporarily depressed, stymied by the difficulties they foresee in solving the problem. Finally the network achieves a breakthrough: the assigned task is accomplished. Exhausted but elated, the team and network terminate the session, experiencing a natural recovery period between meetings. At the conclusion of all meetings, the group participants are likely to have formed a cohesive system as a result of their shared experiences, often (although not necessarily) keeping the network alive long after the formal sessions with the intervention team have ceased. By remaining a supportive, caring, tribal-like group, they may become their own future agents of change, as necessary.

Networking families in crisis is difficult to organize and consequently is used sparingly today, although it continues to be undertaken with specific client populations (Rueveni, 1984). Recent innovations have included networks of family, friends, coworkers, employers, and other concerned persons together confronting a person with a drug or alcohol problem who consistently denies being out of control. Consistent support and caring is coupled with group insistence that the individual look at the substance-abusing behavior. Following the initial confrontation, the newly formed network continues to serve as a problem-solving support group.

SUMMARY

We have considered four diverse kinds of family therapy techniques that supplement the usual approaches to treatment: nonverbal procedures, time-limited procedures, crisis-oriented procedures, and interventions that involve large groups.

In family sculpting, a nonverbal technique, various members are asked to portray how they see the relationships within the family by arranging people in various physical positions in space and time. Family choreography, a related technique, physically recreates interactive patterns within the family and thus opens them to examination and possible change.

Two noteworthy time-limited treatment procedures are the MRI Brief Therapy Project and the solution-focused approach of the Milwaukee Brief Family Therapy Center. As practiced at the MRI, brief family therapy is a pragmatic, strategic, sometimes paradoxical technique for problem resolution in which families learn new, systemic solutions to problems rather than continue the self-defeating "solutions" that become problems in and of themselves. In the related Milwaukee model, the therapist helps clients find "skeleton keys" or formula interventions, after first creating an atmosphere in which change is seen as inevitable.

In multiple impact therapy, a family in crisis (often provoked by the delinquent behavior of an adolescent member) is seen over a two-day period for intensive interaction with a team of mental health professionals. Although essentially a diagnostic procedure, MIT also includes the team's introduction of a number of therapeutic guidelines; the team conducts follow-up studies with the family to evaluate the extent of any therapeutic gains made. Another research-based, crisis-oriented approach, family crisis therapy, is a highly focused technique for mobilizing a family's coping skills to deal with a psychological emergency situation, thereby avoiding psychiatric hospitalization of a family member.

A large-group treatment procedure, multiple family therapy was originally developed for working with hospitalized schizophrenics and their families, but in recent years it has also been used with an outpatient population. It is a form of group therapy in which several families meet regularly to share problems and help each other in the problem-solving process. A variation is the marital-couples group, which meets to discuss common marital problems and to find solutions together. Another kind of large-group approach, social network intervention (network therapy), brings together family, friends, neighbors, and significant others to aid in the patient's treatment and rehabilitation. The aim is to capitalize on the power of the assembled group to induce change in a dysfunctional family system.

Part III

RESEARCH, TRAINING, AND PROFESSIONAL PRACTICE

Chapter Twelve

Research in Family Therapy

Historically speaking, research in family therapy has provided the fertile soil for the blossoming of the field in the last four decades. As we noted in Chapter Four, and as Wynne (1983), himself a pioneer in the field, has observed, working with families in the 1950s was regarded primarily as a research idea; the notion of seeing family members together for therapeutic purposes came later and followed from research discoveries and subsequent theorizing. Wynne recalls that the therapy offered to families in those early years was distinctly intended to facilitate the maintenance of contact with research families. Haley (1978), too, looks back on that decade as a time when it "was taken for granted that a therapist and a researcher were of the same species (although the therapist had a more second-class status)" (p. 73).

Priorities began to change drastically beginning in the 1960s, as clinicians, on the basis of their experiences of working therapeutically with families, generated a multitude of new and exciting clinical techniques, in most cases without benefit of research support. During most of the 1960s as well as the 1970s, with some notable exceptions such as the research of Minuchin, Montalvo, Guerney, Rosman, and Schumer (1967) with delinquent adolescents and their families, family research and family therapy seemed to become different realms, with distinct languages, observational procedures, and philosophical orientations toward inquiry. Inadvertently, Framo's (1972) call in a well-known conference in 1967 for a "dialogue" between family therapist and family researcher attested to the developing polarization.

The 1980s seemed to bring a renewed connection between researcher and therapist, as many practitioners began to pay closer attention to the empirical foundation of the field, particularly in the areas of process and outcome research (Greenberg & Pinsof, 1986). Both researchers and therapists should benefit from the cross-fertilization of ideas. As Wynne (1988) points out, therapists would do well to examine the premises, circumstances, and ingredients of their clinical interventions, and researchers too would profit from moving beyond systematic data collection to becoming more responsive to the more informal conceptual inquiries carried out in the daily practices of their clinical colleagues.

In this chapter we intend to examine the general nature of research inquiry in the sciences and then turn to their applicability to and appropriateness for research in family therapy. We then will elaborate in some detail on research findings in three important areas: classification and assessment, family process research, and research on the effectiveness of family therapy.

SOME METHODOLOGICAL CHALLENGES

Are traditional experimental methods, based on a logical positivist, empirical viewpoint, emphasizing objectivity, the control of variables, and measurability as well as replicability of results, appropriate for family therapy research? Is the step-by-step study of linear cause-and-effect sequences relevant to the systems-based circular or recursive paradigm of today's family therapist? Or, as Gurman (1983b) raises the question, does the use of classical experimental design impose on the clinical data a definition of reality that may be convenient but that may miss the mark in untangling the complexity of systemic phenomena? These issues represent some of the concerns of those who agree that family therapy's assumptions and procedures need to be investigated, but question whether it is appropriate to do so by time-honored research procedures (Keeney & Sprenkle, 1982).

Schwartz and Breunlin (1983) challenge the applicability to family therapy of many of the premises on which the traditional scientific method is based when they observe:

> Underlying traditional research methods is a belief in an *absolute* reality that can be measured objectively, as opposed to the relativistic belief that the version of reality measured will be a function of one's point of reference and of the degree to which the act of measuring affects the phenomenon being measured. The methods of hard science are guided by a faith that

Lyman Wynne, M.D., Ph.D.

> breaking a phenomenon down to its most basic elements yields the most thorough understanding and that it is both possible and useful to distinguish simple causes and effects. (p. 27)

While a number of family therapists (Gurman, 1983a; Kniskern, 1983) defend the use of traditional research methodology, others (Colapinto, 1979; Tomm, 1983), who argue for a "new epistemology," contend that such an approach is derived from linear and reductionistic paradigms and thus would seem to be inappropriate and inadequate in explaining how systems develop, function, and change. We'll return to this issue in greater detail later in this chapter, particularly when we deal with some of the problems surrounding family therapy outcome research.

Family Research and Family Psychopatholgy

Continuing our discussion of the place of research in family therapy, we should note that early research mostly was carried out with small samples, lacked matching control groups, and in general would be considered primitive by today's standards (Wynne, 1983). With some exceptions (such as Lewis, Beavers, Gossett, & Phillips, 1976), relevant rating scales or self-report measures were not yet highly developed for dealing with the special problems involved in family evaluations. A number of studies did attempt to compare family interaction patterns in so-called healthy families and families with at least one disturbed family member (Doane, 1978;

Riskin & Faunce, 1972), but generally speaking failed to deal adequately with the complex methodological issues involved (finding comparable samples, defining "healthy" families, combining samples with mixed diagnoses, pinpointing precisely what aspects of complex interactions should be teased out and measured, using independent judges, and so forth). Efforts to describe single cases (Rabin, 1981), while often instructive, nevertheless were themselves not always generalizable to larger populations.

Goldstein (1988) goes so far as to describe the period from the late 1960s to the late 1970s as representing a kind of "Dark Age" in research on psychopathological family conditions. Direct observational studies of dysfunctional families such as those containing a schizophrenic member, a major research effort barely a decade earlier, seemed to diminish markedly during this period. A fundamental assumption of the earlier studies—that direct observations contrasting families with and without a mental disorder could provide clues to the psychological precursors of that disorder—began to be reappraised a decade later. Two premises—that disturbances in family relationships were the major cause of mental disorders in general, and that each mental disorder resulted from distinctive patterns of family dynamics—also were reassessed because of the research complications they posed.

One major methodological drawback to testing the assumptions arising from such cross-sectional research was that the families were studied long after the disorder in a member had affected the family system. Thus the family interaction data, while it well might have reflected a complex amalgam of family processes, inevitably included some patterns that anteceded the onset of the disorders as well as some that represented various accommodations by family members to the presence of the disorder. Gradually researchers concluded that cross-sectional studies undertaken only after a mental disorder was present were limited in their ability to reveal significant information regarding family etiological processes. In addition, considerable evidence began to accumulate by the late 1960s that schizophrenia, bipolar and unipolar affective disorders, and alcoholism all had strong genetic predispositions, and that psychopharmacological interventions were often effective in reducing symptomatology, also challenging the underlying paradigm of the previous family studies in which family interaction was thought to be the predominant etiological agent and family therapy a potent model of intervention (Goldstein, 1988).

There is currently renewed interest in the relationship between family interaction patterns and the major mental disorders, largely guided by a **vulnerability-stress model** (Nuechterlein & Dawson, 1984). In this model, the genetic predisposition to a disorder such as schizophrenia is recognized as forming the basis for the disorder; the vulnerability is modified by all life events, particularly those of family life, which in turn modify the likelihood of the later expression of the disorder. Family researchers have turned their attention to the interaction between relationships within the family and indexes of vulnerability to specific mental disorders, such as being the offspring of a parent with the disorder. Longitudinal investigations have by and large replaced cross-sectional studies, and families are selected for study prior to the onset of a disorder. Targeted "high risk"

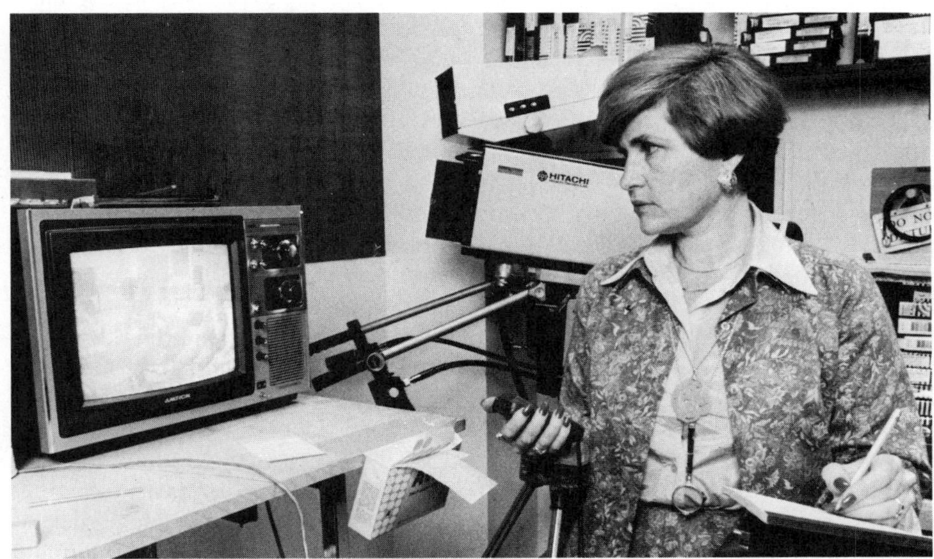

Videotaping family therapy sessions preserves these events for research study. This psychologist is rating certain family interactive patterns along previously determined empirical categories in an effort to clarify what distinguishes the functioning levels of different families.

children of disturbed parents are carefully followed and evaluated for several years, especially as they pass through the risk period for that disorder.

Particularly noteworthy is the UCLA High Risk Study (Goldstein, 1985) in which 64 intact families with a nonpsychotic but emotionally disturbed teenager referred to a university psychology clinic were followed and periodically assessed for 15 years. The incidence of schizophrenia and related disorders within the family was found to be highest in those families classified as high in *communication deviance* (CD)[1] (Wynne, Singer, Bartko, & Toohey, 1977) during the assessment carried out 15 years previously. No cases of schizophrenia were found in families judged in blind diagnostic appraisals to be low in CD. The combination of a high CD score and a high EE (expressed emotion) score (a measure of both negative

1. Communication deviance refers to a family's disordered style of communicating with one another. In risk research that Wynne and his associates (Wynne, 1970; Wynne, Singer, Bartko, & Toohey, 1977) have carried out for two decades, the researchers found that the cognitive capacities of attending and transactionally focusing are consistently impaired in parents of schizophrenics. "Healthy communication" between parents, according to Wynne, Jones, and Al-Khayyal (1982), promotes adaptive behavior in their offspring by providing a model for developing the essential cognitive task of attending, focusing, and remaining task-oriented, as well as a model for communicating ideas and feelings clearly and directly. Wynne's research has application in prevention and early intervention with disturbed families (Wynne, 1983).

family affect expressed toward the patient and/or emotional overinvolvement toward that person) enabled judges to increase their ability to predict those families most likely to manifest schizophrenia and related symptoms in the follow-up period.

The results lend support to the idea that certain communication disturbances and disturbances in the expression of affect within the family antecede the onset of schizophrenia, although, as Goldstein (1988) himself acknowledges, "they do not indicate how these patterns arise or interact with the vulnerability of the child at risk" (p. 287). Subsequent research on the behavioral correlates of relatives' expressed emotions (Cook, Strachan, Goldstein, & Miklowitz, 1989) has suggested that high EE mothers, unlike their low EE counterparts, evoke reciprocal responses in disturbed adolescents; once set off, they are far more likely to engage together in a negative chain of behaviors. One implication from the research, then, is for the design of therapeutic interventions that tend to reduce the joined mother-adolescent dyadic emotional system, correspondingly reducing the risk of further adolescent psychiatric problems.

As a more rigorous set of standards has been adopted in recent years for studying families and their treatment, Stanton (1988) draws the useful distinction between *exploratory research*, breaking new ground, and *confirmatory research*, directed at verifying the efficacy of a particular intervention technique, such as comparing it with a baseline no-treatment control group or with other treatment methods. Both approaches are important, and although the latter may be more amenable to existing research methods—and thus more commonly carried out today—Stanton argues that it must not obscure the need for the development of new methods, which may necessitate a nontraditional research methodology.

CLASSIFYING AND ASSESSING FAMILY FUNCTIONING

Classification is an essential part of the process by which scientists seek to understand and explain large and varied masses of data they accumulate. Furthermore, classification into categories helps researchers to direct and structure the search for new information and provides a framework that enables them to explain their discoveries to one another. In an interdisciplinary area such as family therapy, it is particularly important to develop and refine some systems of classification so that members of different scientific and professional disciplines can communicate more meaningfully.

The efforts to classify family functioning that we are about to discuss all derive from systems theory. That is, they focus on patterns, relationships, and reciprocal interactions within the family unit, although their emphases vary. Kantor and Lehr are particularly intent on differentiating family systems through an analysis of their structural development and transactional styles. Olson and his associates offer a family classification matrix based on underlying dimensions of family functioning. Reiss classifies families according to the way they construct reality and make sense out of their social environment. Beavers attempts to distinguish the processes occurring within families that differentiate those that function competently from those that become dysfunctional. Epstein, Bishop, and Baldwin's McMaster model assesses family coping skills. The Family Environment Scale offered by Moos represents an effort to construct a psychometric scale for depicting a family's social climate.

Kantor and Lehr's Family Typology

Based on the observations of a wide sample of families over a period of nearly a decade, and without attempting to distinguish "normal" from "pathological" families, Kantor and Lehr (1975) provided an early example of exploratory research aimed at developing a system for identifying and classifying types of family structures. In particular, they concerned themselves with how families process information and evolve strategies for regulating distances between one another. How do family subsystems "interface" with one another, they asked, and how does the family unit as a whole communicate with the outside world?

These researchers were able to distinguish three basic family types—open, closed, and random—representing different configurations for structuring both the family's internal relationships as well as its access to, and exchange with, the outside world. No one type appeared to be superior or inferior to the others; no type was found to exist in pure form, although Kantor and Lehr discovered that families cluster around the three categories.

Each family type was found to have its own rules, boundary arrangements, and tactics for achieving and maintaining homeostatic balance. Open families, neither too tightly nor too loosely bounded, are essentially democratic. Honest exchange is encouraged both within the family and with outsiders. Although there is a sense of order, flexibility is given high priority; negotiation is encouraged; adaptation through consensus is endorsed; the rights of individuals are taken for granted; loyalty to oneself and to the family is expected.

Within closed family structures, rules and a hierarchical power structure make individual members subordinate their needs for the benefit of the group. As White (1978) depicts such families, parents make sure that doors are locked, family reading material and television programs are screened, and children scrupulously report their comings and goings. The quest for privacy may border on suspiciousness, and strangers are given a hard look before being allowed access to the family. Rigid daily schedules (wake-up time, mealtimes, bedtime) are apt to be followed. The "core purpose" of such closed families, as Kantor and Lehr define it, is stability through tradition, in contrast to open families who encourage adaptability.

Random families were identified in this research study as fragmented. Each person does whatever he or she wishes, which may or may not be related or connected to what others are doing. There are few, if any, family rules. Boundaries are blurred and easily crossed. Traffic in and out of the family is loosely regulated as everyone, strangers included, comes and goes in an irregular pattern. Mealtimes are seldom scheduled for the family as a whole but are left up to the individual. In a random family, the "core purpose" is identified by Kantor and Lehr as exploration through intuition.

As we noted, Kantor and Lehr do not assume that dysfunctional families necessarily stem from one or another of these structural types. Potentially, each type may be flawed. If closed structures become too rigid, family members may rebel or even bolt from the family and run away. Random family structures run the risk of becoming chaotic. Even open families may be disposed toward schism or divorce if incompatibilities produce excessive strain and create a family impasse (Hoffman, 1981).

Olson's Circumplex Model

A useful "insider" or family member's view of the two central properties of family life—adaptability and cohesion—may be obtained from the assessment technique developed by Olson and his colleagues (Olson, 1986; Olson, Russell, & Sprenkle, 1983; Olson, Sprenkle, & Russell, 1979). Their careful investigation, which extended for over a decade and studied over 1000 families (100 or more in each of seven life-cycle stages), was directed at understanding how families cope with various situational stresses and demands throughout the life cycle. Because diagnosis by family pattern, using standard DSM-III categories, is not very satisfactory, a more applicable classification system for families may emerge from this and related research undertakings.

Olson and his associates have produced a family typology—what they refer to as the Circumplex Model—based on the family's degree of adaptability (its ability to permit changes in its rules, power structure, and role relationships) and cohesion (the emotional bonding of the family members to one another). Olson and his associates argue that a balance on each of these dimensions is most desirable; extremes represent increasingly dysfunctional family patterns. As seen in Figure 12.1, steps along these two dimensions are divided into four levels each, resulting in a four-by-four matrix yielding 16 possible family types. With too much cohesion, the family is enmeshed and its members overly entwined in each other's lives; with too little, the members remain distant, isolated, and disengaged. Excessive adaptability leads to too much change, unpredictability, and possible chaos; too little adaptability may cause rigidity and stagnation. With a 20-item self-report instrument called the Family Adaptability and Cohesion Evaluation Scale (FACES III) (Olson, 1986), family scores on the two dimensions permit placement on the Circumplex Model grid. Research results indicate that high-functioning families show moderate scores on the two dimensions, while low-functioning families reveal extreme scores.

According to this model, balanced family functioning may take one of four forms: flexibly separated, flexibly connected, structurally separated, and structurally connected. Such families are said to combine stability, the flexibility to change whenever necessary, and sufficiently open boundaries to permit effective communication. Note that the four central types are labeled open family systems, and that the outer rings are characterized as closed or random systems, thus linking this model to the typology of Kantor and Lehr (1975).

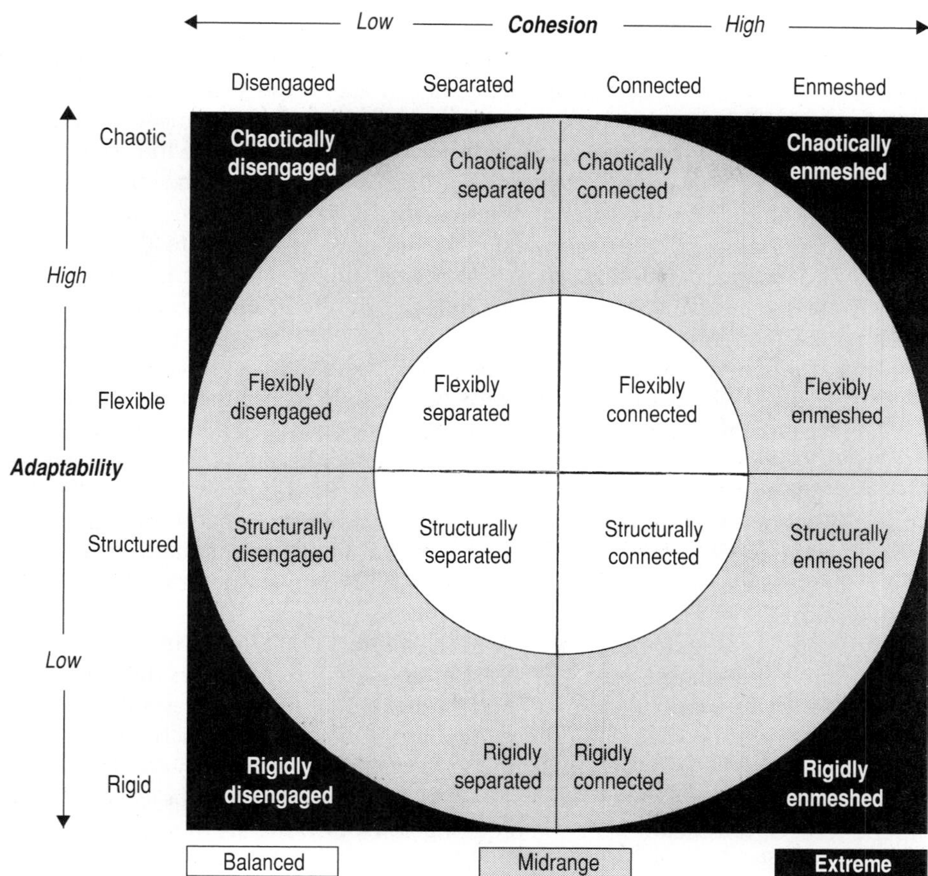

Figure 12.1 The Circumplex Model, representing 16 types of marital and family systems. (Source: Olson, 1986, p. 339)

Reiss's Family Paradigms

Originally intent on discovering through laboratory research how families with schizophrenic members process information (in the hope of learning more about comparable information-processing deficits in the identified patient), David Reiss has moved beyond the study of family cognitive patterns and problem-solving styles. What has emerged from his research efforts—now extending over thirty years and including nonclinical or normal families—is a differentiation of family perceptual and interactive patterns that goes beyond arbitrary functional/dysfunctional distinctions (Oliveri & Reiss, 1982; Reiss, 1981). Reiss's current investigations are directed at discovering how families develop paradigms (in his terms, shared assumptions about the social world), how such family paradigms may be changed, and what happens when a paradigm breaks down.

Beginning in the late 1950s, Reiss presented families with a number of problem-solving tasks (puzzles or card-sorting exercises) and observed how they developed strategies, shared information, and traded ideas with one another in pursuit of solutions. Soon it became clear to him that what was most significant was not how they processed information but how they perceived the laboratory setting in which they were being tested. For example, families with schizophrenic adolescents often perceived danger and a threat to family ties; families with delinquent adolescents tended to view the laboratory as a place to demonstrate distance and independence from one another; and families with normal adolescents were apt to perceive the experience as an opportunity to explore and master a challenging situation together.

Thus, the family's reaction to the unfamiliar experimental situation itself was the crucial determinant of their behavior as a family. Reiss then reasoned that perhaps the laboratory response reflected a general construct with which the family tried to make sense of the world. It was this construct or blueprint or set of fantasies or expectations for dealing with new situations that Reiss labeled the "family paradigm." Just as an individual develops ways to comprehend the meaning of events in the environment, so a family unit—integrating the construing styles of all its members—evolves a mode of perceiving, interpreting, and interacting with the social world.

Reiss distinguishes three dimensions (see Table 12.1) along which characteristics of family paradigms vary: (1) configurations (the way families differ in their experiences of the world as ordered, and the belief that its mysteries are discoverable through reasoned search); (2) coordination (the extent to which they believe the world is equally open to all family members); and (3) closure (the extent to which the family perceives events as familiar and thus interpretable on the basis of past experiences, or novel and fresh and requiring some new means of interpretation).

On the basis of his exploratory research, Reiss (1981) differentiated three ways of constructing reality. **Environment-sensitive families** believe the world is knowable and orderly and expect each member to contribute to its understanding and mastery. **Interpersonal distance-sensitive families** are composed of disengaged members, loners, who strive to demonstrate their autonomy and believe that any attention paid to suggestions of others is a sign of weakness. **Consensus-sensitive families** are made up of enmeshed members who perceive the world as so chaotic and confusing that they must join together, maintain agreement at all times, and in that way protect themselves from danger.

Clearly, in Reiss's typology, it is the environment-sensitive family that is apt to be most problem-free. Its members are able to accept aid and advice from others, benefit from cues from the environment, act individually or jointly, and delay closure in order to make an effective response based on consideration of a number of alternative solutions. In terms of flexibility, the environment-sensitive family resembles the open family system described in Olson's Circumplex Model. Should its family paradigm be threatened as a result of a family crisis, this type of family will attempt to maintain family integrity and overcome adversity together. Reiss (1981) cites the example of a family called upon to deal with the birth of a handicapped child, an event that temporarily threatened the family's notion that the world was predictable and thus comprehensible. By learning all they could about the infant's disability and arranging for the best available treatment, family members once again confirmed for themselves that they live in an orderly, manageable world, adding the realization that certain afflictions or adversities are inevitable but that together they will be able to prevail.

Table 12.1 Summary of Patterns of Association of Family Problem-Solving Behavior with (a) Perceptions of Social Relationships, and (b) Orientations to Kin

High levels of:	*(a)* *. . . were associated with high levels of:*	*(b)* *. . . and with high levels of:*
Configuration		
Belief in a masterable environment	Nonstereotypic view of family Openness to individuals outside the family	Child-parent independence in kin ties
Coordination		
Sense that the environment functions similarly for all members	Nonstereotypic view of family	Child-parent congruence in kin ties Investment in close-knit networks of kin
Closure (delayed)		
View of the environment as source of new and changing experience	Openness to inanimate aspects of the environment	Investment in large networks of kin

(Source: Oliveri & Reiss, 1982, p. 109)

Beavers's Level of Family Functioning

Up to this point we have focused on exploratory research efforts to classify and differentiate family structures and styles. Largely unanswered is the question of how families get that way and whether they are capable of changing or evolving from a less functional pattern to another more functional one. Moreover, baseline data on normal or healthy family functioning is needed. Beavers (1977) and his associates have made a significant contribution by observing and analyzing various forms of negotiation and other transactions within competent families in an effort to shed light on how such processes evolve.

In their research, Lewis, Beavers, Gossett, and Phillips (1976) looked beyond the strengths and weaknesses of individual family members to identify those interactions within a "healthy" family system that make for optimal functioning. Members of intact families (each of which had at least one adolescent but no member identified as a psychiatric patient) were interviewed and their interactions as they carried out a variety of tasks videotaped. While the design of the study had limitations ("healthy" was defined negatively as the absence of psychopathology; subjects were all from white, middle-class, urban homes; videotaped behavior might not have represented their ordinary day-to-day interactions), the findings do expand our understanding of common relationship patterns in competent families.

The research plan required several judges to observe and rate each family's videotaped behavior along five major dimensions and according to a variety of subtopics and themes:

I. Structure of the family
  A. Overt power (how family dealt with influence and dominance)
  B. Parental coalitions (strength of husband-wife alliance)
  C. Closeness (presence or absence of distinct boundaries and degrees of interpersonal distance)
  D. Power structure (ease in determining family "pecking order")

II. Mythology (degree to which a family's concept of itself was congruent with rater's appraisal of family behavior)

III. Goal-directed negotiation (the effectiveness of family negotiations)

IV. Autonomy
  A. Communication of self-concept (degree to which family nourished or discouraged clear communication of feelings and thoughts)
  B. Responsibility (degree to which the family system reflected members' acceptance of responsibility for their own feelings, thoughts, and actions)
  C. Invasiveness (extent to which the family system tolerated or encouraged family members to speak for one another)
  D. Permeability (degree to which the family system encouraged the acknowledgment of the stated feelings, thoughts, and behavior of its members)

V. Family affect
  A. Expressiveness (extent to which the open communication of affect was encouraged within the family system; see Table 12.2)
  B. Mood and tone (ranging from warm and affectionate to cynical and hopeless; see Table 12.2)
  C. Conflict (degree of family conflict and its effect on family functioning)
  D. Empathy (degree to which the family system encouraged members to be sensitive to each other's feelings and to communicate this awareness)

On the basis of these ratings, each family received a score on a global health-pathology scale. The 33 families labeled as healthy were then compared to 70 families with a hospitalized adolescent; 12 families in the former group were studied intensively.

Results indicated that no single quality was unique to highly functional or competent families; a number of variables in combination accounted for family members' special styles of relating to one another. Thus family health was considered not as a single thread but as a tapestry reflecting differences in degree along many dimensions. The capacity of the family to communicate thoughts and feelings and the cardinal role of the parental coalition in establishing the level of functioning of the family stand out as key factors. The parental coalition was found by these researchers to be especially instrumental in providing family leadership and also important in serving as a model for interpersonal relationships.

Table 12.2 Two of 13 Rating Scales Used to Score Family Interaction Patterns

A. *Expressiveness:* Rate the degree to which this family system is characterized by open expression of feelings.

1	1.5	2	2.5	3	3.5	4	4.5	5
Open, direct expression of feelings		Direct expression of feelings despite some discomfort		Obvious restriction in the expression of some feelings		Although some feelings are expressed, there is masking of most feelings		No expression of feelings

B. *Mood and Tone:* Rate the feeling tone of this family's interaction.

1	1.5	2	2.5	3	3.5	4	4.5	5
Unusually warm, affectionate, humorous, and optimistic		Polite, without impressive warmth or affection; or frequently hostile with times of pleasure		Overtly hostile		Depressed		Cynical, hopeless, and pessimistic

(Source: Lewis et al., 1976)

Beavers (Beavers, 1981, 1982; Beavers & Voeller, 1983), in follow-up research, presents convincing evidence that families can be ordered along an infinite linear continuum with respect to their competence. At the low end, he describes leaderless, invasive, chaotic families, with diffuse boundaries between members. Closer to the midpoint of competence, families show rigid interpersonal control, with frequent distancing, projection, and little consequent closeness. At the high end of the scale, families were found to be better structured; they are composed of autonomous individuals who share intimacy and closeness but at the same time respect separateness.

The Beavers Systems Model, an attempt to integrate systems theory and developmental theory, classifies families along two axes rating the stylistic quality of their interactions and their degree of family functioning. As indicated in Figure 12.2, optimal and adequate families are considered competent; midrange, borderline, and severely disturbed families represent progressively poorer functioning levels. In regard to interactive style, members of **centripetal** families view most relationship satisfactions as emanating from within the family; those in **centrifugal** families believe the outside world has more to offer. The arrow shape of the diagram is intended to convey that extremes in style—whether profoundly centripetal or centrifugal—are associated with poor family functioning. Thus, severely dysfunctional families with a centrifugal style are prone to produce sociopathic children (antisocial, irresponsible, egocentric) while those extreme families with a centripetal style run the risk that one or more of their children will become schizophrenic (socially isolated, progressively withdrawn, disorganized). As families become more

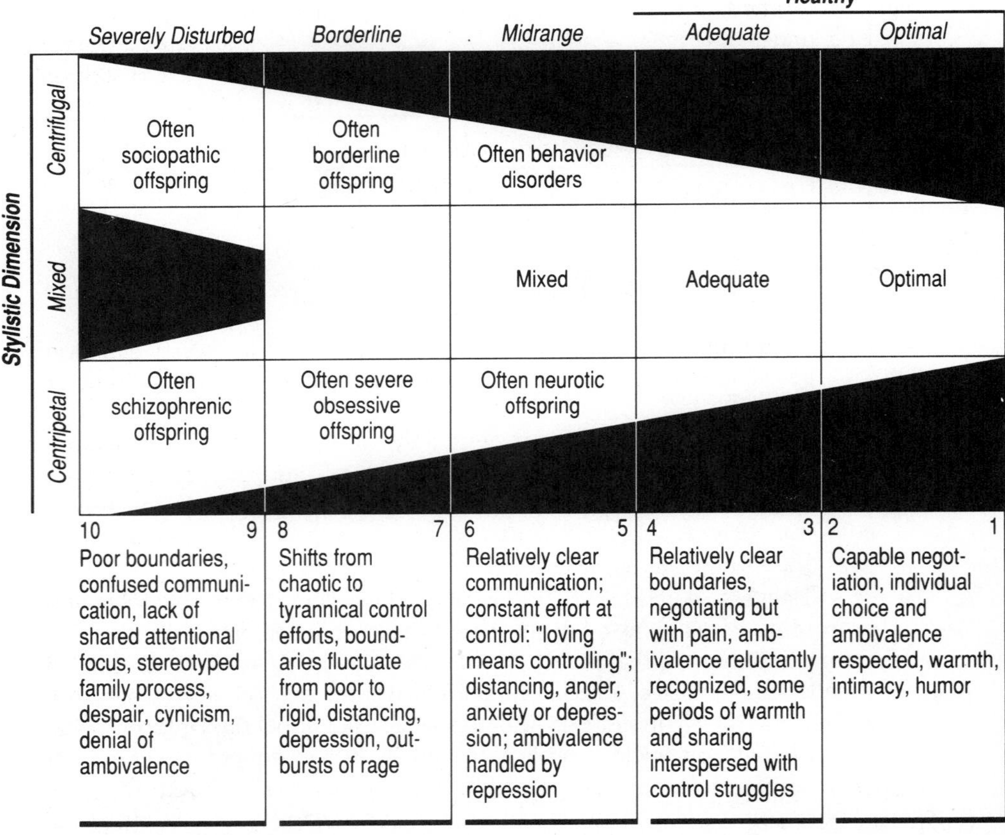

Figure 12.2 The Beavers Systems Model, in the form of a sideways A, with one leg representing centripetal families and the other leg representing centrifugal families. (Source: Beavers & Voeller, 1983, p. 90)

competent or more adaptive, as noted in the diagram, their excessive centripetal or centrifugal styles tend to diminish.

Epstein, Bishop, and Baldwin's McMaster Model

Another long-term systems-based research project, begun in the late 1950s at McMaster University in Hamilton, Ontario, Canada, attends especially to family structure and organization as well as its transactional patterns. Particular heed is paid to how the family develops and maintains itself through its coping skills. The McMaster Model (Epstein, Bishop, & Baldwin, 1982) focuses on those dimensions of family functioning selected, on the basis of research, as having the most impact on the emotional and physical well-being of family members:

I. Basic task area (how the family deals with problems of providing food, money, transportation, shelter)
II. Developmental task area (how they deal with problems arising as a result of changes over time, such as first pregnancies or last child leaving home)
III. Hazardous task area (how they handle crises that arise as a result of illness, accident, loss of income, job change, and such)

To appraise the family's ability to cope with these three task areas, the McMaster group has developed a 53-item self-report questionnaire called the Family Assessment Device (Epstein, Baldwin, & Bishop, 1983). Six aspects of family functioning are probed:

A. Family problem solving (the ability to resolve problems sufficiently well to maintain effective family functioning)
B. Family communication (how, and how well a family exchanges information and affect; also whether communication is clear or masked, direct or indirect)
C. Family roles (how clearly and appropriately roles are defined, how responsibilities are allocated and accountability is monitored in order to sustain the family and support the personal development of its members)
D. Affective responsiveness (the family's ability to respond to a given situation with the appropriate quality and quantity of feelings)
E. Affective involvement (the extent to which the family shows interest in and values the particular activities and interests of its members)
F. Behavior control (the pattern the family adopts for handling dangerous situations, situations involving social interactions within and outside the family, and for satisfying members' psychobiological needs such as eating, sleeping, sex, handling of aggression, and so on)

Based on how each family member responds, family scores are obtained on each of the six scales, and the family's collective health/pathology score is obtained. While this instrument is useful for assessment purposes, further research needs to be carried out on developing subsequent corrective interventions.

Moos's Family Environment Scale

A psychometric evaluative approach introduced by Moos (1974) attempts to assess the impact of the family environment on individual and family functioning. Moos began his research with the assumption that all social climates have characteristics that can be portrayed (and thus measured) accurately. For example, some are more supportive than others, some more rigid, controlling, and autocratic; in others, order, clarity, and structure are given high priority. Moos argues that to a large extent, the family environment regulates and directs the behavior of the people within it. The Family Environment Scale contains 90 statements to be labeled "true" or "false" by the respondent ("Family members really help and support one another"; "Family members often keep their feelings to themselves"; "We fight a lot in our family"). The set of responses characterizes the family climate and its influence on behavior. It provides a framework for understanding the relationships among family members, the kinds of personal growth (for example, intellectual, religious) emphasized in the family, and the family's basic organizational structure.

Ten subscales make up the Family Environment Scale, as indicated in Table 12.3. Three subscales (cohesion, expressiveness, and conflict) are conceptualized as relationship dimensions. They characterize the interpersonal transactions that take place within the family. Five subscales (independence; achievement, intellectual-cultural, and active recreational orientations; moral-religious emphasis) refer to personal development or growth dimensions. Two subscales (organization, control) refer to system maintenance dimensions, providing information about the family structure and its roles. A score is obtained for each subscale and average scores for the family are placed on a family profile. (If desired, the differing perceptions of various family members—for example, parents and children or husband and wife—can be compared for possibly divergent views of the same family environment.)

Table 12.3 Description of Subscales of Moos's Family Environment Scale

	Relationship Dimensions
1. Cohesion	The extent to which family members are concerned and committed to the family and the degree to which family members are helpful and supportive of each other.
2. Expressiveness	The extent to which family members are allowed and encouraged to act openly and to express their feelings directly.
3. Conflict	The extent to which the open expression of anger and aggression and generally conflictual interactions are characteristic of the family.
	Personal Growth Dimensions
4. Independence	The extent to which family members are encouraged to be assertive, self-sufficient, to make their own decisions, and to think things out for themselves.

(continued)

Table 12.3 *(continued)*

5. Achievement orientation	The extent to which different types of activities (for example, school and work) are cast into an achievement-oriented or competitive framework.
6. Intellectual-cultural orientation	The extent to which the family is concerned about political, social, intellectual, and cultural activities.
7. Active recreational orientation	The extent to which the family participates actively in various kinds of recreational and sports activities.
8. Moral-religious emphasis	The extent to which the family actively discusses and emphasizes ethical and religious issues and values.
	System Maintenance Dimensions
9. Organization	How important order and organization are in the family in terms of structuring the family activities, financial planning, and explicitness and clarity in regard to family rules and responsibilities.
10. Control	The extent to which the family is organized in hierarchical manner, the rigidity of family rules and procedures, and the extent to which family members order each other around.

(Source: Moos, 1974)

The family whose profile is shown in Figure 12.3, made up of parents and two children in their early 20s, is strongly upwardly mobile, emphasizing personal development (especially achievement and moral-religious emphasis) above other aspects of family life. These same two factors are deemphasized by the young couple (no children) whose profile is depicted in Figure 12.4. They agree that, for them, relationships are far more important than achievement, conflict is minimal, and control is low. This couple feel very positive about the social environment they have created.

FAMILY THERAPY PROCESS AND OUTCOME RESEARCH

What constitutes therapeutic change? What are the conditions that facilitate or impede such changes? How are those changes best measured? How effective is family therapy in general, and are some intervention procedures more efficacious than others? Do certain specific therapist characteristics and family characteristics influence outcomes? These are some of the questions that researchers in family therapy continue to grapple with in an effort to understand the complex psychotherapeutic process.

For the last 30 years, psychotherapy research has concerned itself with investigating the therapeutic process (the mechanisms of client change) to develop

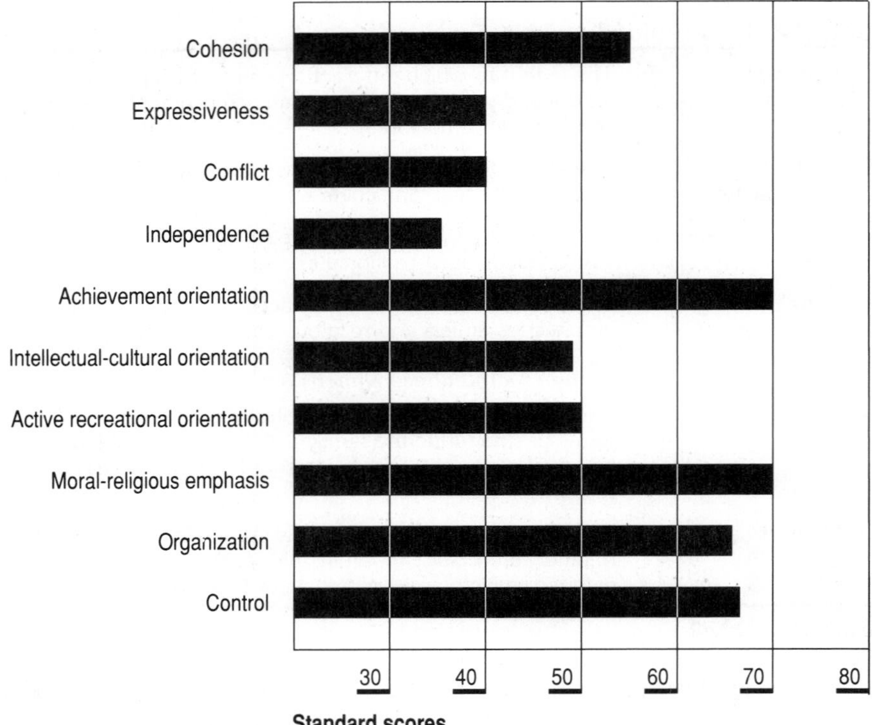

Figure 12.3 Family Environment Scale scores for an achievement-oriented family. (Source: Moos, 1974)

more effective methods of psychotherapy. While the earlier years were devoted largely to outcome research studies in order to confirm the legitimacy of the therapeutic endeavor, "by about 1980 a consensus of sorts was reached that psychotherapy, as a generic treatment process, was demonstrably more effective than no treatment" (VandenBos, 1986, p. 111). Rather than continue single-focus outcome investigations to justify therapeutic efficacy, researchers have turned their attention to comparative outcome studies in which the relative advantages and disadvantages of alternate treatment strategies for clients with different sets of problems are being probed. Increasingly, explorations of process variables are taking place, so that differential outcomes from various therapeutic techniques can be tentatively linked to the presence or absence of specific therapeutic processes.

Process Research

Greenberg and Pinsof (1986) offer the following definition:

> Process research is the study of the interaction between the patient and therapist systems. The goal of process research is to identify the change processes in the interaction between these systems. Process research

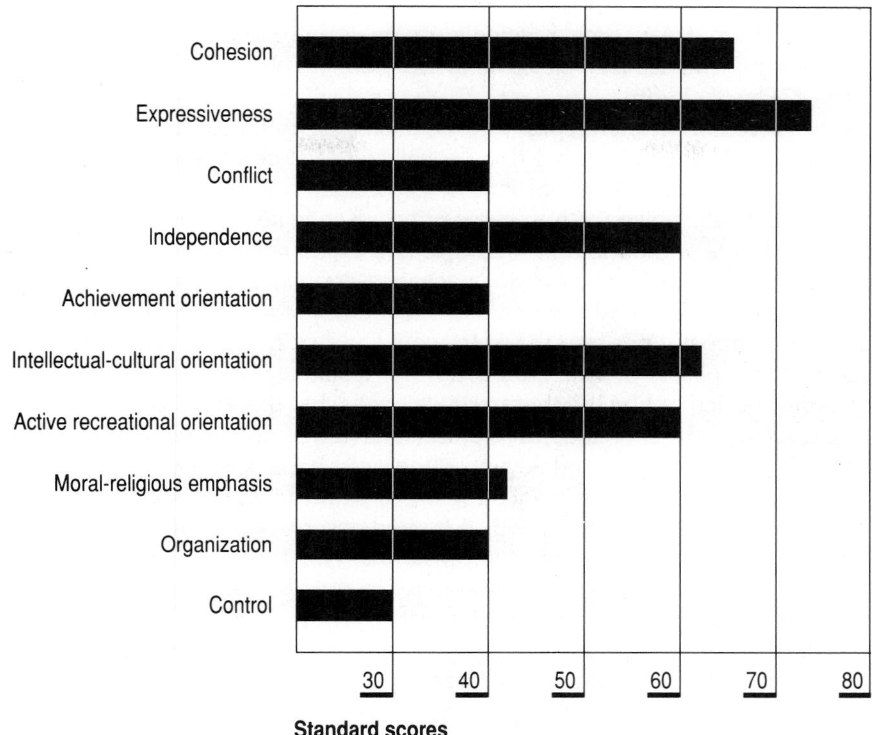

Figure 12.4 Family Environment Scale scores for a higher-relationship, low-control family. (Source: Moos, 1974)

> covers all the behaviors and experiences of these systems, within and outside the treatment sessions, which pertain to the process of change. (p. 18)

Note that in this definition the terms are used broadly. The patient (or client) system, for example, consists of more than the identified patient; other nuclear and extended family members are included, as well as members of other social systems that interact with the client and the family. Similarly, the therapist system might include other therapeutic team members in addition to the therapist who meets with the family. Note too that process research does not simply concern itself with what transpires within the session, but also out-of-session events occurring during the course of family therapy. Finally, the experiences, thoughts, and feelings of the participants are given as much credence as their observable actions. Thus, certain of the self-report methods we described earlier in this chapter may provide valuable input in the process analysis.

Process research attempts to reveal how therapy works, and what factors are associated with improvement or deterioration. For example, a researcher might investigate a specific process, such as joining a particular family in an active and directive way, that resulted in a better therapeutic alliance than joining a similar family in a different way, such as being more passive or more reflective. The results may have significant clinical relevance to practitioners planning future intervention strategies (Pinsof, 1986).

Process research, then, calls for a detailed description of the intended intervention to be employed, along with an equally detailed description of the family to whom it is being applied and its specific problems. The implementation is often extremely difficult, however, and some critics (Keeney & Sprenkle, 1982) argue that efforts to make the therapist's task so consciously deliberate in formulating a change-promoting plan may create "packaged cookbook cures" (p. 16) that are inappropriate to the overall purposes of the therapy. On the other hand, without such a plan, interventions by a therapist would be strictly artistic and idiosyncratic, impossible to replicate or teach to others, nor would we have any inkling of what procedures carried out by the therapist achieved what therapeutic outcomes.

One recent effort to study the verbal behavior of therapists within sessions, and to compare beginning and advanced therapist behavior by means of a Family Therapist Coding System (Pinsof, 1986), appears to be promising. A similar behavioral observation system in which trained observers use some kind of coding system to make notations on therapist and client communication patterns (Hahlweg, 1988) also may be useful in tying specific interventions to specific therapeutic outcomes.

Most researchers would probably agree with Reiss (1988) that family therapy research should be primarily process research. While the temptation to do outcome research—seeking out answers to the practical issue of what works—is understandable, therapists need first to know how, when, and under what conditions the therapy works (Auerswald, 1988). We need to understand better what processes bring about change, and how to identify and measure those processes during the course of family therapy.

Outcome Research

Ultimately, all psychotherapy must provide some kind of answer to the question "Does it help?" Outcome research in family therapy must address the same problems that hinder such research in individual psychotherapy, in addition to the further complications of gauging and measuring the various interactions and changes taking place within a family group. To be meaningful, such research must do more than investigate general therapeutic efficacy; it must also determine the conditions under which family therapy is effective—the types of families, the category of problems or situations, the level of family functioning, the therapeutic techniques, the treatment objectives or goals, and so on. "Does psychotherapy help?" is too vague a question to elicit a useful answer; for example, one could ask, "Compared to what?"—no formal treatment, individual psychotherapy, another form of family therapy? Moreover, the question presumes that psychotherapy is a unitary phenomenon, which it is not; various forms are practiced and subsumed under the general rubric of psychotherapy.

A more precisely stated and thus more useful version of the simple "Does psychotherapy work?" is Paul's (1967) reformulation: "What therapy is most effective for what problems, treated by what therapists, according to what criteria, in what setting?" (p. 111). While data are now available (see following section) to provide some specific answers in the area of family therapy, the question cannot be fully answered at this time, although there are now encouraging signs of sophisticated research efforts to find those specific answers (Hazelrigg, Cooper, & Borduin, 1987). Two decades after Paul's challenge, the overriding question in psychotherapy research remains that of specificity: "What are the specific effects of specific interventions by specified therapists at specific points in time with particular patients with particular presenting problems?" (Gurman, Kniskern, & Pinsof, 1986, p. 601).

Measuring the Effectiveness of Family Therapy. Progress in measuring the outcome of treatment has been slow in developing in the field of family therapy. Several historical factors are involved: (1) family therapy originated in parallel but unrelated ways within different disciplines, each with its own explanatory framework, language, and type of client population (Olson, 1970); (2) most family therapy was practiced in psychiatric (child guidance) or social work (family service agency) settings where the emphasis was more on providing clinical service than conducting research, while psychology—the discipline most apt to engage in psychotherapy research—had not yet made a significant impact on the field (Gurman, 1971); (3) during the first half of this century, the general devaluation of direct intervention with a family system and of any kind of clinical practice by nonphysicians had a pronounced negative effect on interprofessional collaboration (Gurman & Kniskern, 1981c).

In addition to these historical factors, outcome research in family therapy faces some critical methodological problems; the unit of study is large and complex; events that occur during sessions usually result from many factors, making it difficult to identify and control the variables; the family unit is in a state of continuous change; the observer (therapist/researcher) is often part of the system and may change with it; the researcher must consider intrapsychic, relationship, communication, and ordinary group variables as well as taking into account such contextual variables as community, culture, and social pressures (Fox, 1976).

Moreover, philosophical differences regarding the appropriateness of conventional research methodologies must be resolved. Critics such as Tomm (1983) argue that most family therapy research designs reflect the assumptions of logical positivism and, correspondingly, attempt to emulate the traditional scientific methods of the natural sciences based on objective observation. The scientific outlook presumes that observing is a passive rather than an active process, and that it is possible to remain detached and unbiased in one's observations. In the traditional scientific method, by differentiating independent from dependent variables, and by varying the former, hypotheses can be tested regarding what factor causes what outcome.

Yet, according to those who espouse the "new epistemology," the assumptions of the scientific method are incompatible with the following underlying assumptions of family therapy: (1) that many viewpoints of what constitutes reality exist (rather than a single objective reality); (2) that multiple causalities account for most events (not simple cause-and-effect sequences); (3) that the wholeness of the system should be the unit of study (rather than smaller and smaller units to ensure "scientific rigor"); and (4) that the therapist must search for systemic connections (and not explanations based on linear causality). Tomm contends that by breaking phenomena down into smaller and smaller segments in order to make their investigations more precise, scientists may inadvertently destroy the possibility of ever really knowing the phenomenon they set out to study. In the view of many cybernetically influenced family therapists (Colapinto, 1979; Keeney & Sprenkle, 1982; Tomm, 1983), traditional research methodologies are of little use in untangling the complexities of systemic phenomena nor in helping establish a causal relationship between a method of treatment and its effect on the family. Despite such criticisms, the "new epistemologists" have not offered an alternative research methodology.

While many of the criticisms of adhering to a hard science model are well taken, it should be noted that a new paradigm of science is emerging in which the search for an absolute reality has largely been abandoned, replaced by efforts at creating models of reality and then searching for supportive or refuting evidence. Schwartz and Breunlin (1983) question whether it is necessary to throw out the baby (rigor and clear methodology) with the bathwater (outdated assumptions and attitudes about understanding reality). Most family therapists would probably agree with Gurman (1983a) that standard research methods are the only means available for assessing the efficacy of family therapy in an ethically responsible manner. He maintains that outcome researchers do attend to the context by studying the interactions of client, therapist, treatment, and setting variables and by using multiple levels and vantage points for assessing systemic change. To Gurman, then, the charge that psychotherapy researchers are overly linear is inaccurate. He believes there are insufficient grounds for a divorce between standard research (which he says is systems-based) and the "new epistemology."

Early Family Therapy Outcome Studies. Despite enthusiastic claims from practitioners about the effectiveness of their particular approach, in general little if any empirical data were offered to back up the claims during the early years of family therapy. Moreover, those outcome studies that were published tended by and large to be of poor quality. Wells, Dilkes, and Trivelli (1972), reviewing outcome studies published between 1950 and 1970, identified only 18 studies that met their minimal research criteria (three or more families included, outcome measures explicitly stated); of these, only 2 were found to be adequately designed for research purposes. Most of the other studies lacked a no-treatment control group against which to compare changes in the experimental group[2] undergoing family therapy. Some relied on the therapist's evaluation of his or her own work rather than on an independent judge, or on the family members' subjective self-reports at termination. Most studies neglected to test patients before and after therapy or to

2. It is only fair to point out that most of these studies were meant to exemplify a particular treatment approach rather than being specifically designed as research projects. Under such circumstances, it is not surprising that a control group is missing. However, there is the danger that once a method has begun to be practiced and the results published, readers may assume it to be valid and lose sight of the need for careful and systematic scrutiny of its effectiveness (Wells & Dezen, 1978).

carry out adequate follow-up assessments after therapy had terminated. Only the studies of the efficacy of family crisis therapy in preventing hospitalization carried out at the Family Treatment Unit of the Colorado Psychiatric Hospital by Langsley and associates were considered adequate in research design. As reported in Chapter Eleven, these results showed that patients who were treated at the crisis-oriented Family Treatment Unit instead of being hospitalized functioned as well six months later and had avoided hospitalization during that period (Langsley, Pittman, Machotka, & Flomenhaft, 1968).

An increased awareness of and concern with empirical issues began to emerge in the late 1970s, reflected in the more systematic review by Wells and Dezen (1978) of "nonbehavioral" methods and especially the more comprehensive search of family therapy outcome studies by Gurman and Kniskern (1978). The former inquiry examined three types of research undertakings subsumed under family therapy outcome research: (1) uncontrolled, single-group studies ("Does treatment X produce measurable positive changes in population Y?"); (2) comparisons between treatment and no formal treatment ("Does treatment Z produce greater measurable positive changes with a particular client population than if that same group received no treatment?"); and (3) comparisons between alternative forms of treatment ("Which of these treatments, A, B, or C, produces greater measurable positive change with a specific population such as alcoholics?").

With some notable exceptions, such as the carefully carried out single-group studies of Minuchin, Rosman, and Baker (1978) with 50 anorectic adolescents and their families in which follow-ups extending to seven years were conducted, Wells & Dezen (1978) concluded that numerous methodological and practical difficulties (vague and subjective outcome measures; nonrandom assignment of clients; inadequate description of techniques; absence of comparable control groups; use of different outcome criteria in different studies) continued to beset family therapy outcome studies, seriously weakening any conclusions about effectiveness.

Outcome Studies Revisited. In a comprehensive survey of behavioral and nonbehavioral studies in both marital and family therapy, Gurman and Kniskern (1978) examined over 200 studies. More favorably impressed than their predecessors, the reviewers found positive evidence for the effectiveness of family therapy as well as the overall status and quality of family therapy research. Regarding the use of family therapy in situations where there are alternatives, they concluded that "every study to date that has compared family therapy with other types of treatment has shown family therapy to be equal or superior" (p. 835).

Specifically, improvement was reported for 65 percent of the nonbehavioral conjoint marital therapy cases and 73 percent of the family cases. Behavioral family therapies compared with no treatment also produced positive results. As for behavioral marital therapy, Gurman and Kniskern (1981a), in a later review of published research studies, reported impressive gains with mildly or moderately distressed couples but somewhat less persuasive evidence of effectiveness with severely distressed couples or with couples in which one or both partners was seriously emotionally disturbed. These data were convincing enough that these researchers questioned the value of seeing individuals separately for marital problems; couples were found to benefit most when both were involved in therapy, especially when they were seen conjointly.

As for the often difficult empirical and clinical question of what treatment for what problem, Gurman and Kniskern (1981a, 1981c) and more recently Gurman, Kniskern, and Pinsof (1986) offer some definite conclusions based on their literature search:

1. Conjoint treatment for marital discord is clearly the method of choice over the individual, collaborative (each spouse sees a separate therapist), or concurrent (one therapist treats marital partners in separate sessions) approaches.
2. The beneficial effects of both nonbehavioral and behavioral marital/family therapy often occur in treatment of fewer than 20 sessions.
3. Compared to no treatment, nonbehavioral marital/family therapies are effective in approximately two-thirds of all cases.
4. Behavioral marital therapy is about as effective for minimally distressed couples as nonbehavioral methods, somewhat less so when severe dysfunction is involved.
5. Increasing a couple's communication skill, however achieved, is the essence of effective marital therapy.
6. Conjoint, behaviorally oriented sex therapy should be considered the treatment of choice for such problems, especially when severe nonsexual problems do not exist.

In their survey of research, these reviewers found family therapy to be more effective than individual therapy, even for problems that seem more intrapsychic in nature than interpersonal. More specifically:

7. Structural family therapy appears to be particularly helpful for certain childhood and adolescent psychosomatic symptoms.
8. As for the relative efficacy of behavioral and nonbehavioral approaches, no conclusions are justifiable on the basis of published research; however, either strategy is clearly preferable to no treatment at all.
9. No empirical evidence yet exists for the superiority of cotherapy over single-therapist interventions with couples or families.
10. Child management training, a behavioral technique, produces more favorable results with children engaged in antisocial behavior than do nonbehavioral techniques.

Despite such encouraging results, Gurman and his associates warn that a **"deterioration effect"** may operate in marital/family therapy, producing a harmful effect on the clients, especially when they are being treated by a therapist with poor relationship skills, or a therapist who does little to structure or guide the initial phase of therapy, attacks client defenses too early in treatment, fails to intervene in or interpret family confrontation in ongoing treatment, or fails to support the family members in the therapeutic experience. If the therapist is supportive and promotes family interaction, on the other hand, the likelihood of deterioration is reduced.

Some Future Directions. By the mid-1980s, research on both the process and outcomes of family therapy had come to occupy a significant, and also a permanent, place in the field of family and marital therapy. Today there is intense research interest in investigating the effectiveness of various forms of family therapy with different populations (although there remains considerable skepticism that many seasoned practitioners will change their clinical intervention procedures with families based on research results). No longer is it necessary to demonstrate that psychotherapy, as a generic treatment process, is effective. Rather, the research thrust today is to explore "the relative advantages and disadvantages of alternative treatment strategies for patients with different specific psychological or behavioral difficulties (and including in the investigations such factors as cost, length of time necessary to effect change, nature and extent of change, and so forth)" (VandenBos, 1986, p. 111). Such comparative outcome studies most certainly need to include a simultaneous exploration of related process variables in order to continue current efforts to provide some linkage between outcomes achieved by distinctive therapeutic interventions and the presence or absence of specific therapist/client(s) interactive processes.

SUMMARY

Research in family therapy preceded the development of therapeutic intervention techniques, but beginning in the 1960s priorities changed, and the proliferation of techniques outdistanced research. That situation began to equal out in the 1980s, when a renewed family research/therapy connection began to be reestablished. A controversy remains, however, regarding the applicability of scientific methodology to evaluating the effects of family therapy on family functioning.

The study of the relationship between family interaction patterns and family psychopathology, previously based on a cross-sectional research approach, has reemerged in recent years with a longitudinal outlook based on a vulnerability-stress model.

Various research attempts to classify and assess families exist. Most noteworthy are the efforts of Kantor & Lehr to develop a family typology; Olson and his associates to construct their Circumplex Model of family functioning based on the family properties of adaptability and cohesion; Reiss to outline how family paradigms develop; Beavers to depict degrees of family competence; Epstein, Bishop, and Baldwin to classify family coping skills according to the McMaster Model; and Moos to construct his Family Environment Scale.

Both the process and outcome of family therapy interventions have been studied with increased interest in recent years. The former, involved with what mechanisms in the therapist/client(s) encounter produce client changes, requires the higher priority, since the identification of the processes that facilitate change helps ensure greater therapeutic effectiveness. Outcome research, having established that psychotherapy is beneficial, has turned its attention to what specific interventions work most effectively with what client populations. Of particular interest today is the search for the relative advantages and disadvantages of alternative therapeutic approaches for individuals and families with different sets of difficulties.

Chapter Thirteen

Clinical Training and Professional Practice

We have noted a number of times in the previous chapters that preparing to become a family therapist calls for a paradigmatic shift in thinking for a clinician trained in one-to-one psychotherapy. The therapist must learn to view all behavior, including the manifestation of symptoms in an individual, as occurring within a social or familial context. The family system, not the symptomatic person, is the therapeutic unit for achieving change. Moreover, the family therapist is a part of that system, not an outside healer as in many forms of individual treatment. The focus of therapy is present transactions within the family, rather than retrieval and reconstruction of the past. The goal is to modify or change the family's dysfunctional interactive patterns, not simply to interpret or explain them.

A therapist with an individual orientation training to adopt a family focus may be resistant for several reasons: (1) the therapist may see the identified patient as a victim to be supported; (2) he or she may be unwilling to give up exercising control, and may try to remain at the hub of all family interactions; and (3) he or she may find it difficult to learn how to be a participant in the family social system, while avoiding entangling alliances. There is great risk that the individually focused therapist may become absorbed or even enmeshed in the family members' ongoing relationships and, if not careful, lose the necessary sense of balance between being a part of what transpires and maintaining an individual boundary. He or she may begin to believe family members' myths about themselves (for example, that they are jinxed, exploited, or powerless) and adopt their labels for other family members (such as stupid, selfish, unambitious) (Goldenberg, 1973).

On the other hand, new generations of family therapists, particularly if trained in freestanding family institutes, may insist on a family focus to the exclusion of attention to the issues brought to family relationships by individual family members. As we noted in the first chapter, a systems orientation should not preclude an interest in the individual; rather, it broadens that traditional emphasis to attend to the nature of the roles individuals play in their primary relationship networks, such as the family.

BECOMING A FAMILY THERAPIST

Practitioners from a number of mental health and related disciplines—clinical psychology, psychiatry, psychiatric social work, psychiatric nursing, various forms of counseling, the human services—offer direct services to troubled or distressed families today. In some cases, practitioners in these disciplines may find themselves, having gathered a family group together, simply treating the individual members separately but in a family setting. As Haley (1970) has observed (see Table 13.1), such therapists continue to perceive individual psychopathology as their central concern while acknowledging the importance of the family context in which such psychopathology developed. Others find it easier to enlarge their perspective, thus viewing the amelioration of individual intrapsychic conflicts as secondary to improving overall family functioning. In either case, to work in a family-systems approach, the therapist must give up the passive, neutral, nonjudgmental stance developed with so much care in conventional individual psychotherapy. Using a dramatically different approach, the family therapist must become involved in the family's interpersonal processes (without losing balance or independence); support and nurture at some points, challenge and demand at others; attend to (but not overidentify with) members of different ages; and move swiftly in and out of emotional involvements without losing track of family interactions and transaction patterns.

Training Programs

Before 1960, individuals wishing to enter the field of family therapy typically secured the appropriate education and clinical experience in one of the established professions (psychiatry, clinical psychology, psychiatric social work, psychiatric nursing) and then added further specialized training at the postdegree level (Nichols,

1979). With the advent of the family therapy movement (and the boost it provided for practitioners counseling people in troubled marriages) alternative training opportunities developed, and direct entry into the profession, at the master's or doctoral level, became possible.

Training in family therapy today occurs in three basic kinds of settings—degree-granting programs in family therapy, freestanding family therapy training institutes, and university-affiliated programs—which differ significantly in the nature, scope, and desired outcome of the training they offer (Liddle, Breunlin, & Schwartz, 1988). To a large extent, the scope of that training reflects the setting's definition of family therapy.

Table 13.1 A Comparison Between Individual-Oriented and Family-Oriented Family Therapy

Individual-oriented	*Family-oriented*
1. Family therapy is one of many methods of treatment.	1. Family therapy is a new orientation to viewing human problems.
2. The individual's psychopathology is the focus of study and treatment; the family is seen as a stress factor.	2. The disordered family system is seen as needing some family member to express its psychopathology.
3. The identified patient is the victim of family strife.	3. The identified patient contributes to and is an essential part of family strife.
4. The family is a collection of individuals behaving on the basis of past experiences with each other.	4. The present situation is the major causal factor, since current problems must be currently reinforced if they are to continue to exist.
5. Diagnosis and evaluation of the family problem should precede intervention.	5. Immediate action-oriented intervention takes place at the first session, which is usually a time of family crisis, when the family is ripe for change.
6. The therapist is an observer evaluating the family's problems.	6. The therapist is a part of the context of treatment; his or her active participation affects the family system.
7. The therapist brings out clients' feelings and attitudes toward each other; he or she uses interpretation to show them what they are expressing.	7. The therapist uses fewer interpretations; he or she is interested in enhancing positive aspects of the relationships.
8. The therapist talks to one person at a time; family members talk largely to him or her rather than to each other.	8. Family members talk to each other, not the therapist; all members are urged to participate.
9. The therapist takes sides in family conflict, supporting one member (for example, a child, a schizophrenic).	9. The therapist avoids being caught up in factional struggles in the family.
10. Family therapy is seen as a technique for gathering additional information about individuals in the family.	10. Individual psychological problems are seen as social problems involving the total ecological system, including the social institutions in which the family is embedded.

(Source: Haley, 1970)

Degree-granting programs view family therapy as a profession, an orientation for conceptualizing problems people encounter, and as a field or body of knowledge in itself; as a consequence, they offer the most in-depth training. (A list of those programs, approved by the AAMFT for clinical training, appears later in this chapter, as Table 13.5). Freestanding family therapy institutes (see Table 13.2) similarly by and large define family therapy as a profession, a separate and distinct field of knowledge, and as an orientation to human problems. They, too, offer intensive family therapy training, but compared to degree-granting programs the training is less comprehensive, since it tends to be of shorter duration and to be offered to trainees on a part-time basis. With regard to university-affiliated programs, the academic disciplines of psychiatry, psychology, and social work focus on family therapy as one field of study among many, perhaps another therapeutic modality or a field with a body of knowledge and set of clinical skills that are interesting but hardly central to their training mission. Family therapy training in such settings is apt to be less intense and secondary to the overall purposes of the academic program. Thus, as Liddle, Breunlin, and Schwartz (1988) point out, the variety of settings in which training is obtained helps explain why there currently exists a heterogeneous pool of professionals who define and practice family therapy in a multitude of ways.

Table 13.2 A Sample of Freestanding Family Therapy Training Institutes in the United States

Name	*Location*
Boston Family Institute	Brookline, Massachusetts
Family Institute of Cambridge	Cambridge, Massachusetts
Ackerman Institute for Family Therapy	New York, New York
The Center for Family Learning	New Rochelle, New York
Family Institute of Westchester	Mt. Vernon, New York
Philadelphia Child Guidance Center	Philadelphia, Pennsylvania
Eastern Pennsylvania Psychiatric Institute	Philadelphia, Pennsylvania
Haley-Madanes Institute of Washington, D.C.	Rockville, Maryland
Eastern Virginia Family Therapy Institute	Virginia Beach, Virginia
Family Institute of Chicago	Chicago, Illinois
Menninger Foundation	Topeka, Kansas
Houston Family Institute	Houston, Texas
Mental Research Institute	Palo Alto, California
Family Institute of Berkeley	Berkeley, California
Kempler Institute	Costa Mesa, California

Is family therapy a profession, an orientation to human problems, or simply another modality of psychotherapy? The degree-granting programs in marriage and family therapy insist that it is a distinct profession, with its own professional organization (AAMFT), code of ethics, growing body of theory and research, and proliferating graduate programs in family therapy (Sprenkle, 1988). At the same time, they view family therapy as offering a unique systems view or orientation for conceptualizing problems. Graduates of such programs define their professional affiliation as "family therapist." In a similar way, trainees who receive a certificate upon completing a program at a freestanding institution are likely to think in systems terms, and to identify themselves as family therapists. On the other hand, students in university-affiliated programs, while exposed to systems thinking, also learn the discipline's established theoretical traditions as well as its other therapeutic techniques. Graduates of these programs, even if they have a family therapy orientation, are most likely to call themselves by the name of their academic discipline (psychologist, social worker). In some cases, they may even be opposed to thinking of family therapy as a separate discipline. In other cases, however, by obtaining additional postdegree training, some graduates of university programs might adopt a professional identity that incorporates their training as well as their new affiliation.

Advocates of training within university programs, such as Berger (1988), concede that family therapy is still a minor part of most psychology programs, contending that the major conceptual unit and research thrust traditionally has been the individual, isolated from his or her context. On the other hand, Ribordy (1987), an advocate of the traditional, university-based graduate psychology programs, argues that such training offers students an opportunity to integrate systems theory with a variety of other therapy models, as well as encouraging students to examine critically the empirical basis of family therapy. By offering a sampling of various family theorists, these programs expose students to a broader view of the field than they might receive at specialized family institute programs.

Lebow (1987) takes the opposite position, contending that working with couples and families is typically of secondary concern in the customary academic and clinical preparation of psychologists. He argues on behalf of those graduate and postgraduate training programs offered by family institutes (the Ackerman Institute in New York, the Philadelphia Child Guidance Clinic, the Family Institute of Chicago) that prepare students over a period of a year or two for the specific discipline of marital/family therapy. By emphasizing the individual as the focus of study, psychologists have, according to Lebow, generally failed to attend sufficiently to the systems perspective adopted by most of the family therapy field. By way of contrast, he argues that family institute programs are able to employ an interdisciplinary team to fully teach a family therapy model by laying out the theoretical groundwork, presenting a theory and method of intervention, demonstrating the model by master therapists, and supervising trainees as they work with families employing that model.[1]

The controversy is far from being resolved. In a broad survey of existing training facilities in marital/family therapy, Bloch and Weiss (1981) found great diversity with respect to entrance requirements, degrees or certificates awarded on completion, types and forms of supervision and clinical experiences, clinical affiliations, levels of **accreditation**, and so forth. Some training programs aim to produce

1. Freestanding family therapy institutes rarely exist outside of large metropolitan areas, however, thus restricting access for many who seek such training. In addition, most institutes are organized around specific theories and techniques (such as Minuchin and the Philadelphia Child Guidance Center or MRI Brief Therapy Center in Palo Alto), restricting broad family therapy training further.

fully trained practitioners, at least at the journeyman level, while others offer enrichment programs to supplement or improve family therapy skills. Still to be finally determined, and the heart of the issue, is the status of marital/family therapy as a profession. Is marital/family therapy (1) a separate, independent profession; (2) a professional specialty area or subset within the parent mental health profession; (3) a profession that partially overlaps with other mental health professions; or (4) an area of elective study within another mental health profession? The issue is loaded with vocal advocates on all sides (Fenell & Hovestadt, 1986). (It should be noted that the American Board of Professional Psychology—the ABPP—has recently made family psychology a specialty area, alongside clinical, school, and industrial/organizational psychology, for those practitioners who wish to have their competency as family therapists certified.)

The AAMFT, officially designated by the U.S. Department of Health and Human Services to establish certification standards for the accreditation of training programs, primarily supports the position that marital/family therapy is a distinct and separate discipline. Promoting the idea that marital/family therapy is an independent profession or, as a minimum consideration, a professional area developed in conjunction with other mental health professions, AAMFT awards clinical membership only to those persons who meet both the organization's rigorous specialized academic requirements and its supervised professional experience requirements. On the other hand, many practitioners not specifically schooled in marital/family therapy take the position that their professional background plus additional specialized training is sufficient for helping clients experiencing problems in their marriage or family as a whole.

Objectives of Training

While a considerable body of data exists concerning family life, we have seen that there is as yet neither a single theory of family process nor a single set of intervention techniques that is consistently applicable and effective in helping distressed families. Learning family therapy requires theoretical understanding (human development and personality theory; family life-cycle concepts, including cross-cultural studies; psychopathology; research methodology; group dynamics; systems theory; and so on); understanding of ethics and family law; and probably more important, firsthand clinical contact assessing and treating families. Being supervised on a continuous basis while working with families helps hone a student's therapeutic skills as he or she gains invaluable clinical experience (Saba & Liddle, 1986).

Each trainee must find his or her own style of interacting with families and his or her own orientation to what makes for successful therapy. Many authorities continue to agree with Mendelsohn and Ferber's (1972) early assessment that therapeutic skills are best developed in small groups of 5 to 15 trainees who meet regularly with one or two supervisors over a prolonged period of time, such as a year. The opportunity to work therapeutically with a variety of families (with different structures, from different ethnic backgrounds and socioeconomic situations, with different presenting problems) within a training program offering comprehensive **didactic** course work and clinical supervision, seems to be the ideal learning situation. Liddle (1988) underscores the **isomorphic** nature of therapy and training, maintaining that the supervisor's theoretical outlook on how systems operate and families are helped to change is applicable as a guide for how best to train and supervise.

What are the learning objectives of a family therapy training program? Depending on the supervisor's theoretical and therapeutic outlook, goals range from an emphasis on the trainee's personal growth and development to a focus on the acquisition of skills and competencies. As an example of the former, Constantine (1976) describes the training offered to members of different mental health professions at Boston State Hospital, where supervisors strive to "create an environment conducive to growth and learning" (p. 373). The two-year curriculum in this cognitively and experientially oriented program is designed to gradually prepare the trainee to work with families, particularly nonpathological families.

Table 13.3 Checklist of Basic Objectives in Training Family Therapists

Perceptual and conceptual skills	*Executive skills*
1. Recognize and describe interactions and transactions. 2. Describe a family systematically; include assessment of current problem. 3. Recognize effect of family group on oneself. 4. Recognize and describe the experience of being taken into the family system. 5. Recognize one's idiosyncratic reactions to family members.	1. Develop collaborative working relationship with family. 2. Establish therapeutic contract. 3. Stimulate transactions. 4. Clarify communications. 5. Help family members label effects of interactions. 6. Extricate oneself from the family system. 7. Focus on a problem.

(Source: Cleghorn & Levin, 1973)

At the other extreme, Cleghorn and Levin (1973), more behavioral in outlook, set goals of training that are more strictly cognitively based. Particularly useful is their distinction between the behavioral objectives they have for basic-level, advanced, and experienced family therapists. Specifically, these authors distinguish three sets of skills—perceptual, conceptual, and executive—needed by all family therapists at each level of training. Table 13.3 presents a checklist for the trainee's development of basic observational or *perceptual skills* (recognizing interactions and their meaning to and effect on the family members and the family system), *conceptual skills* (formulating the family's problems in systems terms), and therapeutic or *executive skills* (extracting and altering the family's sequences of transactions); these are the skills necessary to be potentially effective with ordinarily functional families who have been exposed to unusual (and presumably temporary) stress. Having developed these basic competencies, the trainee should be able to deal with families exposed to situational problems (for example, shared grief over a death of a family member), helping to mobilize the family's natural restorative devices in working toward a solution. Essentially, the therapist's role is to facilitate constructive problem-solving communication.

Advanced training is required before the therapist can deal successfully with families with chronically fixed, rigid, and unproductive problem-solving transactional patterns. As Table 13.4 suggests, an agent of change must possess different skills from a helper of distressed families. The trainee must learn to catalyze interactions, understand and label relationship messages, and confront family members with what they are doing to each other; he or she must challenge the family to find new solutions, to use its strength as a family in order to take the responsibility for change in its members. Finally, the advanced therapist must be able to judge the effectiveness of his or her interventions and to alter the approach whenever necessary to help the family work with greater efficiency and with less distress.

Table 13.4 Checklist of Advanced Objectives in Training Family Therapists

Perceptual and conceptual skills	*Executive skills*
Regarding the family 1. Conceive of symptomatic behaviors as a function of the family system. 2. Assess family's capacity to change. 3. Recognize that change in a family is more threatening than recognition of a problem. 4. Define key concepts operationally. *Regarding oneself* 1. Deal with feelings about being a change agent, not just a helper. 2. Become aware of how one's personal characteristics influence one's becoming a family therapist. 3. Assess the effectiveness of one's interventions and explore alternatives. 4. Articulate rewards to be gained by family members' making specific changes.	1. Redefine the therapeutic contract periodically. 2. Demonstrate relationship between transactions and the symptomatic problem. 3. Be a facilitator of change, not a member of the group. 4. Develop a style of interviewing consistent with one's personality. 5. Take control of maladaptive transactions by: a. stopping a sequence and labeling the process. b. making confrontations in the context of support. 6. Work out new adaptive behaviors and rewards for them. 7. Relinquish control of the family when adaptive patterns occur.

(Source: Cleghorn & Levin, 1973)

Tomm and Wright (1979) at the University of Calgary endorse the importance of learning perceptual/conceptual and executive skills. In addition, they distinguish certain necessary therapeutic functions a family therapist must learn to perform: decide how most effectively to engage families, identify and explore interpersonal problem areas, facilitate change and help families implement new, adaptive patterns, and determine when and in what way to terminate therapy. As if to illustrate the complexity involved in doing effective family therapy, these authors outline 26 sets of skills needed for the engagement function, 43 for problem identification, 57 for change facilitation, and 15 for termination!

TRAINING AIDS

Family therapy programs use three primary methods for training: (1) didactic presentations, in course work or seminar form, in which trainees learn family therapy's body of knowledge; (2) clinical experiences with families; and (3) supervision, on a regular, ongoing basis, by an experienced family supervisor (Liddle, Breunlin, & Schwartz, 1988). The extent to which each is emphasized, however, varies widely in different settings, depending on the skills, experiences, and viewpoints of those offering the training. While these elements of family therapy training are discussed separately in the following pages, the reader should be aware that in practice a mixture of techniques is used simultaneously, different settings offering different emphases. Reading about families and family theory, observing teachers as they demonstrate work with families, seeing films and videotapes of eminent family therapists at work, all add to abstract knowledge, but in the last analysis the trainee learns experientially—by treating families, under supervision.

Didactic Course Work

Entrants into the field of marital/family therapy typically come from diverse academic backgrounds: psychology, psychiatry, social work, nursing, counselor education, pastoral counseling, and others. Correspondingly, their academic preparation may vary considerably. In an effort to provide some uniform structure for evaluating the relevance and completeness of such training, the AAMFT (1988)[2] has established educational and training guidelines. Its clinical members must have completed the specified number of courses in each of the following areas:

Marital and Family Studies (three-course minimum): Theories of family development, life cycle, subsystems; cross-cultural family studies, sociology of the family.

Marital and Family Therapy (three-course minimum): Family therapy methodology; family assessment; treatment and intervention methods; major clinical theories of marital and family therapy.

2. The AAMFT recognizes three sets of members: students, associates, and clinical members. Students must be currently enrolled in a graduate program in marital and family therapy at a regionally accredited educational institution. Associate members are required to possess at least a master's degree in marital and family therapy from a regionally accredited institution, and must have completed at least eight required courses from the approved list and have had at least one year of supervised experience. Clinical members are expected to have completed all the approved courses, to have had two years of professional work experience in marital and family therapy, and to have successfully completed at least 200 hours of supervision or 1000 hours of marital and family therapy. All applicants are required to have the endorsement of two AAMFT clinical members.

Human Development (three-course minimum): Personality theory; human sexuality; psychopathology; behavior pathology.

Professional Studies (one course): Role of professional organization; legal responsibilities and liabilities; independent practice and interprofessional cooperation; ethics; family law.

Research (one course): Research design; methods; statistics; research in marital and family studies and therapy.

Clinical Practicum (one year, 300 hours): Face-to-face contact with individuals, couples, and families for the purpose of assessment, diagnosis, and treatment.

The didactic component of family therapy training typically includes lectures, group discussion, demonstrations, instructional videotapes, assigned readings, and role playing. The academic courses examine available theories and the existing scientific evidence for a variety of clinical intervention techniques. In some cases, especially in freestanding training centers, courses are team-taught by two supervisors; the teachers not only share the lead in discussion groups but also one may comment to the trainees on what is taking place behind a one-way mirror as the other demonstrates intervention with a real or simulated family. In some cases the trainees' formal course work follows the actual experience of conducting family therapy sessions, in order to avoid premature conceptualizing by trainees before they have had firsthand contact with families. This sequence puts trainees in a better position to integrate family therapy concepts into their understanding of family process (Shapiro, 1975). More often, some introductory lectures, assigned readings, and demonstrations precede the trainees' first clinical experiences; students thus prepared are less likely to be overwhelmed by the abundance of clinical material gathered from the family interview. Following these initial didactic presentations, trainees begin the clinical work of evaluating and treating families while continuing to attend the seminar.

Regardless of the sequence in which the trainee attends didactic seminars, or the method of training used, readings in the field constitute a significant part of the learning experience. Bodin (1969a) has offered a training guide to the literature in family therapy through the 1960s; more recent advances in family therapy are detailed by Erickson and Hogan (1981), Green and Framo (1981), and Piercy, Sprenkle, and Associates (1986). Gurman and Kniskern's (1981b) edited *Handbook of Family Therapy*, Wolman and Stricker's (1983) edited *Handbook of Family and Marital Therapy*, L'Abate's edited *The Handbook of Family Psychology and Therapy* (1985) and Falloon's edited *Handbook of Behavioral Family Therapy* (1988) all offer large collections of papers, usually by experts in their respective areas.

The following journals, among others, help keep students and practitioners abreast of developments in family therapy:

Family Process
Journal of Marital and Family Therapy
Journal of Family Psychology
American Journal of Family Therapy

Family Coordinator
Journal of Marriage and the Family
Journal of Sex and Marital Therapy
International Journal of Family Therapy
Marriage and Family Review
Alternative Life Styles
Family Relations
Family Systems Medicine
Journal of Strategic and Systemic Therapies
American Journal of Orthopsychiatry
The Family Therapy Networker
Journal of Psychotherapy and the Family
Family Therapy Today
Journal of Family Therapy
Professional Psychology

Most of the field's leading theorists have published their theoretical and conceptual ideas in book form: Ackerman (Bloch & Simon, 1982), Boszormenyi-Nagy (Boszormenyi-Nagy & Krasner, 1986; Boszormenyi-Nagy & Spark, 1973), Bowen (1978), Framo (1982), Haley (1976, 1984), Kempler (1981), Minuchin (1974, 1984), Satir (1967, 1972), Selvini-Palazzoli (Selvini-Palazzoli et al., 1989), Watzlawick (1978, 1984), Whitaker (Whitaker & Bumberry, 1988). Finally, it is a worthwhile and at times exciting experience to read verbatim accounts of family therapy sessions (for example, Haley & Hoffman, 1967; Napier & Whitaker, 1978; Papp, 1977; Satir & Baldwin, 1983) following step-by-step what takes place as a master therapist puts theory into practice.

Videotapes

The technological breakthrough that made videotaping possible has provided what has become an indispensable tool for teaching family therapy. Students early in their training have an opportunity to watch master therapists at work with real families; more advanced students can record their own sessions with families for later playback during supervisory meetings. The technique, along with the less frequent use of films, came into general use in the 1950s, as the taboos against breaching the privacy of the therapeutic relationship began to diminish. In the years since, a multitude of videotapes and films demonstrating a variety of techniques with different types of families have been distributed. Together with videotapes of current, ongoing therapy sessions, they now play a significant part in training family therapists because they convey an immediate sense of awareness of the processes by which therapists and families communicate. Family therapy videos and films in particular rely on cinema veritè techniques, allowing the viewer to enter into the multiple verbal and nonverbal transactions going on simultaneously within a family.

Videotapes of master therapists demonstrating their techniques in actual sessions with families are readily available from the following organizations: Boston Family Institute; Philadelphia Child Guidance Center; Ackerman Institute for Family

Therapy; Georgetown University Family Center; the Center for Family Learning in New Rochelle, New York; the South Beach Psychiatric Center in Staten Island, New York; the Institute of Contextual Growth in Ambler, Pennsylvania; the Eastern Pennsylvania Psychiatric Institute; the Haley-Madanes Institute of Washington, D.C.; the Kempler Institute; and the Mental Research Institute in Palo Alto.[3]

Clearly one of the greatest boons to the field of family therapy, videotape has opened new avenues of development in training. For example, supervisors can tape initial sessions with a family for later presentation to students; the tapes give students a basis for noting changes in family interactive patterns as they watch "live" demonstrations of subsequent sessions with the same family (Bodin, 1969b). Tape libraries of family therapy sessions from initial interview to termination and follow-up can be compiled for students to view at their leisure or when confronted with a particular kind of technical problem or therapeutic impasse. Of course, the student can monitor his or her own progressive proficiency by comparing tapes made early and late in training. Away from the emotional intensity of the family session, the trainee can see how he or she presents himself or herself to the family, what was missed or overlooked, what characteristic patterns appear and reappear, what facial expressions belied which family member's verbal communication, and so on (Berger, 1978).

According to Whiffen (1982), videotaping has three unique properties that make it especially valuable in supervision: (1) it freezes time so that every aspect and angle of a crucial sequence is available for posttherapy play and replay by the therapist, impossible to achieve during the session; (2) it enables the therapist to see himself or herself more objectively as a contributor to the whole system, a different perspective from the one available in the midst of the often-bewildering multiple stimuli occurring during the session; and (3) it allows the effect of a therapeutic intervention to be studied and its success evaluated.

A trainee's verbal report of a family therapy session to a supervisor and/or class is subject to the inherent risks of unreliable recall, defensiveness, distortion, and subjective description. The instant replay of the session on tape overcomes these obstacles. Subtle idiosyncratic patterns of interviewing style (for example, avoiding certain topics or retreating from certain emotional expressions) may become more obvious to the trainee after supervisor comments following the viewing of a taped family session. The interplay of verbal and especially nonverbal messages and interactions may become clearer. Not only does the trainee confront his or her own behavior with a family but also the other viewers provide additional corrective feedback. Trainees learn from each other's errors as well as successes. The tape can be played and replayed over and over again, preserved, and retrieved for further study and analysis (Berger, 1978).

By observing trainees with families over closed-circuit television, the supervisor and others retain all of the benefits of a one-way mirror along with a permanent videotaped record of precisely what took place. In some cases, the supervisory

3. All of these centers offer descriptive catalogs of their tapes that are generally available for a period of two to three days and are copyrighted so they may not legally be reproduced. Most insist that the films and tapes be shown only to audiences of students or professionals in the field of family therapy.

sessions themselves are videotaped for later playback as the trainee plans further therapeutic strategies with the family. Videotaped supervision is an especially useful method for developing a trainee's perceptual and cognitive skills (Tomm & Wright, 1982).

Live Supervision

An effective teaching program in family therapy must meld relevant theory with profitable practical experience. However, clinical contact with families is of limited value without regularly scheduled, careful supervision, especially during the early stages of training. Such supervision, provided by highly competent and experienced family therapists who also have teaching skills, may take a number of forms: review of videotapes of trainee sessions with families, either in a trainee/supervisor conference or in a small group session with several trainees and a supervisor (Stier & Goldenberg, 1975); cotherapy, in which a supervisor and a trainee work together with a family (Whitaker & Keith, 1981); observation of a trainee's work through a one-way mirror (Haley, 1976); continuous case conferences during which a trainee presents an outline of his or her work with a client family for several class sessions; and live, on-the-spot supervision in which the supervisor stays in direct communication with the trainee during a session.

Live supervision, in which a supervisor observes an ongoing session through a one-way mirror or watches on a video monitor, introduces a relatively new concept to the supervisory process (Montalvo, 1973); namely, that someone actively guides the therapist's work by providing corrective feedback on what the therapist is doing. The advent of the one-way mirror in the 1950s was a significant breakthrough for clinicians and researchers alike, allowing them to observe live family interviews unobtrusively. By separating the supervisor from the family's ongoing emotional system yet allowing him or her a firsthand look at that system in operation, the one-way mirror added a new dimension to the process of comprehending interaction within the family and between the family and therapist. The supervisor is in an ideal position to note developing patterns, and can think about them more objectively than the therapist who is on the "firing line" (and subject to being caught up in, and becoming part of, the family system). Under these conditions, contributions from the supervisor may represent a force for change in the family (Berger & Dammann, 1982).

The supervisor can intervene in several ways:

1. By calling the therapist out of the room midway through a session for consultation, the therapist then returning with directives to be given to the family (the technique employed by the Milan group in their systemic family therapy, as described in Chapter Nine).
2. By calling the therapist by telephone with suggestions during the treatment process (MRI's Brief Therapy Center approach, discussed in Chapter Eleven).
3. By entering the consultation room during a session with comments and suggestions (used by Minuchin in structural family therapy as an attempt

to reshape or reframe the experience the family is having and thus produce change in their transactional patterns).

4. By using a "bug in the ear" wireless transmitter to communicate directly, and relatively unobtrusively, to the therapist.

When the earphone is used in supervision (Byng-Hall, 1982), the therapist listens through a small "bug" worn in the ear while the supervisor, behind a one-way mirror or at a video monitor, speaks into a microphone. Since the family does not hear the interventions, advocates argue that the technique is superior to the use of the telephone or direct entering of the room by a supervisor. British psychiatrist Byng-Hall (1982) insists that the earphone is the best tool for supervising the therapy process because the flow of interaction is not interrupted and the family responds as if the interventions came from the trainee, not from others. The technique is controversial, however, and runs the risk of overuse by an exuberant supervisor; the trainee may have the feeling of being simply an "echo" of the supervisor or of having his or her concentration interrupted and autonomy invaded. Whether the intervention is by telephone or "bug," Haley (1976) cautions against overindulgence in this procedure, contending that the supervisor should adopt a "call with reluctance" philosophy and offer only one or two very specific suggestions during a session.

According to Byng-Hall (1982), these supervisory interventions are likely to take the form of instructions ("Ask . . . " or "Say to the mother . . . "); suggestions for strategies ("Get father and son to negotiate on that"); efforts to direct the therapist's attention ("Notice how . . . " or "See how they repeat . . . "); moves to increase or decrease intensity ("Encourage mother and father to confront . . . " or "Tell them to stop and listen to one another, instead of . . . "); or perhaps encouragement ("That was well done").

As live supervision in any of the forms just described typically is practiced, the person supervising watches the session from behind a one-way mirror (with or without a group of trainees) and intrudes on the session to make suggestions to the therapist at the very moment that the action is taking place; the objective is to help the trainee get disentangled from recurring, nonproductive interactional sequences with the family in order to regain control and direction of the session. Both parties must feel comfortable with the procedure: the trainee must accept the supervisor's right to intervene if the latter believes that a disservice is done to the family by allowing what is occurring to continue; the supervisor must accept the trainee's right to question or challenge the suggestion and ignore it as he or she sees fit.

In one interesting variation of live supervision, Papp (1980) describes the use of a **Greek chorus** or consultation group (supervisor and other trainees) who watch a session from behind a one-way mirror and periodically send messages into the therapy room, rather like a Greek chorus. This process is particularly appropriate for strategic techniques, in which reframing and prescriptions are offered families; the group is likely to suggest paradoxical interventions in order to provoke, confuse, or challenge a family that appears to them to be resistant to other directives. The therapist can side with the chorus or oppose them; in the latter case, the split can call attention to the family's ambivalence about change, allowing the therapist to capitalize on resistance ("My colleagues seem to think you won't be able to make the change I have suggested, but I think you can").

A basic assumption in live supervision is that any family can direct the therapist away from his or her function as a change agent by maneuvering the therapist into behaving in ways that reinforce the very patterns that brought the members of the family into therapy. The experienced supervisor, not caught up in the action, can help the supervisee correct such missteps at the time they occur. In a sense, the supervisor—as a coach on the sidelines—introduces feedback into the ongoing system, comprising the student therapist and the family.

The advantages of live supervision lie in the timeliness and relevance of supervisor questions or suggestions, and the reduction of possible distortions by the trainee who, in the past, reported later to the supervisor what had taken place during the session. Probably the major disadvantage is the added stress felt by the student being observed. Schwartz, Liddle, and Breunlin (1988) warn against the tendency toward robotization of the trainee, as he or she becomes little more than an automaton, mechanically carrying out the supervisor's every command. According to Loewenstein, Reder, and Clark's (1982) description of themselves as trainees receiving live supervision, the experience can arouse intense emotions; the shame of self-exposure in front of others, the potential loss of self-esteem, loss of a sense of autonomy ("feeling under remote control") and of ego boundaries, problems over compliance and the issue of authority. (The authors also report that the anticipatory fantasies of live supervision were far more frightening than the actual experience and that these fears were greatly reduced over time.) In addition, the student therapist may become too dependent on supervisory interventions, and this may interfere with the evolution of his or her own style (Liddle & Halpin, 1978). Some sense of confidentiality may be jeopardized if the family knows (and it must be told) that it is being observed. Finally, Whitaker (1976c), consistent with his nonplanning approach, is opposed to live supervision, contending that the procedure tends to make the supervisee less self-confident, and more reliant on following a prearranged method rather than relying on the ongoing process for direction.

Despite these objections, authorities such as Haley (1976) consider this method the most effective form of supervision. In the past, all that was revealed about a session was what the student therapist chose to reveal, relying on notes taken during or immediately afterward. With the introduction of audiotapes some 40 years ago, the supervisor could learn what was actually said; videotapes go even farther, revealing both words and actions. But none of these procedures provides guidance at the time the student needs it most—in the act of interviewing. Live supervision not only teaches inexperienced therapists how to do therapy, but also protects client families from incompetent practice.

Cotherapy

Cotherapy—the simultaneous involvement of two therapists in the treatment setting—provides a trainee with an opportunity to work hand-in-glove with a supervisor. Whitaker (1967) routinely used a cotherapist in working with individual schizophrenic patients long before doing so with families; today he is perhaps the leading exponent of the cotherapy model for family treatment. Beyond that, Whitaker uses the therapeutic technique as a training device. Cotherapy is the method of choice for supervision in symbolic-experiential family therapy (Whitaker & Keith, 1981).

Cotherapy has some obvious training advantages. The trainee has an opportunity to learn a distinctive approach at close range and to see an expert in action without taking the full or even the major responsibility for treating the family. The trainee has the added benefit of seeing his or her mentor as a real person who makes mistakes at times, doesn't always understand all that is happening, and isn't always loving—all very reassuring to a beginning family therapist who has felt exactly the same way at times about himself or herself! The supervisor as cotherapist can provide the supervisee with an opportunity to try creative interventions with the family, assured of skillful support and rescue when trouble arises, as it inevitably does. Consistent with Whitaker's experiential outlook, family therapy is taught as a personal experience in this way. The process is emphasized, rather than the discussions of abstract theoretical issues that take place in so many supervisory situations (Napier & Whitaker, 1972).

As a training device, however, cotherapy is not without its disadvantages, real and potential. The trainee may become so identified with the supervisor (especially if the latter's style is colorful and dramatic) that he or she merely mimics the authority figure instead of developing a style more personally authentic. Overdependency on the supervisor for making intervention moves with the family may also become a problem. As Haley (1976) points out, the student acting as cotherapist with a more experienced person may simply sit back and not take responsibility for the case, as he or she must ultimately learn to do. Haley prefers live supervision from behind a one-way mirror so that the trainee can receive immediate assistance whenever needed. He argues that cotherapy is set up to support uncertain therapists, not to aid families.

Indeed, the notion of mutual support is often advanced as a rationale for cotherapy by family therapists who prefer working as a team. For example, Whitaker (Napier & Whitaker, 1978) contends that having a cotherapist allows him to become involved with a family in a way and at a level he would not dare if he worked alone. Whitaker—who equates being a therapist with the pursuit of personal growth—can expose many of his own fantasies and free associations to the family knowing that his cotherapist is a backup person, tied to reality and ready to step in with corrective feedback if that should become necessary. That is, as one therapist becomes emotionally involved with the family, the other waits silently, remaining less involved and more objective than the more active teammate (Napier & Whitaker, 1978). Cotherapists may also support each other by remaining calm in the midst of intense family anxiety. As Rubenstein and Weiner (1967) note, some families readily arouse anxieties in other people and may experience relief in a new situation in which a team of therapists is not easily provoked.

The nature of the relationship between therapists has a powerful impact on the family they are treating. If therapists (whether both experienced or supervisor-supervisee) like, trust, respect, and remain loyal to each other and if their personalities complement each other, they may serve as models for effective and mutually satisfying relationships. In addition, cotherapists in a male-female partnership can serve as gender role models or sometimes as symbolic parents with a well-defined relationship for all family members to observe. The way the cotherapists live their relationship—degrading and undercutting each other or supporting and allowing each other freedom—teaches the family far more about interpersonal relations than what the therapists may say about family relationships. As in a good marriage, the cotherapists need to have a caring and accepting involvement with each other in which both struggle actively to grow; such a relationship allows them to take risks such as fighting in front of a family. According to Napier and Whitaker (1972), witnessing an intense fight can be enormously beneficial for the family in that it teaches the members how to fight and demonstrates that any two people, no matter how close, are likely to have problems with each other. If the therapists display pseudomutuality as an alternative to fighting, their transparent dishonesty may tempt the family to act out the therapists' unexpressed aggression. A family may also attempt to split the cotherapy team who—like parents in an effective coalition—must not permit this to happen. On the other hand, if the therapists are competitive and each one wants consistently to be dominant and win favor from the family, such splitting will likely occur and family therapy will be ineffective (similar to the negative effects of parental conflict on children).

Trainees, especially if assigned difficult families, may find themselves, working alone, to be overwhelmed or "swallowed up" by the family system, seduced or otherwise manipulated by family resistance into maintaining the family status quo. A supervisor's presence during the session may help prevent that from occurring. When supervisor and trainee work as cotherapists, additional supervision, perhaps the bulk of supervision, is likely to take place immediately after and between therapy sessions (Whitaker & Keith, 1981).

PROFESSIONAL ISSUES

Training as a family therapist calls for more than the mastery of clinical skills. The social responsibilities involved in functioning as a professional must be addressed, regardless of where that therapist intends to practice—a mental health center, a private practice setting, a child guidance clinic, a school, a church, or for the courts.

In this final section of the text, we concern ourselves with two continually evolving sets of professional issues—how to ensure the highest quality of professional practice and how to remain alert to ethical standards, particularly as practice shifts from attention to the individual client to the family system as a whole.

Regulating Professional Practice

Most established professions seek some form of legal statute to gain public acceptance and respectability. Statutes in all states control the practice of medicine, law, and psychology, and since 1970 there has been a concerted effort to seek similar legal standards for marital/family therapists, primarily because licensure has become synonymous with professionalism (Huber & Baruth, 1987).

A number of important premises support efforts at licensure (Corey, Corey, & Callanan, 1988; Fretz & Mills, 1980): (1) licensure protects the public by establishing minimum standards of service, since those seeking help might be harmed if treated by incompetent practitioners; (2) it protects the public from ignorance regarding mental health services, helping potential consumers choose practitioners more judiciously; (3) it increases the likelihood that practitioners will be competent, having met the standards to obtain a license; (4) it upgrades the profession by gathering together practitioners committed to improving and maintaining the highest standards of excellence; and (5) it allows the profession to define itself and its activities more clearly, thus becoming more independent. Licensing assures the public that the practitioner has completed an approved educational program, has had an acceptable number of hours of supervised training, and has successfully gone through some screening or evaluative program.[4]

As we indicated earlier in this chapter, an individual seeking professional status in marital/family therapy may earn a graduate and/or professional degree from a university or obtain professional preparation at a center offering specialized training in marital/family therapy. A person who follows the academic route and has obtained the requisite training supervision in a program accredited by the appropriate professional association (for example, the American Psychological Association)[5] may seek either **licensing** or **certification** (according to the law governing practice in a particular state) in his or her specialty.

A licensing law, the more restrictive of the two, regulates who may practice in the state (for example, licensed psychologist, licensed clinical social worker) by defining education and experience criteria, administering qualifying examinations, and stating the conditions under which a license may be revoked (thereby terminating the right to practice) for ethical or other reasons. A certification law, a weaker and less comprehensive form of regulation, simply certifies who has the right to use a particular professional title. Such a law does not restrict practice or define permissible activities but simply guarantees that the title (for example,

4. The criticisms of licensure by some mental health professionals deserve to be noted. Gross (1978) contends that licensure laws are no guarantee of quality or responsible behavior, and that licensure might actually serve to institutionalize a lack of public accountability. By mystifying the therapeutic process, he believes, licensure ensures that consumers receive less information than they are entitled to know. As a profession increases its status, services may cost more, and the profession may fight to protect its domain from competing vendors of similar services. Rather than safeguarding the public, critics maintain, licensure is designed to create and preserve a "union shop." While Corey, Corey, and Callanan (1988) concede that having a license does not assure a professional's services will be beneficial, licensure should not be abandoned. Instead, they propose that ethical standards, continuing education, and peer review be maintained to ensure quality, and that professionals be held accountable through greater disclosure of their procedures, client-therapist contracts, and general efforts to demystify the therapeutic process.

5. Accreditation may be granted to an academic institution by an official accrediting agency (such as the regional Association of Schools and Colleges) or to a field-based training facility by the relevant professional organization.

"psychologist") will be used only by people who meet the standards established by the law. Like the licensing laws, certification laws set up criteria for issuing and revoking certificates; in that sense they help to monitor practice, at least in regard to the use of the title. Both kinds of laws are designed to ensure that practitioners have met certain minimal standards of education, training, and supervised experience. In recent years, regulatory boards in a number of states have mandated the successful completion of certain continuing education courses as a condition of renewal of a license or certificate (Goldenberg, 1983).

Candidates who elect to receive their training as marital/family therapists have fewer credentialing options than other mental health professionals at this time, although the situation is changing. The AAMFT Commission on Accreditation of Marriage and Family Therapy Education, empowered to accredit educational and training programs throughout the United States and Canada, certifies graduate and postdegree clinical training centers in marital and family therapy, usually after making site visits and other careful reviews of the programs (Smith & Nichols, 1979). By 1989 the Commission had accredited 22 masters-level, 9 doctoral, and 10 postdegree training centers (see Table 13.5), with the accreditation of a number of programs still pending. The Commission updates its list quarterly. The list will undoubtedly grow; the committee clearly intends to proceed slowly and with great care in identifying high-quality training programs for accreditation.

Licensing of marital/family therapists is also proceeding slowly, partly because it is easier to establish criteria for licensing the graduates of recognized university programs than those from newly established training programs in freestanding family institutes. In addition, many members of the established mental health professions have opposed an independent profession of marital/family therapy; according to their view, marital/family therapy is but a subspecialty of psychotherapy. However, marital/family therapists argue that traditional professional preparation in the mental health field—especially if it was obtained more than a decade or two ago—generally provides no training in work with families; graduates of such programs should themselves seek additional training and acquire a license in marital/family therapy if they wish to practice in the field. The subject remains controversial and the discussion heated, touching on professional issues such as eligibility for third-party payments from health insurance plans[6] to cover the treatment of marital or family dysfunction as well as the updating of professional skills and conceptual knowledge. Clearly, practitioners accustomed to working with individual clients need further training before working with families. Whether most training institutes as they currently operate provide sufficient training in this area is open to debate.

Marital/family therapy is now regulated in 20 states. Licensing or certifying laws currently exist in Arizona, California, Colorado, Connecticut, Florida, Georgia, Maine, Massachusetts, Michigan, Minnesota, Nevada, New Jersey, North Carolina, Oregon, Rhode Island, South Carolina, Tennessee, Utah, Washington,

6. Several insurance companies, as well as the government-sponsored CHAMPUS program for dependents of military personnel, now recognize AAMFT clinical members as authorized mental health service providers.

and Wyoming. Requirements may vary between states, as may the name accorded the licensee. For example, while Michigan certifies marriage counseling, California refers to marriage, family, and child counselors. In California, as an example, the applicant must possess a two-year master's degree in marriage, family, and child counseling from an academic institution accredited by the Western College Association, or an equivalent accrediting agency, plus at least two years of experience in marriage, family, and child counseling under the supervision of a licensed marriage, family, and child counselor, clinical social worker, licensed psychologist, or licensed physician certified in psychiatry. At present, efforts are under way in nearly half the 50 states to produce legislation to regulate the private practice of marriage and family therapy.

Table 13.5 AAMFT-Accredited Graduate and Postdegree Clinical Training Programs (1989)

Name	*Location*
Accredited Master's Degree Programs	
Abilene Christian University	Abilene, TX
Auburn University	Auburn, AL
Butler University	Indianapolis, IN
Bridgeport, University of	Bridgeport, CT
Brigham Young University	Provo, UT
Connecticut, University of	Storrs, CT
Fuller Theological Seminary	Pasadena, CA
Hahnemann, University of	Philadelphia, PA
Houston at Clear Lake, University of	Houston, TX
Indiana State University	Terre Haute, IN
Kansas State University	Manhattan, KS
Loma Linda University	Loma Linda, CA
Maryland, University of	College Park, MD
Northeast Louisiana University	Monroe, LA
Northern Illinois University	DeKalb, IL
Our Lady of the Lake University	San Antonio, TX
Rhode Island, University of	Kingston, RI
Southern Connecticut State University	New Haven, CT
St. Mary's University	San Antonio, TX
Syracuse University	Syracuse, NY
Virginia Tech University	Falls Church, VA
Wisconsin-Stout, University of	Menomonie, WI
Accredited Doctoral Programs	
Brigham Young University	Provo, UT
Florida State University	Tallahassee, FL
Georgia, University of	Athens, GA
Kansas State University	Manhattan, KS
Minnesota, University of	St. Paul, MN
Purdue University	W. Lafayette, IN
Southern California, University of	Los Angeles, CA

(continued)

Table 13.5 *(continued)*

Texas Tech University	Lubbock, TX
Virginia Tech University	Blacksburg, VA
Accredited Postdegree Programs	
Ackerman Institute for Family Therapy	New York, NY
Bristol Hospital	Bristol, CT
Family & Personal Support Centers	St. Louis, MO
Family Institute of Philadelphia	Philadelphia, PA
Family Service of Milwaukee	Milwaukee, WI
Institute for Comprehensive Family Therapy	Spring House, PA
Kantor Family Institute	Cambridge, MA
Kitchener Interfaith Pastoral Counseling Centre	Kitchener, Ontario
Marriage Council of Philadelphia	Philadelphia, PA
Presbyterian Counseling Service	Seattle, WA

(Source: American Association for Marriage and Family Therapy)

Maintaining Ethical Standards

Beyond legal regulation, professions rely on self-regulation through a variety of procedures—mandatory continuing education as prerequisite for license renewal, peer review, consultation with colleagues, and so forth—to monitor the professional activities of their members. Codes of ethics, in particular, offer standards whose potential violations may provoke both informal and formal discipline (Huber & Baruth, 1987). The former involves pressures colleagues may exert upon violators through consultations regarding questionable practices; the latter may involve censure by professional associations, in extreme cases barring violators from continued membership.

Ethical codes, then, define standards of conduct subscribed to by the members of the profession, aiding members in their decision making with clients whenever possible areas of conflict arise. As Van Hoose and Kottler (1985) point out, such codes help clarify the member's responsibilities to clients as well as society as a whole. Through membership in a professional organization, the member pledges to abide by a set of ethical standards that helps reassure the public that he or she will demonstrate sensible and responsible behavior. In clinical practice, this means guiding members in identifying situations in which an ethical decision is called for with a client (for example, breaking confidentiality to protect the client or another person), formulating an ethical course of action, and implementing an action plan (Huber & Baruth, 1987).

A number of further complications arise as therapy shifts from an individual focus to one that involves a marital/family system. For example, to whom and for whom does the therapist have primary loyalty and responsibility? The identified patient? The separate family members as individuals? The entire family? Only those members who choose to attend? More than academic hairsplitting is involved here.

Hare-Mustin (1980) has warned that "family therapy may be dangerous to your health"; the changes that most benefit the entire family may not in every case be in the best interests of each of its members. By agreeing to participate in family therapy, members may be called upon to subordinate their own individual goals and give up a sense of privacy and confidentiality.

Whether the marital therapist's values are such that he or she chooses to be responsible to the individual as opposed, say, to the marriage, may have significant consequences. To use an example offered by Bodin (1983), suppose a husband is contemplating divorcing his wife, an action his wife opposes. The husband may feel his individual happiness is so compromised by remaining in the marriage that he hopes the therapist attaches greater importance to individual well-being than to maintaining some abstraction called the "family system." The wife, on the other hand, hopes the therapist gives higher priority to collective well-being, helping individuals adjust their expectations for the sake of remaining together. Many therapists caught in such a situation take the position that a strife-torn marriage all but guarantees unhappiness for everyone, including the children. Others argue that the stress and uncertainty of separation and divorce may do irreparable damage to the children and thus the maintenance of family life, imperfect as it is, is preferable to the breakup of the family. As Bodin observes, the therapist's position may have a profound impact not only in terms of the rapport established with the various family members but also on the therapist's formulation of the problems, the goals, the plans for treatment.

Morrison, Layton, and Newman (1982) identify four sets of ethical conflicts in the therapist's decision-making process. We have touched on the first: whose interest should the therapist serve? When working with an individual client, the therapist must decide whether, and to what extent, to involve family members. On the other hand, working with a family, should certain individuals or combinations of family members be seen separately? How should confidentiality be handled under such circumstances?

The second set of ethical dilemmas, according to Morrison, Layton, and Newman, involves the handling of secrets. Should parental secrets (sexual problems) be aired before the family or be brought up in a separate couple's session? How should an extramarital affair—hidden from the spouse but revealed to the therapist in an individual session—be handled? What about family secrets—incest between the father and teenage daughter, or inferred physical abuse of the wife or young children, or child neglect? Here the therapist has legal responsibilities that supersede confidentiality; he or she must report the possibility of abuse or neglect to the police or child welfare authorities, even in the absence of proof. In such a situation, the therapist must make careful observations of family interactions, formulate an ethical course of action, and take steps to ensure the safety and well-being of family members.

A third set of ethical considerations concerns the careful use of diagnostic labeling of individuals, since such labels may ultimately be used by others in litigation (such as child custody disputes) or other forms of intrafamilial power struggles. Fourth, Morrison, Layton, and Newman point to the need for therapists to be aware of their power to increase or decrease marital or family conflict. They must be careful not to impose traditional male-female role expectations that may be disadvantageous to a particular family, or face accusations of bias or sexist attitudes. They also run the risk of being accused of being agents of the parents against the children, the children against the parents, or of one parent against the other. More than most therapists, family therapists must continue to wrestle with the question of whose agent they are.

Undertaking therapeutic work with a family, then, poses a variety of complications with respect to the therapist's professional responsibilities. The help offered to one family member may be harmful or depriving or countertherapeutic to another. A preference for one or the other spouse implies favoritism and, potentially, the loss of necessary impartiality. As Margolin (1982) observes:

> Attempting to balance one's therapeutic responsibilities toward individual family members and toward the family as a whole involves intricate judgments. Since neither of these responsibilities cancels out the importance of the other, the family therapist cannot afford blind pursuit of either extreme, that is, always doing what is in each individual's best interests or always maintaining the stance as family advocate. (p. 790)

In particular, Margolin (1982) identifies six areas of specific ethical concern:

1. Therapist responsibility
2. Confidentiality
3. Client privilege
4. Informed consent and the right to refuse treatment
5. Therapist values
6. Training and supervision

As we have noted, the family therapist, responsible for client welfare, must come to terms with the idea that what is good for one member may not be (temporarily) good for others, and strive to help the system change in a manner reasonably satisfactory to all, to the extent that that is possible.

Confidentiality, protecting the client from unauthorized disclosures by the therapist without prior client consent, has long been a hallmark of individual psychotherapy. In marital/family therapy, some therapists take the position that they must ensure that information given to them in confidence by a family member will be treated as it would be in individual therapy, and thus not be divulged to a spouse or other family member (although they may encourage the individual to share his or her secret in a subsequent conjoint session). Other therapists, in an effort to avoid an alliance with a family member, refuse to see any member separately, in effect insisting that secrets be brought out into the open to the marital partner or family in sessions together. Still other therapists, if they see individually, or talk to by telephone, or receive a written message from a family member, tell the informant beforehand that whatever is divulged may be communicated to the others, if in the judgment of the therapist it would benefit the couple or family. Whatever the procedure, as Corey, Corey, and Callanan (1988) make clear, it is essential to ethical practice that the therapist make his or her stand on confidentiality clear to each family member from the outset of therapy. Except in the case of potential physical harm to a client or to others, as we have previously noted, the therapist is bound to honor client confidentiality.

Client privilege, particularly privileged communication, is closely linked to confidentiality. Privileged communication is a legal right, protecting a client from having his or her confidences revealed from the witness stand during court proceedings without his or her prior consent. Since the privilege belongs to the client, the client's waiving that privilege leaves the therapist with no legal grounds for withholding the information. The issue, however, is who is the client: the individual, the couple, the family? In the case of a divorcing pair, suppose one spouse seeks testimony from the therapist while the other does not wish the information revealed? Gumper and Sprenkle (1981) report a wide variation in statutes between states in who "owns" the right to waive privilege regarding information revealed in conjoint therapy sessions. Because this is often a thorny problem for marital/family therapists, these authors suggest therapists not only acquaint themselves with the laws of their state, but also try to get the couple to agree in writing that in the event of any court action neither will seek disclosures of what transpired in joint sessions with the therapist. Even so, courts may differ in the way they honor such agreements. Generally speaking, the therapist should always demand a written release from a client before revealing any information to others.

The matters of informed consent and the right to refuse treatment have become critical ethical issues in the practice of marital and family therapy. Gill (1982) argues that before families enter therapy they must be adequately informed concerning the nature of the process they are about to undertake. The purposes of the sessions, typical procedures, risks of possible negative outcomes, possible benefits, costs, what behavior to expect from the therapist, the limits of confidentiality, the conditions that might precipitate a referral to another therapist or agency—these issues all require explanation at the outset, before each client agrees to participate. Bray, Shepherd, and Hays (1985) go further, insisting the systems-oriented therapist tell the family that the therapeutic focus will be the family system rather than the specific set of symptoms of the identified patient.

Because specific therapist values (attitudes toward divorce, extramarital affairs, male-female roles in the family or society at large) may be enormously influential in the process of marital or family therapy, therapists must examine their attitudes closely. The danger here is that the therapist might be biased against families whose attitudes differ radically from his or her own, or might side with one family member (say, a father) against the behavior and stated attitudes of other members (say, an adolescent). Most family therapists—deliberately or unwittingly, consciously or unconsciously—proselytize for maintaining a family way of life, which may be inappropriate or worse for a particular warring couple.

Because the therapist is in a position of power, there is the possibility of imposing control over client families or assuming responsibility for defining how change should occur. For example, criticism of structural therapies, such as practiced by Minuchin, has focused on the danger that the role of the therapist as an active agent of change may shift responsibility for change from the family to the therapist (Fieldsteel, 1982). New sets of beliefs and values may be imposed on the family as family members defer their own judgment to the views of the therapist. The possible misuse of power must be examined in such cases.

Similarly, in strategic or systemic therapies, especially when reframing and paradoxical techniques are employed, care must be exercised since the therapist can never be certain how the family will interpret and respond to a particular intervention. Ethical and responsible use of the techniques as we described them in Chapter Nine and as Haley and others carry them out, requires therapist competency and well-thought-out directives based on the role of the symptom within the relationship system, as well as a theoretical and therapeutic approach consistent with the use of paradox (Huber & Baruth, 1987). Although intriguing, paradoxical procedures pose an ethical dilemma; they should never be used indiscriminately or inappropriately or as a spur-of-the-moment ploy simply because nothing else seems to be working. As Weeks and L'Abate (1982) put it, "Paradoxical interventions must be carefully formulated, appropriately timed, convincingly delivered, and followed up. In order to make paradoxical interventions, the therapist must first have skills necessary to make active and direct interventions" (p. 249).

The final ethical issue concerns training and supervision. Margolin (1982) contends that adequate preparation for doing marital/family therapy is still more the exception than the rule for most mental health professionals. Exceeding the bounds of one's competence and experience in assessing and treating marital or family problems is considered unethical. As we have emphasized in this chapter, AAMFT standards have gone a long way toward upgrading training and supervision. The AAMFT (1988) also offers a periodically revised code of ethical principles for marriage and family therapists (see Appendix A), adhered to by all AAMFT members. While it cannot possibly cover all situations, the code does provide a basis for making critical ethical decisions and engaging in responsible professional behavior.

SUMMARY

Becoming a family therapist calls for a paradigmatic shift in thinking for clinicians trained to focus on individual functioning and offer individual psychotherapy. A theoretical understanding of families as social systems, firsthand clinical experience with families, and careful supervision are indispensable elements in a family therapist's education and training. Currently, training occurs in three kinds of settings: degree-granting programs in family therapy, freestanding family therapy training institutes, and university-affiliated graduate programs. The three differ significantly in the nature, scope, and desired outcome of the training they provide. Degree-granting programs in particular view marital/family therapy as a distinct profession, a position supported by the AAMFT, officially designated by the government to certify standards for accreditation in the United States and Canada.

Most training programs direct their efforts at helping trainees develop perceptual, conceptual, and executive skills in working with families. Training aids include (1) didactic course work; (2) the use of master therapist videotapes plus trainee tapes for postsession viewing by the trainee and his or her supervisor and classmates; (3) live supervision through the active guidance by a supervisor who watches the session behind a one-way mirror and offers corrective feedback by telephone, earphone, calling the trainee/therapist out of the therapy session for consultation, or physically entering the session with comments and suggestions; and (4) cotherapy, in which a trainee has an opportunity to work alongside a mentor with a family.

Professional practice in marital/family therapy is regulated by legal statutes and self-regulated by ethical codes, peer review, continuing education, and consultation. Twenty states currently have licensing or certification laws. The AAMFT Commission on Accreditation of Marriage and Family Therapy Education certifies master's-level, doctoral-level, and postdegree programs in marriage and family theapy. The AAMFT ethical code, defining standards of conduct for members of the profession, offers guidance in identifying clinical situations in which the therapist must make ethical decisions, and offers principles on which those decisions can best be based.

Appendix

Code of Ethical Principles for Marriage and Family Therapists, *by the American Association for Marriage and Family Therapy*[1]

The Board of Directors of the American Association for Marriage and Family Therapy (AAMFT) hereby promulgates, pursuant to Article II, Section (1)(C) of the Association's Bylaws, the Revised AAMFT Code of Ethical Principles for Marriage and Family Therapists, effective August 1, 1988.

The AAMFT Code of Ethical Principles for Marriage and Family Therapists is binding on all Members of AAMFT (Clinical, Student, and Associate) and on all AAMFT Approved Supervisors.

If an AAMFT Member or an AAMFT Approved Supervisor resigns in anticipation of or during the course of an ethics investigation, the Ethics Committee will complete its investigation. Any publication of action taken by the Association will include the fact that the Member attempted to resign during the investigation.

Marriage and family therapists are encouraged to report alleged unethical behavior of colleagues to appropriate professional associations and state regulatory bodies.

1. Responsibility to clients

Marriage and family therapists are dedicated to advancing the welfare of families and individuals, including respecting the rights of those persons seeking their assistance, and making reasonable efforts to ensure that their services are used appropriately.

1.1 Marriage and family therapists do not discriminate against or refuse professional service to anyone on the basis of race, sex, religion, or national origin.

1. *AAMFT Code of Ethical Principles for Marriage and Family Therapists*, by the American Association for Marriage and Family Therapy. Copyright 1988 by the American Association for Marriage and Family Therapy. Reprinted by permission.

1.2 Marriage and family therapists are cognizant of their potentially influential position with respect to clients, and they avoid exploiting the trust and dependency of such persons. Marrriage and family therapists therefore make every effort to avoid dual relationships with clients that could impair their professional judgment or increase the risk of exploitation. Examples of such dual relationships include, but are not limited to, business or close personal relationships with clients. Sexual intimacy with clients is prohibited. Sexual intimacy with former clients for two years following the termination of therapy is prohibited.

1.3 Marriage and family therapists do not use their professional relationship with clients to further their own interests.

1.4 Marriage and family therapists respect the right of clients to make decisions and help them to understand the consequences of these decisions. Marriage and family therapists clearly advise a client that a decision on marital status is the responsibility of the client.

1.5 Marriage and family therapists continue therapeutic relationships only so long as it is reasonably clear that clients are benefiting from the relationship.

1.6 Marriage and family therapists assist persons in obtaining other therapeutic services if a marriage and family therapist is unable or unwilling, for appropriate reasons, to see a person who has requested professional help.

1.7 Marriage and family therapists do not abandon or neglect clients in treatment without making reasonable arrangements for the continuation of such treatment.

1.8 Marriage and family therapists obtain informed consent of clients before taping, recording, or permitting third party observation of their activities.

2. Confidentiality

Marriage and family therapists have unique confidentiality problems because the "client" in a therapeutic relationship may be more than one person. The overriding principle is that marriage and family therapists respect the confidences of their client(s).

2.1 Marriage and family therapists cannot disclose client confidences to anyone, except: (1) as mandated by law; (2) to prevent a clear and immediate danger to a person or persons; (3) where the marriage and family therapist is a defendant in a civil, criminal or disciplinary action arising from the therapy (in which case client confidences may only be disclosed in the course of that action); or (4) if there is a waiver previously obtained in writing, and then such information may only be revealed in accordance with the terms of the waiver. In circumstances where more than one person in a family is receiving therapy, each such family member who is legally competent to execute a waiver must agree to the waiver required by sub-paragraph (4). Absent such a waiver from each family member legally competent to execute a waiver, a marriage and family therapist cannot disclose information received from any family member.

2.2 Marriage and family therapists use client and/or clinical materials in teaching, writing, and public presentations only if a written waiver has been received in accordance with sub-principle 2.1(4), or when appropriate steps have been taken to protect client identity.

2.3 Marriage and family therapists store or dispose of client records in ways that maintain confidentiality.

3. Professional competence and integrity

Marriage and family therapists are dedicated to maintaining high standards of professional competence and integrity.

3.1 Marriage and family therapists who (a) are convicted of felonies, (b) are convicted of misdemeanors (related to their qualifications or functions), (c) engage in conduct which could lead to conviction of felonies, or misdemeanors related to their qualifications or functions, (d) are expelled from other professional organizations, (e) have their licenses or certificates suspended or revoked, (f) are no longer competent to practice marriage and family therapy because they are impaired due to physical or mental causes or the abuse of alcohol or other substances, or (g) fail to cooperate with the Association at any stage of an investigation of an ethical complaint of his/her conduct by the AAMFT Ethics Committee or Judicial Council, are subject to termination of membership or other appropriate action.

3.2 Marriage and family therapists seek appropriate professional assistance for their own personal problems or conflicts that are likely to impair their work performance and their clinical judgment.

3.3 Marriage and family therapists, as teachers, are dedicated to maintaining high standards of scholarship and presenting information that is accurate.

3.4 Marriage and family therapists seek to remain abreast of new developments in family therapy knowledge and practice through both educational activities and clinical experiences.

3.5 Marriage and family therapists do not engage in sexual or other harassment or exploitation of clients, students, trainees, employees, colleagues, research subjects, or actual or potential witnesses or complainants in ethical proceedings.

3.6 Marriage and family therapists do not attempt to diagnose, treat, or advise on problems outside the recognized boundaries of their competence.

3.7 Marriage and family therapists attempt to prevent the distortion or misuse of their clinical and research findings.

3.8 Marriage and family therapists are aware that, because of their ability to influence and alter the lives of others, they must exercise special care when making public their professional recommendations and opinions through testimony or other public statements.

4. Responsibility to students, employees, and supervisees

Marriage and family therapists do not exploit the trust and dependency of students, employees, and supervisees.

4.1 Marriage and family therapists are cognizant of their potentially influential position with respect to students, employees and supervisees, and they avoid exploiting the trust and dependency of such persons. Marriage and family therapists therefore, make every effort to avoid dual relationships that could impair their professional judgment or increase the risk of exploitation. Examples of such dual relationships include, but are not limited to, provision of therapy to students, employees, or supervisees, and business or close personal relationships with students, employees, or supervisees. Sexual intimacy with students or supervisees is prohibited.

4.2 Marriage and family therapists do not permit students, employees or supervisees to perform or to hold themselves out as competent to perform professional services beyond their training, level of experience, and competence.

5. Responsibility to the profession

Marriage and family therapists respect the rights and responsibilities of professional colleagues; carry out research in an ethical manner; and participate in activities which advance the goals of the profession.

5.1 Marriage and family therapists remain accountable to the standards of the profession when acting as members or employees of organizations.

5.2 Marriage and family therapists assign publication credit to those who have contributed to a publication in proportion to their contributions and in accordance with customary professional publication practices.

5.3 Marriage and family therapists who are the authors of books or other materials that are published or distributed should cite appropriately persons to whom credit for original ideas is due.

5.4 Marriage and family therapists who are the authors of books or other materials published or distributed by an organization take reasonable precautions to ensure that the organization promotes and advertises the materials accurately and factually.

5.5 Marriage and family therapists, as researchers, must be adequately informed of and abide by relevant laws and regulations regarding the conduct of research with human participants.

5.6 Marriage and family therapists recognize a responsibility to participate in activities that contribute to a better community and society, including devoting a portion of their professional activity to services for which there is little or no financial return.

5.7 Marriage and family therapists are concerned with developing laws and regulations pertaining to marriage and family therapy that serve the public interest, and with altering such laws and regulations that are not in the public interest.

5.8 Marriage and family therapists encourage public participation in the designing and delivery of services and in the regulation of practitioners.

6. Financial Arrangements

Marriage and family therapists make financial arrangements with clients and third party payors that conform to accepted professional practices and that are reasonably understandable.

6.1 Marriage and family therapists do not offer or accept payment for referrals.

6.2 Marriage and family therapists do not charge excessive fees for services.

6.3 Marriage and family therapists disclose their fee structure to clients at the onset of treatment.

6.4 Marriage and family therapists are careful to represent facts truthfully to clients and third party payors regarding services rendered.

7. Advertising

Marriage and family therapists engage in appropriate informational activities, including those that enable laypersons to choose marriage and family services on an informed basis.

7.1 Marriage and family therapists accurately represent their competence, education, training, and experience relevant to their practice of marriage and family therapy.

7.2 Marriage and family therapists claim as evidence of educational qualifications in conjunction with their AAMFT membership only those degrees (a) from regionally-accredited institutions or (b) from institutions recognized by states which license or certify marriage and family therapists, but only if such regulation is accepted by AAMFT.

7.3 Marriage and family therapists assure that advertisements and publications, whether in directories, announcement cards, newspapers, or on radio or television, are formulated to convey information that is necessary for the public to make an appropriate selection. Information could include: (1) office information, such as name, address, telephone number, credit card acceptability, fee structure, languages spoken, and office hours; (2) appropriate degrees, state licensure and/or certification, and AAMFT Clinical Member status; and (3) description of practice.

7.4 Marriage and family therapists do not use a name which could mislead the public concerning the identity, responsibility, source, and status of those practicing under that name and do not hold themselves out as being partners or associates of a firm if they are not.

7.5 Marriage and family therapists do not use any professional identification (such as a professional card, office sign, letterhead, or telephone or association directory listing), if it includes a statement or claim that is false, fraudulent, misleading, or deceptive. A statement is false, fraudulent, misleading, or deceptive if it (a) contains a material misrepresentation of fact; (b) fails to state any material fact necessary to make the statement, in light of all circumstances, not misleading; or (c) is intended to or is likely to create an unjustified expectation.

7.6 Marriage and family therapists correct, wherever possible, false, misleading, or inaccurate information and representations made by others concerning the marriage and family therapist's qualifications, services, or products.

7.7 Marriage and family therapists make certain that the qualifications of persons in their employ are represented in a manner that is not false, misleading, or deceptive.

7.8 Marriage and family therapists may represent themselves as specializing within a limited area of marriage and family therapy, but may not hold themselves out as specialists without being able to provide evidence of training, education, and supervised experience in settings which meet recognized professional standards.

7.9 Only marriage and family therapist Clinical Members, Approved Supervisors, and Fellows—**not** Associate Members, Student Members, or organizations—may identify these AAMFT designations in public information or advertising materials.

7.10 Marriage and family therapists may not use the initials AAMFT following their name in the manner of an academic degree.

7.11 Marriage and family therapists may not use the AAMFT logo and the abbreviated initials AAMFT. The Association (which is the sole owner of its name, logo, and the abbreviated initials AAMFT) and its committees and regional divisions, operating as such, may use the name, logo and the abbreviated initials AAMFT. A regional division of AAMFT may use the AAMFT insignia to list its individual Clinical Members as a group (e.g., in the Yellow Pages); when all Clinical Members practicing within a directory district have been invited to list themselves in the directory, any one or more members may do so.

7.12 Marriage and family therapists use their membership in AAMFT only in connection with their clinical and professional activities.

Violations of this Code should be brought in writing to the attention of the AAMFT Committee on Ethics and Professional Practices at the central office of AAMFT, 1717 K Street, N.W., Suite 407, Washington, DC 20006.

Glossary

accommodating A therapeutic tactic, used primarily by structural family therapists, whereby the therapist attempts to make personal adjustments in order to adapt to the family style, in an effort to build a therapeutic alliance with the family.

accreditation The granting of status to an academic institution or training program, certifying that its offerings are in accord with the standards established by the accrediting body.

acting out The enactment of unconscious feelings, impulses, and tensions through overt behavioral acts, usually of a dysfunctional nature.

alignments Clusters of alliances between family members within the overall family group; affiliations and splits from one another, temporary or permanent, occur in pursuit of homeostasis.

baseline A stable, reliable performance level, against which changes, particularly of a behavioral nature, can be compared.

behavioral The viewpoint that objective and experimentally verified procedures should be the basis for modifying maladaptive, undesired, or problematic behaviors.

behavioral analysis An assessment procedure in which a therapist identifies the targeted behavior to be changed, determines the factors currently maintaining the behavior, and formulates a treatment plan that includes specific criteria for measuring the success of the change effort.

behavioral marital therapy Training couples in communication skills, the exchange of positive reinforcements, cognitive restructuring, and problem-solving skills in order to facilitate marital satisfaction.

behavioral parent-skills training Training parents in behavioral principles and the use of contingency management procedures in altering or modifying undesirable behavior in their children.

blank screen In psychoanalytic therapy, the passive, neutral, unrevealing behavior of the analyst, onto which the patient may project his or her fantasies.

boundary An abstract delineation between parts of a system or between systems, typically defined by implicit or explicit rules regarding who may participate and in what manner.

brief family therapy Short-term treatment that focuses on resolving the presenting problem rather than viewing that problem as a symptom of an underlying disorder.

calibration Setting of a limit in a system, determining the range in which it may operate and how much deviation will be tolerated.

centrifugal Tending to move outward or away from the center; within a family, forces that push the members apart, especially when the family organization lacks cohesiveness.

centripetal Tending to move toward the center; within a family, forces that bind or otherwise keep the members together so that they seek fulfillment from intrafamilial rather than outside relationships.

certification A statutory process established by a government agency, usually a state, granting permission to persons, having met predetermined qualifications, to call themselves by a particular title, and prohibiting the use of that title without a certificate.

circular causality The view that causality is nonlinear, occurring instead within a relationship context and by means of a network of interacting loops; any cause is thus seen as an effect of a prior cause, as in the interactions within families.

circular questioning An interviewing technique aimed at eliciting differences in perception about events or relationships from different family members, particularly regarding points in the family life cycle when significant coalition shifts and adaptations occurred.

classical conditioning A form of learning in which a previously neutral stimulus, through repeated pairing with a stimulus that ordinarily elicits a response, eventually elicits the response by itself.

closed system A self-contained system with impermeable boundaries, operating without interactions outside the system, resistant to change and thus prone to increasing disorder.

coalitions Covert alliances or affiliations, temporary or long-term, between certain family members against others in the family.

cognitive Pertaining to mental processes, such as thinking, remembering, perceiving, and planning.

cognitive behavior therapy A set of therapeutic procedures that attempts to change feelings and actions by modifying or altering faulty thought patterns or destructive self-verbalizations.

complementarity The degree of harmony in the meshing of family roles, as between husband and wife; to the extent that the roles dovetail satisfactorily, the partners are able, together, to provide and receive satisfactions from the relationship.

complementary A type of dyadic transaction or communication pattern in which inequality and the maximization of differences exist (for example, dominant/submissive) and in which each participant's response provokes or enhances a counterresponse in the other in a continuing loop.

conductor A type of family therapist who is active, aggressive, charismatic, and who openly and directly confronts the family's dysfunctional interactive patterns.

conjoint Involving two or more family members seen together in a therapy session.

conjoint sex therapy Therapeutic intervention with a couple in an effort to treat their sexual dysfunction.

consensus-sensitive families Enmeshed families who view the world as unpredictable and therefore dangerous unless they maintain agreement at all times and on all issues.

contextual Pertaining to circumstances or situations in which an event took place; as a therapeutic approach, an emphasis on relational determinants, entitlements and indebtednesses across generations that bind families together.

contingency contract An agreement made by two or more family members specifying the circumstances under which one is to do something for another, so that they may exchange rewarding behavior with one another.

contracts As used by behavioral family therapists, written agreements between family members to make specific behavior changes in the future.

cotherapy The simultaneous involvement of two therapists, often for training purposes, in working with an individual, couple, or family.

counterparadox In systemic family therapy, placing the family in a therapeutic double bind in order to counter the members' paradoxical interactions.

countertransference According to psychoanalytic theory, the analyst's unconscious emotional responses to a patient that may interfere with objectivity.

cybernetics The study of methods of feedback control within a system, especially the flow of information through feedback loops.

defense mechanism According to psychoanalytic theory, the process, usually unconscious, whereby the ego protects the individual from conscious awareness of threatening and therefore anxiety-producing thoughts, feelings, and impulses.

deterioration effect The finding, in psychotherapy research, that a certain proportion of clients are worse off after treatment than before.

detouring coalition A mother-father-child triad in which conflict between the parents is avoided or rerouted by focusing attention on the child.

detriangulate The process of withdrawing from a family role of buffer or go-between with one's parents, so as to not be drawn into alliances with one against the other.

developmental tasks Problems to be overcome and conflicts to be mastered at various stages of the life cycle, enabling movement to the next developmental stage.

didactic Used for teaching purposes.

differentiation of self The separation of one's intellectual and emotional functioning; the greater the distinction, the better one is able to resist being overwhelmed by the emotional reactivity of his or her family, and is thus less prone to dysfunction.

disengagement A family organization with rigid boundaries, in which members are isolated and feel unconnected to each other, each functioning separately and autonomously and without involvement in the day-to-day transactions within the family.

double-bind concept The view that an individual who receives an important contradictory message about which he or she is unable to comment, is in an impossible situation; if this message is repeated over time, the individual may respond in kind and/or show signs of schizophrenia.

dyad A liaison, temporary or permanent, between two persons.

dysfunctional Abnormal or impaired in the ability to accommodate to or cope with stress.

ego According to psychoanalytic theory, the mediator between the demands of the instinctual drives (id) and the social prohibitions (superego); thus, the rational, problem-solving aspect of personality.

emotional cutoff The flight from unresolved emotional ties to one's family, typically manifested by withdrawing or running away from the family, or denying its current importance in one's life.

emotional divorce Marked emotional distance between marital partners, both of whom are immature, although one may accentuate the immaturity and the other deny it by acting overly responsible.

enactment In structural family therapy, a facilitating intervention in which the family is induced to enact or play out its relationship patterns spontaneously during a therapeutic session, allowing the therapist to observe and ultimately to develop a plan for restructuring future transactions.

encounter group A kind of therapeutic group in which intense interpersonal experiences are promoted in order to produce insight, personal growth, and sensitivity to the feelings and experiences of others.

enmeshment A family organization in which boundaries between members are blurred and members are overconcerned and overinvolved in each other's lives, making autonomy impossible.

entropy The tendency of a system to go into disorder, and if unimpeded, to reach a disorganized and undifferentiated state.

environment-sensitive families Families in which the members share the belief that they can cope with the world because it is knowable, orderly, and predictable.

epistemology The study of the origin, nature, and methods, as well as the limits, of knowledge; thus, a framework for describing and conceptualizing what is being observed and experienced.

ethnicity The defining characteristics of a cultural subgroup, transmitted over generations and reinforced by the expectations of the subgroup in which the individual or family maintains membership.

existential A philosophical view that people define their lives through the choices they make; they must accept responsibility for those choices, and therefore for their existence.

experiential The therapeutic approach in which the therapist reveals himself or herself as a real person and uses that self in interacting with a family.

extended family An enlarged and interpersonally complex family unit made up of a nuclear family (a married couple and their children) plus relatives (grandparents, aunts and uncles, cousins) with consanguine ties.

extinction The elimination of behavior as a result of nonreinforcement.

family choreography The charting of shifting transactional patterns within a family through a succession of family sculpting exercises.

family context therapy Bell's therapeutic effort to enhance a family's environment, in order to improve overall family functioning.

.mily crisis therapy A crisis-oriented therapeutic approach in which the family as a system is helped to restore its previous level of functioning; in some cases, with schizophrenia, hospitalization can be avoided.

family group therapy The intervention technique developed by Bell based on social-psychological principles of small-group behavior.

family life chronology An experiential technique in which clients retrace their family history, particularly the family's relationship patterns, to better understand current family functioning.

family life cycle The series of stages or events that mark a family's life, offering an organizing schema for viewing the family as a system proceeding through time.

family of origin The family into which one is born or adopted.

family paradigm A family's shared assumptions about the social environment, determining its priorities, self-image, and strategies for dealing with the outside world.

family projection process The mechanism by which parental conflicts and immaturities are transmitted, through the process of projection, to one or more of the children.

family reconstruction An auxiliary therapeutic approach developed by Satir, whereby family members are guided back through stages of their lives in order to discover and unlock dysfunctional patterns from the past.

family sculpting A physical arrangement of the members of a family in space, with the placement of each person determined by an individual family member acting as "director"; the resulting tableau represents that person's symbolic view of family relationships.

family systems theory The theory advanced by Bowen that emphasizes the family as an emotional unit or network of interlocking relationships best understood from an historical or transgenerational perspective.

feedback The reinsertion into a system of the results of its past performance, as a method of controlling the system.

feedback loops Those circular mechanisms by which information about a system's output is continuously reintroduced back into the system, initiating a chain of subsequent events.

first-order changes Changes within a system that do not alter the basic organization of the system itself.

functional analysis A behavioral assessment of a problem in order to determine what interpersonal or environmental contingencies elicit the problematic behavior and how to extinguish or reduce its occurrence.

functional family therapy A therapeutic approach based on systems theory, cognitive theory, and behavioral principles in which clients are helped to understand the function or interpersonal payoff of certain of their behaviors as a prelude to substituting more effective ways to achieve the same results.

fusion The merging of the intellectual and emotional aspects of a family member, paralleling the degree to which that person is caught up in, and loses a separate sense of self in, family relationships.

general systems theory The study of the relationship of interactional parts in context, emphasizing their unity and organizational hierarchy.

genogram A schematic diagram of a family's relationship system, in the form of a genetic tree, usually including at least three generations, used in particular by Bowen and his followers to trace recurring behavior patterns within the family.

Gestalt family therapy A form of experiential family therapy, loosely based on the principles of Gestalt psychology, that focuses on here-and-now experiences in an effort to heighten self-awareness and increase self-direction.

Greek chorus A live form of supervision in which a consultation group observes a family session from behind a one-way mirror, and from time to time sends messages back to the therapy room.

group therapy A form of psychotherapy in which several people are treated simultaneously by a therapist, and in addition are helped therapeutically through their interactions with one another.

homeostasis A dynamic state of balance or equilibrium in a system, or a tendency toward achieving and maintaining such a state in an effort to ensure a stable environment.

human potential movement The therapeutic movement concerned with expanded sensory awareness, enrichment of life experiences, and fulfillment of the potential for creativity and joy within each individual.

hypothesizing As used by systemic therapists, the process by which a team of therapists form suppositions, open to revision, regarding how and why a family's problems have developed and persisted; in advance of meeting the family, in order to facilitate asking relevant questions and organizing incoming information.

identified patient The family member with the presenting symptom; thus, the person who initially seeks treatment or for whom treatment is sought.

information processing The gathering, distilling, organizing, storing, and retrieving of information through a system or between that system and larger systems.

interlocking pathology Multiple forms of disability or dysfunction within and between family members that are interdependent in the ways in which they are expressed, maintained, and controlled.

interpersonal distance-sensitive families Disengaged families whose members refuse to depend on each other, out of fear that dependence reflects personal weakness and insecurity.

intrapsychic Within the mind or psyche; used especially in regard to conflicting forces.

introjects Imprints or memories from the past, usually based on unresolved relationships with one's parents, that continue to impose themselves on current relationships, particularly with a spouse or one's children.

invariant prescription A single, unchanging verbal directive issued to all parents with symptomatic children, intended to help the parents and children break out of collusive and destructive "games" and establish clearer and more stable intergenerational boundaries.

isomorphic Exhibiting a similar form or parallel process.

joining The therapeutic tactic of entering a family system by engaging its separate members and subsystems, gaining access in order to explore and ultimately to help modify dysfunctional aspects of that system.

licensing A statutory process established by a government agency, usually a state, granting permission to persons having met predetermined qualifications to practice a specific profession.

linear causality The view that a nonreciprocal relationship exists between events in a sequence, so that one event causes the next event, but not vice versa.

live supervision The active guidance of a therapist while at work by an observer or team of observers who offer suggestions by telephone, earphone, or after calling the therapist out of the consultation room.

marital quid pro quo An initial rule arrangement or bargain between husband and wife regarding the ways in which they intend to define themselves vis-à-vis one another in the marital relationship.

marital schism A disturbed marital situation characterized by family disharmony, self-preoccupation, the undermining of the spouse, and frequent threats of divorce by one or both partners.

marital skew A disturbed marital situation in which one partner dominates the family to an extreme degree, and in which the marriage is maintained at the expense of the distortion of reality.

metacommunication A message about a message, typically nonverbal (a smile, a shrug, a nod, a wink), offered simultaneously with a verbal message, structuring, qualifying, or adding meaning to that message.

metarules A family's unstated rules regarding how to interpret or, if necessary, to change its rules.

mimesis A tactic used particularly by structural family therapists, who attempt to copy or mimic a family's communication and behavioral patterns in order to gain acceptance by the family members.

modeling In social learning theory, a way of acquiring new behavior based on the imitation of that behavior observed in others to have led to positive or desired consequences.

multigenerational transmission process The process, occurring over several generations, in which poorly differentiated persons marry similarly differentiated mates, ultimately resulting in offspring suffering from schizophrenia or other severe mental disorders.

multiple family therapy A form of therapy in which members of several families meet together as a group to work on individual as well as family problems.

multiple impact therapy A crisis-focused form of intervention in which members of a single family are seen all together or in various combinations for intensive interaction with a team of professionals over a two-day period.

negative feedback The flow of corrective information from the output of a system back into the system in order to attenuate deviation and keep the system functioning within prescribed limits.

negative reinforcement The termination of or escape from an aversive event or situation, as a result of performing some desired behavior.

negentropy The tendency of a system to remain flexible and open to new input, necessary for change and survival of the system.

network therapy A form of therapy, typically carried out in the home of a patient (for example, a schizophrenic recently discharged from a hospital), in which family members, friends, neighbors, and other involved persons participate in treatment and rehabilitation.

neuro-linguistic programming A therapeutic approach that draws attention to certain linguistic principles and observable neurological correlates of internal thought processes in an effort to program changes in individuals.

neutrality A nonjudgmental therapist position intended to enable the therapist to avoid being caught up in family "games" through coalitions or alliances.

nuclear family A family composed of a husband, wife, and their offspring, living together as a family unit.

nuclear family emotional system An unstable, fused family's way of coping with stress, typically resulting in marital conflict, dysfunction in a spouse, or psychological impairment of a child; their pattern is likely to mimic the patterns of past generations and to be repeated in future generations.

object relations theory The theory that the basic human motive is the search for satisfying object relationships, and that parent-child patterns, especially if frustrating or unfulfilling, are internalized as introjects and imposed on current family relationships.

open system A system with more-or-less permeable boundaries that permits interaction between the system's component parts or subsystems.

operant conditioning A form of learning in which correct or desired responses are rewarded or reinforced, thus increasing the probability that these responses will recur.

operant interpersonal therapy A marital therapy approach based on operant conditioning theory, particularly the exchange between partners of positive rewards.

organization The notion that the components of a system relate to each other in some consistent fashion, and that the system is structured by those relationships.

paradigm A set of assumptions, delimiting an area to be investigated scientifically and specifying the methods to be used to collect and interpret the forthcoming data.

paradoxical communication A way of communicating that is internally inconsistent and contradictory, as in a double-bind message.

paradoxical intervention A therapeutic technique whereby a therapist gives a client or family a directive he or she wants resisted; a change takes place as a result of defying the directive.

pathogenic Pathology-producing.

permeability The ease or flexibility with which members can cross subsystem boundaries within the family.

phenomenological The view that to fully understand the causes of another person's behavior requires an understanding of how he or she subjectively experiences the world, rather than of the physical or objective reality of that world.

phobia An intense, irrational fear of a harmless object or situation that the individual seeks to avoid.

positive connotation A reframing technique whereby positive motives are ascribed to family behavior patterns because these patterns help maintain family balance and cohesion; as a result, the family is helped to view each other's motives more positively.

positive feedback The flow of information from the output of a system back into the system in order to amplify deviation from the state of equilibrium, thus leading to instability and change.

positive reinforcement A reward that strengthens a response and increases the probability of its recurrence.

power Influence, authority, and control over an outcome.

prescribing the symptom A paradoxical technique in which the client is directed to voluntarily engage in the symptomatic behavior; as a result, the client is put in the position of rebelling and abandoning the symptom or obeying, thereby admitting it is under voluntary control.

pretend techniques Paradoxical interventions based on play and fantasy, in which clients are directed to "pretend" to have a symptom; the paradox is that if they are pretending, the symptom may be reclassified as voluntary and unreal, thus able to be altered.

process A series of linked behavioral transactions occurring over a particular period of time.

projective systems The unrealistic expectations, carried over from childhood, of people with relationship difficulties.

pseudomutuality A homeostasis-seeking relationship between and among family members that gives the surface appearance of being open, mutually understanding, and satisfying, when in fact it is not.

psychoanalysis A comprehensive theory of personality development and set of therapeutic techniques developed by Sigmund Freud in the early 1900s.

psychodrama A form of group therapy in which participants role-play themselves or significant others in their lives to achieve catharsis or to resolve conflicts and gain greater spontaneity.

psychodynamics The interplay of opposing forces within an individual as the basis for understanding that person's motivation.

psychosomatic A physical disorder caused or aggravated by chronic emotional stress, usually involving a single organ system under autonomic nervous system innervation.

punctuation The communication concept that each participant in a transaction believes whatever he or she says is caused by what the other says, in effect holding the other responsible for his or her reactions.

reactors Therapist whose style is subtle and indirect, and who prefers to observe and clarify the family process rather than serve as an active, aggressive, or colorful group leader.

redundancy principle Repetitive behavioral sequences within a family.

reframing Relabeling behavior by putting it into a new, more positive perspective ("Mother is trying to help" rather than "She's intrusive"), thus altering the context in which it is perceived and inviting new responses to the same behavior.

reinforcement A response, in the form of a reward or of punishment, intended to change the probability of the occurrence of another person's previous response.

relabeling Verbal redefinition of an event in order to make dysfunctional behavior seem more reasonable and understandable, intended to provoke in others a more positive reaction to that behavior.

retribalization In network therapy, the effort to create or strengthen tribal-like bonds between members of a family in order to facilitate their ability to seek solutions to family crises.

rituals Family activities designed to mark a significant occasion or transition in family life; therapists may prescribe rituals to be enacted by the family in order to provide clarity or insight into their roles and relationships.

scapegoat A family member, likely to be the identified patient, cast in the role that exposes him or her to criticism, blame, punishment, or scorn.

schizophrenia A group of severe mental disorders characterized by withdrawal from reality, blunted or inappropriate emotion, delusions, hallucinations, incoherent thought and speech, and an overall breakdown in personal and social functioning.

schizophrenogenic mother A cold, domineering, possessive but rejecting mother (usually married to an inadequate, passive husband) whose behavior toward her son is thought to be a determining factor in his schizophrenic behavior.

second-order changes Fundamental changes in a system's organization and function.

shaping A form of behavioral therapy, based on operant conditioning principles, in which successive approximations of desired behavior are reinforced until the desired behavior is achieved.

sibling position The birth order of children in a family, which influences their personalities as well as their interactions with future spouses.

single-parent-led family A family led by a single custodial parent, most often a woman, as a result of divorce, death of a spouse, desertion, or never having married.

social learning theory The theory that a person's behavior is best understood when the conditions under which the behavior is learned are taken into account.

societal regression The notion that society responds emotionally in periods of stress and anxiety, offering short-term "band-aid" solutions, rather than seeking more rational solutions that lead to greater individuation.

stable coalition A fixed or inflexible union between family members that becomes a dominant force in the family's everyday functioning.

stepfamily A linked family system created by the marriage of two persons, one or both of whom has been previously married, in which one or more children from the earlier marriage(s) live with the remarried couple.

strategic A therapeutic approach in which the therapist develops a specific plan or strategy and designs interventions aimed at solving the presenting problem.

structural A therapeutic approach directed at changing or realigning the family organization or structure in order to alter dysfunctional transactions and clarify subsystem boundaries.

structural map A symbolic representation of a family's organizational structure, particularly its boundaries and coalitions, used in structural family therapy to plan interventions.

subsystem An organized, coexisting component within an overall system, having its own autonomous functions as well as a specified role in the operation of the large system; within families, a member can belong to a number of such units.

suprasystem A higher-level system in which other systems represent component parts and play subsystem roles.

symbiosis An intense attachment between two or more individuals, such as a mother and child, to the extent that the boundaries between them becomes blurred, and they respond as one.

symmetrical A type of dyadic transaction or communication pattern characterized by equality and the minimization of differences; each participant's response provokes a similar response in the other, sometimes in a competitive fashion.

symmetrical escalation A spiraling competitive effect in the communication between two people whose relationship is based on equality, so that vindictiveness leads to greater vindictiveness in return, viciousness to greater viciousness, and so forth.

system A set of interacting units or component parts that together make up a whole arrangement or organization.

systemic family therapy A therapeutic approach in which the family, as an evolving system, is viewed as continuing to use an old epistemology that no longer fits its current behavior patterns; the therapist indirectly introduces new information into the family system and encourages alternative epistemologies to develop.

therapeutic double bind A general term for a variety of paradoxical techniques in which clients are directed to continue to manifest their presenting symptoms; caught in a bind, they must give up the symptom or acknowledge control over it.

time out A behavioral technique for extinguishing undesirable or inappropriate behavior by removing the reinforcing consequences of that behavior; the procedure is used primarily with children.

token economy A program in which tokens (points, gold stars) are dispensed contingent upon the successful completion of previously designated desired behaviors; the accumulated tokens can be redeemed later for money or special privileges.

tracking A therapeutic tactic associated with structural family therapy, in which the therapist deliberately attends to the symbols, style, language, and values of the family, using them to influence the family's transactional patterns.

transference In psychoanalytic treatment, the unconscious shifting to the analyst of a patient's feelings, drives, attitudes, and fantasies, displaced from reactions to significant persons in the patient's past.

triad A three-person relationship.

triadic family therapy A therapeutic approach in which the therapist, as a third person, acts as go-between in working with a couple, in order to disrupt the partners' chronic relationship patterns.

triangle A three-person system, the smallest stable emotional system; a two-person emotional system, under stress, will recruit a third person into the system to lower the intensity and anxiety and gain stability.

triangulation A process in which each parent demands that a child ally with him or her against the other parent during parental conflict.

undifferentiated family ego mass An intense, symbiotic nuclear family relationship; an individual sense of self fails to develop in members because of the existing fusion or emotional "stuck-togetherness."

vulnerability-stress model The viewpoint that a predisposition or vulnerability to a severe mental disorder, such as schizophrenia, is inherited; its ultimate manifestation is determined by how that vulnerability is later modified by life events, especially those involving the family.

wholeness The systems view that combining units, components, or elements produces an entity greater than the sum of its parts.

References

Ackerman, N. J. (1984). *A theory of family systems.* New York: Gardner Press.

Ackerman, N. W. (1937). The family as a social and emotional unit. *Bulletin of the Kansas Mental Hygiene Society, 12*(2).

Ackerman, N. W. (1956). Interlocking pathology in family relationships. In S. Rado & G. Daniels (Eds.), *Changing conceptions of psychoanalytic medicine.* New York: Grune & Stratton.

Ackerman, N. W. (1958). *The psychodynamics of family life.* New York: Basic Books.

Ackerman, N. W. (1966). *Treating the troubled family.* New York: Basic Books.

Ackerman, N. W. (1970). *Family therapy in transition.* Boston: Little, Brown.

Ackerman, N. W. (1972). The growing edge of family therapy. In C. Sager & H. Kaplan (Eds.), *Progress in group and family therapy.* New York: Brunner/Mazel.

Alexander, J., & Parsons, B. V. (1982). *Functional family therapy.* Pacific Grove, CA: Brooks/Cole.

Alger, I. (1976a). Integrating immediate video playback in family therapy. In P. J. Guerin, Jr. (Ed.), *Family therapy: Theory and practice.* New York: Gardner Press.

Alger, I. (1976b). Multiple couple therapy. In P. J. Guerin, Jr. (Ed.), *Family therapy: Theory and practice.* New York: Gardner Press.

American Association for Marriage and Family Therapy. (1988). *Code of ethical principles for marriage and family therapists.* Washington, DC: AAMFT.

American Association for Marriage and Family Therapy. (1988). *AAMFT membership requirements.* Washington, DC: AAMFT.

Andolfi, M. (1979). *Family therapy: An interactional approach.* New York: Plenum.

Aponte, H. (1976). Underorganization in the poor family. In P. J. Guerin, Jr. (Ed.), *Family therapy: Theory and practice.* New York: Gardner Press.

Aponte, H. (1987). The treatment of society's poor: An ecological perspective on the underorganized family. *Family Therapy Today, 2,* 1–7.

Aponte, H., & Van Deusin, J. M. (1981). Structural family therapy. In A. S. Gurman & D. P. Kniskern (Eds.), *Handbook of family therapy.* New York: Brunner/Mazel.

Auerswald, E. H. (1988). Epistemological confusion and outcome research. In L. C. Wynne (Ed.), *The state of the art in family therapy research: Controversies and recommendations.* New York: Family Process Press.

Aylmer, R. C. (1988). The launching of the single young adult. In B. Carter & M. McGoldrick (Eds.), *The changing family life cycle: A framework for family therapy* (2nd ed.). New York: Gardner Press.

Back, K. W. (1974). Intervention techniques: Small groups. In M. R. Rosenzweig & L. W. Porter (Eds.), *Annual Review of Psychology, 39,* 367–387.

Bandler, R., & Grinder, J. (1975). *The structure of magic* (Vol. 1). Palo Alto, CA: Science and Behavior Books.

Bandler, R., Grinder, J., & Satir, V. M. (1976). *Changing with families.* Palo Alto, CA: Science and Behavior Books.

Bandura, A. (1977). *Social learning theory.* Englewood Cliffs, NJ: Prentice-Hall.

Barnhill, L. H., & Longo, D. (1978). Fixation and regression in the family life cycle. *Family Process, 17,* 469–478.

Barton, C., & Alexander, J. (1981). Functional family therapy. In A. S. Gurman & D. P. Kniskern (Eds.), *Handbook of family therapy.* New York: Brunner/Mazel.

Bateson, G. (1958). *Naven* (2nd ed.). Stanford, CA: Stanford University Press.

Bateson, G. (1972). *Steps to an ecology of mind.* New York: E. P. Dutton.

Bateson, G., Jackson, D. D., Haley, J., & Weakland, J. (1956). Towards a theory of schizophrenia. *Behavioral Science*, *1*, 251–264.

Beavers, W. R. (1977). *Psychotherapy and growth: Family systems perspective.* New York: Brunner/Mazel.

Beavers, W. R. (1981). A systems model of family for family therapists. *Journal of Marital and Family Therapy*, *7*, 229–307.

Beavers, W. R. (1982). Healthy, midrange, and severely dysfunctional families. In F. Walsh (Ed.), *Normal family processes.* New York: Guilford Press.

Beavers, W. R., & Voeller, M. N. (1983). Family models: Comparing and contrasting the Olson circumplex with the Beavers model. *Family Process*, *22*, 85–98.

Bednar, R. L., Burlingame, G. M., & Masters, K. S. (1988). Systems of family treatment: Substance or semantics? In M. R. Rosenzweig & L. W. Porter (Eds.), *Annual Review of Psychology*, *39*, 401–434.

Beels, C., & Ferber, A. (1969). Family therapy: A view. *Family Process*, *8*, 280–332.

Bell, J. E. (1961). Family group therapy (Public Health Monograph No. 64). Washington, DC: U.S. Government Printing Office.

Bell, J. E. (1975). *Family therapy.* New York: Aronson.

Bell, J. E. (1976). *A theoretical framework for family group therapy.* In P. J. Guerin, Jr. (Ed.). *Family therapy: Theory and practice.* New York: Gardner Press.

Bell, J. E. (1983). Family group therapy. In B. B. Wolman & G. Stricker (Eds.), *Handbook of family and marital therapy.* New York: Plenum.

Belle, D. (Ed.). (1982). *Lives in stress: Women and depression.* Beverly Hills, CA: Sage Publications.

Berger, M. (1988). Academic psychology and family therapy training. In H. A. Liddle, D. C. Breunlin, & R. C. Schwartz (Eds.), *Handbook of family therapy training and supervision.* New York: Guilford Press.

Berger, M. M. (Ed.). (1978). *Videotape technique in psychiatric training and treatment* (rev. ed.). New York: Brunner/Mazel.

Berger, M. M., & Dammann, C. (1982). Live supervision as context, treatment, and training. *Family Process*, *21*, 337–344.

Berkowitz, B. P., & Graziano, A. M. (1972). Training parents as behavior therapists: A review. *Behavior Research and Review*, *10*, 297–317.

Bernard, J. (1974). *The future of marriage.* New York: World.

Bertalanffy, L. von. (1968). *General systems theory: Foundation, development, applications.* New York: Braziller.

Bion, W. R. (1961). *Experiences in groups.* New York: Basic Books.

Bloch, D. A. (1985). The family as a psychosocial system. In S. Henao & N. P. Grose (Eds.), *Principles of family systems in family medicine.* New York: Brunner/Mazel.

Bloch, D. A., & LaPerriere, K. (1973). Techniques of family therapy: A conceptual frame. In D. A. Bloch (Ed.), *Techniques of family psychotherapy: A primer.* New York: Grune & Stratton.

Bloch, D. A., & Simon, R. (Eds.). (1982). *The strength of family therapy: Selected papers of Nathan W. Ackerman.* New York: Brunner/Mazel.

Bloch, D. A., & Weiss, H. M. (1981). Training facilities in marital and family therapy. *Family Process, 20*, 133–146.

Bodin, A. M. (1969a). Family therapy training literature: A brief guide. *Family Process, 8*, 729–779.

Bodin, A. M. (1969b). Videotape in training family therapists. *The Journal of Nervous and Mental Disease, 148*, 251–261.

Bodin, A. M. (1981). The interactional view: Family therapy approaches of the Mental Research Institute. In A. S. Gurman & D. P. Kniskern (Eds.), *Handbook of family therapy.* New York: Brunner/Mazel.

Bodin, A. M. (1983). Family therapy. Unpublished manuscript.

Boscolo, L., Cecchin, G., Hoffman, L., & Penn, P. (1987). *Milan systemic family therapy: Conversations in theory and practice.* New York: Basic Books.

Boszormenyi-Nagy, I. (1987). *Foundations of contextual therapy: Collected papers of Ivan Boszormenyi-Nagy.* New York: Brunner/Mazel.

Boszormenyi-Nagy, I., & Framo, J. L. (Eds.). (1965). *Intensive family therapy: Theoretical and practical aspects.* New York: Harper & Row.

Boszormenyi-Nagy, I., & Krasner, B. R. (1986). *Between give and take: A clinical guide to contextual therapy.* New York: Brunner/Mazel.

Boszormenyi-Nagy, I., & Spark, G. M. (1973). *Invisible loyalties: Reciprocity in intergenerational family therapy.* New York: Harper & Row.

Boszormenyi-Nagy, I., & Ulrich, D. (1981). Contextual family therapy. In A. Gurman & D. Kniskern (Eds.), *Handbook of family therapy.* New York: Brunner/Mazel.

Bowen, M. (1960). A family concept of schizophrenia. In D. D. Jackson (Ed.), *The etiology of schizophrenia.* New York: Basic Books.

Bowen, M. (1966). The use of family theory in clinical practice. *Comprehensive Psychiatry, 7*, 345–374.

Bowen, M. (1975). Family therapy after twenty years. In S. Arieti, D. X. Freedman, & J. E. Dyrud (Eds.), *American handbook of psychiatry V: Treatment* (2nd ed.). New York: Basic Books.

Bowen, M. (1976). Theory in the practice of psychotherapy. In P. J. Guerin, Jr. (Ed.), *Family therapy: Theory and practice.* New York: Gardner Press.

Bowen, M. (1977). Family systems theory and society. In J. P. Lorio & L. McClenathan (Eds.), *Georgetown family symposia: Volume II (1973–1974)*. Washington, DC: Georgetown Family Center.

Bowen, M. (1978). *Family therapy in clinical practice.* New York: Aronson.

Bradt, J. O. (1988). Becoming parents: Families with young children. In B. Carter & M. McGoldrick (Eds.), *The changing life cycle: A framework for family therapy* (2nd ed.). New York: Gardner Press.

Bray, J. H., Shepherd, J. N., & Hays, J. R. (1985). Legal and ethical issues in informed consent to psychotherapy. *American Journal of Family Therapy, 13*, 50–60.

Breunlin, D. C. (1988). Oscillation theory and family development. In C. J. Falicov (Ed.), *Family transitions: Continuity and change over the life cycle.* New York: Guilford Press.

Broderick, C. B., & Schrader, S. S. (1981). The history of professional marriage and family counseling. In A. S. Gurman & D. P. Kniskern (Eds.), *Handbook of family therapy.* New York: Brunner/Mazel.

Broderick, C. B., & Smith, J. (1979). The general systems approach to the family. In W. R. Burr, R. Hill, F. I. Nye, & I. L. Reiss (Eds.), *Contemporary theories about the family* (Vol. 2). New York: Free Press.

Brody, E. M. (1974). Aging and family personality: A developmental view. *Family Process, 13*, 23–38.

Bross, A., & Benjamin, M. (1982). Family therapy: A recursive model of strategic practice. In A. Bross (Ed.), *Family therapy: Principles of strategic practice.* New York: Guilford Press.

Buckley, W. Q. (1967). *Sociology and modern systems theory.* Englewood Cliffs, NJ: Prentice-Hall.

Byng-Hall, J. (1982). The use of the earphone in supervision. In R. Whiffen & J. Byng-Hall (Eds.), *Family therapy supervision: Recent developments in practice.* London: Academic Press.

Cannon, W. B. (1932). *The wisdom of the body.* New York: W. W. Norton.

Carter, B., & McGoldrick, M. (1988). Overview: The changing family life cycle—A framework for family therapy. In B. Carter & M. McGoldrick (Eds.), *The changing family life cycle: A framework for family therapy* (2nd ed.). New York: Allyn and Bacon, Inc.

Carter, E. A., & McGoldrick, M. (1980). *The family life cycle: A framework for family therapy.* New York: Gardner Press.

Cleghorn, J. M., & Levin, S. (1973). Training family therapists by setting learning objectives. *American Journal of Orthopsychiatry, 43*, 439–446.

Colapinto, J. (1979). The relative value of empirical evidence. *Family Process, 18*, 427–441.

Colapinto, J. (1982). Structural family therapy. In A. M. Horne & M. M. Ohlsen (Eds.), *Family counseling and therapy.* Itasca, IL: F. E. Peacock.

Constantine, L. L. (1976). A multiple goal-directed training program in family therapy. *Family Process, 15,* 373–387.

Constantine, L. L. (1978). Family sculpture and relationship mapping techniques. *Journal of Marriage and Family Counseling, 4*(2), 13–24.

Constantine, L. L. (1986). *Family paradigms: The practice of theory in family therapy.* New York: Guilford Press.

Cook, W. L., Strachan, A. M., Goldstein, M. J., & Miklowitz, D. J. (1989). Expressed emotion and reciprocal affective relationships in families of disturbed adolescents. *Family Process, 28,* 337–348.

Cooper, S. (1974). Treatment of parents. In S. Arieti & G. Caplan (Eds.), *American handbook of psychiatry II: Child and adolescent psychiatry, sociocultural and community psychiatry* (2nd ed.). New York: Basic Books.

Corey, G., Corey, M. S., & Callanan, P. (1988). *Issues and ethics in the helping professions.* Pacific Grove, CA: Brooks/Cole.

Cromwell, R. E., Olson, D. H., & Fournier, D. G. (1976). Diagnosis and evaluation in marital and family counseling. In D. H. Olson (Ed.), *Treating relationships.* Lake Mills, IA: Graphic.

Dell, P. F. (1982). Beyond homeostasis: Toward a concept of coherence. *Family Process, 21,* 21–42.

deShazer, S. (1985). *Keys to solution in brief therapy.* New York: W. W. Norton.

Dicks, H. V. (1967). *Marital tensions.* New York: Basic Books.

Dilts, R., Grinder, J., Bandler, R., Cameron-Bandler, L., & DeLozier, J. (1980). *Neuro-linguistic programming* (Vol. 1). Cupertino, CA: Meta Publications.

Dinkmeyer, D., & McKay, G. D. (1976). *Systematic training for effective parenting.* Circle Pines, MN: American Guidance Service.

Doane, J. (1978). Family interaction and communication deviance in disturbed and normal families: A review of research. *Family Process, 17,* 357–376.

Duhl, F. J., Kantor, D., & Duhl, B. S. (1973). Learning, space, and action in family therapy: A primer of sculpture. In D. A. Bloch (Ed.), *Techniques of family psychotherapy: A primer.* New York: Grune & Stratton.

Duvall, E. M. (1957). *Family development.* Philadelphia: Lippincott.

Duvall, E. M. (1977). *Marriage and family development* (5th ed.) New York: Lippincott.

Duvall, E. M., & Hill, R. (1948). *Report to the committee on the dynamics of family interaction.* Washington, DC: National Conference on Family Life.

Duvall, E. M., & Miller, B. C. (1985). *Marriage and family development* (6th ed.). New York: Harper & Row.

Edelman, M. W. (1987). *Families in peril: An agenda for social change.* Cambridge, MA: Harvard University Press.

Epstein, N., Baldwin, L. M., & Bishop, D. S. (1983). The McMaster family assessment device. *Journal of Marital and Family Therapy, 9*, 171–180.

Epstein, N., Bishop, D. S., & Baldwin, L. M. (1982). McMaster Model of family functioning: A view of the normal family. In F. Walsh (Ed.), *Normal family processes.* New York: Guilford Press.

Epstein, N., Schlesinger, S. E., & Dryden, W. (1988). Concepts and methods of cognitive-behavioral family treatment. In N. Epstein, S. E. Schlesinger, & W. Dryden (Eds.), *Cognitive-behavioral therapy with families.* New York: Brunner/Mazel.

Erickson, G. D., & Hogan, T. P. (1981). *Family therapy: An introduction to theory and technique* (2nd ed.). Pacific Grove, CA: Brooks/Cole.

Fairbairn, W. R. (1954). *An object-relations theory of personality.* New York: Basic Books.

Falicov, C. J. (Ed.). (1988). *Family transitions: Continuity and change over the life cycle.* New York: Guilford Press.

Falloon, I. R. H. (Ed.). (1988). *Handbook of behavioral family therapy.* New York: Guilford Press.

Falloon, I. R. H., & Liberman, R. P. (1982). Behavioral therapy for families with child management problems. In M. Textor (Ed.), *Family pathology and its treatment.* New York: Aronson.

Falloon, I. R. H., & Lillie, F. J. (1988). Behavioral family therapy: An overview. In I. R. H. Falloon (Ed.), *Handbook of behavioral family therapy.* New York: Guilford Press.

Fenell, L., & Hovestadt, A. J. (1986). Family therapy as a profession or professional specialty: Implications for training. *Journal of Psychotherapy and the Family, 1*(4), 25–40.

Fieldsteel, N. D. (1982). Ethical issues in family therapy. In M. Rosenbaum (Ed.), *Ethics and values in psychotherapy: A guidebook.* New York: Free Press.

Fisch, R., Weakland, J., & Segal, L. (1982). *The tactics of change: Doing therapy briefly.* San Francisco: Jossey-Bass.

Fishman, H. C. (1988). Structural family therapy and the family life cycle: A four-dimensional model for family assessment. In C. J. Falicov (Ed.), *Family transitions: Continuity and change over the life cycle.* New York: Guilford Press.

Fox, R. E. (1976). Family therapy. In I. B. Weiner (Ed.), *Clinical methods in psychology.* New York: Wiley.

Framo, J. L. (1972). *Family interaction: A dialogue between family researchers and family therapists.* New York: Springer.

Framo, J. L. (1973). Marriage therapy in a couples group. In D. A. Bloch (Ed.), *Techniques of family psychotherapy: A primer.* New York: Grune & Stratton.

Framo, J. L. (1976). Family of origin as a therapeutic resource for adults in marital and family therapy: You can and should go home again. *Family Process, 15,* 193–210.

Framo, J. L. (1978). In-laws and out-laws: A marital case of kinship confusion. In P. Papp (Ed.), *Family therapy: Full-length case studies.* New York: Gardner Press.

Framo, J. L. (1981). The integration of marital therapy with sessions with family of origin. In A. S. Gurman & D. P. Kniskern (Eds.), *Handbook of family therapy.* New York: Brunner/Mazel.

Framo, J. L. (1982). *Explorations in marital and family therapy: Selected papers of James L. Framo.* New York: Springer.

Franks, C. M., & Wilson, G. T. (Eds.). (1975). *Annual review of behavior therapy: Theory and practice* (Vol. III). New York: Brunner/Mazel.

Fretz, B. R., & Mills, D. H. (1980). *Licensing and certification of psychologists and counselors.* San Francisco: Jossey-Bass.

Freud, S. (1955). Analysis of a phobia in a five-year-old boy (1909). *The standard edition of the complete psychological works of Sigmund Freud* (Vol. 10). London: Hogarth.

Freud, S. (1959). Fragments of an analysis of a case of hysteria (1905). *Collected papers* (Vol. 3). New York: Basic Books.

Fromm-Reichmann, F. (1948). Notes on the development of treatment of schizophrenics by psychoanalytic psychotherapy. *Psychiatry, 11,* 253–273.

Fulmer, R. (1988). Lower-income and professional families: A comparison of structure and life cycle process. In B. Carter & M. McGoldrick (Eds.), *The changing family life cycle: A framework for family therapy* (2nd ed.). New York: Gardner Press.

Gazda, G. M. (1975). Group psychotherapy and group counseling: Definitions and heritage. In G. M. Gazda (Ed.), *Basic approaches to group psychotherapy and group counseling.* Springfield, IL: Charles C Thomas.

Gill, S. J. (1982). Professional disclosure and consumer protection in counseling. *Personnel and Guidance Journal, 60,* 443–446.

Gilligan, C. (1982). *In a different voice: Psychological theory and women's development.* Cambridge, MA: Harvard University Press.

Goldenberg, H. (1973). *Is training family therapists different from clinical training in general?* Paper presented at the American Psychological Association annual meeting, Montreal, Canada, 1973.

Goldenberg, H. (1983). *Contemporary clinical psychology* (2nd ed.). Pacific Grove, CA: Brooks/Cole.

Goldenberg, H., & Goldenberg, I. (1990). *Counseling today's families.* Pacific Grove, CA: Brooks/Cole.

Goldenberg, I., & Goldenberg, H. (1975). A family approach to psychological services. *American Journal of Psychoanalysis, 35*, 317–328.

Goldenberg, I., & Goldenberg, H. (1983). Historical roots of contemporary family therapy. In B. B. Wolman & G. Stricker (Eds.), *Handbook of family and marital therapy.* New York: Plenum.

Goldner, V. (1985). Feminism and family therapy. *Family Process, 24*, 13–47.

Goldstein, M. J. (1985). Family factors that antedate the onset of schizophrenia and related disorders: The results of a fifteen-year prospective longitudinal study. *Acta Psychiatrica Scandinavia*, 71, 7–18.

Goldstein, M. J. (1988). The family and psychopathology. In M. R. Rosenzweig & L. W. Porter (Eds.), *Annual Review of Psychology, 39*, 283–299.

Gordon, S. B., & Davidson, N. (1981). Behavioral parent training. In A. S. Gurman & D. P. Kniskern (Eds.), *Handbook of family therapy.* New York: Brunner/Mazel.

Green, R. J., & Framo, J. L. (Eds.). (1981). *Family therapy: Major contributions.* New York: International Universities Press.

Greenberg, G. S. (1977). The family interactive perspective: A study and examination of the work of Don D. Jackson. *Family Process, 16*, 385–412.

Greenberg, L. S., & Pinsof, W. M. (Eds.). (1986). *The psychotherapeutic process: A research handbook.* New York: Guilford Press.

Gritzer, P. H., & Okun, H. S. (1983). Multiple family group therapy: A model for all families. In B. B. Wolman & G. Stricker (Eds.), *Handbook of family and marital therapy.* New York: Plenum.

Gross, S. J. (1978). The myth of professional licensing. *American Psychologist, 33*, 1009–1016.

Group for the Advancement of Psychiatry. (1970). *The field of family therapy* (Report No. 78). New York: Group for the Advancement of Psychiatry.

Guerin, P. J., Jr. (1976). Family therapy: The first twenty-five years. In P. J. Guerin, Jr. (Ed.), *Family therapy: Theory and practice.* New York: Gardner Press.

Gumper, L. L., & Sprenkle, D. H. (1981). Privileged communication in therapy: Special problems for the family and couples therapist. *Family Process, 20*, 11–23.

Gurin, G., Veroff, J., & Feld, S. (1960). *Americans view their mental health.* New York: Basic Books.

Gurman, A. S. (1971). Group family therapy: Clinical and empirical implications for outcome research. *International Journal of Group Psychotherapy, 21*, 174–189.

Gurman, A. S. (1979). Dimensions of marital therapy: A comparative analysis. *Journal of Marital and Family Therapy, 5*, 5–18.

Gurman, A. S. (1983a). Family therapy and the new epistemology. *Journal of Marital and Family Therapy*, *9*, 227–234.

Gurman, A. S. (1983b). The old hatters and the new wavers. *The Family Therapy Networker*, 7(4), 36–37.

Gurman, A. S., & Klein, M. (1980). Marital and family conflicts. In A. M. Brodsky & R. Hare-Mustin (Eds.), *Women and psychotherapy*. New York: Guilford Press.

Gurman, A. S., & Kniskern, D. P. (1978). Research on marital and family therapy: Progress, perspectives, and prospect. In S. L. Garfield & A. E. Bergin (Eds.), *Handbook of psychotherapy and behavior change: An empirical analysis* (2nd ed). New York: Wiley.

Gurman, A. S., & Kniskern, D. P. (1981a). Family therapy outcome research: Knowns and unknowns. In A. S. Gurman & D. P. Kniskern (Eds.), *Handbook of family therapy*. New York: Brunner/Mazel.

Gurman, A. S., & Kniskern, D. P. (Eds.). (1981b). *Handbook of family therapy*. New York: Brunner/Mazel.

Gurman, A. S., & Kniskern, D. P. (1981c). The outcome of family therapy: Implications for practice and training. In G. Berenson & H. White (Eds.), *Annual review of family therapy* (Vol. 1.). New York: Human Sciences Press.

Gurman, A. S., Kniskern, D. P., & Pinsof, W. M. (1986). Research on the process and outcome of marital and family therapy. In S. Garfield & A. Bergin (Eds.), *Handbook of psychotherapy and behavior change* (3rd ed.). New York: Wiley.

Gurman, A. S., & Knudson, R. M. (1978). Behavior marriage therapy: I. A psychodynamic-systems analysis and critique. *Family Process*, *17*, 121–138.

Hahlweg, K. (1988). Statistical methods for studying family therapy process. In L. C. Wynne (Ed.), *The state of the art in family therapy research: Controversies and recommendations*. New York: Family Process Press.

Hahlweg, K., Baucom, D. H., & Markman, H. (1988). Recent advances in therapy and prevention. In I. R. H. Falloon (Ed.), *Handbook of behavioral family therapy*. New York: Guilford Press.

Haley, J. (1963). *Strategies of psychotherapy*. New York: Grune & Stratton.

Haley, J. (1970). Family therapy. *International Journal of Psychiatry*, *9*, 233–242.

Haley, J. (1971a). Approaches to family therapy. In J. Haley (Ed.), *Changing families: A family therapy reader*. New York: Grune & Stratton.

Haley, J. (1971b). Family therapy: A radical change. In J. Haley (Ed.), *Changing families: A family therapy reader*. New York: Grune & Stratton.

Haley, J. (1973). *Uncommon therapy: The psychiatric techniques of Milton H. Erickson, M.D.* New York: W. W. Norton.

Haley, J. (1976). *Problem-solving therapy*. San Francisco: Jossey-Bass.

Haley, J. (1978). Ideas which handicap therapists. In M. M. Berger (Ed.), *Beyond the double-bind: Communication and family systems, theories, and techniques with schizophrenics.* New York: Brunner/Mazel.

Haley, J. (1979). *Leaving home: Therapy with disturbed young people.* New York: McGraw-Hill.

Haley, J. (1984). *Ordeal therapy: Unusual ways to change behavior.* San Francisco: Jossey-Bass.

Haley, J. (1988). Personal communication.

Haley, J., & Hoffman, L. (1967). *Techniques of family therapy.* New York: Basic Books.

Hare-Mustin, R. T. (1978). A feminist approach to family therapy. *Family Process, 17*, 181–194.

Hare-Mustin, R. T. (1980). Family therapy may be dangerous to your health. *Professional Psychology, 11*, 935–938.

Hare-Mustin, R. T. (1987). The problem of gender in family therapy theory. *Family Process, 26*, 15–27.

Hatcher, C. (1978). Intrapersonal and interpersonal models: Blending Gestalt and family therapies. *Journal of Marriage and Family Counseling, 4*, 63–68.

Hazelrigg, M. D., Cooper, H. M., & Borduin, C. M. (1987). Evaluating the effectiveness of family therapies: An integrative review and analysis. *Psychological Bulletin, 101*, 428–442.

Heiman, J. R., LoPiccolo, L., & LoPiccolo, J. (1981). The treatment of sexual dysfunction. In A. S. Gurman & D. P. Kniskern (Eds.), *Handbook of family therapy.* New York: Brunner/Mazel.

Hines, P. M. (1988). The family life cycle of poor black families. In B. Carter & M. McGoldrick (Eds.), *The changing family life cycle: A framework for family therapy* (2nd ed.). New York: Gardner Press.

Ho, M. K. (1987). *Family therapy with ethnic minorities.* Newbury Park, CA: Sage Publications.

Hoffman, L. (1981). *Foundations of family therapy.* New York: Basic Books.

Hoffman, L. (1988). The family life cycle and discontinuous change. In B. Carter & M. McGoldrick (Eds.), *The changing family life cycle* (2nd ed.). New York: Gardner Press.

Howells, J. G. (1975). *Principles of family psychiatry.* New York: Brunner/Mazel.

Huber, C. H., & Baruth, L. G. (1987). *Ethical, legal, and professional issues in the practice of marriage and family therapy.* Columbus, OH: Merrill.

Imber-Black, E. (1988). *Families and larger systems: A family therapist's guide through the labyrinth.* New York: Guilford Press.

Jackson, D. D. (1957). The question of family homeostasis. *Psychiatric Quarterly Supplement, 31*, 79–90.

Jackson, D. D. (1959). Family interaction, family homeostasis, and some implications for conjoint family therapy. In J. Masseman (Ed.), *Individual and family dynamics.* New York: Grune & Stratton.

Jackson, D. D. (Ed.). (1960). *The etiology of schizophrenia.* New York: Basic Books.

Jackson, D. D. (1965a). Family rules: Marital quid pro quo. *Archives of General Psychiatry, 12*, 589–594.

Jackson, D. D. (1965b). The study of the family. *Family Process, 4*, 1–20.

Jacobson, N. S. (1981). Behavioral marital therapy. In A. S. Gurman & D. P. Kniskern (Eds.), *Handbook of family therapy.* New York: Brunner/Mazel.

Jacobson, N. S., & Margolin, G. (1979). *Marital therapy: Strategies based on social learning and behavior exchange principles.* New York: Brunner/Mazel.

Jacobson, N. S., & Martin, B. (1976). Behavioral marital therapy. *Psychological Bulletin, 83*, 540–556.

Kanner, L. (1962). Emotionally disturbed children: A historical review. *Child Development, 33*, 97–102.

Kantor D., & Lehr, W. (1975). *Inside the family.* San Francisco: Jossey-Bass.

Kaplan, H. S. (1974). *The new sex therapy: Active treatment of sexual dysfunction.* New York: Brunner/Mazel.

Kaplan, M. L., & Kaplan, N. R. (1978). Individual and family growth: A Gestalt approach. *Family Process, 17*, 195–206.

Karpel, M. A. (1986). Questions, obstacles, contributions. In M. A. Karpel (Ed.), *Family resources: The hidden partner in family therapy.* New York: Guilford Press.

Kaslow, F. W. (1980). History of family therapy in the United States: A kaleidoscopic view. *Marriage and Family Review, 3*, 77–111.

Kaye, K. (1985). Toward a developmental psychology of the family. In L. L'Abate (Ed.), *The handbook of family psychology and therapy* (Vol. 1). Homewood, IL: Dorsey Press.

Kazdin, A. E. (1984). *Behavior modification in applied settings* (3rd ed.). Homewood, IL: Dorsey Press.

Keeney, B. P. (1983). *Aesthetics of change.* New York: Guilford Press.

Keeney, B. P., & Sprenkle, D. H. (1982). Ecosystemic epistemology: Critical implications for the aesthetics and pragmatics of family therapy. *Family Process, 21*, 1–19.

Keeney, B. P., & Thomas, F. N. (1986). Cybernetic foundations of family therapy. In F. P. Piercy, D. H. Sprenkle, & Associates (Eds.), *Family therapy sourcebook.* New York: Guilford Press.

Keith, D. V., & Whitaker, C. A. (1982). Experiential/symbolic family therapy. In A. M. Horne & M. M. Ohlsen (Eds.), *Family counseling and therapy.* Itasca, IL: F. E. Peacock.

Kempler, W. (1974). *Principles of gestalt family therapy.* Costa Mesa, CA: The Kempler Institute.

Kempler, W. (1981). *Experiential psychotherapy with families.* New York: Brunner/Mazel.

Kempler, W. (1982). Gestalt family therapy. In A. M. Horne & M. M. Ohlsen (Eds.), *Family counseling and therapy.* Itasca, IL: F. E. Peacock.

Kerr, M. E. (1981). Family systems theory and therapy. In A. S. Gurman & D. P. Kniskern (Eds.), *Handbook of family therapy.* New York: Brunner/Mazel.

Kerr, M. E., & Bowen, M. (1988). *Family evaluation: An approach based on Bowen theory.* New York: W. W. Norton.

Kinder, B. N., & Blakeney, P. (1977). Treatment of sexual dysfunction: A review of outcome studies. *Journal of Clinical Psychology, 33*, 523–530.

Kniskern, D. P. (1983). The new wave is all wet. *The Family Therapy Networker*, 7(4), 38, 60–62.

L'Abate, L. (Ed.). (1985). *The handbook of family psychology and therapy* (Vols. I & II). Homewood, IL: Dorsey Press.

L'Abate, L., & Frey, J., III. (1981). The E-R-A model: The role of feelings in family therapy reconsidered: Implications for a classification of theories in family therapy. *Journal of Marital and Family Therapy, 7*, 143–150.

Langsley, D. G., & Kaplan, D. M. (1968). *The treatment of families in crisis.* New York: Grune & Stratton.

Langsley, D. G., Machotka, P., & Flomenhaft, K. (1971). Avoiding mental hospital admission: A follow-up study. *American Journal of Psychiatry, 127*, 1391–1394.

Langsley, D. G., Pittman, F. S., Machotka, P., & Flomenhaft, K. (1968). Family crisis therapy: Results and implications. *Family Process, 7*, 145–158.

Laqueur, H. P. (1973). Multiple family therapy: Questions and answers. In D. A. Bloch (Ed.), *Techniques of family psychotherapy.* New York: Grune & Stratton.

Laqueur, H. P. (1976). Multiple family therapy. In P. J. Guerin, Jr. (Ed.), *Family therapy: Theory and practice.* New York: Gardner Press.

Lazarus, A. A. (1977). Has behavior therapy outlived its usefulness? *American Psychologist, 32*, 550–554.

Lebow, J. L. (1987). Training psychologists in family therapy in family institute settings. *Journal of Family Psychology, 1*, 219–231.

Lerner, G. (1986). *The creation of patriarchy.* New York: Oxford University Press.

Leslie, L. A. (1988). Cognitive-behavioral and systems models of family therapy: How compatible are they? In N. Epstein, S. E. Schlesinger, & W. Dryden (Eds.), *Cognitive-behavioral therapy with families.* New York: Brunner/Mazel.

Levant, R. F. (Ed.). (1986). *Psychoeducational approaches to family therapy and counseling.* New York: Springer.

Lewis, J. M., Beavers, W. R., Gossett, J. T., & Phillips, V. A. (1976). *No single thread: Psychological health in family systems.* New York: Brunner/Mazel.

Liberman, R. P. (1970). Behavioral approaches to family and couple therapy. *American Journal of Orthopsychiatry, 40*, 106–118.

Liberman, R. P., Wheeler, E., deVisser, L. A. J. M., Kuehnel, J., & Kuehnel, T. (1980). *Handbook of marital therapy: A positive approach to helping troubled relationships.* New York: Plenum.

Liberman, R. P., Wheeler, E., & Sanders, N. (1976). Behavioral therapy for marital disharmony: An educational approach. *Journal of Marriage and Family Counseling, 2*, 383–395.

Liddle, H. A. (1987). Family psychology: The journal, the field. *Journal of Family Psychology, 1*, 5–22.

Liddle, H. A. (1988) Systemic supervision: Conceptual overlays and pragmatic guidelines. In H. A. Liddle, D. C. Breunlin, & R. C. Schwartz (Eds.), *Handbook of family therapy training and supervision.* New York: Guilford Press.

Liddle, H. A., Breunlin, D. C., & Schwartz, R. C. (Eds.). (1988). *Handbook of family therapy training and supervision.* New York: Guilford Press.

Liddle, H. A., & Halpin, R. J. (1978). Family therapy training and supervision: A comparative review. *Journal of Marriage and Family Counseling, 4*, 77–98.

Lidz, R., & Lidz, T. (1949). The family environment of schizophrenic patients. *American Journal of Psychiatry, 106*, 332–345.

Lidz, T., Cornelison, A., Fleck, S., & Terry, D. (1957). The intrafamilial environment of schizophrenic patients: II. Marital schism and marital skew. *American Journal of Psychiatry, 114*, 241–248.

Loewenstein, S. F., Reder, P., & Clark, A. (1982). The consumers' report: Trainees' discussion of the experience of live supervision. In R. Whiffen & J. Byng-Hall (Eds.), *Family therapy supervision: Recent developments in practice.* London: Academic Press.

LoPiccolo, J., & LoPiccolo, L. (Eds.). (1978). *Handbook of sex therapy.* New York: Plenum.

Low, P., & Low, M. (1975). Treatment of married couples in a group run by a husband and wife. *International Journal of Group Psychotherapy, 25*, 54–66.

Lowe, R. N. (1982). Adlerian/Dreikursian family counseling. In A. M. Horne & M. M. Ohlsen (Eds.), *Family counseling and therapy.* Itasca, IL: F. E. Peacock.

Luepnitz, D. A. (1988). *The family interpreted: Feminist theory in clinical practice.* New York: Basic Books.

MacGregor, R. (1971). Multiple impact psychotherapy with families. In J. G. Howells (Ed.), *Theory and practice of family psychiatry.* New York: Brunner/Mazel.

MacGregor, R., Ritchie, A. N., Serrano, A. C., & Schuster, F. P. (1964). *Multiple impact therapy with families.* New York: McGraw-Hill.

MacKinnon, L. (1983). Contrasting strategic and Milan therapies. *Family Process, 22,* 425–440.

Madanes, C. (1981). *Strategic family therapy.* San Francisco: Jossey-Bass.

Madanes, C. (1984). *Behind the one-way mirror: Advances in the practice of strategic therapy.* San Francisco: Jossey-Bass.

Madanes, C., & Haley, J. (1977). Dimensions of family therapy. *The Journal of Nervous and Mental Disease, 165,* 88–98.

Malcolm, J. (1978). A reporter at large: The one-way mirror. *New Yorker,* May 15, 39–114.

Manus, G. (1966). Marriage counseling: A technique in search of a theory. *Journal of Marriage and the Family, 28,* 449–453.

Margolin, G. (1982). Ethical and legal considerations in marital and family therapy. *American Psychologist, 37,* 788–801.

Martin, P. A., & Bird, W. H. (1963). An approach to the psychotherapy of marriage partners: The stereoscopic technique. *Psychiatry, 16,* 123–127.

Masters, J. C., Burish, T. G., Hollon, S. D., & Rimm, D. C. (1987). *Behavior therapy: Techniques and empirical findings* (3rd ed.). New York: Harcourt Brace Jovanovich.

Masters, W. H., & Johnson, V. E. (1970). *Human sexual inadequacy.* Boston: Little, Brown.

McGoldrick, M. (1988a). Ethnicity and the family life cycle. In B. Carter & M. McGoldrick (Eds.), *The changing family life cycle: A framework for family therapy* (2nd ed.). New York: Gardner Press.

McGoldrick, M. (1988b). Women and the life cycle. In B. Carter & M. McGoldrick (Eds.), *The changing family life cycle: A framework for family therapy* (2nd ed.). New York: Gardner Press.

McGoldrick, M., Anderson, C. M., & Walsh, F. (1989). *Women in families: A framework for family therapy.* New York: W. W. Norton.

McGoldrick, M., & Gerson, R. (1985). *Genograms in family assessment.* New York: W. W. Norton.

McGoldrick, M., Pearce, J. K., & Giordano, J. (1982). *Ethnicity and family therapy.* New York: Guilford Press.

Mednick, M. T. (1987). Single mothers: A review and critique of current research. In S. Oskamp (Ed.), *Family processes and problems: Social psychological aspects.* Newbury Park, CA: Sage Publications.

Meichenbaum, D. (1977). *Cognitive behavior therapy.* New York: Plenum.

Meissner, W. W. (1978). The conceptualization of marriage and family dynamics from a psychoanalytic perspective. In T. J. Paolino & B. S. McCrady (Eds.), *Marriage and marital therapy: Psychoanalytic, behavioral, and systems perspectives.* New York: Brunner/Mazel.

Mendelsohn, M., & Ferber, A. (1972). A training program. In A. Ferber, M. Mendelsohn, & A. Napier (Eds.), *The book of family therapy.* New York: Science House.

Midelfort, C. F. (1957). *The family in psychotherapy.* New York: Viking Press.

Miller, J. G. (1978). *Living systems.* New York: McGraw-Hill.

Minuchin, S. (1974). *Families and family therapy.* Cambridge, MA: Harvard University Press.

Minuchin, S. (1982). Foreword. In J. R. Neill & D. P. Kniskern (Eds.), *From psyche to system: The evolving therapy of Carl Whitaker.* New York: Guilford Press.

Minuchin, S. (1984). *Family kaleidoscope.* Cambridge, MA: Harvard University Press.

Minuchin, S., & Fishman, H. C. (1981). *Family therapy techniques.* Cambridge, MA: Harvard University Press.

Minuchin, S., Montalvo, B., Guerney, B. G., Jr., Rosman, B. L., & Schumer, F. (1967). *Families of the slums: An exploration of their structure and treatment.* New York: Basic Books.

Minuchin, S., Rosman, B. L., & Baker, L. (1978). *Psychosomatic families: Anorexia nervosa in context.* Cambridge, MA: Harvard University Press.

Mittelman, B. (1948). The concurrent analysis of married couples. *Psychoanalytic Quarterly, 17,* 182–197.

Montalvo, B. (1973). Aspects of live supervision. *Family Process, 12,* 343–359.

Moos, R. H. (1974). *Combined preliminary manual: Family, work, and group environment scales.* Palo Alto, CA: Consulting Psychologists Press.

Morris, S. B., Alexander, J. F., & Waldron, H. (1988). Functional family therapy. In I. R. H. Falloon (Ed.), *Handbook of behavioral family therapy.* New York: Guilford Press.

Morrison, J. K., Layton, D., & Newman, J. (1982). Ethical conflict in decision making. In J. C. Hansen & L. L'Abate (Eds.), *Values, ethics, legalities, and the family therapist.* Rockville, MD: Aspen Publications.

Mudd, E. H. (1951). *The practice of marriage counseling.* New York: Association Press.

Napier, A. Y., & Whitaker, C. A. (1972). A conversation about co-therapy. In A. Ferber, M. Mendelsohn, & A. Y. Napier (Eds.), *The book of family therapy.* New York: Science House.

Napier, A. Y., & Whitaker, C. A. (1978). *The family crucible.* New York: Harper & Row.

Neill, J. R., & Kniskern, D. P. (Eds.). (1982). *From psyche to system: The evolving therapy of Carl Whitaker.* New York: Guilford Press.

Nerin, W. F. (1986). *Family reconstruction: Long day's journey into light.* New York: W. W. Norton.

Nerin, W. F. (1989). You can go home again. *The Family Networker, 13*(1), 54–55.

Neugarten, B. (1976). Adaptation and the life cycle. *The Counseling Psychologist, 6*, 16–20.

Nichols, M. (1984). *Family therapy: Concepts and methods.* New York: Gardner Press.

Nichols, W. C. (1979). Introduction to Part I. Education and training in marital and family therapy. *Journal of Marital and Family Therapy, 5* (3), 3–5.

Nichols, W. C. (1988). *Marital therapy: An integrative approach.* New York: Guilford Press.

Nichols, W. C., & Everett, C. A. (1986). *Systemic family therapy: An integrative approach.* New York: Guilford Press.

Nuechterlein, K. H., & Dawson, M. E. (1984). A heuristic vulnerability/stress model of schizophrenic episodes. *Schizophrenia Bulletin, 10*, 300–312.

Oliveri, M. E., & Reiss, D. (1982). Family styles of construing the social environment: A perspective on variation among nonclinical families. In F. Walsh (Ed.), *Normal family processes.* New York: Guilford Press.

Olson, D. H. (1970). Marital and family therapy: Integrative reviews and critique. *Journal of Marriage and Family Counseling, 4*, 77–98.

Olson, D. H. (1986). Circumplex model VII: Validation studies and FACES III. *Family Process, 26*, 337–351.

Olson, D. H., Russell, C. S., & Sprenkle, D. H. (1980). Marital and family therapy: A decade review. *Journal of Marriage and the Family, 42*, 973–993.

Olson, D. H., Russell, C. S., & Sprenkle, D. H. (1983). Circumplex model of marital and family systems: VI. Theoretical update. *Family Process, 22*, 69–83.

Olson, D. H., Sprenkle, D. H., & Russell, C. S. (1979). Circumplex model of marital and family systems: Cohesion and adaptability dimensions, family types, and clinical applications. *Family Process, 18*, 3–28.

Papero, D. V. (1983). Family systems theory and therapy. In B. B. Wolman & G. Stricker (Eds.), *Handbook of family and marital therapy.* New York: Plenum.

Papp, P. (1976). Family choreography. In P. J. Guerin, Jr. (Ed.), *Family therapy: Theory and practice.* New York: Gardner Press.

Papp, P. (1977). *Family therapy: Full-length case studies.* New York: Gardner Press.

Papp, P. (1980). The Greek chorus and other techniques of paradoxical therapy. *Family Process, 19*, 45–57.

Papp, P. (1984). Setting the terms for therapy. *The Family Therapy Networker, 8*(1), 42–47.

Patterson, G. R. (1971). *Families: Application of social learning to family life.* Champaign, IL: Research Press.

Patterson, G. R., & Reid, J. (1970). Reciprocity and coercion: Two facets of social systems. In C. Neuringer & J. Michael (Eds.), *Behavior modification in clinical psychology.* New York: Appleton-Century-Crofts.

Patterson, G. R., Reid, R. B., Jones, R. R., & Conger, R. E. (1975). *A social learning approach to family intervention, Vol. I: Families with aggressive children.* Eugene, OR: Castalia.

Patterson, G. R., Weiss, R. L., & Hops, H. (1976). Training of marital skills. In H. Leitenberg (Ed.), *Handbook of behavior modification and behavior therapy.* New York: Prentice-Hall.

Pattison, E. M. (1981). Clinical applications of social network therapy. *International Journal of Family Therapy, 3*, 241–320.

Paul, G. L. (1967). Outcome research in psychotherapy. *Journal of Consulting Psychology, 31*, 109–188.

Paul, N. L. (1974). The use of empathy in the resolution of grief. In J. Ellard, V. Volkan, & N. L. Paul (Eds.), *Normal and pathological responses to bereavement.* New York: MSS Information Corporation.

Peake, T. H., Borduin, C. M., & Archer, R. P. (1988). *Brief psychotherapies: Changing frames of mind.* Newbury Park: Sage Publications.

Peck, J. S., & Manocherian, J. (1988). Divorce in the changing family life cycle. In B. Carter & M. McGoldrick (Eds.), *The changing family life cycle: A framework for family therapy* (2nd ed.). New York: Gardner Press.

Perls, F. S. (1969). *Gestalt therapy verbatim.* Lafayette, CA: Free People Press.

Perry, H. S. (1982). *Psychiatrist of America: The life of Harry Stack Sullivan.* Cambridge, MA: Harvard University Press.

Piercy, F. P., Sprenkle, D. H., & Associates. (1986). *Family therapy sourcebook.* New York: Guilford Press.

Pinsof, W. M. (1986). The process of family therapy: The development of the Family Therapist Coding System. In L. Greenberg & W. M. Pinsof (Eds.), *The psychotherapeutic process: A research handbook.* New York: Guilford Press.

Pittman, F. S. (1987). *Turning points: Treating families in transitions and crisis.* New York: W. W. Norton.

Preto, N. G. (1988). Transformation of the family system in adolescence. In B. Carter & M. McGoldrick (Eds.), *The changing family life cycle: A framework for family therapy* (2nd ed.). New York: Gardner Press.

Rabin, C. (1981). The single-case design in family therapy evaluation research. *Family Process*, *20*, 351–366.

Rait, D. (1988). Survey results. *The Family Therapy Networker*, *12*(1), 52–56.

Reiss, D. (1981). *The family's construction of reality.* Cambridge, MA: Harvard University Press.

Reiss, D. (1988). Theoretical versus tactical inferences: Or, how to do family psychotherapy research without dying of boredom. In L. C. Wynne (Ed.), *The state of the art in family therapy research: Controversies and recommendations.* New York: Family Process Press.

Ribordy, S. C. (1987). Training family therapists within an academic setting. *Journal of Family Psychology*, *1*, 204–218.

Riskin, J., & Faunce, E. (1972). An evaluative review of family interaction research. *Family Process*, *11*, 365–456.

Ritchie, A. (1971). Multiple impact therapy: An experiment. In J. Haley (Ed.), *Changing families: A family therapy reader.* New York: Grune & Stratton.

Rosenberg, J. B. (1983). Structural family therapy. In B. B. Wolman & G. Stricker (Eds.), *Handbook of family and marital therapy.* New York: Plenum.

Rosenblatt, B. (1971). Historical perspective of treatment modes. In H. E. Rie (Ed.), *Perspectives in child psychiatry.* Chicago: Aldine-Atherton.

Rubenstein, D., & Weiner, O. R. (1967). Co-therapy teamwork relationships in family psychotherapy. In G. H. Zuk & I. Boszormenyi-Nagy (Eds.), *Family therapy and disturbed families.* Palo Alto, CA: Science and Behavior Books.

Rubenstein, E. (1948). Childhood mental disease in America: A review of the literature before 1900. *American Journal of Orthopsychiatry*, *18*, 314–321.

Rueveni, U. (1979). *Networking families in crisis.* New York: Human Sciences Press.

Rueveni, U. (Ed.). (1984). Application of networking in family and community. *International Journal of Family Therapy*, *6*(2).

Saba, G. W., & Liddle, H. A. (1986). Perceptions of professional needs, practice patterns and initial issues facing family therapy trainees and supervisors. *Journal of Family Therapy*, *14*, 109–122.

Sager, C. J. (1966). The treatment of married couples. In S. Arieti (Ed.), *American handbook of psychiatry* (Vol. III). New York: Basic Books.

Sager, C. J., Brown, H. S., Crohn, H., Engel, T., Rodstein, E., & Walker, L. (1983). *Treating the remarried family.* New York: Brunner/Mazel.

Satir, V. M. (1964). *Conjoint family therapy.* Palo Alto, CA: Science and Behavior Books.

Satir, V. M. (1967). *Conjoint family therapy* (rev. ed.). Palo Alto, CA: Science and Behavior Books.

Satir, V. M. (1972). *Peoplemaking.* Palo Alto, CA: Science and Behavior Books.

Satir, V. M. (1982). The therapist and family therapy: Process model. In A. M. Horne & M. M. Ohlsen (Eds.), *Family counseling and therapy.* Itasca, IL: F. E. Peacock.

Satir, V. M., & Baldwin, M. (1983). *Satir step by step: A guide to creating change in families.* Palo Alto, CA: Science and Behavior Books.

Schwartz, R., & Breunlin, D. (1983). Why clinicians should bother with research. *The Family Therapy Networker*, *7*(4), 22–27.

Schwartz, R. C., Liddle, H. A., & Breunlin, D. C. (1988). Muddles in live supervision. In H. A. Liddle, D. C. Breunlin, & R. C. Schwartz (Eds.), *Handbook of family therapy training and supervision.* New York: Guilford Press.

Segal, L. (1982). Brief family therapy. In A. M. Horne & M. M. Ohlsen (Eds.), *Family counseling and therapy.* Itasca, IL: F. E. Peacock.

Segal, L. (1987). What is a problem? A brief family therapist's view. *Family Therapy Today*, *2*(7), 1–7.

Segal, L., & Bavelas, J. B. (1983). Human systems and communication theory. In B. B. Wolman & G. Stricker (Eds.), *Handbook of family and marital therapy.* New York: Plenum.

Selvini-Palazzoli, M. (1978). *Self-starvation.* New York: Aronson.

Selvini-Palazzoli, M. (1980). Why a long interval between sessions? The therapeutic control of the family-therapist suprasystem. In M. Andolfi & I. Zwerling (Eds.), *Dimensions of family therapy.* New York: Guilford Press.

Selvini-Palazzoli, M. (1986). Towards a general model of psychotic family games. *Journal of Marital and Family Therapy*, *12*, 339–349.

Selvini-Palazzoli, M., Boscolo, L., Cecchin, G. F., & Prata, G. (1978). *Paradox and counterparadox: A new model in the therapy of the family in schizophrenic transaction.* New York: Aronson.

Selvini-Palazzoli, M., Boscolo, L., Cecchin, G. F., & Prata, G. (1980). Hypothesizing–circularity–neutrality: Three guidelines for the conductor of the session. *Family Process*, *19*, 3–12.

Selvini-Palazzoli, M., Cirillo, S., Selvini, M., & Sorrentino, A. M. (1989). *Family games: General models of psychotic processes in the family.* New York: W. W. Norton.

Shapiro, R. J. (1975). Problems in teaching family therapy. *Professional Psychology*, *6*, 41–44.

Shean, G. (1978). *Schizophrenia: An introduction to research and theory.* Cambridge, MA: Winthrop.

Sherman, R., & Fredman, N. (1986). *Handbook of structured techniques in marriage and family therapy.* New York: Brunner/Mazel.

Simon, R. (1984). Stranger in a strange land: An interview with Salvador Minuchin. *The Family Therapy Networker, 6*(6), 22–31.

Simon, R. (1987). Goodbye paradox, hello invariant prescription: An interview with Mara Selvini-Palazzoli. *The Family Therapy Networker, 11*(5), 16–33.

Simon, R. M. (1972). Sculpting the family. *Family Process, 11*, 49–57.

Singleton, G. (1982). Bowen family systems theory. In A. M. Horne & M. M. Ohlsen (Eds.), *Family counseling and therapy.* Itasca, IL: F. E. Peacock.

Skinner, B. F. (1953). *Science and human behavior.* New York: Macmillan.

Skynner, A. C. R. (1976). *Systems of family and marital psychotherapy.* New York: Brunner/Mazel.

Skynner, A. C. R. (1981). An open-systems, group analytic approach to family therapy. In A. S. Gurman & D. P. Kniskern (Eds.), *Handbook of family therapy.* New York: Brunner/Mazel.

Slavson, S. R. (1964). *A textbook in analytic group psychotherapy.* New York: International Universities Press.

Sluzki, C. E. (1978). Marital therapy from a systems theory perspective. In T. J. Paolino & B. S. McCrady (Eds.), *Marriage and marital therapy: Psychoanalytic, behavioral, and systems theory perspectives.* New York: Brunner/Mazel.

Smith, V. G., & Nichols, W. C. (1979). Accreditation in marital and family therapy. *Journal of Marital and Family Therapy, 5*, 95–100.

Speck, R. V., & Attneave, C. L. (1973). *Family networks.* New York: Pantheon.

Sprenkle, D. H. (1988). Training and supervision in degree-granting graduate programs in family therapy. In H. A. Liddle, D. C. Breunlin, & R. C. Schwartz (Eds.), *Handbook of family therapy training and supervision.* New York: Guilford Press.

Stanton, M. D. (1981). Strategic approaches to family therapy. In A. S. Gurman & D. P. Kniskern (Eds.), *Handbook of family therapy.* New York: Brunner/Mazel.

Stanton, M. D. (1988). The lobster quadrille: Issues and dilemmas for family therapy research. In L. C. Wynne (Ed.), *The state of the art in family therapy research: Controversies and recommendations.* New York: Family Process Press.

Stier, S., & Goldenberg, I. (1975). Training issues in family therapy. *Journal of Marriage and Family Therapy, 1*, 63–68.

Stierlin, H. (1972). *Separating parents and adolescents.* New York: Quadrangle.

Stierlin, H. (1977). *Psychoanalysis and family therapy.* New York: Aronson.

Stierlin, H., Simon, F. B., & Schmidt, G. (Eds.). (1987). *Familiar realities: The Heidelberg Conference.* New York: Brunner/Mazel.

Stierlin, H., & Weber, G. (1989). *Unlocking the family door: A systemic approach to the understanding and treatment of anorexia nervosa.* New York: Brunner/Mazel.

Strelnick, A. H. (1977). Multiple family group therapy: A review of the literature. *Family Process*, *16*, 307–325.

Stuart, R. B. (1969). Operant-interpersonal treatment of marital discord. *Journal of Consulting and Clinical Psychology, 33, 675–682.*

Stuart, R. B. (1976). An operant-interpersonal program for couples. In D. H. L. Olson (Ed.), *Treating relationships.* Lake Mills, IA: Graphic.

Stuart, R. B. (1980). *Helping couples change: A social learning approach to marital therapy.* Champaign, IL: Research Press.

Stuart, R. B., & Lott, L. A. (1972). Behavioral contracting with delinquents: A cautionary note. *Journal of Behavior Therapy and Experimental Psychiatry*, *3*, 161–169.

Sullivan, H. S. (1953). *The interpersonal theory of psychiatry.* New York: W. W. Norton.

Sundberg, N., Tyler, L. E., & Taplin, J. R. (1973). *Clinical psychology: Expanding horizons* (2nd. ed.). Englewood Cliffs, NJ: Prentice-Hall.

Terkelson, K. G. (1980). Toward a theory of the family life cycle. In E. A. Carter & M. McGoldrick (Eds.), *The family life cycle: A framework for family therapy.* New York: Gardner Press.

Thaxton, L., & L'Abate, L. (1982). The "second wave" and the second generation: Characteristics of new leaders in family therapy. *Family Process*, *21*, 359–362.

Thibaut, J. W., & Kelley, H. H. (1959). *The social psychology of groups.* New York: Wiley.

Todd, T. C. (1988). Behavioral and systemic family therapy. In I. R. H. Falloon (Ed.), *Handbook of behavioral family therapy.* New York: Guilford Press.

Toman, W. (1961). *Family constellation: Its effects on personality and social behavior.* New York: Springer.

Tomm, K. M. (1983). The old hat doesn't fit. *The Family Therapy Networker*, 7(4), 39–41.

Tomm, K. M. (1984a). One perspective on the Milan approach: Part I. Overview of development, theory, and practice. *Journal of Marital and Family Therapy*, *10*, 113–125.

Tomm, K. M. (1984b). One perspective on the Milan approach: Part II. Description of session format, interviewing style, and interventions. *Journal of Marital and Family Therapy*, *10*, 253–271.

Tomm, K. M., & Wright, L. M. (1979). Training in family therapy: Perceptual, conceptual, and executive skills. *Family Process*, *18*, 227–250.

Tomm, K. M., & Wright, L. M. (1982). Multilevel training and supervision in an outpatient service program. In R. Whiffen & J. Byng-Hall (Eds.), *Family therapy supervision: Recent developments in practice.* London: Academic Press.

Towards a differentiation of self in one's family. (1972). In J. L. Framo (Ed.), *Family interaction: A dialogue between family researchers and family therapists.* New York: Springer.

Ulrich, D. N. (1983). Contextual and marital therapy. In B. B. Wolman & G. Stricker (Eds.), *Handbook of family and marital therapy.* New York: Plenum.

Umbarger, C. C. (1983). *Structural family therapy.* New York: Grune & Stratton.

Van Hoose, W. H., & Kottler, J. A. (1985). *Ethical and legal issues in counseling and psychotherapy* (2nd ed.). San Francisco: Jossey-Bass.

VandenBos, G. R. (1986). Psychotherapy research: A special issue. *American Psychologist, 41,* 111–112.

Visher, E. B., & Visher, J. S. (1988). *Old loyalties, new ties: Therapeutic strategies with stepfamilies.* New York: Brunner/Mazel.

Wachtel, E. F., & Wachtel, P. L. (1986). *Family dynamics in individual psychotherapy: A guide to clinical strategies.* New York: Guilford Press.

Walrond-Skinner, S. (1976). *Family therapy: The treatment of natural systems.* London: Routledge & Kegan Paul.

Walsh, F. (1988). The family in later life. In B. Carter & M. McGoldrick (Eds.), *The changing family life cycle: A framework for family therapy* (2nd ed.). New York: Gardner Press.

Walters, M., Carter, B., Papp, P., & Silverstein, O. (1989). *The invisible web: Gender patterns in family relationships.* New York: Guilford Press.

Watson, J. B., & Rayner, R. (1920). Conditioned emotional reactions. *Journal of Experimental Psychology, 3,* 1–14.

Watzlawick, P. (1978). *The language of change.* New York: Basic Books.

Watzlawick, P. (1984). *The invented reality.* New York: W. W. Norton.

Watzlawick, P., Beavin, J. H., & Jackson, D. D. (1967). *Pragmatics of human communication.* New York: W. W. Norton.

Watzlawick, P., Weakland, J. H., & Fisch, R. (1974). *Change: Principles of problem formation and problem resolution.* New York: W. W. Norton.

Waxler, N. (1975). The normality of deviance: An alternative explanation of schizophrenia in the family. *Schizophrenia Bulletin, 14,* 38–47.

Weakland, J. (1976). Communication theory and clinical change. In P. J. Guerin, Jr. (Ed.), *Family therapy: Theory and practice.* New York: Gardner Press.

Weathers, L., & Liberman, R. P. (1975). The family contracting exercise. *Journal of Behavior Therapy and Experimental Psychiatry, 6,* 208–214.

Weeks, G. R., & L'Abate, L. (1982). *Paradoxical psychotherapy: Theory and technique.* New York: Brunner/Mazel.

Weiss, R. S. (1985). Men and the family. *Family Process*, *24*, 49–58.

Wells, R. A., & Dezen, A. E. (1978). The results of family therapy revisited: The nonbehavioral methods. *Family Process*, *17*, 251–274.

Wells, R. A., Dilkes, T. C., & Trivelli, N. (1972). The results of family therapy; A critical review. *Family Process*, *11*, 189–207.

Whiffen, R. (1982). The use of videotape in supervision. In R. Whiffen & J. Byng-Hall (Eds.), *Family therapy supervision: Recent developments in practice.* London: Academic Press.

Whitaker, C. A. (1967). The growing edge in techniques of family therapy. In J. Haley & L. Hoffman (Eds.), *Techniques of family therapy.* New York: Basic Books.

Whitaker, C. A. (1975). Psychotherapy of the absurd: With a special emphasis on the psychotherapy of aggression. *Family Process*, *14*, 1–16.

Whitaker, C. A. (1976a). A family is a four-dimensional relationship. In P. J. Guerin, Jr. (Ed.), *Family therapy: Theory and practice.* New York: Gardner Press.

Whitaker, C. A. (1976b). The hindrance of theory in clinical work. In P. J. Guerin, Jr. (Ed.), *Family therapy: Theory and practice.* New York: Gardner Press.

Whitaker, C. A. (1976c). Comment: Live supervision in psychotherapy. *Voices*, *12*, 24–25.

Whitaker, C. A. (1977). Process techniques of family therapy. *Interaction*, *1*, 4–19.

Whitaker, C. A., & Bumberry, W. M. (1988). *Dancing with the family: A symbolic-experiential approach.* New York: Brunner/Mazel.

Whitaker, C. A., & Keith, D. V. (1981). Symbolic-experiential family therapy. In A. S. Gurman & D. P. Kniskern (Eds.), *Handbook of family therapy.* New York: Brunner/Mazel.

Whitaker, C. A., & Malone, T. P. (1953). *The roots of psychotherapy.* New York: Blakiston.

White, S. L. (1978). Family theory according to the Cambridge Model. *Journal of Marriage and Family Counseling*, *4*, 91–100.

Whiteside, M. F. (1982). Remarriage: A family developmental process. *Journal of Marital and Family Therapy*, *8*, 59–68.

Wiener, N. (1948). Cybernetics. *Scientific American*, *179*(5), 14–18.

Williamson, D. S. (1981). Personal authority via termination of the intergenerational hierarchical boundary: A "new" stage in the family life cycle. *Journal of Marital and Family Therapy*, *7*, 441–452.

Williamson, D. S. (1982). Personal authority via termination of the intergenerational hierarchical boundary: Part II. The consultative process and the therapeutic method. *Journal of Marital and Family Therapy*, *8*, 23–37.

Wolman, B. B., & Stricker, G. (Eds.). (1983). *Handbook of family and marital therapy*. New York: Plenum.

Wynne, L. C. (1970). Communication disorders and the quest for relatedness in families of schizophrenics. *American Journal of Psychoanalysis*, *30*, 100–114.

Wynne, L. C. (1983). Family research and family therapy: A reunion? *Journal of Marital and Family Therapy*, *9*, 113–117.

Wynne, L. C. (Ed.). (1988). *The state of the art in family therapy research: Controversies and recommendations*. New York: Family Process Press.

Wynne, L. C., Jones, J. E., & Al-Khayyal, M. (1982). Healthy family communication patterns: Observations in families "at risk" for psychopathology. In F. Walsh (Ed.), *Normal family processes: Implications for clinical practice*. New York: Guilford Press.

Wynne, L. C., Ryckoff, I. M., Day, J., & Hirsch, S. I. (1958). Pseudomutuality in the family relationships of schizophrenics. *Psychiatry*, *21*, 205–220.

Wynne, L. C., & Singer, M. T. (1963). Thought disorder and family relations of schizophrenics, I and II. *Archives of General Psychiatry*, *9*, 191–206.

Wynne, L. C., Singer, M. T., Bartko, J. J., & Toohey, M. L. (1977). Schizophrenics and their families: Research on parental communication. In J. M. Tanner (Ed.), *Developments in psychiatric research*. London: Hodden & Stoughton.

Yalom, I. D. (1985). *The theory and practice of group psychotherapy* (3rd ed.). New York: Basic Books.

Yapko, M. D. (1988). An interview with Virginia M. Satir, M. A., A. C. S. W. *The Milton H. Erickson Newsletter*, *8*(3), 3, 11–16.

Zeig, J. K. (Ed.). (1980). *A teaching seminar with Milton H. Erickson*. New York: Brunner/Mazel.

Zimmerman, J., & Sims, D. (1983). Family therapy. In C. E. Walker & M. C. Roberts (Eds.), *Handbook of clinical child psychology*. New York: Wiley.

Zuk, G. H. (1976). Family therapy: Clinical hodgepodge or clinical science? *Journal of Marriage and Family Counseling*, *2*, 299–303.

Zuk, G. H. (1981). *Family therapy: A triadic based approach* (rev. ed.). New York: Human Sciences Press.

Zuk, G. H., & Boszormenyi-Nagy, I. (Eds.). (1967). *Family therapy and disturbed families*. Palo Alto, CA: Science and Behavior Books.

Zuk, G. H., & Rubenstein, D. (1965). A review of concepts in the study and treatment of families with schizophrenics. In I. Boszormenyi-Nagy & J. L. Framo (Eds.), *Intensive family therapy: Theoretical and practical aspects*. New York: Harper & Row.

Name Index

Subject Index

Credits

(These pages constitute an extension of the copyright page)

Chapter Two

16, Figure 2.1 from Figure 7.2, p. 148, from *Marriage and Family Development*, 5th Ed., by Evelyn Millis Duvall. Copyright ©1957, 1962, 1967, 1971, 1977 by J. B. Lippincott Company. By permission of Harper & Row, Publishers, Inc. Based on data from the U.S. Bureau of Census and from the National Center for Health Statistics, Washington, D.C. **18, 24, 25,** Tables 2.1, 2.2, and 2.3 from Betty Carter and Monica McGoldrick, *The Changing Family Life Cycle: A Framework for Family Therapy, Second Edition*. Copyright ©1989 by Allyn and Bacon. Reprinted with permission.

Chapter Three

39, Figure 3.1 from "The Study of the Family," by D. D. Jackson, *Family Process*, 1965, *4*, 1-20. Reprinted by permission. **42,** Figure 3.2 from *Living Systems*, by J. G. Miller. Copyright 1978 by McGraw-Hill, Inc. Reprinted by permission.

48, Figure 3.3 from *Families and larger systems*, by E. Imber-Black. Copyright 1988 by Guilford Press. Reprinted by permission.

Chapter Four

55-57, Table 4.1 from *Marriage and Family Development*, 5th Edition, by Evelyn Millis Duvall, pp. 127-129. Copyright ©1957, 1962, 1967, 1971, 1977 by J. B. Lippincott Company. By permission of Harper & Row, Publishers, Inc. **62,** Figure 4.1 from Sundberg/Tyler/Taplin, *Clinical Psychology: Expanding Horizons*, 2nd Ed., ©1973, p. 101. Reprinted by permission of Prentice-Hall, Inc., Englewood Cliffs, New Jersey. Based on the theory presented by Miller, 1971. **62,** Table 4.2 from Table 10.1 in *Americans View Their Mental Health* by Gerald Gurin, Joseph Veroff, and Sheila Feld, ©1960 by Basic Books, Inc., Publishers, New York. Reprinted by permission. **80,** Tables 4.4 and 4.5 from *The Field of Family Therapy*, GAP Report No. 78. Copyright 1970 by the Group for the Advancement of Psychiatry, Inc. Reprinted by permission of the Committee on the Family, Group for the Advancement of Psychiatry.

Chapter Five

106-107, Quotes from *Between Give and Take: A Clinical Guide to Contextual Therapy*, by Boszormenyi-Nagy and Krasner. Copyright ©1986 by Brunner/Mazel, Inc. Reprinted with permission.

Chapter Six

122, Quotes from *Dancing with the Family*, by Whitaker and Bumberry. Copyright ©1988 by Brunner/Mazel, Inc. Reprinted with permission. **127-130,** Quotes from *Experiential Psychotherapy within Families* by W. Kempler. Copyright ©1981 by Brunner/Mazel, Inc. Reprinted with permission.

Chapter Seven

150, **153**, Figure 7.2 and quote reprinted from *Family Evaluation: An Approach Based on Bowen Theory* by Kerr, M. E. and Bowen, M., with the permission of W. W. Norton & Company, Inc. Copyright ©1988 by W. W. Norton & Company, Inc.

Chapter Eight

175, Figures 8.2 and 8.3 reprinted by permission of the publishers from *Families and Family Therapy* by Salvador Minuchin, Cambridge, Mass.: Harvard University Press, Copyright ©1974 by the President and Fellows of Harvard College.

Chapter Ten

222, **224,** Figure 10.1 and Table 10.2 from "An Operant Interpersonal Program for Couples," by R. B. Stuart. In D. H. L. Olsen (Ed.), *Treating Relationships*. Copyright 1976 by Graphic Publishing Company. Reprinted by permission. **228,**

Table 10.4 from "Behavioral Therapy for Families with Child Management Problems," by I. R. H. Falloon and R. P. Liberman. In M. Textor (Ed.), *Helping Families with Special Problems*. Copyright 1983 by Jason Aronson, Inc. Reprinted by permission. **230,** Figure 10.2 from *Families: Application of Social Learning to Family Life*, by G. R. Patterson. Copyright 1971 by Research Press Company. Reprinted by permission. **232,** Figure 10.3 reprinted with permission from *Journal of Behavior Therapy and Experimental Psychiatry*, *6*, L. Weathers and R. P. Liberman, "The Family Contracting Exercise," Copyright 1975, Pergamon Press, Ltd.

Chapter Twelve

269, Figure 12.1 from "Circumplex model VII: Validation studies and FACES III." by D. H. Olson. In *Family Process*, 1986, *26*, 337-351. Copyright 1986 by *Family Process*. **271,** Table 12.1 from "Family Styles of Construing the Social Environment: A Perspective on Variation among Nonclinical Families," by M. E. Oliveri and D. Reiss. In *Normal Family Processes* by F. Walsh (Ed.). Copyright ©1982 by The Guilford Press. Reprinted by permission. **273,** Table 12.2 from *No Single Thread: Psychological Health in Family Systems*, by J. M. Lewis, W. R. Beavers, J. T. Gossett, and V. A. Phillips. Copyright 1976 by Brunner/Mazel, Inc. Reprinted by permission. **274,** Figure 12.2 from "Family models: Comparing and contrasting the Olson circumplex with the Beavers model," by W. R. Beavers and M. N. Voeller. In *Family Process*, 1983, *22*, 85-98. Copyright 1983 by *Family Process*. **276, 278, 279,** Table 12.3, Figure 12.3, and Figure 12.4 from *Combined Preliminary Manual: Family, Work, and Group Environment Scales*, by R. H. Moos. Copyright 1974 by Consulting Psychologists Press. Reprinted by permission.

Chapter Thirteen

289, Table 13.1 adapted from "Family Therapy," by J. Haley, *International Journal of Psychiatry*, 1970, *9*, 233-242. Reprinted by permission. **294, 294,** Tables 13.3 and 13.4 from "Training Family Therapists by Setting Learning Objectives," by J. M. Cleghorn and S. Levin, *American Journal of Orthopsychiatry*, 1973, *43*(3), 439-446. Copyright ©1973 by the American Orthopsychiatric Association, Inc. Reproduced by permission.

PHOTO CREDITS

p. **9**, University of California; p. **34**, ©Bruce Talamon/People Magazine; p. **75**, John E. Bell; p. **94**, The Ackerman Institute for Family Therapy; p. **101**, James L. Framo; p. **105**, Ivan Boszormenyi-Nagy; p. **119**, Carl Whitaker; p. **125**, ©Keld Traejaer; p. **133**, John Nakles; p. **155**, Murray Bowen; p. **172**, ©Bruce Talamon/People Magazine; p. **173**, Anthony A. Bottone; p. **192**, The Milton Erickson Foundation, Inc.; p. **200**, Jason Aronson, Inc.; p. **201**, Luigi Boscolo; p. **218**, Robert Liberman; p. **227**, Kennel-Ellis Photography; p. **243**, Bernard Gotfryd, ©1978 by Newsweek, Inc.; p. **263**, Lyman C. Wynn; p. **265**, ©Bruce Talamon/People Magazine